Mountain Biking
Pennsylvania

Rob Ginieczki

FALCON®

GUILFORD, CONNECTICUT
HELENA, MONTANA
AN IMPRINT OF THE GLOBE PEQUOT PRESS

*A*FALCONGUIDE®

Cover photo by Jamie Bloomquist.
All black-and-white photos by author unless otherwise noted.

Library of Congress Cataloging-in-Publication Data
Ginieczki, Rob, 1971-
Mountain biking Pennsylvania / Rob Ginieczki.
   p. cm. -- (A Falcon guide)
Includes index.
ISBN 1-56044-861-X
1. All terrain cycling--Pennsylvania--Guidebooks. 2. Pennsylvania--Guidebooks. I. Title. II. Series.
GV1045.5.P4 G56 2000

                                      917.4804'44--dc21
                                                  CIP

 Text pages printed on recycled paper.

Manufactured in the United States of America
First Edition/Second Printing

CAUTION

Outdoor recreational activities are by their very nature potentially hazardous. All participants in such activities must assume the responsibility for their own actions and safety. The information contained in this guidebook cannot replace sound judgment and good decision-making skills, which help reduce risk exposure, nor does the scope of this book allow for disclosure of all the potential hazards and risks involved in such activities.

    Learn as much as possible about the outdoor recreational activities in which you participate, prepare for the unexpected, and be cautious. The reward will be a safer and more enjoyable experience.

Contents

Dedication vi

Acknowledgments vii

Map Legend viii

Statewide Locator Map ix

Get Ready to Crank! 1

    Pennsylvania State Parks, Forests, and Game Lands 3

    Allegheny National Forest 4

    Penn's Woods 4

    Hunting Season 5

How to Use This Guide 6

Duct Tape and Other Important Stuff 10

Ethics of the Trail 10

The Rides

Laurel Highlands

  1 Moraine State Park 12

  2 Youghiogheny River Rail-Trail 15

  3 Sugarloaf Surprise 21

  4 Sugar Run Sneak 24

  5 Laurel Hill Lung-Buster 27

  6 Mount Davis 31

  7 Mountain View Trail 35

  8 Jones Mill Run 39

  9 Roaring Run Ramble 42

10 Powdermill Loop 45

11 Laurel Summit Loop 49

12 Lower Beam Loop 53

13 Taggart's Traverse 56

14 Wolf Rocks 60

15 Ghost Town Trail 64

Allegheny Plateau

16 Rockton Mountain 67

17 Parker Dam State Park 70

18 Big Springs Draft 74

19 Gore Vista 77

20 Little Toby Rail-Trail 80

21 Garocii Quarry Switchback Trail 84

22 Big Mill Creek 87

23 Beaver Meadows 90

24 Lower Buzzard Swamp 93

25 Upper Buzzard Swamp 96

26 Kelly Pines Powerhouse 99
27 Willow Creek ATV Trail 102
28 Brush Hollow 105
29 Minister Creek 108
30 Thundershower Surprise 111
31 Rimrock Ramble 114

Endless Mountains

32 Commissioner Run 118
33 Potato City Singletrack 122
34 Middle Ridge Trail 125
35 Asaph Classic 129
36 Bee Tree Trail 133
37 Wild Apple to Bake Oven 136
38 The Grand Canyon 140
39 Big Trestle Trail 145
40 Black Forest Shay Trail 149
41 Pump Station to Shady Grove 152
42 Ruth Will Trail 157
43 Tamarack Tower 161

Ridge and Valley Province

44 Cowbell Hollow 166
45 Boiling Springs 171
46 Tunnel Mountain Trail 174
47 Little Flat Fire Tower 178
48 Rattlesnake Mountain 181

Valleys of the Susquehanna

49 Deep Hollow 186
50 Blue Knob 190
51 Pigeon Hills 194
52 Hidden Tunnel Trail 197
53 Roaring Run 202
54 Big Springs to Bear Pond 206
55 Grave Ridge to Rocky Pass 211
56 Three Mile Trail 216
57 Chimney Rocks 219
58 Rocky Ridge 223
59 Lake Redman 227
60 Spring Valley 231
61 Devils Race Course 234
62 Stony Valley Rail-Trail 237

Coastal Piedmont and Dutch Country

63 Kelly's Run Pinnacle 242
64 Cornwall Fire Tower 246
65 Governor Dick to Dinosaur Rock 249
66 Roadkill Hill 253
67 Blue Marsh Lake Loop 256
68 French Creek 260
69 Wicked Wissahickon Valley 265
70 Pine Run Preamble 269
71 The Edge 272
72 Delaware Canal Path 278
73 South Mountain 282
74 Ironton Railroad 286
75 Homestead Trail 290
76 Jacobsburg Jive 294

Lehigh Valley and Pocono Plateau

77 Bob's Option 299
78 Summit Hill 303
79 Switchback Gravity Railroad 307
80 The American Standard 310
81 Broad Mountain 314
82 Lehigh Gorge 317
83 Pohopoco Tract 321
84 Wolf Swamp 326
85 Bradys Lake 329
86 High Knob to Pecks Pond 332
87 Maple Run Ramble 335
88 Promised Land 338
89 Shanerburg Run 342
90 Worlds End Trail 347
91 High Knob Vista 351

A Short Index of Rides 355
Appendix A: Land Management Contacts 358
Appendix B: Maps and Guides 358
Appendix C: Camping 359
Appendix D: Pennsylvania's Weather 359
Glossary 360
About the Author 362

Dedication

Taggart Schubert
Whose spirit endures in the wild
In the coyote's howl
On the wings of hawks up high
Long may you run Tag, long may you run.

Acknowledgments

Thanks to the following people for helping make this book a reality:

- All the folks at Bikesport in Trappe, including owner Rich Politz, Mark "Pork Roll" Taylor, and Matt Kary, who helped me out with all my technical, mechanical, and mental problems.
- Ed Hall for doing the same at Bikewerks in Harleysville.
- Karl Rosengarth for the kind use of his abode and the twilight urban-assault tour of his town.
- Beth Gorny for enduring friendship and encouragement on the trail.
- All the fellas at Dirt Rag Magazine and their annual Retro-ride.
- Laurel Hill State Park Ranger Doug Finger for sharing a ride and for all his professional help in the Laurel Summit–Hidden Valley area.
- Dean Leone for sharing his local insight and secret finds in the Jim Thorpe area.
- Jay DeJesus for his soul-sharing and trials teaching.
- Mike Gruver for the ride down one of the last free-flowing rivers in the U.S.
- Ed and Ted Patton for the use of their awesome facility.
- My mom, Nancy, and sister, Christie, for their editing, and for their emotional and spiritual support.
- Great Spirit for the creation of beautiful wilderness and the spiritual energy that makes me whole.

Map Legend

Interstate		Campground	
U.S. Highway		Picnic Area	
State Highway/County Road		Buildings	
Forest Road		Peak/Elevation	x 4,507 ft.
Interstate Highway		Gate	
Paved Road		Parking Area	
Gravel Road		Fire Tower	
Unimproved Road		Railroad Track	
Trail (singletrack)		Cliffs/Bluff	
Main Trail		Power/Telephone Line	
Trailhead		Forest Boundary	
Route Marker		County Boundary	
Waterway		Pipeline	
Intermittent Waterway/Creek		Boardwalk	
Lake/Reservoir		Radio Tower	
Swamp		Map Orientation	N
Mining Site		Scale	0 0.5 1 MILES
Bridge		City	
Spring		Point of Interest/Vista	
Waterfall		Boulders	

Statewide Locator Map

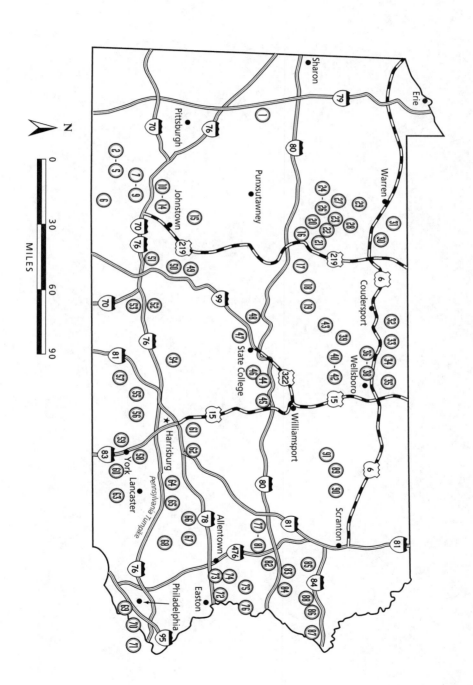

Get Ready To Crank!

Pennsylvania, home to some of the finest woodland riding in the lower 48 states, is a mecca for technical mountain biking. Like the slickrock of Utah, the high mountain passes of the San Juans, the alpine meadows of Bozeman, Montana, or the sagebrush drainages of Jackson, Wyoming, Pennsylvania has its very own special and unique features. Traditional east-coast riding is tough and technical, and Pennsylvania may very well be the best place to hone your rock-hopping and stump-jumping skills. Not only does Pennsylvania offer varied terrain, but the state's history has helped shape the trails into what they are today. In order for you to fully appreciate the rides and understand their incredible natural and historical features we must first take a ride back in time, back when mountain bikes were made from mastodon bones.

Ice sheets and glaciers, which covered two-thirds of the state, carved out the face of the landscape and deposited moraines. Scars and features like lakes, swamps, and bogs are still visible on the landscape today and can be found along many of the rides, especially in the Pocono Plateau. Most of the rock in Pennsylvania is a sandstone or shale composite, since Pennsylvania was at one time ocean-front property. A mix of sedimentary and metamorphic rock litters the trails throughout the state. Fossils are found in the shale north of the Delaware Water Gap, and Skolithos worm burrows are easily observed in the Montalto quartzite in the Michaux State Forest. The cliffs that survived glaciation and erosion offer some of the best climbing in the state. Limestone caves are abundant in the Ridge and Valley Province. The Wind Cave, which is the largest plate-tectonic cave east of the Mississippi, is east of York on the Susquehanna River. Needless to say, there's plenty of rock out there to keep any rider happy.

As the ice retreated, the trees grew in thick. Not long after, Native Americans roamed these forested hills, living a life of spiritual unity with the land. It was in these deep, dark forests that tribal members of the Iroquois Six Nations (Cayuga, Mohawk, Oneida, Onondaga, Seneca, and Tuscarora) shared their reverence for the land until the white man landed on the Atlantic shore. Many places and towns throughout the state have kept their original Native American names, such as Shickshinny, Macanaqua, Monongahela, Susquehannock, and Tyoga. The history of Native Americans runs very deep in Pennsylvania and their legacy remains in the names of places, the arrowheads in the fields, and the footpaths of brave warriors.

With the white man came many things both good and bad. Important folks like William Penn and Conrad Weiser were influential in dealing with the Native Americans, but in the end the Indians lost their pristine forests and abundant hunting grounds. Settlers imported domestic livestock and slowly began to clear the state for grazing and farming lands. Ancient stone walls are still found in second-generation forests throughout many regions. These dividing structures were built from rocks cleared from the fields.

Clearing the land meant conflict with native wild animals, including woodland bison, wolves, mountain lions, and river otters.

The biggest change to Penn's Woods came with the industrial exploitation of the land. Pennsylvania was well known for its copious supply of natural raw materials. The coal mines in the upper Lehigh Valley (Rides 78-79) held some of the finest veins of hard anthracite coal. Coal was important to industry as well as to residents in the ever-growing city of Philadelphia. Canals were built along the Lehigh and Delaware Rivers (Rides 72, 82) and barges shipped coal to the city. Coal was also mined in the western part of the state and supplied industry with the softer bituminous coal. Strip mines and tunnel mines abound throughout the state, and much of the Pennsylvania Game Commission land is reclaimed mining operations (see Ride 43). Iron ore was mined in the central regions of the state. Blast furnaces smelted iron from ore in the early stages of steel production. Many of these massive furnaces can still be found, well preserved, in places like Pine Grove Furnace State Park and on the Ghost Town Trail in Nanty Glo (Rides 15, 55, 56). Limestone was another important resource, mined and crushed for the cement industry in the Allentown region (Ride 74).

"Black Gold" was first discovered at Drakes Well near Oil City in the Allegheny Plateau. This was the first oil well in the United States, and sparked a prospecting boom in the region. Shallow oil fields that lie just below the plateau were tapped all over the area. The remains of this once prosperous industry are evident on the Kelly Pines Powerhouse (Ride 26). There are many oil rigs still operating today along the trails in the Allegheny Plateau, draining the last few drops from the ground. With all the drilling for oil, a few prospectors also hit natural gas. These wells became important once prospectors devised a way of containing the pressure of these reserves. The north central mountains abound with gas wells, especially around the Tamarack Tower (Ride 43), which sits atop one of the largest natural underground gas fields in the United States.

Ultimately it was the lumber industry that dramatically changed the landscape and all things that lived within it. Timber was a plentiful product that was easy to find and process. No digging, drilling, or prospecting was necessary. The trees were just there for the cutting, and transportation was courtesy of Mother Nature. Upon exploring the north-central regions of the state, Conrad Weiser went on to say that the forests were so dense that if the sun shone through at all, it would be in an area no larger than your hand. Monolithic white pine and hemlock trees were felled at an astounding rate. Where streams had a heavy enough flow, dams were built and logs were "splashed" down to the mills in the valleys. Narrow gauge railroads were built into remote drainages and linked with other railways in the valleys.

Many of the trails throughout the state use these old logging railroad grades and pathways (Rides 38, 39, 42, 46, 54). The tall, straight, and girthy pine and hemlock logs were important to the shipbuilding industry, and many sailing ship masts came from these woods. The thick, red bark from the hemlocks was used in the process of tanning leather hides, which were soaked in large vats of tannic acid. Many tanneries sprung up around lumber mills and vice versa, and small villages soon began to grow. The villages of Tannery on the Lehigh Gorge (Ride 82) and Wells Tannery near the Hidden Tunnel Trail (Ride 52) are perfect examples of this once prosperous business.

During the Great Depression, young men working under President Roosevelt's Civilian Conservation Corps built trails and structures throughout the state. Many of the stone projects from the 1930s still remain today; the CCC trails offer a motherlode of sweet, woodland singletrack. Numerous stone dams and pavilions can be observed at state picnic areas and parks such as Parker Dam State Park (Ride 17). The best rides in the state follow some of these hand-cut trails. This combination of the exploration and exploitation of Penn's Woods has left us with many pristine trails and paths to ride. From original Native American footpaths to the industrial canals and railways to the sweat of the CCC workers, Pennsylvania is endowed with spectacular trails of historical significance.

PENNSYLVANIA STATE PARKS, FORESTS, AND GAME LANDS

Pennsylvania state parks, forests, and game lands are some of the most beautiful lands in the state. Most of the 91 rides in this guide travel through one of these three types of state land. Each division has its own rules and guidelines on land usage. Most of the state parks are located in special areas that harbor unique geologic features and offer camping. Many state parks surround a body of water, a few parks boast showers, rustic cabin rentals, and bike and boat rentals. A handful of Pennsylvania's 108 state parks are actually open to mountain biking and are found in this guide. All other trails found within state park boundaries are off-limits to mountain bikes. State parks do in fact make great base camps for many of the rides listed in the guide. I highly recommend getting the free Pennsylvania State Parks and Forests map. This map highlights all the state park, forest, and game land areas and offers a detailed list of the amenities found at each state park and state forest. The Land Management Contacts Appendix lists the phone numbers and e-mail information for these three agencies.

The wild and wonderful state forests contain many outstanding mountain bike trails. With 20 independent state forests totaling over 2 million acres, it's easy to pedal away from civilization. The largest continuous cluster of state forest lands located in the north-central mountains is probably the most remote and wild in the entire state. State forests—often discarded lands of the early twentieth century timber companies—hold many hidden treasures: waterfalls, caves, cliffs, virgin forest, high mountain cranberry bogs, rare plants, native brook trout, reclusive bear, and elk. Although the forests are managed to provide a continuous supply of timber, there are 44 Natural Areas and 13 Wild Areas designated to preserve the unique natural beauty and rugged character of certain locations. These areas are open to foot traffic only, in order to preserve the unique plants and animals. Some of the finest views are found in the state forests, many of which are covered in this guide.

State game lands make up the third group of state-owned lands open to public recreation. These smaller tracts of land were primarily set aside for the preservation of hunting in the state. Some of these lands are reclaimed strip mines and make for some tricky and interesting trail riding. State game lands are not open to camping and are basically regarded as day use areas. Many habitat projects can be observed along the rides that pass through these tracts, including ponds, swamps, food plots, and tree plantings. The game lands represent ideal habitats for our game birds and animals and are heavily used during the fall hunting seasons.

Some rides follow trails on public utility lands belonging to the power, gas, and oil companies; a few others ride on local county park lands. Although utility lands are unrestricted for mountain bike recreation, local parks have their own specific land use guidelines. The Army Corps of Engineers is another land manager that allows mountain biking on some holdings. Consult the appendix for phone numbers of these specific county and government land managing agencies to learn more about their rules and regulations, as some trails are open on a conditional basis.

ALLEGHENY NATIONAL FOREST

Located in the northwestern region of the state, this government land holding is managed by the USDA Forest Service. The sale of commercial oil first began here, in Titusville, back in 1859. Since then oil, natural gas, and some of the largest stands of black cherry in the world have become the profitable natural resources of the forest. As a result there are many paths, trails, and roads to explore here. The Allegheny National Forest is divided into four ranger districts and boasts over 600 miles of trail open to mountain bikes! Included in this astounding figure are the numerous ATV, snowmobile, and cross-country ski trails. Campgrounds, recreation areas, and regulations in the forest are found on the Allegheny National Forest Region map, which can be purchased through the information in the Appendix.

PENN'S WOODS

The woods in Pennsylvania are a wonderful and beautiful place with many hidden treasures for the adventurous explorer. To ride in these woods, you must be in harmony with nature; good karma is the stuff that'll get you home. The woods here are relatively safe but they do possess a few dangers worth noting, the first being water. Water is something easy to find just about anywhere in the state. Springs abound in the high mountain country, and just about anywhere you turn you're bound to hit water. Water crossings, though, can be downright dangerous, especially in the spring thaw when streams, creeks, and rivers are running much higher than normal. Never underestimate the power and force of water. Potable water presents another dilemma because the water sources and quality are not monitored.

Many of the springs are suitable for drinking but the chance of ingesting giardia still exists. All water should be treated by filtering or boiling to avoid the "bovine bowel."

Lightning is another powerful force of nature, and mid-summer thunderstorms can be quite dangerous in the high mountains. Exposed areas, especially along ridge tops, are highly susceptible to lighting strikes. Tornadoes have become more prevalent throughout the state. The evidence of their wicked wrath can be observed on rides 17, 86, and 88, vivid and frightening reminders of nature's fury. Keep an eye to the sky and avoid threatening weather. Trees can pose a danger if you are stuck in a violent storm with strong winds. In Mother Nature's housecleaning, sometimes whole trees and large limbs come crashing down. I've cheated death a few times in storms; it's an experience you'll want to avoid.

The woods are blessed with animals and insects, some of which can be harmful. The black bear is generally a very reclusive and timid animal, except of course when you come ripping around a blind singletrack and scare a mama bear with cubs. Frightened or cornered bears are dangerous and you should make every effort to respect their space. Although the state has not yet formally acknowledged the presence of mountain lions, the increased sightings of mountain lions in the state are worth mentioning. The eastern diamondback rattlesnake, or timber rattler, and the copperhead are poisonous, reclusive, and spectacular reptiles. The timber rattler lives in the rocky regions of the higher mountains and is rarely seen, mainly due to its fantastic camouflage. The copperhead is another master of disguise and lives in cool, lush woodlands near rocks and water. Both reptiles are protected and should be respected.

Various wasps, hornets, and bees can pose a problem for the allergic rider. White-faced hornets build beautiful paper nests, usually in pine trees. Bump into one of these and you'll never forget the experience. The same goes for yellow jackets, who usually build their underground homes in soft, loamy soils. A few spiders such as the wolf spider have been known to give a mean bite when handled and bull elk in the north central mountains can get a bit testy during the fall rut. Treat all animals with respect and they will generally do the same for you.

Finally, the chance of getting turned around and lost in these woods is a real possibility, especially if you are poor at following directions. The old phrase "just walk down hill, follow a stream and eventually you'll come out to a road" holds true in Penn's Woods. Get familiar with the ride and grab hold of the extra maps listed in the ride. With these tools and a bit of common sense, you should have no problems finding your way.

HUNTING SEASON

Anyone venturing on these rides during the hunting season needs to be aware of open hunting seasons and to wear florescent orange. The general hunting seasons run from mid-October to late January. The antlered deer season runs for two weeks, beginning the first Monday after Thanksgiving; this is the most dangerous part of hunting season, and, if you need to be in the woods during this time, make yourself seen and heard. Contact the Pennsylvania Game Commission on season dates, as they change from year to year.

How to Use This Guide

The guide was designed as just that, a guide. It will not hold your hand, pedal your bike, fix your flat, or save you from ravenous wild beasts on the trail. The purpose is to offer an adventurous experience in the great outdoors of Pennsylvania and to test your personal mettle on a mountain bike. If you are unsure of your riding and outdoor skills, seek a guide or more experienced friend to assist you on these rides. Some trails are obscure and remote, requiring strong navigational, first aid, and backcountry skills. Remember you are the only one responsible for yourself. The rides have been organized by region: Laurel Highlands, Allegheny Plateau, Endless Mountains, Ridge and Valley Province, Valleys of the Susquehanna, Coastal Piedmont and Dutch Country, and the Lehigh Valley and Pocono Plateau region. The guide has been carefully formatted to offer you all the essential information needed to locate, enjoy, and successfully complete all 91 rides. Listed below are the category headings and a description of what they entail.

Number and name of the ride: For ease of referencing, rides have been numbered and named. The numbers follow a sequential order through seven specific regions within the state, from the southwest to the northeast. The names of the rides come from many sources. Some rides are named after a specific trail traversed during the ride, others are named after important natural or geologic features, and some take on long-time local names.

Location: The general area where the trailhead can be found and its direction and distance from a prominent town. It is from this town that directions are given to the trailhead under the Access heading.

Distance: The ride's length in miles and type of ride (out and back, one way, or loop). Almost every ride in this guide is a loop, the way it should be.

Time: A rough estimate of how long it would take an intermediate rider to complete the ride, pedaling throughout the entire experience. This number has a high and low range to better judge the ride but does not include time allotted for rest stops or exploration of the unique features found along the ride. Many rides have awesome highlights that beg for additional exploratory time, so plan for it. Conditional factors can greatly influence the time needed to complete a ride as well. Sudden rain storms, snow, windfallen trees, and mechanical difficulties are just a few of the adversities you may face. Be prepared for the worst.

Tread: This gives you a basic idea of what types of trail and surfaces you will find. Trails are composed of a broad and spicy mix: paved road, dirt road, cinder rail-trail, grassy old woods roads (includes logging roads and most doubletrack), ATV trail, jeep (four-wheel drive) road, and, of course, stellar singletrack are all well represented. The trail composites vary from sand, loam, mica, clay, and hardpacked dirt to boulder-strewn rock gardens. A variety of rock exists in Pennsylvania, from slick shale to grippy sandstones and conglomerates.

Aerobic level: A basic description of the level of physical effort demanded by the ride. The categories are easy, moderate, and difficult, and are relative to your personal level of fitness. A more detailed description of these three categories can be found on page 8.

Technical difficulty: This lists the objective hazards found along the ride and what skill level is needed to keep the rubber side down. The rides are rated on a scale of 0 to 5, 5 being the most difficult. As with the Aerobic level, this rating is relative to your own level of technical skill. A more detailed description of this scale can be found on page 9.

Highlights: A quick glance at the spectacular sites found along the ride. This section lists points of interest, both natural and man-made.

Land status: A listing of the agencies which own or manage the land on which the ride travels. Most of the rides cruise on state lands (park, forest, or game lands), with a few running in county parks, utility right-of-ways, and the Allegheny National Forest. Most agencies offer maps to the lands they manage and can be contacted with the information listed in the Land Management Contacts Appendix.

Maps: This section lists the United States Geologic Survey (USGS) maps associated with the ride. Many USGS maps are out of date and do not show the actual trails that the ride follows. Use the USGS and land agency maps in conjunction with the maps in this guide to form a better picture of the route. I suggest that you use a USGS county map which covers a lot more terrain than the 7.5-minute quadrangle maps. The land agency maps are also listed in this section and can be located with the information from the Maps and Guides Appendix. Even though this guidebook provides outstanding detailed maps, additional maps aid in finding your way and exploring other side trails listed in the ride. You gotta have maps!

Access: This tells you how to get to the trailhead. These are detailed driving directions from the prominent town listed in the Location section. The Pennsylvania Atlas and Gazetteer is an indispensable tool in finding all the rides because it shows all the small side roads and dirt roads in the state. More important, you can mark the trailhead locations in this detailed guide for return visits to that killer ride.

Notes on the trail: An armchair tour through all the dirt, grime, blood, sweat, and gears of the ride. This section may also include the brief history of the area and the incredible features you will find along the way. It will then take you on a written journey, painting a vivid picture of the trail and its surroundings. Highlighted information and key landmarks are all described in detail. Occasional options are listed for ride alterations.

The Ride: This scroll of numbers, resembling an audit sheet, is your detailed mileage log of the ride. This accurate listing assists in finding the proper turn to keep you on track. If you don't have a computerized bicycle odometer, it might be a good time to visit your local bike shop and pick one up. Better yet, have them install it so that it is as accurate as possible. Find out how to tweak it so that it jives with the guidebook.

RATING THE RIDES

This guide was designed to assist in finding the ideal ride for you by rating the rides under two separate categories: **Aerobic level**—the physical effort required to push the pedals across the varied terrain throughout the ride, and **Technical difficulty**—the level of bike handling skill (and mental balance) needed to keep the rubber side down. These may be the most difficult and subjective sections to write, so the following descriptions will explain the two categories and their ratings. In choosing a ride, you should also take into account additional conditional factors such as length of the ride, terrain, weather, and trail conditions.

AEROBIC LEVEL RATINGS

Most mountain biking is not just "aerobic." The anaerobic, full-body workout received from horsing a 25-pound bicycle through rough terrain is downright difficult. Hill climbs will have your heart throbbing and the flats will require finesse. On the flip side, many of the more scenic rides follow some of the easiest grades. Pennsylvania's topography is varied and diverse—mountainous climbs are brutal and the rocky ridge-tops can be wicked. Valley cruises and rocking hills are beautiful and typically more flat.

Easy: Flat or gently rolling terrain with no steep or prolonged climbs.

Moderate: Some hills with climbs that may be short and steep or longer and more gradual in grade. Usually contains more challenging terrain that requires some extra effort.

Strenuous: Multiple or sustained climbs over steep terrain and burly sections of demanding technical trail. Requires riding the granny gear and a high level of endurance, power, and cardiac fitness. Some hiking may be required of the adventurous but less fit rider.

TECHNICAL DIFFICULTY RATINGS

Riding in Pennsylvania typically requires a vast array of technical skills. Although the state may not have thousands of feet of vertical climbing, Pennsylvania contains some of the most intense and technical singletrack in the lower 48 states. Technical difficulty is rated on a scale from 0-5, easiest to most difficult. The objective ratings listed are a combination of the type of obstacles and the frequency in which they occur, using the hardest section encountered as the ride rating. Use this rating in conjunction with the Elevation profile to get a feel for the length of technical sections throughout the ride. Some rides may have difficult technical ratings but the actual technical sections may be very short and easily hiked through. I have used plus (+) and minus (-) symbols to help clarify the gray areas between various levels of difficulty.

Level 0: Flat, smooth trail similar to paved road. May be hard-packed cinder or asphalt.

Level 1: Smooth tread, paved or dirt road and cinder rail-trail with occasional lumps, bumps, and technical obstacles. Requires basic bike handling skills and is easily negotiated by riders of all ages and levels.

Level 2: Mostly smooth tread with wide, hard-packed single track and/or dirt and old woods roads. Some sections may contain small ruts and loose sand, dirt or gravel trail surfaces.

Level 3: Irregular tread with some rough sections including occasional rocks, roots, logs, water bars, and loose trail surfaces. May include short but steep ascents and descents. Rideable lines are more readily recognized through these sections.

Level 4: Rough tread with few smooth areas. More obscure lines through technical singletrack. May have steeper and more sustained climbs. Contains a variety of obstacles including rocks, roots, logs, water bars, off camber sections, loose sand and rock, and bar-grabbing singletrack. Rideable lines are more obscure and difficult.

Level 5: Sustained and extreme sections of gnarly trail with objective hazards like rock gardens, slick roots, burly boulders, logs, deep water bars and quagmire mud. Extreme climbs, descents, and hair-raising off-camber sections. These are trails others fear to walk on!

ELEVATION PROFILES

The elevation graphs presented here are designed to aid in route-finding and to present a visual cross-section of the ride. The trail type and technical difficulty of sections throughout the ride are also well-defined with the appropriate icons and markings. The trail type used on the trail map corresponds to the trail type on the elevation profile. There are various, very small sections in both the trail type and the difficulty rating descriptions that do not appear on the actual graph due to their short length. These minute differences are described in detail in the ride section. Each elevation profile has an elevation shown in feet and a distance shown in miles. Some hills and descents may look steeper than they appear in reality due to the sizing of the diagram to fit the guide. Most of the elevation profiles also pinpoint landmarks and special points of interest along the ride. Use these features to aid in your route-finding and enjoyment of the ride. Depicted below is an example of the elevation profile and its different features:

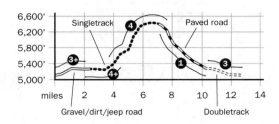

The descriptions and ratings for the rides are as accurate as possible. Personal taste, skill, and level of adventure differ from person to person. Get to know the guide and use this information as a starting point. As with alpine, ice, and rock climbing, half the fun is finding the route and trying to stay on it. Like everything in life, the trails are in a constant state of change. In the woods the only thing you can expect is the unexpected.

Duct Tape and Other Important Stuff

There are a few items a rider must not overlook when heading out on any of the following trails; a small first aid kit, tools, water, food, and of course duct tape. Although there are berries, buds, bark, and roadkill, there's nothing like having an energy bar to pull you through a brain-frying bonk. Water is a readily available commodity but drinking from untreated sources is an invitation for a parasitic party in you lower intestine. Bring sufficient water to hydrate and/or flush debris from gnarly diggers. Barring that you will enjoy the dab-free ride, there may be a point where you donate you epidermis and other bodily fluids back to the earth. A small first aid kit (or roll of duct tape) may never be needed but will always be handy in the event of a disaster. A rider also needs tools and, more importantly, to know how to use them. Carry tubes, plenty of them, especially if you run a low tire pressure and ride technical stuff. This is serious 'snakebite' country. It's also handy to have a pump, tire levers, patch kit, Allen wrenches and the ultimate—duct tape. I could write another book on the uses of duct tape, but lets just say it has saved many riders from a long hike out of the backwoods.

Ethics of the Trail

Mountain biking carries with it a special code of ethics. It would be utopian if all riders displayed courtesy and respect for the land and the creatures they share it with. Following the six basic ideals designed by the International Mountain Biking Association (IMBA), a rider will be much more in tune with their environment and experience a oneness with the trail. So here it is, the mountain biking code of ethics.

IMBA RULES OF THE TRAIL

The International Mountain Bicycling Association (IMBA) is a non-profit advocacy organization dedicated to promoting mountain biking that's environmentally sound and socially responsible. IMBA's work keeps trails open and in good condition for everyone.

These rule of the trail are reprinted with permission from IMBA.

1. Ride on open trails only. Respect trail and road closures (ask if not sure), avoid possible trespass on land, obtain permits and authorization as may be required. Federal and state wilderness areas are closed to cycling. The way you ride will influence trail management decisions and policies.

2. Leave no trace. Be sensitive to the dirt beneath you. Even on open (legal) trails avoid riding immediately after heavy rains or when the trail surface is soft and muddy. In some locations, muddy trails are unavoidable. Recognize different types of soils and trail construction. Practice low impact cycling. This also means staying on existing trails and not creating new ones. Be sure to pack out at least as much as you pack in.

3. Control your bicycle. Inattention for even a second can cause problems. Obey all bicycle speed regulations and recommendations.

4. Always yield trail. Give your fellow trail users plenty of advance notice when you're approaching. A friendly greeting (or bell) is considerate and works well; don't startle others. Show your respect when passing by slowing to a walking pace or even stopping, particularly when you meet horses. Anticipate other trail users around corners or in blind spots.

5. Don't scare animals. All animals are startled by an unannounced approach, a sudden movement, or a loud noise. This can be dangerous for you, others, and the animals. Give animals extra room and time to adjust to you. When passing horses, use special care and follow the directions from the horseback riders (ask if uncertain). Running cattle and disturbing wildlife is a serious offense. Leave gates as you found them, or as marked.

6. Plan ahead. Know your equipment, your ability, and the area in which you are riding—and prepare accordingly. Be self-sufficient at all times, keep your equipment in good repair, and carry all necessary supplies for changes in weather or other conditions. A well-executed trip is a satisfaction to you and not a burden or offense to others. Always wear a helmet.

The information in this guide is as complete, accurate, and up-to-date as possible. If you should find otherwise, please contact Rob Ginieczki, c/o Falcon Publishing, P.O. Box 1718, Helena, MT 59624.

Laurel Highlands

Located in the southwestern region of the state, this lower section of the Allegheny mountains is beautiful and rugged. Containing the highest mountain in Pennsylvania, Mount Davis, this region boasts some of the burliest hill climbs, sweetest singletrack, and longest descents in the state. On the outskirts of Pittsburgh in the Forbes State Forest, the rides in this historical region touch on many geologic features. Noted for its prolific stands of ridgetop mountain laurel, this region really comes alive in mid-June. Spectacular bursts of white and pink flowers contrast against the deep-forest green foliage in a natural display that rivals any other in the state.

Moraine State Park

Location:	Moraine State Park, 28 miles north of Pittsburgh.
Distance:	6.4-mile loop.
Time:	30 minutes to 1 hour.
Tread:	Wild singletrack through dense, young woodland; mostly nice hardpacked dirt, but mind you, the trail is littered sporadically with rocks. Going 'sailing' here isn't always a lake activity!
Aerobic level:	Moderate. There are loads of short, steep hill climbs that require some pedaling effort and momentum. Definitely a 'bumpy' ride.
Technical difficulty:	There are copious amounts of boulders throughout the ride. Nice part is that they are soft, rounded, and well-worn (until you fall on them!).
Highlights:	Lakeside riding; swimming; boat rental; marina; camping; 7-mile paved, family bike path; lots of food concessions, including a marina restaurant.
Land status:	Pennsylvania State Parks, Department of Conservation and Natural Resources.
Maps:	DCNR Moraine State Park map; Moraine State Park Mountain Bike Trail map.

Access: From Pittsburgh take Interstate 79 north to exit 29 and take U.S. Highway 422 east to the Moraine State Park South Shore exit. Once you exit, turn around and get onto U.S. Highway 422 west, to the North Shore exit. Get off at the North Shore exit and follow the signs for the Davis Hollow Marina. Approximately 1 mile before the marina is the intersection of Mount Union Road and North Shore Drive; turn left onto Mount Union Road. Drive about 0.5 mile before turning into the second parking lot on the right. This lot is the trailhead.

Notes on the trail: A long, long time ago, back when cavemen mountain bikers wore turtle shells for helmets and frames were made from Mastadon bones, the Wisconsin ice sheet stretched down into Pennsylvania. As the ice receded and mountain bike technology improved, huge deposits of rock rubble and boulders were left at their terminus. This glacial moraine is extremely evident at Moraine State Park, and has not only made for a unique geologic feature but also made for a radical riding surface.

This ride is the product of an incredible effort by local riders who volunteered to design, build and maintain a mountain bike trail within the state park. From the trailhead lot, you can visibly see the huge deposits of smooth glacial stone. The ride begins in these rounded boulders and follows the powerline cut for a short way. A steep and switchbacked descent will test your agility and technical prowess as you work your way out to the Davis Hollow Marina. An old woods road climb and more singletrack wind you back up to Alexander Ridge Road, where intensely tight and rolling singletrack brings you again into the moraine field, and back to the trailhead. It's quite a strenuous little loop, with some sweet carved berms and fast, scary singletrack.

Moraine State Park offers more that just a cool mountain biking loop. After hitting the loop a few times, cool off in the lake at the swimming beach or rent a sailboat. Campsites are available, and I hear that the fishing is great. Also worth checking out are the 7-mile paved family bicycle path that cruises along the north shore to the marina restaurant, the wind-surfing area, and the countless snack bars throughout the park. This place is still hopping in the winter with ice skating, ice boating, cross-country skiing, snowmobiling, and sledding. One would never know that at one time this area was once a huge strip mine and an environmental nightmare. Due in part to the concerted efforts of the state, it is now an outdoor recreator's paradise!

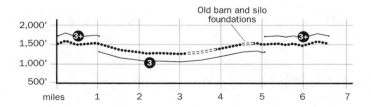

Moraine State Park

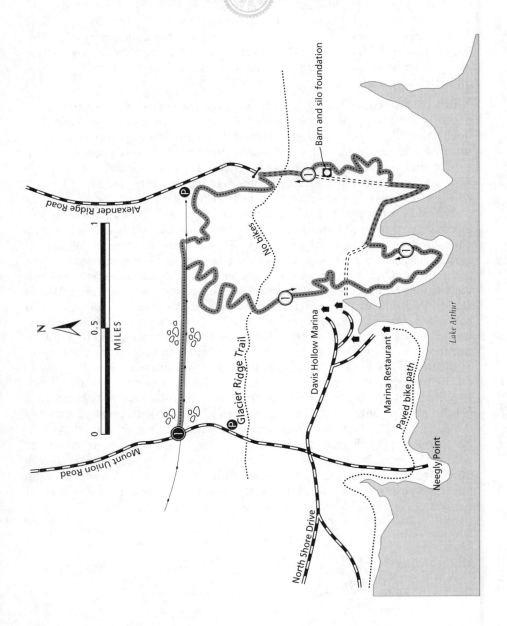

0.0 From the parking lot, follow the trail as it leaves the upper right corner of the lot, out onto the power line cut. The trail will weave in, around, and over the huge rocks as it climbs, descends, and reascends.

0.8 Turn right, into the woods, and get ready to rail some sweet, technical, switchbacked singletrack.

1.6 The Glacier Ridge Trail cuts across, this trail is closed to mountain bikes.

2.0 Trail forks. Keep left at the fork and climb the hill.

2.3 Cross the dirt road and continue to descend on the fat singletrack. You will soon drop down near the shoreline and follow along the lake.

3.1 Turn right onto the dirt old woods road, following it around as it switchbacks left up the hill.

3.8 Take a hard right onto singletrack and climb a steep series of switchbacks.

4.5 After passing an old barn and silo foundations in the woods on your left, you will come back out to the dirt road. Turn right up the dirt road, continuing to climb until you get to the gate (Alexander Ridge Road). Turn left just before the gate, over a dirt mound. Once over the mound, turn hard left, following the trail as it begins to descend down a rolling section of technical singletrack.

5.2 Turn left at the T intersection.

5.5 This is the end of the loop and the point where you exit out onto the power line. Turn left onto the power-line cut and grunt out over the glacial moraine.

6.4 Trailhead.

Youghiogheny River Rail-Trail

Location:	Ohiopyle State Park.
Distance:	0 to 33.5 miles out and back.
Time:	2 to 6 hours.
Tread:	An ultrasmooth, hardpacked cinder surface. Perfect for any type of bike and also the tow-behind child carts.
Aerobic level:	Easy. This is a rail-trail with about a 5 percent grade. The only way you know you're going downhill is by looking at the directional flow of the river.
Technical difficulty:	0. Remember, this is a rail-trail. It's a great beginner ride.
Highlights:	Two huge old railroad bridges, views of the river and rapids, cliffs to explore, great family trail or training ride, incredible photo opportunity at the gorge.

Youghiogheny River Rail-Trail

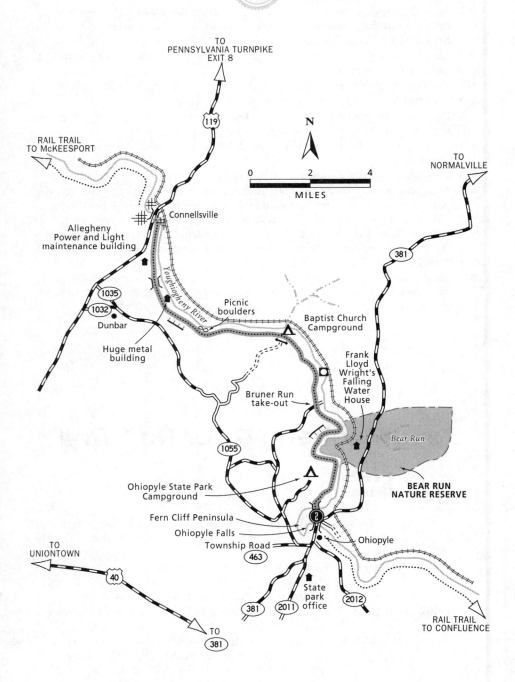

TO
PENNSYLVANIA TURNPIKE
EXIT 8

119

N

0   2   4
MILES

RAIL TRAIL
TO McKEESPORT

TO
NORMALVILLE

Connellsville

Allegheny
Power and Light
maintenance building

381

1035

1032

Dunbar

Picnic
boulders

Baptist Church
Campground

Huge metal
building

Frank
Lloyd
Wright's
Falling
Water
House

Bruner Run
take-out

1055

Bear Run

Ohiopyle State Park
Campground

BEAR RUN
NATURE RESERVE

Fern Cliff Peninsula

Ohiopyle Falls

Ohiopyle

Township Road

463

TO
UNIONTOWN

40

State
park
office

381   2011   2012

TO
381

RAIL TRAIL
TO CONFLUENCE

Land status: Ohiopyle State Park, Department of Conservation and Natural Resources, Pennsylvania Rails to Trails right-of-way.

Maps: USGS Mill Run, Connellsville, South Connellsville; Pennsylvania Rails to Trails guide map; DCNR Ohiopyle State Park map.

Access: As you enter the Ohiopyle Valley from the north on Pennsylvania Highway 381, turn right just after crossing the railroad tracks into the Fern Cliff Peninsula parking area. This is the trailhead.

Notes on the trail: This is one of the most scenic rail-trails in Pennsylvania. The ride may be tailored to any distance and is a great family cruise for those young and budding trail riders. There is much to do at this incredible outdoor location. Ohiopyle is a full-service town built around the unique features of the Yough River. The Fern Cliff Peninsula is an incredible place for a short afternoon hike and vantage points along the shore allow you to watch kayakers shooting the rapids. The Falling Waters House built by Frank Lloyd Wright is just up the road, as is the beautiful Bear Run Nature Preserve. Camping is available at the state park campground or at one of the many campgrounds along Pennsylvania 381. Many of these campsites fill up during the summer months, so call ahead for reservations. A visit here would not be complete, though, without a rafting trip down the Yough River. The town has numerous bike rental shops, so if someone in your group doesn't have a set of wheels, you can pick them up in town.

This rail-trail is part of a greater project to connect Pittsburgh with Washington, D.C. It's pretty amazing to think about riding a bike between these two points in the peacefulness of the woods. The rail-trail continues north to McKeesport and south to Confluence, but this section is the most scenic and interesting.

The ride crosses two new bridges constructed on the original rock railroad piers. From the trailhead you soon find yourself a hundred feet above the Yough River, where you can watch rafters and kayakers exiting the Railroad Rapid. It's a truly beautiful spot and a great photo opportunity as well. Traveling along the trail in the cover of the tree canopy, you will be treated to views of majestic moss-covered cliffs and occasional views of the Lower Yough's rapids. Further along you'll see the old Baptist Church campground

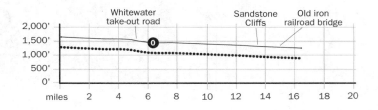

The Entrance Rapids, the middle Yough.

Laurel Highlands covered bridge.

and the huge "picnic" boulders down in the river. With only a mile to go, you cross the long train bridge that spans the valley town of Dunbar. Connellsville, your terminus, is a quaint town, complete with bike shop.

THE RIDE

0.0 From the parking lot, the rail-trail begins (continues) in the upper right corner of the lot.

0.2 Cross over the beautiful old rail bridge spanning the gorge above the Yough River. Take some time to check out the boaters as they make their way down the river.

4.0 Pass a series of 80 to 100-foot-high cliffs located up the mountain on your left.

5.8 Carefully ride across the paved road. This is the commercial take-out for boaters riding the Lower Yough. Huge buses come barreling down this one-lane road, so cross with extreme caution!

6.6 A nice view of the river from a strange bend in the trail. At one time the trail must have washed out here. A fancy retaining wall now prevents further erosion.

9.1 Pass a gated road on your left and the Baptist Church campground on the right.

12.9 Pass by the huge "picnic" boulders located down in the river on the right.

13.6 Pass another set of huge sandstone cliffs on the left.

14.5 Keep left at the fork, passing above a huge metal building.

15.0 Pass a classic old train bridge.

Riders spanning the gorge over the middle Youghigheny, on the Youghigheny Rail-Trail.

15.3 Cross over the huge rail bridge that takes you above the outskirts of Dunbar.

16.2 Pass Allegheny Power Company maintenance yard on the left.

16.5 You are now at the end of the ride in Connellsville. From this point, return back to Ohiopyle State Park. If you need grub in town or want to visit the bike shop, turn left from the wooden rail-trail bulletin board and ride down along Crawford Avenue.

33.5 Trailhead. (Not enough mileage for you? There is additional riding across the river at the visitor center. The rail-trail continues Southeast from the visitor center to Confluence, a one-way ride of 9.5 miles.)

Sugarloaf Surprise

Location:	Ohiopyle State Park.
Distance:	4.3-mile loop.
Time:	30 minutes to 1 hour.
Tread:	All singletrack on well-maintained snowmobile trails. The surface is mainly hardpack with a few short sections of grass and loose rock.
Aerobic level:	Easy to moderate. The climbs are on a relatively mellow grade and you enjoy the steeper sections on the descent. This is a rolling ride that would be great for just about any rider.
Technical difficulty:	1+. There are a few short downhill sections with small loose stones, but these are about halfway through the ride and are easily negotiated at a slower speed.
Highlights:	Mountain-top ridge ride; great woodland scenery; near the little town of Ohiopyle, which has the best white water in Pennsylvania.
Land status:	Pennsylvania State Parks, Department of Conservation and Natural Resources.
Maps:	USGS Ohiopyle; DCNR Ohiopyle State Park map.

Access: From traveling south on Pennsylvania 381 and crossing the Youghiogheny River, you will pass briefly through Ohiopyle. Note the parking areas on your right. As town abruptly ends, turn left on the paved road (Pennsylvania Road 2012) that climbs out of the valley, splitting two parking lots. Continue driving 4 miles up the road to the Sugarloaf snowmobile and mountain bike parking area. Turn right and park here. The trailhead is located at the large wooden map in the parking lot.

Notes on the trail: This ride can be tailored to suit most riders. The terrain is challenging enough for the novice but offers a super-fast ride for the intermediate and experienced rider. The rolling terrain combined with a relatively fast and smooth surface makes this ride a blast for any rider.

A large wooden map near the trailhead shows all of the trails that loop around the ridge tops. A slightly tricky start will soon have you on your way to enjoying these beautiful and well-maintained trails. The short climb takes you up between the saddle of two separate knobs. A loop around the east knob will bring you back to the saddle where an awesome descent awaits. The trail then completes its loop around Sugarloaf Knob, bringing you back

Sugarloaf Surprise

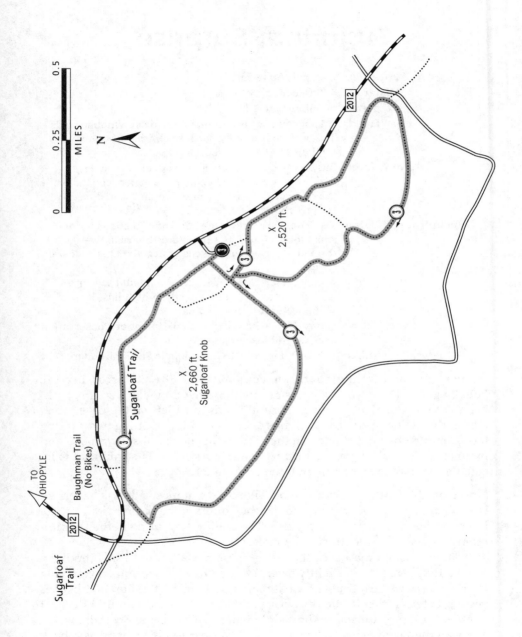

to the trailhead parking area. Try extending your fun by riding the loop backward or just plain looping it again.

Since this ride is just above Ohiopyle, don't miss out on the great amenities this cool town has to offer. From the bike shops to the food stops, it has everything a weekend warrior needs to get by without roughing it too badly. You'll find campgrounds north on Pennsylvania Highway 381 as well as the beautiful Bear Run Nature Reserve, which is a popular hiking and backpacking spot. Across from Bear Run is the famous Frank Lloyd Wright Falling Waters House situated on the waterfalls. You can visit countless waterfalls in Ohiopyle State Park and camp atop Kentucky–Tharp Knob. This campground is frequently filled to capacity, so reservations are recommended. Of course your trip would not be complete without a stop at the Dogwood, where the local river rats hang to sink a few to the sounds of Neil Young.

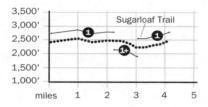

THE RIDE

0.0 Start at the wooden trail sign. Ride around behind the sign about 20 yards and turn left, climbing up a dirt singletrack trail. The trail will end at the top left of this big grassy slope.

0.1 Turn left at the four-way intersection. In about 30 yards the trail will fork. Keep left at the fork, continuing to climb. You will soon swing around to the huge grassy slope and should be able to see your car in the trailhead parking lot below.

1.0 After dropping down into the little valley and climbing back up, turn right at the right-hand trail spur. If you cross the gravel road, you missed the turn.

1.6 Turn left at the T intersection.

2.0 Turn left at the T intersection. Then, after about 30 yards, turn left at the four-way intersection and begin the fun descent. You will now be riding down behind the south face of Sugarloaf Knob. (Note: Turning right at the four-way intersection would take you back to the trailhead parking lot.)

3.2 Turn right at the T intersection onto the Sugarloaf Trail, beginning a slow climb back to the trailhead lot. During the summer the fields on both sides of the trail are full of wildflowers that attract all kinds of colorful birds and butterflies.

4.3 Back at the trailhead.

4

Sugar Run Sneak

Location:	Ohiopyle State Park.
Distance:	5.8 miles one way.
Time:	20 to 60 minutes.
Tread:	Incredible, steep, wooded singletrack that turns into ultrasmooth rail-trail.
Aerobic level:	Easy. It's is a one-way downhill ride!
Technical difficulty:	2+. The first 2 miles contain all the super-fun stuff with rocks, roots, and logs. There are also two new railroad timber bridges that may be mossy or slick. The other 4 miles are on the rail-trail.
Highlights:	A one-way ride designed for whitewater and mountain bike adventurers; spectacular waterfall.
Land status:	Ohiopyle State Park, Department of Conservation and Natural Resources.
Maps:	USGS Fort Necessity; DCNR Ohiopyle State Park map.

Access: From the town of Ohiopyle, head south on Pennsylvania Highway 381. Once across the bridge, turn right onto Pennsylvania Road 2019 and climb the steep hill. After passing the Jonathan Run parking area, keep right at the fork to the Bruner Run take-out. Turn right into the Old Mitchell Place parking area. This is the trailhead.

Notes on the trail: A visit to the Ohiopyle Valley would not be complete for any true adventurer without a trip down the rugged Lower Yough. The Lower Yough is no easy float trip, and when the water is running, the hydraulics get hungry! If you are up for shooting Class III and IV rapids, have a boat as well as a mountain bike, this is your ride. A local volunteer worked with the state park officials to design and build a singletrack trail that will legally take you from the parking lot down to the rail-trail. This was a smart move by the state as they were able to successfully accommodate the hiker and mountain biker.

 Since this is a one-way ride, you will need three forms of transportation (preferably a car, a bike, and a boat). If you have a boat, lock it up in town. If you are renting, make reservations so it'll be ready for you. Now get in the car (with bikes, of course) and cruise on up to the trailhead. Hop out at the trailhead, grab your white water gear bag and get on your mountain bike. Once in town, lock up the bike, buy the all-important shuttle pass, shoot the foam, and get a lift from Bruner Run take-out to your car. With boat secured, head back down into town to rack the bike. It's like Old Milwaukee: it really just doesn't get any better than this!

Sugar Run Sneak

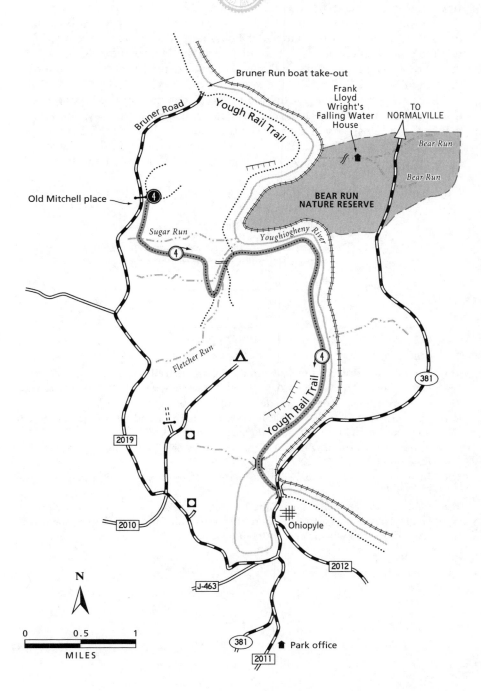

Bruner Run boat take-out

Frank Lloyd Wright's Falling Water House

TO NORMALVILLE

Bruner Road

Yough Rail Trail

Bear Run

Bear Run

BEAR RUN NATURE RESERVE

Old Mitchell place

Sugar Run

Youghiogheny River

Fletcher Run

381

Yough Rail Trail

2019

2010

Ohiopyle

2012

J-463

N

0   0.5   1

MILES

381

Park office

2011

For those who may not be prepared to tackle the gut-wrenching, bone-crunching hungry hydraulics, you will need two vehicles to complete the ride (unless you wish to ride it backward). Leave a car in town and take another one up to the trailhead. Bikes are not banned on the roads back up to the trailhead, but the chances of becoming roadkill are very high! You want to stay off these roads due to the poorly paid bus drivers who, incidentally, are extreme kayakers with no real regard for human life, including their own!

Please respect the rules of the park and do not ride on the linking hiking trails, as they are off-limits to mountain bikes. Oh, and by the way, don't forget to buy a shuttle pass if you are running the river. The bus driver will make you walk all the way up Bruner Run road with your boat if you don't have your pass—an experience you may never forget, if you live to tell about it!

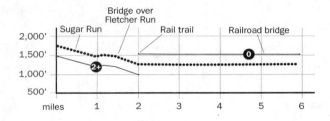

THE RIDE

0.0 From the lot, ride back out toward the road. The trail begins on the edge of the woods on the left. Look hard, as the entrance may be obscured by the foliage.

0.5 Cross over Sugar Run on wooden railroad tie bridge.

1.5 After crossing over Fletcher Run on a wooden railroad tie bridge, merge left onto the Jonathan Run Trail and continue to descend.

1.8 If the water is running, look for the sweet waterfall off to the left on Fletcher Run.

2.0 Turn right onto the Yough Rail-Trail and ride to town, crossing that beautiful bridge that spans the great gorge.

5.8 Ride out through the Fern Cliff Peninsula parking area and turn right on Pennsylvania Highway 381. Carefully cross the bridge and ride down into town. Lock the wheels and clutch a paddle!

Laurel Hill Lung-Buster

Location: Ohiopyle State Park.

Distance: 16-mile loop.

Time: 3 to 5 hours.

Tread: Mostly great, hardpacked singletrack with a few road and paved road sections mixed in.

Aerobic level: Strenuous. With 1,680 vertical feet gained in about 6 miles, this ride has the highest vertical climb in Pennsylvania. It brings you from the river valley to the mountain summits. Most of the elevation is in the first 3 miles, where the climb is very steep and sustained.

Technical difficulty: 2+. The trail is well worn and wide in places, but there are some tricky steep hills and loose rock sections you will need to negotiate both going up and coming down.

Highlights: Highest vertical climb in Pennsylvania; quad-burning climb with a brake-smoking descent; nice vista; best whitewater location in Pennsylvania, great little outdoor town.

Land status: Pennsylvania State Parks, Department of Conservation and Natural Resources.

Maps: USGS Ohiopyle; DCNR Ohiopyle State Park map.

Access: As you enter the Ohiopyle Valley from the north on Pennsylvania Highway 381, across the Youghiogheny River you will pass briefly through town. Note the parking areas on your right. As town abruptly ends, turn left onto the paved road (Pennsylvania Road 2012) that climbs out of the valley,

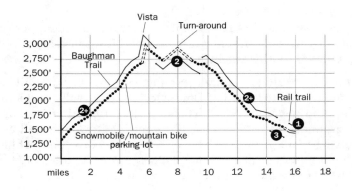

Laurel Hill Lung-Buster

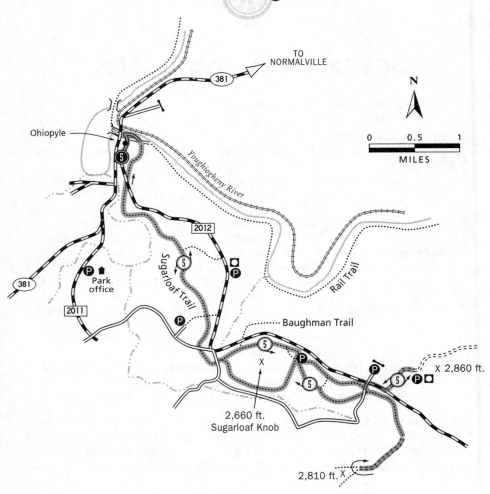

splitting two parking lots. The trailhead is located in the upper parking lot on the left, across from the shower house, and just south of the white water outfitters on the southwest side of town.

Notes on the trail: The Yough (pronounced "Yock") is a wild river that flows through the little town of Ohiopyle. The river valley, which sits 1,700 feet below the towering ridges, is rich in history. This area was once the hunting grounds of the Delaware, Shawnee, and Iroquois nations, and the town gets its name from the Native American word "ohiopehhle," which means "white, frothy water." General George Washington's 1754 attempt to capture Fort Duquesne via the Yough River was thwarted by the rugged and

The Ohiopyle Falls, Ohiopyle State Park.

somewhat ominous-looking falls, which forced him to find an alternative means of attack. More recently, when the railroad was built, scores of people from Pittsburgh would come to visit the falls on summer weekends. Eventually the state park and quaint town of Ohiopyle were established. Local legend has it that the cave under the falls extends to Kentucky.

This ride combines incredible scenery and killer terrain. Beginning in Ohiopyle, you embark on the arduous climb out of the valley. Be careful as you ride on Pennsylvania Road 2012; the river tour buses scream up and down this hill! Once on the singletrack climb, the solitude of the woods and the great forest scenery are a pleasant distraction from the constant grind to the ridge tops. Atop the ridge, the trail takes you to the high point at 2,892 feet, just below the old fire tower that once stood on the true summit. An out-and-back trip to the southwest corner of the park will lead you to a maze of old park trails and illegal ATV trails. Make sure you have a map, compass, extra water, and a lot of daylight if you choose to explore this spider web. On the return trip you can explore new singletrack before dropping down the steep, long, and somewhat sketchy descent back to the river. A short jaunt through town will have you back at the trailhead, where a wet'n'wild trip down the Yough may be in order.

THE RIDE

0.0 From the upper parking lot, head up the mountain on Pennsylvania Road 2012. Watch for the river guide buses and cars that come tearing up and down this road.

0.2 Turn right onto dirt singletrack, the Sugarloaf Trail. It would be a smart idea to read the trail on the way up, as you will be screaming down it on the descent.

2.5 Cross over the horse trail and continue straight on up the mountain.

3.1 Turn left onto the partially paved and gravel road. In approximately 0.1 mile, the trail reenters the woods on the right: turn right here.

3.4 After crossing the dirt road, the trail becomes a grassy doubletrack and forks, soon turning to dirt singletrack. Keep left at the fork, on the Sugarloaf Trail. You will soon pass the Baughman Trail on the left.

4.5 Trail comes to a four-way intersection, just before the snowmobile/mountain bike trailhead and parking lot. Turn right at the four-way intersection, following the red blazes that climb the hill. Once on top of the hill you will turn left at another four-way intersection. Shortly after that (about 30 yards) keep left at the fork. Not as complicated as it sounds!

5.5 Turn left on the gravel road then turn right on the paved road (Pennsylvania 2012).

5.8 Turn left up the rocky four-wheel drive road to the summit parking lot on the right. The view west is Laurel Ridge with an elevation of 2,887 feet. From here you will need to return back down the four-wheel drive road, turn right on Pennsylvania 2012, and then turn left onto the gravel road (back to the point at mile 5.5).

6.1 Turn left up dirt singletrack, ascending the steep hill into the woods.

7.0 Turn right at the T intersection, following the snowmobile orange diamond blazes.

8.0 At this point you will reach a fork in the trail. Turn around and head back the way you came. (An optional extension is to explore the maze of trails that lead off from the fork ahead. The free mountain bike map, which is available at the park office, shows a vague representation of these trails. But beware! This mess of interlaced trails can become quite confusing. I am serious about the map and compass!)

8.9 Turn onto the left-hand spur trail and begin the climb back up through the field.

9.5 Cross the gravel road and, once on the other side, turn left at the fork.

10.1 Turn left at the T intersection.

10.5 Left at the T intersection. Approximately 30 yards after, turn left at the four-way intersection and get ready for some serious, fast, sweet singletrack.

11.7 Turn left onto Sugarloaf Trail. Soon the trail crosses the gravel road and picks up again in the woods on the other side.

12.0 Turn left on the gravel road. In approximately 0.1 mile, the trail reenters the woods on the right: turn right here.

12.6 Cross over the horse path trail. This is where the psycho downhill begins!

15.1 Cross over Pennsylvania 2012 (watch for those cars and buses!). The trail continues a rippin' descent down to the river.

15.3 Turn left on the rail-trail cinder path and follow it out to the visitor center and train station.

15.6 From the visitor center, turn left onto Sherman Road. This will run you behind the backside of town, past the only pizza joint in a 30-mile radius, and back to the trailhead parking area.

16.0 Trailhead parking lot. Now go run the river!

Mount Davis

Location:	28 miles south of Somerset.
Distance:	11.1-mile loop.
Time:	1 to 2 hours.
Tread:	Fire roads for the most part, with a fun section of grassy doubletrack and very short sections of paved road.
Aerobic level:	Moderate. There is one sustained, moderate hill climb out of the bottom of North Wolf Rocks Road that can be a bit of a challenge. The rest of the ride is on fairly level ground that rolls lazily between the two ridge tops.
Technical difficulty:	1. The only technical section of the whole ride is the 1.5-mile-long Shelter Rock Trail, which is a bumpy mix of grassy trail, small sections of loose gravel, and muddy puddles.
Highlights:	Highest natural point in Pennsylvania (elevation 3,213 feet), scenic vistas, unique rock formations, interpretive stations, observation tower.
Land status:	Forbes State Forest, Department of Conservation and Natural Resources.
Maps:	USGS Mount Davis; DCNR Forbes State Forest map.

Access: Mount Davis is not the easiest place to get to, and a detailed forest map and the *Pennsylvania Atlas and Gazetteer* will help considerably in finding this location. From Somerset, travel south on Pennsylvania Highway 281 to New Centerville. From here take Pennsylvania Highway 653 south, passing through Rockwood to Garrett. From here take U.S. Highway 219 south, passing through Meyersdale to Salisbury. In Salisbury turn right onto Pennsylvania Highway 669, heading south to West Salisbury. Once across the bridge (Cassleman River), turn right onto Pennsylvania Road 2003 and head to the village of Saint Paul. When you get to Saint Paul there will be a road entering from the left (Pennsylvania Road 2003; the only left-hand

Mount Davis

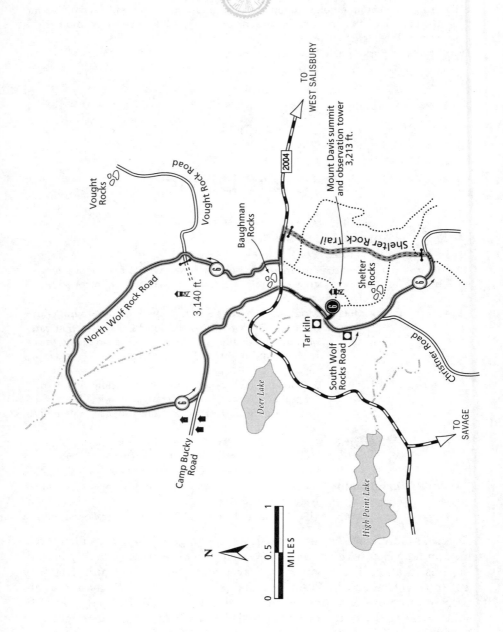

TO
WEST SALISBURY

2004

Mount Davis summit
and observation tower
3,213 ft.

Vought
Rocks

Vought Rock Road

Baughman
Rocks

Shelter Rock Trail

North Wolf Rock Road

3,140 ft.

Shelter
Rocks

Tar kiln

Christner Road

South Wolf
Rocks Road

Camp Bucky
Road

Deer Lake

TO
SAVAGE

High Point Lake

N

MILES

0   0.5   1

road spur since West Salisbury), turn left here and continue on Pennsylvania 2003. Pennsylvania 2003 turns into Pennsylvania 2004; the distance from Saint Paul to the summit of Mount Davis is 4 miles. As you crest the summit, notice the huge blue sign marking the summit pass; after this you will turn left onto South Wolf Rocks Road. Follow this road down for 1 mile and turn left into the observation tower parking lot road. This is the trailhead.

Notes on the trail: Who wouldn't want to ride on the highest point in Pennsylvania? The Mount Davis Natural Area and neighboring Negro Mountain are rich in both natural and local history and also contain unique geologic features. Although the air isn't any thinner here, it's a special place to take a spin and check out the sights. The area received its name from John Davis, a Civil War vet, land surveyor, and naturalist who spent most of his time studying the diversity of life on and around the mountain. The mountains here were never settled, due to the poor soil conditions, strange weather, and quantity of rock that littered the woods.

As settlers moved west, the Alleghenies presented a challenge to their passage. The Cumberland Trail was one of the main passageways through the hills at the time; its route is now followed by U.S. Highway 40. The two mountains also seem to trap storm clouds that contribute to the 40 inches of annual rainfall and 4-foot snow depths. Unique rock formations are found all around these areas, the most unusual being the circular stone patterns found atop Mount Davis. These circular patterns are the result of thousands of years of frost action, which heaves the stones from the earth to form the circles. Across the road is Negro Mountain which has a lot of its own strange history. The name dates back to the French and Indian War, when a brave black man died while fighting off the Indians who were attacking his companions. His unmarked grave is somewhere on the hill, now appropriately named after him for his valiant efforts. The Baughman Rocks and the Tar Kiln site are also worth checking out for their bizarre and historical significance.

Enough said about history! Let's talk mountain biking. The ride begins on an easy fire road before turning into the doubletrack Shelter Trail that follows the east end of the Natural Area. A jump across Pennsylvania Road 2004 will have you sailing down North Wolf Rocks Road, only to harshly repay your descent with an equal climb back up the shoulder of Negro Mountain. A short stop at the eerie Baughman Rocks will be the last point of interest before heading back to the trailhead. There is no water here, but there are restrooms. Oh, by the way, there are a lot of rattlesnakes off the beaten path; watch where you walk and place your hands!

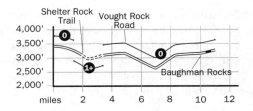

THE RIDE

0.0 From the Observation Tower parking lot, head back out the entrance road and turn left onto South Wolf Rocks Road.

0.2 Pass the historic Tar Kiln site on your right. The huge stone may be hard to see if a lot of ferns are still standing. A closer inspection will reveal the depression and trough in this huge stone used to extract pitch from pine trees.

0.5 Pass the High Point View scenic vista. From this wooden platform you can look way out over the valley. The lake in front of you is High Point Lake. Note the quarry off the southeast shore.

0.7 Turn left at the road fork, following South Wolf Rocks Road.

1.7 Turn left onto a dirt and grass doubletrack, and pass around the gate. Note the large wooden Mount Davis Natural Area sign on your left. You will soon pass the Wildcat Spring sign on your left—if the spring is running and you choose to drink from it, be sure to purify the water (as always).

2.2 Pass the Shelter Rock Trail on the left. This would be a great side trip on foot, as no bikes are allowed into the Natural Area. The hike into the rocks takes about 20 minutes.

3.3 Turn left onto Pennsylvania Road 2004. At mile 3.6, turn right onto the gravel North Wolf Rocks Road. Be careful crossing on Pennsylvania 2004, as it is heavily used.

4.7 Vought Rocks Road turns off to the right. Keep straight on North Wolf Rocks Road. A 1.5-mile side trip (one way) down Vought Rocks Road will take you to the vista and Vought Rocks formation.

7.0 You have now reached the bottom of the descent on North Wolf Rocks Road. Now it's time to pay back for the fun freewheeling ride, as you begin the long sustained climb back up the mountain.

8.3 Keep left as a gravel road (Camp Bucky Road) joins in from the right. Note the cabins and trailers back on Camp Bucky Road.

10.1 Turn left onto Pennsylvania 2004. Approximately 200 yards on your left is the Baughman Rocks handicapped parking area. Turn left here. Walk your bike back along the 40-yard trail to the rock formation and read about the rock's eerie history. Return back out to Pennsylvania 2004, this time turning right. In approximately 200 yards, turn left onto South Wolf Rocks Road, the main road to Mount Davis's summit.

11.1 Turn left onto the observation area parking lot road. Return to the trailhead.

Mountain View Trail

Location: 12 miles west of Somerset.

Distance: 9.9-mile loop.

Time: 1 to 3 hours.

Tread: Majority of the ride is on some of the most beautiful grassy singletrack in the state, with a few sections of old jeep road doubletrack.

Aerobic level: Moderate. There are many short, moderate climbs as you weave in and out of the beautiful Shafer Run drainage. Of course this also means that there are many short, fun downhills as well.

Technical difficulty: 2+. There are some hidden surprises in the grassy sections, like sunken rocks and holes. A few of the climbs and descents have some rocky sections that may be challenging.

Highlights: Beautiful mountain and valley ride, a ski hut available to mountain bikes, remote with very little traffic, many wildlife viewing opportunities.

Land status: Forbes State Forest, Pennsylvania Department of Conservation and Natural Resources.

Maps: USGS Bakersville; Laurel Highlands Snowmobile Trail System map; DCNR Forbes State Forest map.

Access: From Somerset, head west on Pennsylvania Highway 31. After passing Kooser State Park on your left (approximately 10 miles), travel another 2.5 miles and turn left on Fire Tower Road (gravel). Approximately 300 yards on your right is the huge trailhead parking lot.

Notes on the trail: The setting for this ride is in the Laurel Highlands cross-country ski trail system, which is an incredible network of well-maintained, wooded trails on state forest land. This is a spectacular ride for the adventurous novice as well as the hard-core hammerhead. The ski trails are relatively wide and the summer mountain bike traffic has started to carve a nice singletrack into the grassy surface. The best thing about these trails is that the state forest service encourages mountain biking on them to help keep vegetation down. This results in less maintenance work for the trail crew folks who already do an outstanding job of maintaining this awesome trail system.

The ride begins with a gradual climb through a spider web of trails atop a small knoll and down into the Shafer Run drainage. At the junction of three trails you will discover a beautiful rustic backcountry warming hut.

Mountain View Trail

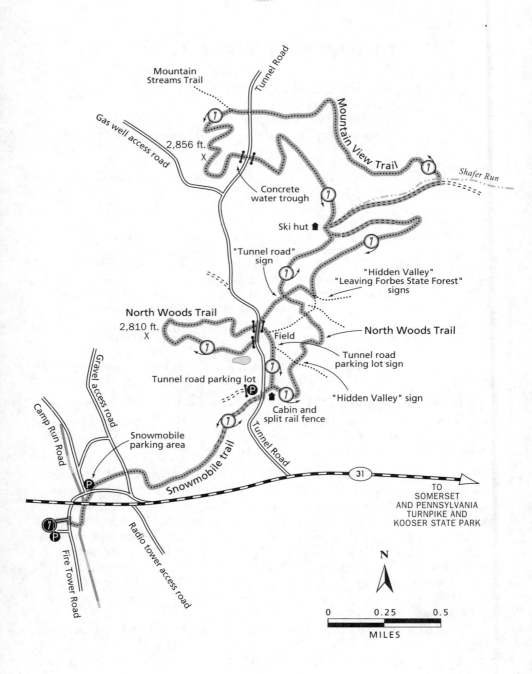

Mountain Streams Trail

Tunnel Road

Mountain View Trail

Shafer Run

Gas well access road

2,856 ft. X

Concrete water trough

Ski hut

"Tunnel road" sign

"Hidden Valley"
"Leaving Forbes State Forest"
signs

North Woods Trail

2,810 ft. X

Field

North Woods Trail

Tunnel road parking lot sign

Tunnel road parking lot

"Hidden Valley" sign

Gravel access road

Camp Run Road

Snowmobile parking area

Cabin and split rail fence

Snowmobile trail

Tunnel Road

31

TO SOMERSET AND PENNSYLVANIA TURNPIKE AND KOOSER STATE PARK

Radio tower access road

Fire Tower Road

N

0   0.25   0.5

MILES

This great shelter is used by the skiers all winter and makes for a great storm shelter during a midsummer thundershower. Please be kind when visiting this place and remember to close and latch the door behind you when you leave. A fast descent along Shafer Run has you soon climbing to the north end of its headwaters.

A remote summit at 2,856 feet may offer a scenic vista if you are there before the leaf-out in spring or drop in late fall. Atop this high point you may notice an abundance of wildlife, as turkeys and hawks are often seen here. An awesome descent takes you back to the hut where an old logging road switchbacks you out of the drainage for the last time. Across the web of trails again, you'll pass over Tunnel Road for the second time to visit the beauty of a high mountain pond. One more moderate climb will bring you to the final descents, past the brown cabin and back to the trailhead. Throughout the ride you will cross over the Laurel Highlands Hiking Trail marked with yellow blazes, which is off-limits to mountain bikes.

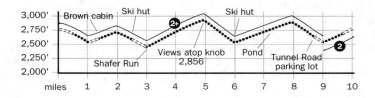

THE RIDE

0.0 From the lot, cross over Fire Tower Road and turn left on the pipeline.

0.2 Carefully cross Pennsylvania Highway 31 and turn right on the dirt and gravel road. You will pass the huge Laurel Hill snowmobile parking lot on your left. As the lot tapers down to the road, turn left onto the marked snowmobile trail as it enters the woods. Not long after, you will cross over the Laurel Highlands Hiking Trail, marked by yellow blazes, and a gravel road.

1.1 Left onto Tunnel Road (gravel) and continue to climb. You will pass a brown cabin on your right and a small section of wooden split-rail fence. You will also notice the triple white paint markers noting the state forest corner boundary. Turn right here, pass around the split rail fence, and head up into the woods.

1.2 You come to a four-way intersection. A sign for Hidden Valley will be on your right. You will continue straight on the North Woods Trail, ascending the hill.

1.4 Come to another four-way intersection. Continue to ride straight on the Horner/ North Woods Trail. You will also notice two signs, one for Hidden Valley on your right and another for the Mountain View / Shafer Run Trails and rest area.

1.8 After descending the hill you will come to an intersection. Keep left at the first fork, then keep right at the second fork (the North Woods Trail breaks off from here). Then keep left at the last fork, riding onto the Shafer Run Trail. In 0.1 mile you will cross a four-way intersection. Note the Tunnel Road sign on your left and continue straight.

2.4 Turn left at the T intersections and then hook a hard right on the grassy doubletrack jeep road. You will be following Shafer Run as it flows down out of the mountains. Check out the backcountry hut if you have the time – remember to close it up when you leave.

3.0 Turn left onto the Mountain View Trail immediately after crossing over Shafer Run. Begin a long, mellow climb out of the valley on the old woods road. Notice also the Laurel Highlands Trail as it crosses over the Mountain View Trail.

4.1 Pass around two gates and over Tunnel Road. A sign notes both the Mountain View and the Mountain Streams Trails. Make sure to keep left at the Y intersection, staying on the Mountain View Trail. You will soon wrap around to the summit knob at 2,856 feet (mile 4.5).

4.9 Pass around two more gates and over Tunnel Road again and continue on the Mountain View Trail. Note the concrete water trough building on your right at the gate. You will now embark on one of the sweetest singletrack descents back down to the backcountry hut. Be careful not to turn off onto the yellow-blazed Laurel Highlands Trail.

5.7 Back at the hut you will want to take the easy left up and out in front of you that slowly ascends the hill. You are now on the Shafer Run Trail. It begins as a grassy woods road, slowly turning to singletrack and taking a hard switchback about halfway up the mountain.

6.8 Turn hard right as the trail comes in from behind you (you'll know you missed the turn if you see the signs that read "Hidden Valley" and "Leaving Forbes State Forest"). Then you will want to continue straight as another trail forks to the left.

7.1 Cross over four-way intersection (yes, you have been here before at mile 1.9) and ascend toward Tunnel Road. The Laurel Highlands Hiking Trail joins for a few hundred feet just before you turn left on Tunnel Road.

7.2 Turn right onto North Woods Trail and pass around the gate. You will soon be passing the pond on your left.

8.4 Exit the woods, pass around the gate, cross Tunnel Road, and continue on around the next gate across the road. You will soon come out into a grassy field: keep to its right edge. Look for the sign saying "Tunnel Road Parking Lot" and follow the trail as it begins to descend parallel to Tunnel Road.

8.7 Back at another four-way intersection, turn right, following the sign to the Tunnel Road parking lot. Soon you will dump out onto Tunnel Road where you will turn left, passing the cabin on your left. Reenter the snowmobile trail on your right, and retrace your route back to the trailhead.

9.5 Cross the gravel road and pass the Laurel Highlands Hiking Trail.

9.7 Exit the snowmobile trail from the woods, and turn right onto the gravel road. Turn left at the pipeline cut and carefully cross Pennsylvania Highway 31.

9.9 Travel up the pipeline a bit and turn right, crossing Fire Tower Road, and ride into the trailhead parking lot. A truly classic ride!

Jones Mill Run

Location:	12 miles west of Somerset.
Distance:	4.6-mile loop.
Time:	30 minutes to 1 hour.
Tread:	A fine blend of rich woodland singletrack including a touch of rock and root. The pipeline and fire road sections are rarely traveled, so they too are singletrack in nature.
Aerobic level:	Easy to moderate. The climbs are gradual and nontechnical, allowing for an easier pedal up the hills. The downhills are well worth the payment of the climb, and the short flat sections will have you rolling along with effortless ease.
Technical difficulty:	2. The ride does involve some thinking through minor rock and root sections. Aside from that, it is a short and sweet ride. When the trail is wet, it may be a bit more challenging due to root sections and a wooden bridge crossing, so be alert for any change in conditions.
Highlights:	Beautiful woodland ride including a section through spruce and pine forest, a historic fire tower, and Kooser State Park amenities, including camping.
Land status:	Forbes State Forest, Pennsylvania Department of Conservation and Natural Resources.
Maps:	USGS Seven Springs; Laurel Highlands Snowmobile Trail System map; DCNR Forbes State Forest map.

Access: From Somerset, head west on Pennsylvania Highway 31. After passing Kooser State Park on your left (approximately 10 miles), travel another 2.5 miles and turn left onto Fire Tower Road (gravel). Approximately 300 yards on your right is the trailhead parking lot.

Notes on the trail: What a great beginner's ride! It is short and mostly singletrack with two easy climbs and some really fun downhills. You can bail out at the 2.5-mile mark or cruise endless possibilities on other spur trails. But expert riders, fear not, for this is extreme singletrack speed! The terrain is mellow enough to crank hard on the uphills, yet the downhill with its twisted turns will offer more than enough gravitational pull. With other rides leaving from the same trailhead, this is a great warm-up loop to link with another trail.

As you leave the trailhead, you are treated to a mellow hill climb up a nice smooth singletrack located on the pipeline. From its high point the trail

Jones Mill Run

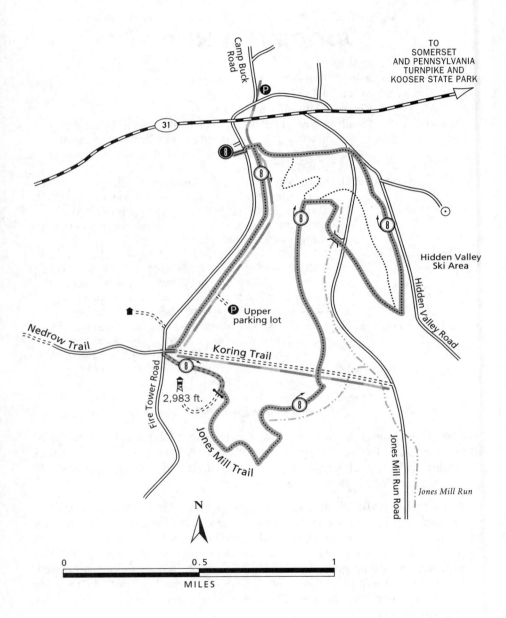

TO
SOMERSET
AND PENNSYLVANIA
TURNPIKE AND
KOOSER STATE PARK

Camp Buck Road

31

Hidden Valley
Ski Area

Hidden Valley Road

Nedrow Trail

Upper
parking lot

Koring Trail

Fire Tower Road

2,983 ft.

Jones Mill Trail

Jones Mill Run Road

Jones Mill Run

N

0   0.5   1

MILES

turns away from the roads and starts to head up to the old fire tower. For a great side trip, continue up the grassy road, around the cable, and on up to check out the old fire tower. The Jones Mill Run Trail splits off from the grassy fire road and begins a beautiful descent on twisty singletrack, crossing the grassy Koring Trail. From here a short climb brings you up to a flat trail that crosses a snowmobile bridge and heads out toward Hidden Valley Ski Area. An abrupt left turn will take you through a beautiful spruce and pine forest that leads you back down to the trailhead.

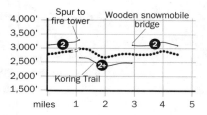

THE RIDE

0.0 From the lot, cross Fire Tower Road and immediately turn right onto the pipeline. Begin the mellow climb up the pipeline on the singletrack.

0.5 Cross a gravel road which is the entrance to the upper trailhead parking lot.

0.8 Take an easy left onto the Jones Mill Run Trail, not the hard left on to the Koring Trail (pipeline). Pass around the gate on the grassy fire road.

1.0 The road forks, keep to the right. Sixty feet before the cable gate across the fire road is the continuation of the Jones Mill Run Trail. Turn left onto the Jones Mill Run Trail. (A super short side trip up the gated, grassy fire road will take you to the old fire tower. This tower is one of the better preserved fire towers in the state and still has the old ranger's cabin alongside.)

1.8 Cross the Koring Trail (grassy pipeline) and begin to ascend on the great singletrack.

2.6 A trail will merge from the left and you will shortly come to a fork where you will want to keep right. This all takes place in a beautiful section of spruce forest.

2.9 Cross the wooden snowmobile bridge and Jones Mill Run Road. Watch the wooden bridge as it may become slippery when wet.

3.3 Pass a spur trail on your left. About 70 yards later you will come to a second spur trail on the left. Turn left here and continue on through another beautiful section of spruce forest that parallels Hidden Valley Road. You know you missed the turn if you come out onto a paved road (Hidden Valley Road).

4.0 Cross Jones Mill Run Road again. The trail picks up on the other side, marked by a set of split-rail fence posts and red blazes on the trees. This is your final descent. Watch for hikers on the Laurel Highlands Hiking Trail as it crosses down below.

4.6 Ride straight across the pipeline and Fire Tower Road to the trailhead lot.

Roaring Run Ramble

Location: 12 miles west of Somerset.

Distance: 10.7-mile loop.

Time: 1 to 2 hours.

Tread: This is one of the finest singletrack rides in Pennsylvania, with some sections of doubletrack and dirt fire road.

Aerobic level: Easy to moderate. The trail is somewhat rolling with a few short climbs and one long, mellow ascent. One minute you're on the gas and the next you're freewheeling down through incredible singletrack.

Technical difficulty: 2 +. There are a few rocks along the top sections of the McKenna Trail. The Nedrow Trail is mainly coarse gravel and rock mixed in with hardpacked dirt, which may make it slow going for some folks. Nothing here is too difficult for the willing novice; it's just the right mix for the intermediate rider, and, of course, there's singletrack sweetness for the seasoned pro.

Highlights: Classic 3-star ride with some of the finest singletrack in Pennsylvania; beautiful scenery aside the Roaring Run Natural Area; the eerie Nedrow cemetery.

Land status: Forbes State Forest, Pennsylvania Department of Conservation and Natural Resources.

Maps: USGS Seven Springs; Laurel Highlands Snowmobile Trail System map; DCNR Forbes State Forest map, Roaring Run Natural Area map.

Access: From Somerset, head west on Pennsylvania Highway 31. After passing Kooser State Park on your left (approximately 10 miles), travel another 2.5 miles and turn left on Fire Tower Road (gravel). Approximately 300 yards on your right is the trailhead parking lot.

Notes on the trail: This is a "must do" ride. The beauty of the Roaring Run Natural Area is reason enough to spin your tires through this incredible section of woods. As with most natural areas in Pennsylvania, Roaring Run was at one time a tract of land owned and used by logging companies. Evidence of man's intervention on the landscape is obvious on the McKenna Trail as it traverses the ridge top. Old stone farm walls and young stands of third-growth forest are all that remain of what was once a pasture. Areas that were logged more recently show evidence of thick vegetation like blackberry bushes and younger saplings and seedlings that are reclaiming the land back to a mature forest.

The Roaring Run headwaters are now protected within the boundaries of the 3,593 acre preserve, which also supports a healthy native brook trout stream. Although Roaring Run is not in pristine condition, its reclaimed natural beauty is a good demonstration of the state's power to take great strides in preserving ecological areas for recreation.

The ride begins with a climb up the McKenna Trail, where you roll along the summit ridge past the remains of old stone farm walls. A great descent brings you down to the low point of the ride where an old logging road brings you past the eerie memorial marker and up to the Nedrow cemetery. More sweet singletrack awaits as you cross over on the Hillside Trail and roll along the southern shoulder of the drainage. Returning back across the Hillside Trail, the route steepens abruptly, bringing you back onto the McKenna Trail. The final descent is a blast as you zip down the tight singletrack section to the trailhead. A classic ride with a stellar finish!

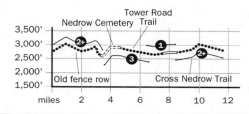

THE RIDE

0.0 From the parking lot, head due south up the grassy field. Keep the woods close to your right as the singletrack trail begins to appear. You will also see a sign for the McKenna Trail as it leads up into the woods, marked by red blazes.

0.5 Trail turns hard right. Continue to climb, following the red blazes.

1.1 Turn right at the fork. Continue to follow the red blazes on the McKenna Trail.

1.5 Pass by huge rock piles, remains of the old pasture fence.

2.1 Pass a left-hand trail. Keep straight following the Painter Rock-McKenna Trail sign.

2.9 Turn left at trail spur and begin to descend, following the red blazes down to the Nedrow Trail. Do not follow the blue blazes straight.

3.8 Pass Painter Rock–McKenna Trail sign on the left and continue on the gravel old woods road. Soon you will pass a strange stone monument for three people who were killed at this spot January 19, 1896. Strange indeed!

4.1 Go left at the fork in the road marked by a sign for the Roaring Run parking area, which is on the right. The Nedrow Trail continues on the woods road as it turns left. Soon you will pass the old Nedrow cemetery. Some of the old washed-out limestone headstones date back to the early 1800s.

4.7 Turn right on the Hillside Trail, following the red blazes and the cross-country skier marker, and begin to descend. Note the old house foundations on both the right and left sides of the trail.

Roaring Run Rumble

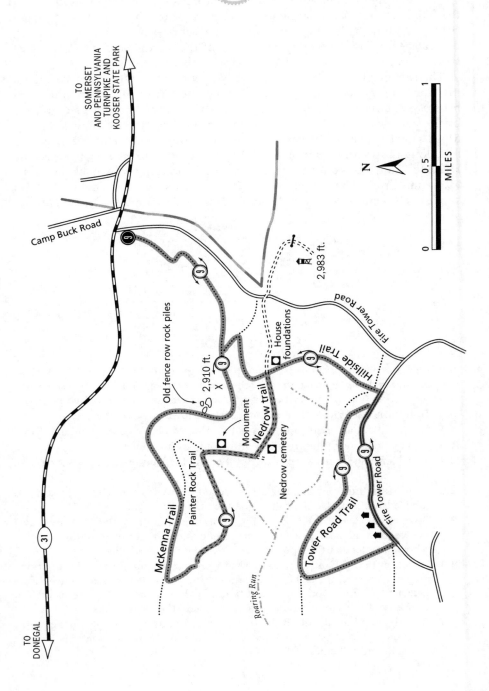

TO
SOMERSET
AND PENNSYLVANIA
TURNPIKE AND
KOOSER STATE PARK

Camp Buck Road

31

TO
DONEGAL

N

MILES

0   0.5   1

Old fence row rock piles

2,910 ft.
X

2,983 ft.

Fire Tower Road

House
foundations

Hillside Trail

McKenna Trail

Painter Rock Trail

Monument

Nedrow trail

Nedrow cemetery

Roaring Run

Tower Road Trail

Fire Tower Road

5.5 Pass a blue-blazed trail on the right and shortly after turn right onto Fire Tower Road. Once on the Fire Tower Road, ride about 200 yards and turn right, back into the woods following the red blazes.

6.7 Keep left at the trail fork, staying on the red-blazed trail.

7.4 Turn left on Fire Tower Road, passing some cabins on your left.

8.3 Turn left back onto the Hillside Trail, staying on the red-blazed trail.

9.1 Cross over Nedrow Trail (gravel road) and ascend the steep hill.

9.4 Left at the trail intersection to the McKenna Trail. In approximately 0.2 of a mile you will turn right onto the McKenna Trail and begin your return descent to the trailhead.

10.7 Exit the woods into the field to the trailhead parking lot. A classic indeed!

Powdermill Loop

Location:	Linn Run State Park, 10 miles south of Ligonier.
Distance:	13.8-mile loop.
Time:	2 to 4 hours.
Tread:	The trail varies from singletrack, doubletrack, grassy road, paved road, four-wheel drive, and ATV trails.
Aerobic level:	Strenuous. There is a killer climb out of the valley up onto the ridge tops, but the true test comes when you climb out of Powdermill Run along its rugged creek banks.
Technical difficulty:	4. You'll find numerous rough and rugged sections to contend with, from the heinous Powdermill Run section to the loose and sketchy Quarry Trail downhill. Rocks and loose terrain abound.
Highlights:	Remote and rugged riding, 840-foot vertical climb, scenic vista, folklore "medicinal" spring, rustic rental cabins.
Land status:	Linn Run State Park, Forbes State Forest. Department of Conservation and Natural Resources.
Maps:	USGS Seven Springs, Stahlstown, Ligonier, Bakersville; Laurel Highlands Snowmobile Trail System map; PW&S Railroad Bike Trail map; DCNR Forbes State Forest map.

Access: From Ligonier travel south on U.S. Highway 30 to Pennsylvania Highway 381. Turn right onto Pennsylvania 381 and head south 3 miles to Rector. In the small village of Rector, turn left onto Linn Run Road. After about 3 miles you will come to the park office. Continue past the office for

Powdermill Loop

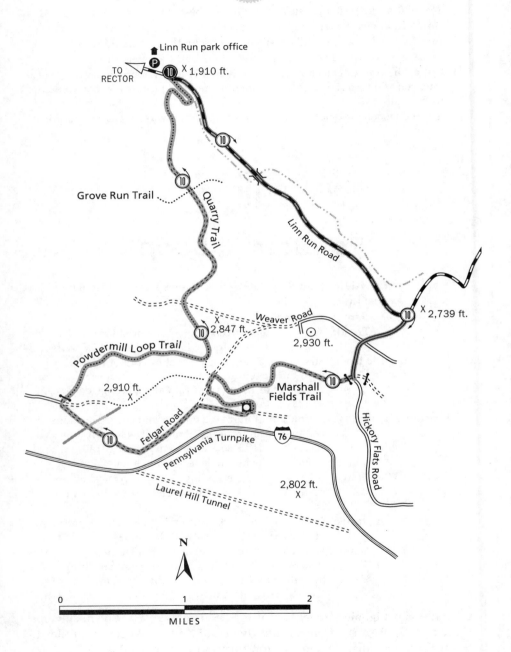

Linn Run park office
TO RECTOR
P
10 X 1,910 ft.

Grove Run Trail

Quarry Trail

Linn Run Road

10

Weaver Road
X 2,847 ft.
⊙ 2,930 ft.

Powdermill Loop Trail

10 X 2,739 ft.

2,910 ft. X

Marshall Fields Trail
10

Felgar Road

Hickory Flats Road

Pennsylvania Turnpike
76

Laurel Hill Tunnel
2,802 ft. X

N

0   1   2
MILES

about 0.2 mile and park on the left in the huge gravel parking area. This is the trailhead.

Notes on the trail: This ride takes you way away from civilization, so it's important to carry the knowledge and gear to fix your bike and yourself in the event of the unforeseen. The chances of bumping into another human being here are quite slim. There's a nice vista (even though it's out over the Pennsylvania Turnpike) that includes Laurel Hill. As you can see by the curves of the turnpike, the road cut straight through the Laurel Hill Mountain at one time. The tunnel is still there in its entirety and is used by the Pennsylvania Department of Transportation to store salt and equipment. The vista is atop a man-made hill of blasted rock left from the re-routing of the turnpike to its present-day location. Down in Linn Run State Park, you'll find beautiful rustic cabins to rent and the infamous "medicinal" spring, which local lore claims has healed ailments. All I can tell you is that it's darn cold and tastes great! So fill your water bottles to the brim because lots of strenuous climbing makes this ride a true mountain-man experience.

The ride begins way down in the lush valley of Linn Run. You start by ascending the paved road on an arduous hill climb. Over the next 3.5 miles you grind your way to the top to gain 840 vertical feet. Slowly, you wind your way back deep into the woods on mellow fire roads and gated doubletrack. You top out again on the man-made vista to see the sights, then it's back to the grind, literally, up the gnarly Felgar Road and into the heinous Powdermill Run. The final descent is well earned as you scream down a sketchy logging road to the valley floor. A tough trail for tough riders.

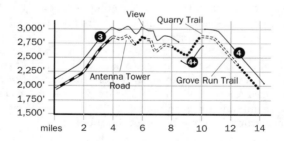

THE RIDE

0.0 From the trailhead lot, turn left and begin the long, arduous climb up Linn Run Road.

1.4 Cross over Linn Run on the grated bridge. Watch this bridge if it is wet–it can become dangerously slippery.

3.4 Take a hard right onto Hickory Flats Road. Enjoy the cruise out on this relatively flat dirt road, but watch for vehicles.

The "Dirt Rag" crew on a retro-ride.

4.0 Pass Weaver Road on the left and right; continue straight on Hickory Flats Road.

4.3 After passing the Laurel Highlands Hiking Trail (note the yellow blazes), turn right on the dirt doubletrack, the Marshall Fields Trail. Pass around a gate and continue on.

5.2 Pass a lefthand road spur that goes to the antenna tower.

5.8 Keep left at the fork, ascending a short, loose, rocky, steep hill. You will soon come out into an open field area. Hug the left edge of the field as you come around to the flat-topped vista. From here you should be able to look out over the Pennsylvania Turnpike and across to Laurel Hill. The hill you are on is the rubble from rerouting the turnpike, and from this vantage you can see how the turnpike used to go through the old Laurel Hill tunnel. You should also be able to see the antenna tower to the north. Keep to the left as a rough, rocky road descends around the north side of the rubble pile.

6.1 As the rocky road turns around the rubble pile and heads toward the turnpike, the road forks. Keep right at the fork and continue on the dirt doubletrack that runs parallel with the turnpike, heading westbound.

6.6 Turn left at the T intersection, onto Felgar Road (dirt four-wheel-drive road). You will soon pass around huge road-blocking boulders that the locals constantly relocate with their trucks and chains.

7.5 Pass a pipeline on the right.

8.1 Turn hard right on the dirt road, then turn quickly left down a grassy, overgrown old woods road. You will soon pass around a gate at the bottom. Grind your way up and out of the Powdermill Run.

9.8 Turn left at the T intersection on the Quarry Trail.

10.4 Cross over the old Weaver Road. The grassy Quarry Trail comes out to a gravel logging road. Keep to the left as the trail and logging road merge, and get ready to descend. Note the memorial in the woods on the left to a fella who "died by accident."

11.7 Cross over the Grove Run Trail and continue to descend as the trail gets steeper and the water bars get bigger (Big Air Ahead!).

13.8 Pass around the gate and cross Linn Run Road to the trailhead.

Laurel Summit Loop

Location:	Linn Run State Park, 10 miles south of Ligonier
Distance:	11.7-mile loop.
Time:	1 to 2 hours.
Tread:	The first 3.5 miles are on relatively flat dirt road; the next 7 miles are on grassy doubletrack. The grassy old woods road has two beautifully distinct hardpacked lines. The last mile runs along the flat, wide, hardpacked dirt of the old Pittsburgh, Westmoreland, and Somerset (PW&S) rail grade.
Aerobic level:	Easy. This route follows the relatively flat grade of Laurel Summit Road before dropping down onto the Beam Run Trail, which rolls roughly along the contour. A small climb out on the old PW&S grade will bring you back to the trailhead. The only challenge for the novice is that this is a moderately long ride.
Technical difficulty:	1+. The Beam Run Trail has a few areas of rough surface that contain embedded rock, loose stones, and mud puddles, and the initial descent from Laurel Summit Road presents small difficulties through a rocky and rutted logging road. The Laurel Summit Road and PW&S rail grade are flat, fast, hardpacked dirt surfaces with no technical difficulties.
Highlights:	Beam Run Rocks, scenic vista, rock climbing, remote woodland trail, wildlife viewing opportunities, picnic area with spring water.
Land status:	Laurel Summit State Park, Forbes State Forest, Department of Conservation and Natural Resources.
Maps:	USGS Bakersville, Ligonier; Laurel Highlands Snowmobile Trail System map; PW&S Railroad Bike Trail map; DCNR Forbes State Forest map.

Laurel Summit Loop

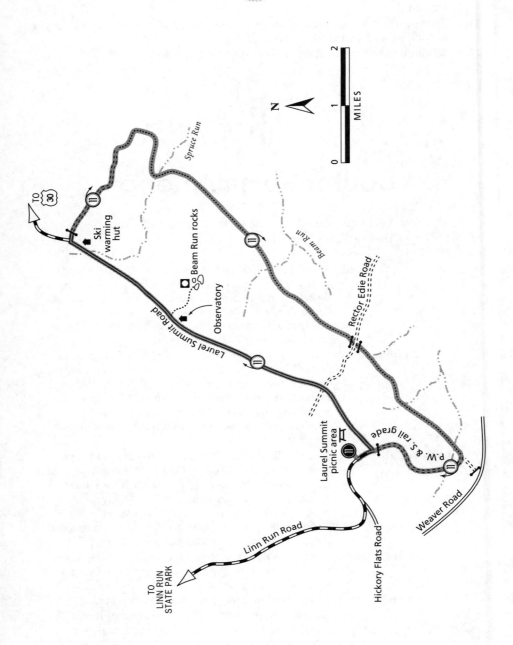

TO 30

Ski warming hut

Spruce Run

Beam Run rocks

Beam Run

Observatory

Laurel Summit Road

Rector Edie Road

Laurel Summit picnic area

P.W. & S. rail grade

Weaver Road

Linn Run Road

Hickory Flats Road

TO LINN RUN STATE PARK

N

MILES
0 1 2

The pedalin' park ranger, Doug Finger, at Linn Run State Park.

Access: From Ligonier travel south on U.S. Highway 30 to Pennsylvania Highway 381. Turn right onto Pennsylvania 381 and head south 3 miles to Rector. In the small village of Rector, turn left on Linn Run Road. After about 3 miles you will come to the park office; continue past the office, climbing Linn Run Road for another 3.5 miles. Near the summit the road bends left and is joined from the right by Hickory Flats Road. Continue on for 0.5 mile and turn left into the Laurel Summit picnic area. This is the trailhead.

Notes on the trail: This loop is a sweet ride in that it offers a great woodland riding experience tucked back in the historical hills of the Laurel Highlands. The history of Laurel Summit dates back to the exploits of timber and mining companies whose sole interest was in taking all they could from the land. After they stripped the hills of their old-growth trees and mined the bluestone, the state purchased the ground to begin building the state forests as we know them today. Outdoor recreation is the only human activity you'll find now at Laurel Summit, and many folks come here from all around to unwind.

Beginning at the Laurel Summit picnic area, you head out on the smooth, mellow surface and grade of Laurel Summit Road. About 2 miles out is an interesting side trip to the Beam Run Rocks that is well worth your time. This unique formation of quartzite sandstone has some of the most interesting pillar and gendarme formations in Pennsylvania. You'll also find a beautiful vista atop the rock cliff which offers an expansive view southeast over the mountains. Unless you're a solid boulder rider, you'll have to walk the 5 minutes into the cliff, because the sandstone boulders are quite stout!

Back on the road, the trail breaks off onto the Beam Run Trail, a bumpy and rutted logging road that makes up the bulk of the technical riding. An awesome traverse along the contours of Laurel Ridge offers a deep-woods feel and the chance to see some native wildlife. Rector Edie Road crossing offers a bail-out opportunity but a moderate hill climb is the price you'll pay for the short cut. Turning right on the old PW&S grade will take you past the old rock cut, back up to the trailhead. The trailhead is a day use area only but camping is available at Kooser State Park. Stop in at the Linn Run State Park office down at the bottom of Linn Run road, for directions and a map.

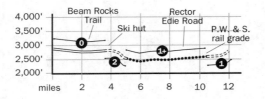

THE RIDE

0.0 From the trailhead lot, ride out to Linn Run Road and turn left.

0.1 Turn left onto Laurel Summit Road.

0.9 Pass Rector Edie Road.

2.2 After passing the hidden driveway of the observatory, there will be a small parking area on the right. This is the trailhead for Beam Run Rocks. A short 5-minute walk will take you to the sandstone cliff. Be careful around the edge; people have died here!

3.4 After passing the ski warming hut and patrol cabin, turn right onto the logging road, pass around a gate, and begin the descent.

4.0 Pass the vertical trail markers for the Laurel Highlands Hiking Trail (off limits to bikes) that are inscribed "PA Turnpike 9 miles."

8.7 Cross over Rector Edie Road. This is a possible bail-out point if you turn right on Rector Edie and then left on Laurel Summit Road.

8.8 Pass around a gate.

10.6 Turn right at T intersection onto the PW&S rail grade. You will soon pass through a rock-cut along the way.

11.5 Pass around a gate (ridable on the right side) and continue straight on out as the road surface changes from dirt to pavement (Linn Run Road).

11.7 Turn right at the Laurel Summit picnic area and trailhead.

Lower Beam Loop

Location:	Linn Run State Park, 10 miles south of Ligonier.
Distance:	8.5-mile loop.
Time:	1 to 2 hours.
Tread:	A fine blend of singletrack, doubletrack, old woods road, and fire roads. The trails are mainly hardpacked dirt, but there is a rocky, loose descent on the Beam Run Road trail. Also, the forest service has laid in some huge ballast rock along a section of the Pittsburgh, Westmorland, and Somersetn (PW&S) rail grade that may present an annoying challenge.
Aerobic level:	Easy to moderate. There are steep descents with mild climbs, the way a good mountain bike loop should be run.
Technical difficulty:	2. The descent on the Beam Run Road Trail can be a small challenge to the novice rider. The old woods road is rutted and rocky. The weird section of ballast can also prove to be slightly difficult.
Highlights:	Great woodland ride for the experienced novice on up to the honed hammerhead, the historic PW&S railroad grade, great wildlife viewing opportunities.
Land status:	Laurel Summit State Park, Laurel Ridge State Park, Forbes State Forest, Department of Conservation and Natural Resources.
Maps:	USGS Bakersville, Ligonier; Laurel Highlands Snowmobile Trail System map; PW&S Railroad Bike Trail map; DCNR Forbes State Forest maps.

Access: From Ligonier travel south on U.S. Highway 30 to Pennsylvania Highway 381. Turn right onto Pennsylvania 381 and head south 3 miles to Rector. In the small village of Rector, turn left on Linn Run Road. After about 3 miles you will come to the park office, continue past the office. Climbing Linn Run Road another 3.5 miles. Near the summit the road bends left and is joined from the right by Hickory Flats Road. Continue on for 0.5 mile and turn left into the Laurel Summit picnic area. This is the trailhead.

Notes on the trail: The Laurel Summit day use area is a great place to start numerous hikes and rides that spiderweb out from this ridge-top location. There are restrooms, spring water, and charcoal pits for stoking up some coals for that after-the-ride T-bone! Expect to see a few cars parked here, as it is an outdoor hot-spot. Things change once you're out on the trail, where there are many opportunities for peace and solitude.

Lower Beam Loop

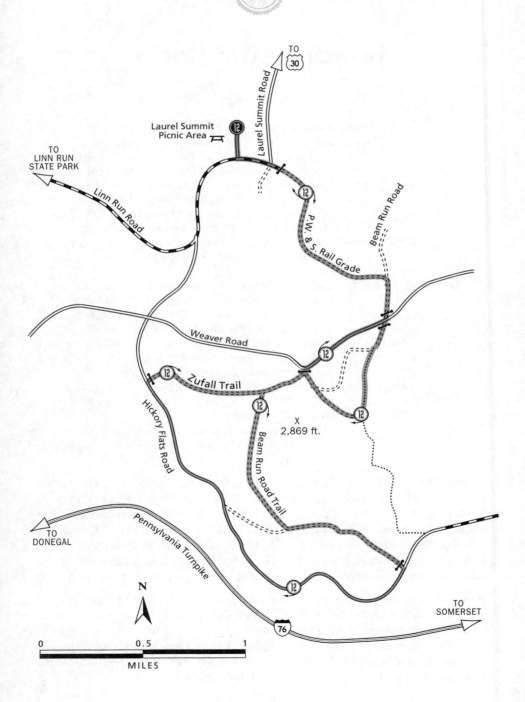

TO 30

Laurel Summit Road

Laurel Summit Picnic Area

TO LINN RUN STATE PARK

Linn Run Road

P.W. & S. Rail Grade

Beam Run Road

Weaver Road

Zufall Trail

Hickory Flats Road

X 2,869 ft.

Beam Run Road Trail

TO DONEGAL

Pennsylvania Turnpike

TO SOMERSET

76

N

0   0.5   1

MILES

The ride begins on Laurel Summit and runs out along the historic Pittsburgh, Westmoreland, and Somerset (PW&S) railroad grade. Built back in 1899, this grade was used to haul timber and bluestone from the once abundant resources atop Laurel Hill Mountain. It wasn't long before they mined and logged the hills bare. This was the first parcel purchased in what is today the Forbes State Forest. The cuts you see through the rock were made when the original builders blasted out these sections to maintain the railroad grade. The trail passes through a tough section of huge ballast, climbs the hill, and crosses around two gates. A forked trail heads over a dirt berm where you can enjoy the hardpacked singletrack section. Some more climbing ensues, just before the doubletrack bombs down the Beam Run Road Trail. A mellow climb back out on Hickory Flats Road will bring you across the Zufall Trail and down Weaver Road. A return trip back on the PW&S rail grade will have you back to the trailhead for that T-bone on the barbecue!

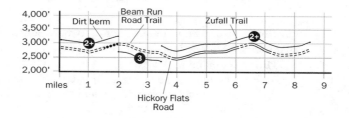

THE RIDE

0.0 From the trailhead lot, ride out to Linn Run Road and turn left.

0.1 Continue straight as the road turns hard left. You will soon pass around a gate that is ridable on the left. This is the PW&S rail grade.

1.0 The trail will appear to fork. Keep right (straight) at the fork, riding the rough ballast roadbed up to the steep hill climb.

1.4 Pass around a gate and cross Weaver Road (dirt). Pass around a second gate and continue to climb up past a large open grassy area.

1.7 Keep left (straight) at the fork, crossing over a dirt berm onto the singletrack. The singletrack will shortly bear to the right and ascend a short hill.

2.0 Turn left onto the gravel road. In approximately 300 yards you will turn left, as the trail reenters the woods. This entrance is about 100 feet before the gate, on the left.

2.3 Turn left at the fork, onto the Beam Run Road Trail. Bomb the rocky, rutted old woods road to the bottom.

3.0 Trail passes through a large grassy field. Hug the field on the left as trail reenters the woods on the other side of the field. Watch for those groundhog holes!

3.2 Turn left at T intersection, onto a grassy old woods road and continue to descend.

3.7 After passing around a gate, turn right onto Hickory Flats Road and begin the mellow climb back to the Summit.

5.9 Turn right on the Zufall Trail and pass around the gate.

6.5 Turn (merge) left onto the Beam Run Road Trail. In approximately 0.2 mile turn left onto the gravel road and pass around the gate. Once around the gate, turn right onto Weaver Road.

7.1 Turn left, pass around the gate, and descend into the rocky ballast below on the PW&S railroad grade. You are now retracing your route back to the trailhead.

8.5 After passing around the gate, continue straight on the paved road to the Laurel Summit picnic area on the right.

Taggart's Traverse

Location:	Laurel Summit State Park, 10 miles south of Ligonier.
Distance:	33.3-mile loop.
Time:	5 to 8 hours.
Tread:	Old woods roads, logging roads, dirt roads, paved roads, snowmobile trails, and a touch of singletrack make up the route.
Aerobic level:	Strenuous. Due to the distance and amount of vertical climbing (2,300 feet) it's not your average stroll through the woods. Endurance will be your best friend, as will plenty of food, water, and good maps.
Technical difficulty:	3. The short singletrack sections present the most challenge but they are mellow at that.
Highlights:	Full-day excursion with endless side-trip possibilities, wilderness experience; Laurel Hill State Park amenities include swimming lake, food concession, restrooms, fishing.
Land status:	Forbes State Forest, Laurel Summit State Park, Laurel Hill State Park, Department of Conservation and Natural Resources.
Maps:	USGS Bakersville, Ligonier, Seven Springs, Kingwood; Laurel Highlands Snowmobile Trail System map; PW&S Railroad Bike Trail map; DCNR Forbes State Forest map.

Access: From Ligonier travel south on U.S. Highway 30 to Pennsylvania Highway 381. Turn right onto Pennsylvania 381 and head south 3 miles to Rector. In the small village of Rector, turn left on Linn Run Road. After about 3 miles you will come to the park office; continue past the office, climbing Linn Run Road for another 3.5 miles. Near the summit the road bends left and is joined from the right by Hickory Flats Road. Continue on for 0.5 mile and turn left into the Laurel Summit picnic area. This is the trailhead.

Notes on the trail: This trail has "epic" written all over it. It's definitely not an easy ride as it travels through remote sections of Forbes State Forest. Competent first-aid and backcountry bicycle repair skills are of extreme importance. Help can only be found at the Pennsylvania Highway 31 crossover and down at Laurel Hill State Park. Ride with a level head and let the spirits of the forest guide your soul.

Beginning north of the Pennsylvania Turnpike, the trail snakes its way down and out to a snowmobile bridge spanning the turnpike. The bridge is off-limits to bikes and horses (but not foot traffic). I won't tell you how I got across, but let's just say I followed the rules and it doesn't take too much creativity!

On the south side of the turnpike, miles of trail lie ahead. A combination of pipeline cuts, singletrack, and forest roads lead you down to Pennsylvania 31. A bit of climbing ensues before the final 800-foot drop down into Laurel Hill State Park on the Ridge Trail. (At the time of printing the Ridge Trail was a designated snowmobile/mountain bike trail. If the Ridge Trail should close to mountain bikes, continue to follow Jones Mill Run Road to a T intersection and turn left, which will take you to Laurel Hill State Park.) Once in the comfort of Laurel Hill State Park, enjoy all it has to offer. Scenic lake views, swimming, food, and a shady place to rest are just some of the great things here.

The return trip has you retracing many parts of your original route and you do so to gain Beltz Road above the park's northern boundary. From here you traverse along the Red Oak Trail and down onto the Koring Trail. Back across Pennsylvania 31, Tunnel Road presents a moderate challenge as you climb back up toward the turnpike. Back on the north side of the turnpike, a parting summit view and the Marshall Fields Trail bring you back to Laurel Summit picnic area and the trailhead.

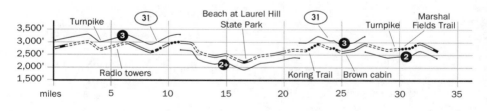

THE RIDE

0.0 From the trailhead, turn right on Linn Run Road.

0.5 Keep left at the road fork, taking Hickory Flats Road (dirt).

1.1 Turn right onto Weaver Road (dirt).

1.8 You will pass a road to the antenna towers on your left and then cross a pipeline cut. Keep an easy left at the strange X-type four-way intersection.

2.3 Pass around a set of huge road-blocking boulders.

2.9 Turn left at the four-way intersection. Note the old steel gate.

Taggart's Traverse

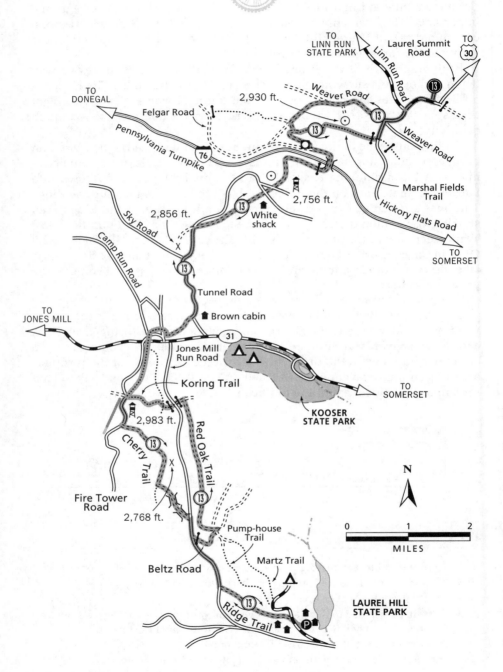

TO
LINN RUN
STATE PARK

Laurel Summit
Road

TO
30

Linn Run Road

13

TO
DONEGAL

Felgar Road

2,930 ft.

Weaver Road

13

Pennsylvania Turnpike

76

13

Weaver Road

Marshal Fields
Trail

Hickory Flats Road

2,756 ft.

Sky Road

2,856 ft.

13

White
shack

Camp Run Road

X

13

TO
SOMERSET

Tunnel Road

Brown cabin

TO
JONES MILL

31

Jones Mill
Run Road

Koring Trail

KOOSER
STATE PARK

TO
SOMERSET

2,983 ft.

Cherry Trail

13

Red Oak Trail

X

Fire Tower
Road

13

2,768 ft.

N

Pump-house
Trail

Martz Trail

0   1   2

MILES

Beltz Road

Ridge Trail

13

LAUREL HILL
STATE PARK

P

3.1 Turn right at the T intersection and ascend the short, steep, rocky road to the summit views of the turnpike. Keep to the left as you climb up on top of the flat grassy field. Follow the extremely rocky road that descends around the back left side of the flat-topped summit.

3.4 As you come around below the huge rubble pile (these are the rock tailings left from carving out a new path for the turnpike), turn left at the spur trail following the turnpike eastbound. Note the old steel gate as you enter the woods.

3.9 Come to a bridge spanning the turnpike. Trail continues on the south side.

4.0 Turn hard right on the wide, rocky trail that climbs as it follows the turnpike westbound. You'll also pass around a gate.

4.5 Trail pulls away from the turnpike through a large open field with rubble piles. Follow the main pathway through the field and out left as it picks up an old woods road and begins a slight climb.

5.2 After passing a huge radio tower, you'll cross over a gravel road. Keep going straight. Note the old fire tower tucked back in on your left.

5.5 Cross another gravel road and continue straight onto a pipeline cut. Note the old white shack on your left.

6.1 Cross another gravel road and continue straight.

6.6 Turn left onto Tunnel Road (dirt). Note orange diamond blazes on the trees on your right.

7.4 After passing a cinder-block horse watering trough on your right, you'll pass Sky Road on your right as well. Enjoy the fast, smooth descent ahead!

8.5 Toward the bottom of the descent and after passing a little brown cabin on your left, you will be turning right onto a logging road. Keep straight as it climbs.

9.2 Cross a gravel road after a steep ascent.

9.5 Trail dumps out into a big open field. Continue down to the right, joining the gravel road. Just before it empties out onto Pennsylvania Highway 31 (paved road) turn left at the telephone pole with the big white transformer box. Carefully cross Pennsylvania 31 and continue on the other side, ascending the pipeline singletrack.

10.5 You'll come to a slightly confusing six-way intersection. Take an easy left onto Fire Tower Road and continue to climb.

11.4 After passing the Laurel Highlands Hiking Trail, you will soon turn left onto a gated old woods road (Cherry Trail) descending to a 2,769-foot summit knob.

12.4 As you continue descend from the summit knob, turn left at the old woods road spur and continue to descend (Cherry Trail).

13.0 Cross over a wooden snowmobile bridge and begin a short climb.

13.5 Cross a second wooden snowmobile bridge, pass around a gate, and turn right on Jones Mill Run Road. Note: You'll soon pass Beltz Road on the left. Make a mental note as you will be returning this way.

14.7 Turn left onto the Ridge Trail and begin your final descent into Laurel Hill State Park.

15.9 Dump out onto a gravel road, bearing left and passing multiple cabins.

16.1 Turn right onto Buck Run Road (paved).

16.4 Turn left down into the parking lot that'll take you down to the beach. Enjoy a mid-ride swim or just the beauty of the lakeside setting. From here you will need to retrace your route back to Beltz Road (back at mile 13.6).

19.2 Turn right onto Beltz Road and pass around a gate.

19.9 Pass a spur trail on the right. The old woods road bends hard left shortly thereafter. A bit after that, keep left at the trail fork (obscured by summer foliage?!), riding on the contour along the Red Oak Trail.

22.1 Keep left at the trail fork.

22.4 Keep left as you enter an open field area. Turn left down the old woods road and pass around a gate. Cross Jones Mill Run Road and pass around a second gate. You are now on the Koring Trail.

23.2 Take a hard right onto the pipeline. Note the brown gas well company shed. You are now retracing your route back to the turnpike bridge.

24.2 Cross Pennsylvania 31, carefully! Once across, turn right at the telephone pole onto a gravel road. As the field edge narrows down to the road, the trail begins again on your left up into the woods.

25.1 Turn left onto Tunnel Road and begin the long climb. Note the brown cabin on your right.

27.1 Turn right onto the pipeline trail. You will cross gravel roads and pass towers.

29.1 Old woods road turns right into a large clearing; ride back across and parallel with the turnpike, heading eastbound.

29.6 After passing around the gate, find your way back to the other side and turn left.

30.1 After the old open gate, turn right at the T intersection and climb the rough, rocky trail around and up. Keep to the right field edge and continue on with a short, steep descent.

30.4 Pass a trail spur to the left. Keep straight on the Marshall Fields Trail.

31.9 After passing a gate, turn left on Hickory Flats Road (dirt), passing Weaver Road.

33.3 Trailhead.

Wolf Rocks

Location:	Laurel Summit State Park, 10 miles south of Ligonier.
Distance:	4.1-mile loop.
Time:	30 minutes to 1 hour.
Tread:	Some of the most gnarly, ridable boulders in Pennsylvania are found here. The trail surface is all boulder, with sporadic splotches of loamy singletrack.
Aerobic level:	Strenuous. The ride is a total pump-fest. Arms, legs, heart, head, back, and bladder all take a severe beating on this ride, so don't let the mileage fool you!

Technical difficulty:	5. This trail eats bikes and feels no remorse for snagging the occasional skin snack. Blood and pain are just part of the ride. During the warmer months rattlers abound among the rocks, so plain'n' simple don't dab. Remember, pain is temporary; glory is forever . . . ride hard!
Highlights:	Scenic vista, unique rock formations, killer trails riding, most technical ride in the region, Laurel Summit picnic area amenities.
Land status:	Laurel Summit State Park, Forbes State Forest, Department of Conservation and Natural Resources.
Maps:	USGS Ligonier; Laurel Highlands Snowmobile Trail System map; DCNR Forbes State Forest map.

Access: From Ligonier travel south on U.S. Highway 30 to Pennsylvania Highway 381. Turn right on Pennsylvania 381 and head south 3 miles to Rector. In the small village of Rector, turn left on Linn Run Road. After about 3 miles you will come to the park office. Continue past the office, climbing Linn Run Road another 3.5 miles. Near the summit the road bends left and is joined from the right by Hickory Flats Road. Continue on for 0.5 mile and turn left into the Laurel Summit picnic area. This is the trailhead.

Notes on the trail: This is a short but "suppa-sweet" technical ride through the rugged flat, atop Laurel Hill. The topography itself is generally flat, but it's what's on the trail that presents the ultimate challenge. Large rocks and small boulders test your ability to negotiate through this unforgiving trail. Make sure you have plenty of tubes or a patch kit because you may flat. Tube "snakebites" aren't the only snakebites to be wary of—Wolf Rocks is home to a number of timber rattlesnakes that occasionally glare at psychotic mountain bikers. Just respect their space and admire their awesome beauty. Rattlesnakes are a protected species in Pennsylvania and under no circumstances should they be handled or harmed. The chances of getting bit by a rattlesnake are ten times less than of getting struck by lightning, unless of course you dance the funky-chicken in front of its den.

At the trailhead lot, look for a sign post for the Wolf Rocks Trail in the middle of the back edge of the lot. From here, it's a mellow start as there are few boulders, but slippery roots sprawl out across the trail at odd angles. As the trail narrows down the rocks grow in size and quantity. Your tenacious first left turn will take you into the heart of the bone-breaking boulders, as you hammer your way out to the rockpile vista. Once at Wolf Rocks, enjoy the natural playground Mother Nature has provided and rest up for the return ride out. The ride out is as demanding as it was going in, but take some time to enjoy the scrub oak, ferns, and low-bush blueberry that line the trail. A rough ride for crazy cowboys on steel steeds.

Wolf Rocks

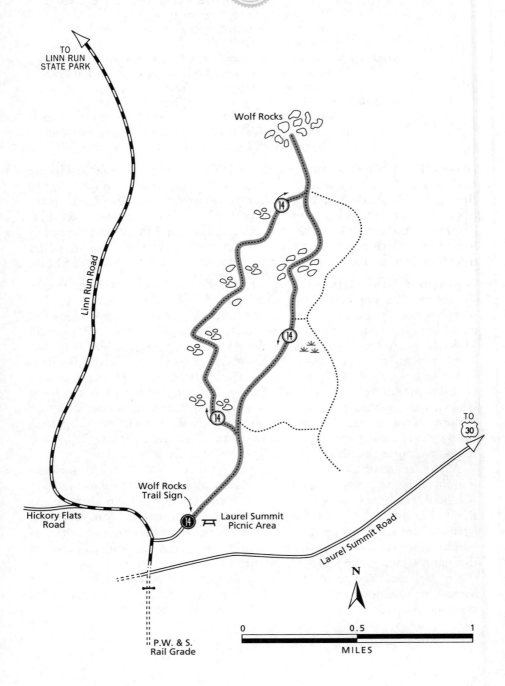

TO
LINN RUN
STATE PARK

Linn Run Road

Wolf Rocks

14

14

14

Wolf Rocks
Trail Sign

14

Laurel Summit
Picnic Area

Hickory Flats
Road

TO
30

Laurel Summit Road

N

P.W. & S.
Rail Grade

0   0.5   1

MILES

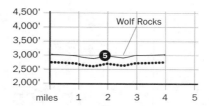

THE RIDE

0.0 From the back of the trailhead parking lot, notice the wooden trail sign for the Wolf Rocks Trail. This is where you enter the woods and begin the ride.

0.5 Turn left at a four-way intersection, following the faint red blazes. Buckle up for the ride ahead.

2.1 Turn left at the four-way intersection.

2.3 Wolf Rocks. Return the way you came and continue straight at the 4-way intersection, which is at mile 2.5.

3.1 Pass a spur trail on the left and continue straight

3.5 Continue straight at the four-way intersection—almost home!

4.1 Trailhead.

The "easy" section along Wolf Rocks.

Ghost Town Trail

Location: 12 miles north of Johnstown.

Distance: 11.7 miles one way.

Time: 30 minutes to 2 hours.

Tread: The original railbed of crushed limestone constitutes the surface of this trail.

Aerobic level: Easy. There is a barely noticeable 3-percent grade that runs uphill from Dilltown to Nanty Glo, making your return ride downhill.

Technical difficulty: This is a rail-trail, so there are no technical difficulties.

Highlights: Remains of old mining ghost towns, old open strip mines, awesome creek-side ride, well shaded, best preserved iron furnace in the state, bike shops and rentals.

Land status: Pennsylvania Game Commission, Indiana and Cambria County Parks.

Maps: USGS New Florence, Vintondale, Nanty Glo; Indiana and Cambria County Parks: Ghost Town Trail map.

Access: From Johnstown, take Pennsylvania Highway 403 north and cross U.S. Highway 22. One mile after crossing U.S. 22, you will be in the small village of Dilltown. The parking area is well marked on the left by a large pavilion and signs for the Ghost Town Trail. Park here; this is the western trailhead where the ride begins. To access the eastern trailhead where the ride ends, return south on Pennsylvania 403 to US 22. Take US 22 east for 10 miles to Pennsylvania Luania Highway 271. Take Pennsylvania 271 north for 2 miles to the town of Nanty Glo. Follow the signs to the Ghost Town Trail parking access area.

Notes on the trail: A truly historic and casual ride along the beautiful Black Lick Creek, this trail has the remains of five ghost towns along its course as well as evidence of coal mines and iron furnaces. After discovering the natural riches of the area, settlers constructed the Eliza Furnace in Vintondale. It remains one of the best-preserved iron furnaces in Pennsylvania and one of the few with blast coils still intact. Further down the trail is the Bracken mine and ghost town. At one time Bracken was a small village of 12 houses, a one-room schoolhouse, and a company store. All that remains now are a few random foundations. Not far from here is the Twin Rocks mine, located south of the main trail. Nanty Glo, at the trail's terminus, was settled by Irish, Welsh, Scots, and English immigrants in the 1890s.

Ghost Town Trail

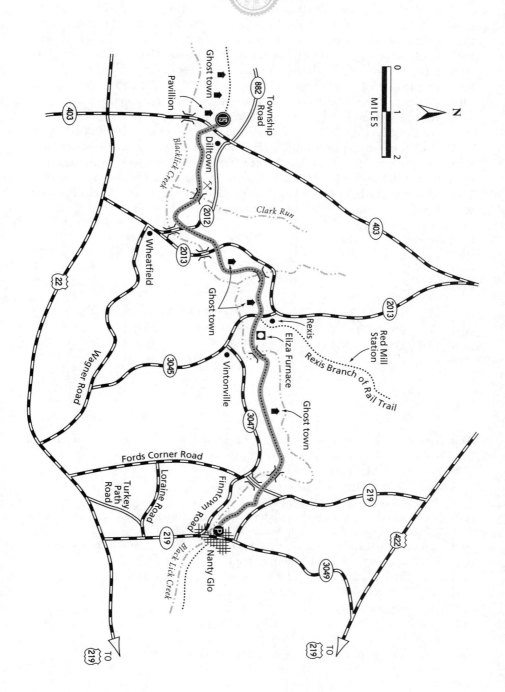

Originally named Glenglade, the town's name changed in 1901 to Nant-y-glo, Welsh for "valley of coal."

The valley is rich in folklore and carries two unique tales. Eliza Furnace is supposedly haunted by Dave Ritter, one of the two men who constructed the furnace, who hanged himself there. A second tale is of a great train robbery that took place on the Rexis Branch of the Ghost Town Trail (the spur branch at mile 6.0). The story claims that two men robbed two Clover Mine employees of a safe containing over $33,000 intended for the Clover Mine payroll. The robbers were found, convicted, and electrocuted a year later, yet the safe and money were never recovered.

Today the Black Lick Creek Valley rail line is traveled by foot or by bicycle, and the sounds of a once industrious little valley are now replaced with the quiet gurgle of the Black Lick Creek. You may notice the leach of the mines into the creek by the tan-orange discoloration of the creek stones. The trail has more bike shops per linear mile than any other trail in Pennsylvania, and all sell and rent bikes and accessories. You will feel very secure riding along the trail knowing that you'll never be more than 4 miles from a bicycle shop. Restrooms are available at Dilltown, Vintondale, and Nanty Glo. Remember, this is a one-way ride so unless you have a vehicle at the other end you will need to retrace your route.

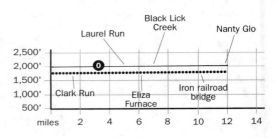

THE RIDE

0.0 Beginning in the village of Dilltown, start the trail at the huge outdoor pavilion and head east, carefully crossing Pennsylvania Highway 403.

1.6 Cross the bridge over Clark Run.

3.7 Carefully cross over the paved road.

5.2 Cross the bridge over Laurel Run.

6.0 Keep right at the trail fork. The left fork is the Rexis Branch, which runs for 2.5 miles to Red Mill Station, where the bridge is out.

6.2 Carefully cross over the paved road. The impressive Eliza Furnace is on your left. Restrooms are located here as well.

7.0 Cross the bridge over Black Lick Creek.

8.5 Carefully cross over the paved road.

9.9 Pass through a unique cut-rock gorge.

10.1 Cross over the old black iron railroad bridge.

11.1 Carefully cross over the paved road.

11.7 Nanty Glo terminus and access parking area.

Allegheny Plateau

Located in the northwestern section of the state, this region is comprised mainly of the Allegheny National Forest and the Moshannon and Elk State Forests. Rolling plateau riding, unique geologic formations, and a dash of early industrial history are some of the outstanding features of this area. Although the local oil industry has subsided, the timber industry is alive and well throughout the woodlands. Many of the rides in the Allegheny National Forest are close to towns that offer accommodations. Some of the more remote rides travel through the Moshannon State Forest, making for a more rugged, wilderness experience. Either way you can't go wrong with any of the classic rides in the region.

Rockton Mountain

Location: 14 miles northwest of Clearfield.

Distance: 11.1-mile loop.

Time: 1.5 to 3 hours.

Tread: A rugged mix of rocky and rooted singletrack, rough old woods roads, doubletrack, and a small section of forest road.

Aerobic level: Moderate. The ride makes subtle changes in elevation but the hard terrain eats away at you. This ride gives you an upper-body workout throughout its entire length.

Technical difficulty: 3. The trail never gets into extreme technical terrain, but the challenges it presents persist throughout the entire ride. There are few smooth sections that offer any kind of reprieve, so buckle up—it's gonna be a bumpy ride.

Highlights: Technical ridge-top ride, great wildlife viewing, entire route blazed for your route-finding convenience.

Land status: Pennsylvania State Forest; Department of Conservation and Natural Resources.

Maps: USGS Elliott Park; DCNR Pennsylvania State Forest: Moshannon State Forest map.

Rockton Mountain

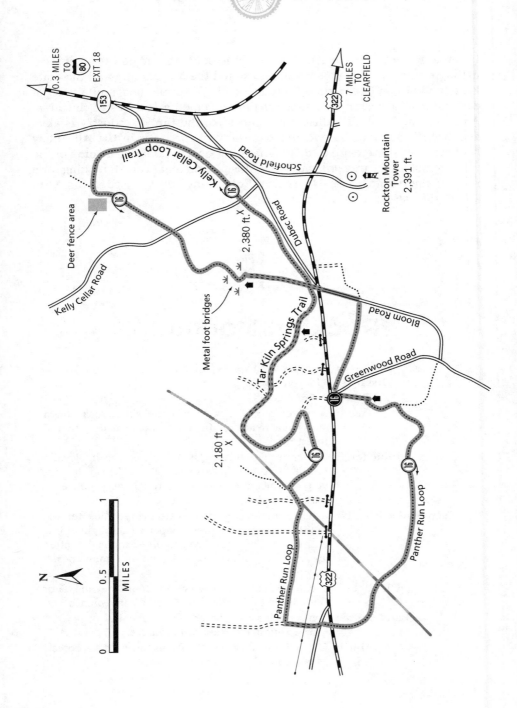

0.3 MILES TO **80** EXIT 18

153

7 MILES TO CLEARFIELD

322

Rockton Mountain Tower 2,391 ft.

Schofield Road

Kelly Cellar Loop Trail

16

16

Deer fence area

Kelly Cellar Road

Dubec Road

2,380 ft. X

Metal foot bridges

Tar Kiln Springs Trail

Bloom Road

Greenwood Road

16

2,180 ft. X

16

16

Panther Run Loop

Panther Run Loop

322

N

0   0.5   1

MILES

Access: From Clearfield take U.S. Highway 322 west for 9 miles to Greenwood Road, which is the third dirt road on the left after the fork with Pennsylvania Highway 153. It is marked by a wooden sign stating "Rockton Mountain Trail System." Turn left onto Greenwood Road and park in the lot on your immediate right behind the DCNR sign.

Notes on the trail: A cross-country ski trail system in winter, the Rockton Mountain trail system is a superb mountain bike trail network. Not only are riders having a blast on the many trails, but they are helping the state forest service maintain the trails by keeping them clear and the grasses down. This is one of a few places where the state is catching on to the benefits of mountain bikers.

Rockton Mountain is relatively flat and broad but has its fill of rock along the trail. The ride is well marked with blazes and brown fiberglass posts, so following the route should be easier. The bumpy ride begins as the singletrack hobbles its way westward out to U.S. Highway 322. The tread doesn't let up as the trail cuts back into the woods to the Tar Kiln Springs Trail. If you've had enough at this point, head back to the trailhead by following the mileage directions, but think of all that great trail you'll be missing . . . and it actually gets a bit easier, so ride on. A spin around the Kelly Cellar Loop Trail returns you to the final singletrack across the mountain to the trailhead. A sustained but most enjoyable ride.

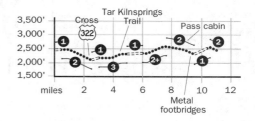

THE RIDE

0.0 From the trailhead lot, begin on the sandy, grass-lined doubletrack road at the mouth of the parking lot. Note the fiberglass post with the number "1."

0.2 The trail breaks off right from the sandy doubletrack onto divine singletrack.

0.4 Keep right at the fork and marker number 13.

1.7 Cross an old woods road.

2.3 Carefully cross U.S. Highway 322, noting marker number 19. Soon after cross a gravel road and continue straight on an old woods road at marker number 21.

2.6 After crossing under the power line, turn right onto the singletrack at marker 23.

3.0 Cross an old woods road and soon after (mile 3.3) cross a gravel road.

3.6 Ride across a wide, grassy pipeline and continue straight at marker number 33, which also indicates the Panther Run Loop (PRL). Be careful not to turn left at this intersection.

4.4 Turn hard left onto the Tar Kiln Springs Trail (TKS) at marker number 34. If you need to bail out, turn right onto the woods road and follow it for 0.2 mile to return to the trailhead.

5.0 The trail turns right onto an old woods road; follow the blazes.

5.4 The trail turns right onto an old four-wheel drive road; continue to follow the blazes.

6.4 Cross an old woods road passing marker number 37.

7.2 Cross Kelly Cellar Road.

8.0 Turn left at the T intersection and follow the blazes. Soon after, the trail turns left onto a singletrack trail. Note the deer fence 200 yards on the right.

8.7 Cross Kelly Cellar Road.

9.1 The trail turns 90 degrees left into the woods, back onto some singletrack.

9.5 After crossing a series of metal footbridges, pass a cabin on the right and follow the woods road out of the hollow.

10.0 Pass around a gate; turn right onto US 322 and ride for 60 yards. Cross US 322 and continue on Bloom Road (four-wheel drive road).

10.3 Turn right onto the blazed singletrack trail.

11.0 Trailhead.

Parker Dam State Park

Location:	17 miles north of Clearfield.
Distance:	12.9-mile loop.
Time:	2 to 4 hours.
Tread:	A strange mix of old woods roads, wide grassy singletrack, easy root-and-rock covered singletrack, forestry road, and a small section of paved road.
Aerobic level:	Easy to moderate. The ride follows a rolling topography with a bunch of short but mild climbs.
Technical difficulty:	1+. There are small sections of bumpy singletrack throughout the ride as well as a slow grassy surface on some trail segments. Considered a mild ride by most, it's a great novice-level adventure.
Highlights:	Beaver dams, evidence of the massive tornado destruction of 1985, swimming, boating, and fishing at the lake, camping and cabin rentals on site, food and boat rental concessions, and a great environmental education building and program with evening and weekend activities.
Land status:	Pennsylvania State Parks and Pennsylvania State Forest, Department of Conservation and Natural Resources.
Maps:	USGS Penfield; Parker Dam State Park mountain biking map.

Access: From Clearfield take U.S. Highway 322 west, which joins with Pennsylvania Highway 153. Continue north on Pennsylvania 153 as it breaks off from US 322, 5 miles from Clearfield. From the fork, travel 7 more miles and turn right onto Mud Run Road. Follow the signs to Parker Dam State Park. Go 2.5 miles and turn right into the main parking area adjacent to the ranger station. The trail starts from the parking area.

Notes on the trail: The Parker Dam State Park is rich in logging history. This area was originally covered with towering pines and hemlocks that drew the lumber and tanning industries. The land was first timbered in 1875 under contract to William Parker, who began cutting the banks along Laurel Run. It was during this time that splash dams were the most effective way of transporting big timber to mills. These dams were constructed to store water that would be released downstream onto the logs that lay in the creekbed. The flooding of the stream would float the timber to the mills that lay downstream. In the case of Laurel Run, the mills were located on the Bennett's Branch of the Sinnemahoning Creek.

By the late 1800s most of the white pine was cut and the land changed hands to the Elk Tanning Company, which used the hemlock and chestnut bark for tanning hides. In 1903 the Central Pennsylvania Lumber Company purchased over 4,500 acres of mainly hemlock timber from the Elk Tanning Company and built logging-gauge railroads up Laurel, Little Laurel, and Moose Runs. The area had been decimated by 1930 and was sold to the Commonwealth of Pennsylvania. The Civilian Conservation Corps (CCC) built the area into a recreation park as you see it today. An authentic reproduction of the old log slide and an interpretive sign on the logging era are located along the road to the campground.

The park tour begins along the lake, works its way back up through the cabin area and ascends Sullivan Ridge. A great descent down wild blackberry-lined trail leads over a deep dirt berm and out to the beaver-dammed Abbot Hollow Run. A climb through a beautiful stand of quaking aspens turns onto Bushkirk Road, which slowly descends to the Abbot Hollow Trail. As you climb back up into the drainage, you soon pass through the regrowth of the 1985 tornado that ripped through the upper part of this hollow. The line of destruction is visible where the shrub growth is replaced with mature trees near the crest of Sullivan Ridge. Descending back toward the trailhead, a final loop climbs up and out onto the Skunk Trail, which finishes with a short but sweet singletrack section through older-growth pines.

When you finish the ride, check out the environmental education building near the lake. If the season permits, a swim in the lake is most enjoyable after a gritty ride through the park. The location makes a prime base camp for the other local rides such as the Rockton Mountain ride and the trails in the Moshannon State Forest.

Parker Dam State Park

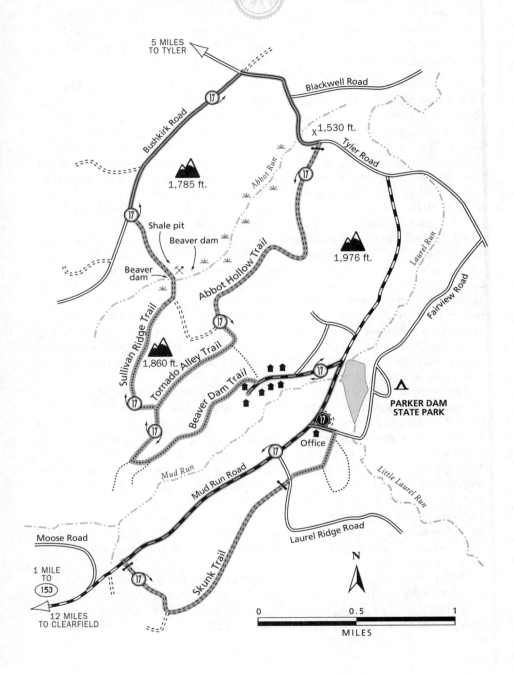

5 MILES TO TYLER

Blackwell Road

Bushkirk Road

X 1,530 ft.

Tyler Road

1,785 ft.

Abbot Run

1,976 ft.

Shale pit

Beaver dam

Abbot Hollow Trail

Beaver dam

Laurel Run

Fairview Road

Sullivan Ridge Trail

1,860 ft.

Tornado Alley Trail

Beaver Dam Trail

PARKER DAM STATE PARK

Office

Mud Run

Little Laurel Run

Mud Run Road

Laurel Ridge Road

Moose Road

N

Skunk Trail

1 MILE TO 153

12 MILES TO CLEARFIELD

0   0.5   1

MILES

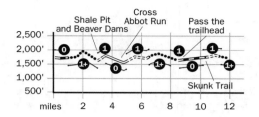

THE RIDE

0.0 From the parking area turn right onto Mud Run Road.

0.4 After passing the lake, turn left on the paved park road that heads up to the cabins. This road is just opposite the spillway and the CCC camp building.

0.9 Bear right onto the Beaver Dam Trail marked by the large wooden post.

1.6 After passing a trail spur to the left that leads to the beaver dams, take a hard right onto the Sullivan Ridge Trail and ascend the hill.

1.8 Turn left onto the trail spur, following the Sullivan Ridge Trail, and continue to climb.

2.7 At the four-way intersection continue straight onto the Abbot Hollow Trail. Carefully cross over a deep, dirt berm and mud hole.

3.0 After passing a beaver dam on the left and an open-pit shale mine on the right, keep left at a fork on the woods road.

3.3 Turn right at the T intersection onto Bushkirk Road.

4.3 Turn right at the four-way intersection onto Tyler Road.

4.9 Turn right onto the old woods road spur. Pass around an old wooden gate and a wooden post marked "A. H." for the Abbot Hollow Trail.

6.3 Turn left at the trail spur that is marked by a wooden post that says "To Cabins," and climb the hill.

7.5 Pass a trail spur to the left (that leads to the cabins) and continue on the main trail as it bends right (the Tornado Alley Trail).

8.1 Continue straight at the right-hand trail spur (now on the Sullivan Ridge Trail) and descend the hill, retracing the ride back to the trailhead.

9.0 Merge left onto the paved road at the cabins.

9.4 Turn right onto Mud Run Road.

9.8 Pass the trailhead and continue down Mud Run Road.

11.1 Turn left onto the gated old woods road, marked "Skunk Trail" on a wooden post.

11.4 Turn left at a grassy woods road spur, marked by a wooden post with the initial "S" and an arrow pointing left.

12.3 Pass around a gate, carefully cross Laurel Ridge Road, and resume the trail on the other side.

12.9 Turn left at the T intersection with the paved campground road and ride it out to the trailhead.

Big Springs Draft

Location:	26 miles northeast of Clearfield.
Distance:	12.7-mile loop.
Time:	2 to 4 hours.
Tread:	Rugged, rocky, technical singletrack, grassy old woods and forest road.
Aerobic level:	Moderate. The elevation gains are insignificant when compared to the long, technical singletrack sections. A full-body workout is guaranteed on this ride.
Technical difficulty:	4. Over half of the ride follows some of the best technical singletrack in the region. Rock gardens, downed trees, off-camber trail, and loose tread are just a few of the gnarly obstacles you'll encounter on this classic route.
Highlights:	Long sections of stellar technical singletrack, great wildlife viewing, one of the most remote woodland areas in Pennsylvania.
Land status:	Pennsylvania State Forest. Department of Conservation and Natural Resources.
Maps:	USGS Devils Elbow; DCNR Pennsylvania State Forest: Moshannon State Forest map, Quehanna Trail map.

Access: From Clearfield, take Pennsylvania Highway 879 north 20 miles. Just before the town of Karthaus, turn left onto Pennsylvania Road 1011 and head north to Piper (Quehanna Boot Camp). After passing the Quehanna Boot Camp, travel for 4 miles to the intersection of Wykoff Run Road and Quehanna Highway (Pennsylvania Road 1011). Turn left at this intersection onto the dirt road, which soon dead-ends and offers ample parking. This dead-end road is the trailhead.

Notes on the trail: The Quehanna Wild Area is a most spectacular tract of Pennsylvania woods. Ravaged by man's destructive logging practices and the tornadic forces of nature, this place is definitely "wild." This 50,000-acre area was originally state forest lands that were transferred to the Curtiss Wright Corporation for jet engine and nuclear research in the mid 1950s. In 1966 the land was given back to the state and has since been designated a Wild Area. I guess if you pull a night ride here and notice that the critters glow in the dark, you'll know what they did with all that spent nuclear waste.

The ride begins with some stout singletrack on the Wykoff Trail. Getting more burly by the mile, the route dives down to the Devils Elbow and

Big Springs Draft

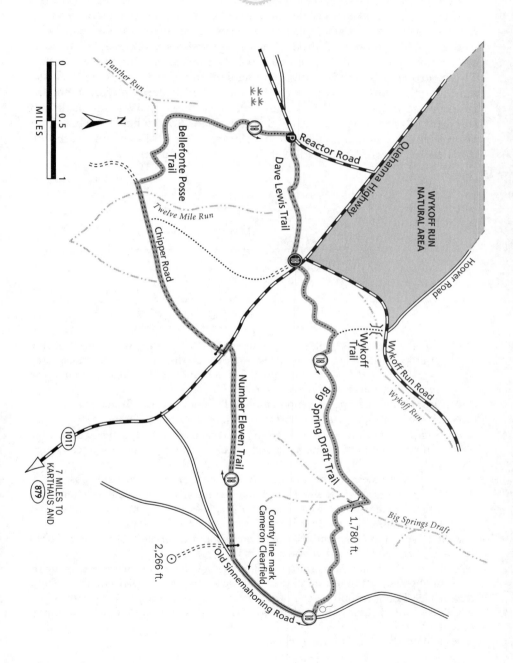

crosses Big Springs Draft and then climbs again on some of the toughest but most enjoyable singletrack. After passing the old stone-built spring and a prolific grove of huckleberry bushes, the ride cruises out along forest road to the grassy Number Eleven Trail. After carefully crossing the desolate Quehanna Highway, stoke up some speed as you descend the Chipper Road to the next singletrack. Climbing back into the woods, the Posse Trail soon passes through beautiful open scrub oak and mountain blueberry patches. This is a rough place to be caught in a violent thunderstorm; there was also massive tornado that touched down and flattened acres of forest not far from this spot back in 1985, so, keep an eye to the sky. Weaving back into stands of tall conifers, the ride exits onto Reactor Road where a nice, rolling old woods road meanders back to the trailhead. For a full-day epic, combine this ride with Gore Vista (Ride 19) for a 25.8-mile adventure.

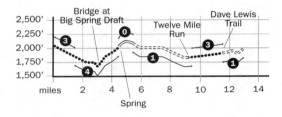

THE RIDE

0.0 From the trailhead lot, ride out to Quehanna Highway and turn right. Ride for 0.1 mile, cross Quehanna Highway, and pick up the singletrack cross-country ski trail marked by a wooden post. This obscure trail is hidden among the pines and is the crux of the entire ride.

1.0 Turn right at the T intersection onto the Big Springs Draft Trail.

3.0 Cross a footbridge over Big Springs Draft, at the Devils Elbow.

4.4 After passing a large, stone spring, turn left onto the gravel road and soon after turn right onto Old Sinnemahoning Road. The spring is a great huckleberry spot.

5.0 Cross the Cameron-Clearfield county line marked by the roadside post.

5.3 Turn right onto the old woods road, marked heavily with blue blazes, and pass around a gate on to Number Eleven Trail. (What I want to know is what happened to trails one through ten?)

7.2 Turn left onto Quehanna Highway and soon after (mile 7.3) turn right onto Chipper Road, a gated doubletrack road.

9.2 After a dip in the road, carefully follow the blue blazes as they break off right, and head up into the woods on singletrack. This is the Bellefonte Posse Trail.

11.4 After passing around a gate, the trail comes to a clearing near Reactor Road. Take a hard right onto Dave Lewis Trail and follow the blue-blazed grassy doubletrack.

12.7 Reluctantly return to the trailhead.

Gore Vista

Location:	26 miles northeast of Clearfield.
Distance:	13.1-mile loop.
Time:	2 to 4 hours.
Tread:	Rugged, rocky, technical singletrack, grassy old woods and forest road.
Aerobic level:	Moderate. The ride changes little in elevation but a full-body workout is guaranteed. The technical riding keeps the heart rate up and the mind sharp.
Technical difficulty:	3 + . Over half the ride follows some of the finest technical singletrack in the region. Rock gardens, windfallen trees, off-camber trail, and loose tread are just a few of the great objective hazards on this classic route.
Highlights:	Long sections of stellar technical singletrack, beautiful pure stands of white birch trees, true solitude, the commanding Gore Vista, great wildlife viewing, one of the most remote woodland areas in Pennsylvania.
Land status:	Pennsylvania State Forest; Department of Conservation and Natural Resources.
Maps:	USGS Devils Elbow, Driftwood; DCNR Pennsylvania State Forest: Moshannon State Forest map, Elk State Forest map, Quehanna Trail map.

Access: From Clearfield, take Pennsylvania Highway 879 north 20 miles. Just before the town of Karthaus, turn left onto Pennsylvania Road 1011 and head north to Piper (Quehanna Boot Camp). After passing the Quehanna Boot Camp, travel for 4 miles to the intersection of Wykoff Run Road and Quehanna Highway (Pennsylvania 1011). Turn left at this intersection onto the dirt road, which soon dead-ends and offers ample parking. This dead-end road is the trailhead.

Notes on the trail: This ride travels through the beautifully rugged woodlands surrounding the Wykoff Run Natural Area. The route is actually a series of cross-country ski trails through the heart of the Quehanna Wild Area, which encompasses 50,000 acres of some of the most remote and untouched land in Pennsylvania. It wasn't always untouched—loggers cut every inch of forest, fires burned the rich soil layer, and the land was left for dead. But Mother Nature has an uncanny way of breathing the life back into almost anything, and this woodland couldn't be a finer example of her handiworks.

Gore Vista

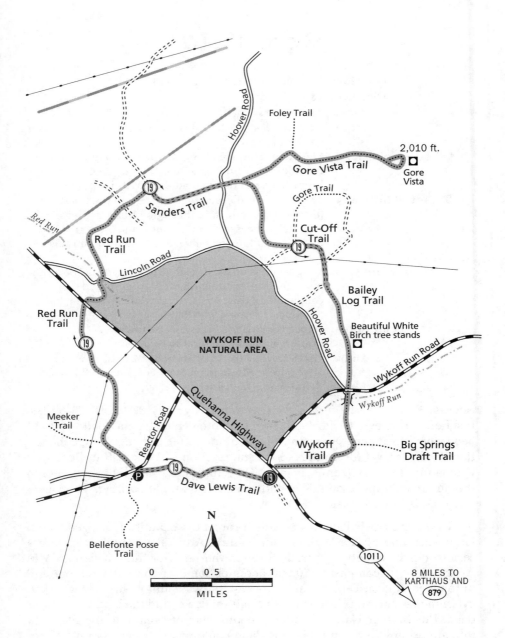

Foley Trail

Hoover Road

2,010 ft.

Gore Vista Trail

Gore Vista

Gore Trail

19

Sanders Trail

Red Run

Red Run Trail

Cut-Off Trail

19

Lincoln Road

Bailey Log Trail

Hoover Road

Red Run Trail

Beautiful White Birch tree stands

19

WYKOFF RUN NATURAL AREA

Wykoff Run Road

Meeker Trail

Quehanna Highway

Wykoff Run

Reactor Road

Wykoff Trail

Big Springs Draft Trail

P

19

Dave Lewis Trail

19

Bellefonte Posse Trail

N

1011

8 MILES TO KARTHAUS AND 879

0   0.5   1

MILES

A divine ride in itself, this outstanding loop can be linked with Big Springs Draft (Ride 18) to create a killer, full-day adventure. But let's start with the armchair ride through this route. From the trailhead, a great warm-up takes you along the rolling Dave Lewis doubletrack. After you cross Reactor Road, the riding gets better. Four miles of the most pristine singletrack floats through beautiful woodland. A short link on doubletrack along the Sanders Trail leads to more outstanding singletrack, which takes you to the remote Gore Vista Trail. It's not uncommon to sit here for hours, communing with the natural world and recharging you spiritual connections.

Returning back to the Sanders Trail, the obscure Cut-Off Trail is a short cut to the Gore Trail. Enjoy the dense canopy of sapling trees that crowd out this old woodland logging trail. The spectacular grove of white birches is a sight to behold, even on the most darkest of days when the trees seem to emit their own light. This is a rare and special sight in Pennsylvania. But you're not done yet, as the ride spices up a bit after entering the Wykoff Trail. Two miles of burly trail await your technical finesse and end-of-the-ride stamina. As you cross the Quehanna Highway and head back to your car, think back to all the spectacular sights and sounds you experienced on the ride.

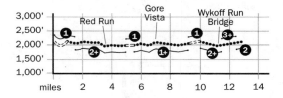

THE RIDE

0.0 From the trailhead area, begin riding west on the Dave Lewis Trail, a grassy doubletrack.

1.3 Cross Reactor Road diagonally left and continue on the sweet singletrack of the Red Run Trail.

1.8 Turn right at the junction with the Meeker Trail, still following the Red Run Trail.

2.4 Cross under the power line diagonally right.

3.0 Carefully turn left on Quehanna Highway and ride for 150 yards before turning right onto the singletrack that heads back into the woods.

3.5 Turn right onto Lincoln Road; ride for 150 yards crossing over Red Run, and turn left to continue on the beautiful singletrack.

4.4 At a clearing and prominent intersection, continue straight into the woods following the singletrack.

4.9 Turn right at the T intersection onto the Sanders Trail (old woods road), marked by a wooden post.

5.4 Cross Hoover Road; soon after, keep left at the fork (mile 5.6) and head out on the Gore Vista Trail. Note the wooden post and make a strong mental note of this intersection.

6.1 Pass the Foley Trail on the left, noting the small wooden sign nailed high on the tree.

7.0 Take either fork as they form a loop out to the impressive Gore Vista. Enjoy the solitude of this beautiful vista looking out over the Wykoff Run drainage. From here return back to the intersection of the Sanders Trail (remember mile 5.4).

8.5 Turn left at the T intersection (the one you were supposed to commit to memory).

9.3 Come to a clearing and turn left onto an old woods road. Soon after (mile 9.5) keep right at the fork onto the semi-overgrown woods road, the Cut-Off Trail.

9.8 Cross under the power line.

10.1 Cross a four-way intersection and continue straight, noting the wooden sign stating "Wykoff Road, 1 mile." Soon you will pass through a stand of beautiful white birch trees.

11.2 Turn left onto Hoover Road, immediately crossing Wykoff Run Road, and follow the blue-blazed singletrack (Wykoff Trail) back into the woods. Once in the woods, pass over a wooden footbridge at Wykoff Run– A nice place to soak the quads and check for crawdads.

11.9 Turn right at the wooden post onto the Wykoff Trail.

13.1 Carefully cross Quehanna Highway and follow the blue blazes through the woods to the trailhead.

Little Toby Rail-Trail

Location:	7.5 miles southwest of Ridgeway.
Distance:	21.8 miles out and back.
Time:	1 to 5 hours.
Tread:	The entire ride follows the cinder-covered original railbed grade.
Aerobic level:	Easy. It's a great ride for families, young riders, and the tow-behind kid carts.
Technical difficulty:	0. It's a rail-trail.
Highlights:	The historic Ridgeway-to-Clearfield rail grade, historic quarry operation ruins, numerous ghost towns, swinging span bridge over Toby Creek.
Land status:	Pennsylvania Game Commission, Tri-County Rails to Trails.
Maps:	USGS Carman; Tri-County Rails to Trails–Clarion/Little Toby Trail map.

The swinging bridge along The Little Toby Rail-Trail.

Little Toby Rail-Trail

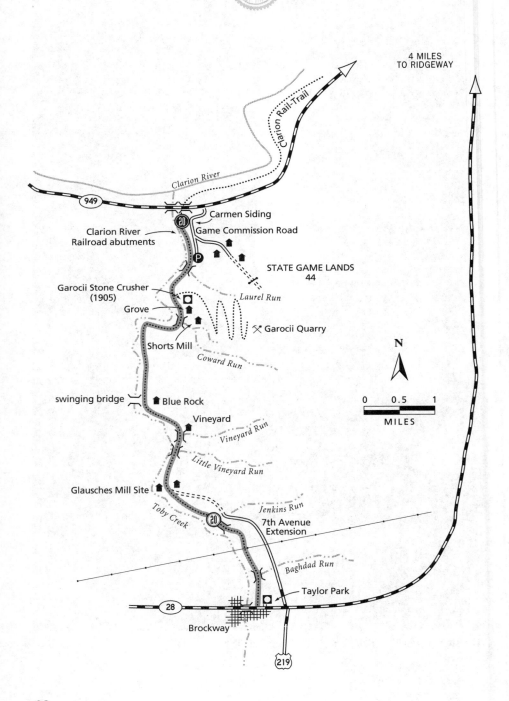

4 MILES
TO RIDGEWAY

Clarion Rail-Trail

Clarion River

949

Carmen Siding

20

Clarion River
Railroad abutments

Game Commission Road

P

STATE GAME LANDS
44

Garocii Stone Crusher
(1905)

Grove

Laurel Run

Garocii Quarry

Shorts Mill

Coward Run

N

swinging bridge

Blue Rock

Vineyard

Vineyard Run

0   0.5   1

MILES

Little Vineyard Run

Glausches Mill Site

Toby Creek

20

Jenkins Run

7th Avenue
Extension

Baghdad Run

28

Taylor Park

Brockway

219

Access: From Ridgeway, travel southwest on Pennsylvania Highway 949 for 7.5 miles to Game Commission Road. Turn left onto Game Commission Road and travel for approximately 200 yards. Park on the right at a large wooden sign that says "Carman Siding Access Area." This is the trailhead.

Notes on the trail: This ride is part of an ever-expanding network of rail-trail along this section of the old Pennsylvania Railroad. The ride begins at the old Carman siding and passes through some of the most historic points along the entire tract. Built in 1885 as part of the Pennsylvania Railroad, the Ridgeway-Clearfield branch stretches 45 miles and was used to haul timber from the mills in the northern region to the main rail lines that lie further south. In 1968 the last train passed through the valley; four years later the tracks were removed and the Pennsylvania Game Commission purchased sections of the adjoining lands. The ride follows the Little Toby Creek, which is a designated trout stream. The creek feeds the Clarion River, which has been designated by Congress as a Wild and Scenic River.

From Carman Siding, the trail passes the old stone abutments of the Clarion River Railroad. Not long after, you'll see the massive remains of the Garocii stone crusher built in 1905. Next, the trail passes three ghost towns where even the building foundations are disappearing. The swinging bridge over the Little Toby is a nice stop since there aren't many bridges of this type left. A few bridge crossings follow as the ride terminates in the quaint town of Brockway. This is leisurely ride with a host of interesting stops along the way.

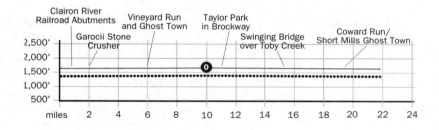

THE RIDE

0.0 Enter the rail-trail by taking the short, twisty singletrack just to the right of the large wooden sign. Once across the small wooden bridge, turn left onto the rail-trail.

0.6 Pass under the old Clarion River Railroad trestle abutments. Soon after, pass two sets of yellow poles at a game commission parking area.

2.0 Pass the Garocii stone crusher ruins built in 1905. Take some time to check it out. The quarry is way above the valley and can be reached by taking the Garocii Quarry Switchback Trail, or hiking up the Switchback Trail, (Ride 21).

2.5 Pass over Coward Run and Shorts Mill ghost town.

4.8 Pass the swinging bridge over the Little Toby Creek on the right and the Blue Rock ghost town on the left.

5.9 Cross Vineyard Run, the site of an old sawmill and the ghost town of Vineyard. Soon after pass over Little Vineyard Run.

7.0 Pass a few cabins and cross an access road at the site of Glausches Mill.

8.5 Cross the bridge over Jenkins Run.

9.6 Cross under a set of double power lines.

10.3 Cross the bridge over Baghdad Run.

10.9 Terminate at a beautiful pavilion and park in Brockway. Return from whence you came.

21.8 Trailhead.

Garocii Quarry Switchback Trail

Location:	7.5 miles southwest of Ridgeway.
Distance:	8.7-mile loop.
Time:	2 to 4 hours.
Tread:	The perfect blend of great singletrack and fire roads. The singletrack sections are mostly hardpacked, with the occasional rock.
Aerobic level:	Moderate. The initial 800-foot climb is quite stiff, and although the elevation gain is spread out over 4 miles, there is a section around the 2.5-mile mark that rises sharply.
Technical difficulty:	2. The killer singletrack section off the top of the quarry has a few obstacles to contend with and the switchbacks are to be treated with care. The loose nature of these sharp turns is unforgiving, as are the big trees that lie over their edge.
Highlights:	The historic ruins of the Garocii Stone Quarry and Stone Crusher, Little Toby Rail-Trail, 2 miles of the area's best switchback singletrack, bouldering on massive boulders, exploring mini-caves between the massive blocks, great wildlife viewing.
Land status:	Pennsylvania Game Commission.
Maps:	USGS Carman; Pennsylvania Game Commission SGL 44 map.

Access: From Ridgeway travel southwest on Pennsylvania Highway 949 for 7.5 miles to Game Commission Road. Turn left onto Game Commission Road and travel for 1.6 miles, passing the game commission maintenance buildings on the right. Cross the rickety old wooden bridge and park in the lot at the end of the road by the gate. This lot is the trailhead.

Notes on the trail: A truly classic ride! Founded by Dave Love, the owner of Love's Canoe in Ridgeway, it is a shining example of the ideal mountain bike ride. If stout climbs and sweet singletrack are what you crave, then this is the honey pot. The ridge-top singletrack passes an optional but worthy spur trail that drops down through massive sandstone boulders. These mono-lithic rocks litter the hillside, forming small caves and interesting climbing problems. The trail meanders by the man-made quarry and ancient steam engine. The engine was used to lower the quarried rock to the stone crusher found at the bottom of the hill. Oak trees now grow through the old steam engine, making it a permanent fixture atop the quarry. The question is, how did they get that colossal beast up there?

The ride begins down in the valley with a slow climb up to the flat-topped ridge. Soon you hit the wall, where the road rises sharply and your quads start screaming. After the second right-hand road, the ride lets up for a bit before a final, sharp climb to the top. A few turns on some gas well roads leads to the semi-obscure, sweet singletrack. A mile-long descent ends at a T intersection; turn left and begin climbing a bit to the quarry and steam engine. The final leg is the awesome switchback that fires off the mountain. Loose, tight turns require lots of finesse as the trail drops fast elevation and empties out at the stone crusher ruins. A short cruise on the Little Toby Rail-Trail leads to the Game Commission Road and the trailhead.

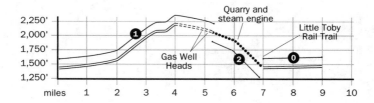

THE RIDE

0.0 From the game lands parking lot, ride south and pass around the steel gate. You start to gain some elevation on the dirt road.

3.1 Turn right at the second righthand dirt road.

3.9 Keep right at the fork and climb the short but steep grade.

4.4 Follow the road as it bends left at a large blue gas well head.

4.8 Turn right at the T intersection and head into a clearing marked by another blue gas well head. The dirt road will enter some woods and descend a bit.

5.1 Pass another gas well head and a lefthand road. Continue straight on the road which turns into all grass with a singletrack line down the one side. Soon after (mile 5.2), turn left onto the somewhat obscure singletrack trail. Here comes the honey!

Garocii Quarry Switchback Trail

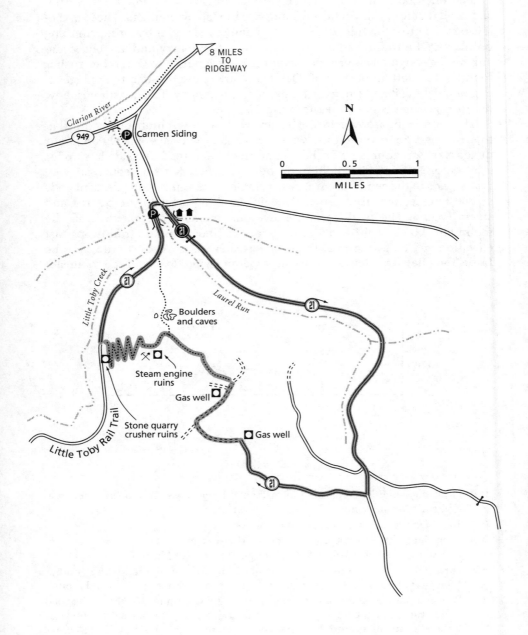

8 MILES
TO
RIDGEWAY

N

Clarion River

949 Carmen Siding

0   0.5   1
MILES

Little Toby Creek

21

Laurel Run

21

Boulders
and caves

Steam engine
ruins

Gas well

Stone quarry
crusher ruins

Gas well

Little Toby Rail Trail

21

6.0 Turn hard left at a T intersection after the killer descent. Follow the small, orange circle blazes as they climb a bit to the quarry. If you turn right here the trail continues down past the huge sandstone boulders and caves. Following the trail all the way down the mountain will bring you out to the Little Toby Rail-Trail.

6.3 The trail bends 90 degrees hard right at the top of the quarry, following the lip of this cavernous hole. The old steam engine is about 50 yards left of this turn and about 30 yards back from the edge of the quarry. Vultures are a common sight here as they glide in the thermals afforded by the south-facing cliffs.

6.4 Hop over the dirt berm and follow the trail as it turns 90 degrees left. The trail then wraps around right and into a large depression, finally turning 180 degrees left. This is the first in the series of switchbacks.

7.0 Pass the Garocii stone crusher ruins on the left and the remains of the rock slide area. Turn right onto the Little Toby Rail-Trail.

8.3 Pass over Laurel Run on a bridge, through a set of yellow poles and bear right as the dirt road wraps around to the game commission maintenance buildings, following the dirt road right, at the T intersection.

8.7 Trailhead.

Big Mill Creek

Location:	2.5 miles west of Ridgeway.
Distance:	6.3-mile loop.
Time:	1 to 2 hours.
Tread:	Beautiful hardpacked singletrack and grassy power line roads.
Aerobic level:	Easy to moderate. The initial climb up to the singletrack trail is a heinous strain even though it's on the paved road. Once atop the hill, the trail is a mellow roll until the final sweet descent back into the valley.
Technical difficulty:	2. The rolling singletrack and grassy roads offer the typical bumps and rocky obstructions commonly associated with trail riding. Mild by most standards.
Highlights:	Tight, twisty singletrack with a sweet downhill finish through an older growth stand of conifers; Sandy Beach Recreation Area.
Land status:	Allegheny National Forest.
Maps:	USGS Portland Mills.

Access: From Ridgeway take Laurel Mill Road (Pennsylvania Highway 688) west 3.3 miles to Sandy Beach Recreation Area. Park anywhere in the lots on the left at this township recreation area. This is the trailhead.

Big Mill Creek

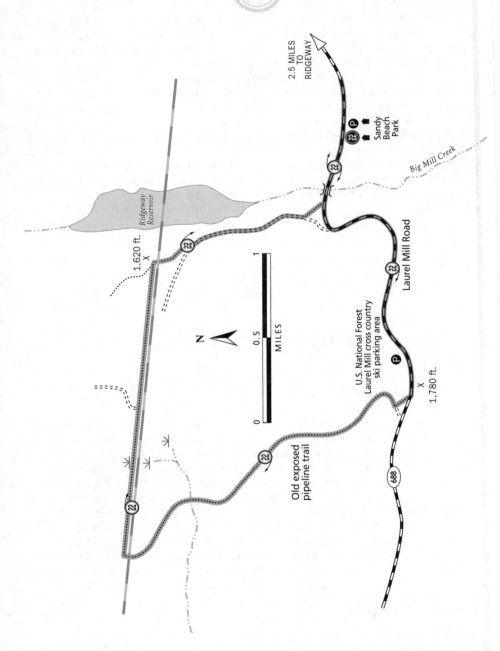

2.5 MILES TO RIDGEWAY

Sandy Beach Park

Big Mill Creek

Ridgeway Reservoir

1,620 ft. X

Laurel Mill Road

N

0   0.5   1

MILES

U.S. National Forest
Laurel Mill cross country
ski parking area

X
1,780 ft.

Old exposed
pipeline trail

Notes on the trail: This ride was once part of the Ridgeway Mountain Bike Race course. The original course went deep into the National Forest and crossed some private tracts of land. Vegetation has now grown back along the abandoned pipelines and covered parts of the trail, but the front half of the ride still survives and offers some great riding. The course passes along old pipeline singletrack which has exposed the old pipe due to the heavy amount of riding. Skilled bike handling is a must to avoid the heinous tire-slides on the old, slippery steel pipe that would otherwise toss you from your bike.

From the Sandy Beach recreation area, the ride heads out on a stout hill climb up the paved road. With a mile of climbing and some serious elevation gain behind you, the best is yet to come. Two miles of rolling singletrack along the old pipeline are a blast as the trail leapfrogs the exposed pipeline, which has been polished clean by plenty o' knobbies. The route then swings out onto the power line where it rolls along the grassy doubletrack. Watch out for the usual hidden surprises like chuck holes and obscure rocky sleepers. And just when you thought it was getting good, it gets better, much better. The trail drops off sharply on a short but rocky singletrack and then peels off into the woods on a smooth hardpacked trail shrouded in towering hemlocks. On the way down, the ride passes the Ridgeway Reservoir and coasts back out to the highway. It's only a matter of a few hundred yards until you're back at the trailhead.

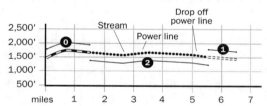

THE RIDE

0.0 From the Sandy Beach Recreation Area, take Pennsylvania Highway 688 left and climb the steep and sustained hill. Be careful on the road!

1.5 After passing the National Forest Laurel Mill cross-country ski area, turn right onto the obscure singletrack (approximately 200 yards). After 100 yards, at an exposed pipeline, the trail bends 90 degrees right and follows the partially exposed pipeline along a wooded singletrack.

2.7 Cross a small stream.

3.3 Turn right onto the power line, following the faint grassy trail.

3.8 Cross a very swampy area at a dip in the power line.

5.1 As the power line drops off sharply toward Big Mill Creek, ride down 40 yards from the crest of the hill and turn right onto the singletrack trail that soon widens as it enters the woods.

5.6 Merge left onto the old woods road after crossing over the dirt berm.

6.2 Turn left at the obscure fork, riding over a dirt berm and back out to Pennsylvania 688. Turn left onto Pennsylvania 688.

6.3 Turn right into the trailhead.

Beaver Meadows

Location:	5 miles north of Marienville.
Distance:	12.2-mile loop.
Time:	1 to 3 hours.
Tread:	A few miles of beautiful singletrack leads to an ATV trail. Doubletrack and snowmobile trail mix in and out for the next few miles, turning to hardpack dirt and gravel roads to finish out the ride.
Aerobic level:	Easy. The terrain is relatively flat with two easy hill climbs. Some of the doubletrack is grass-covered, causing more rolling resistance. A great ride for an adventurous novice.
Technical difficulty:	1. There are no sections of difficult technical riding. As with any mountain bike ride, there are a few rocks and roots, but that's half the fun!
Highlights:	Beaver ponds, waterfowl lakes, swamp crossing, primitive campground, secret blueberry patch, close to town.
Land status:	Allegheny National Forest.
Maps:	USGS Lynch.

Access: From Marienville, follow Job Corps Road north for 5 miles. Turn right at the Forest Service sign for Beaver Meadows Recreation Area. Park in the first parking area on the right, next to the restrooms, not in the campground area.

Notes on the trail: This is a fast ride with mixed terrain and minimal elevation gain. Beaver Meadows Recreation Area is an awesome base camp from which to explore any of the rides in this region. Its proximity to town is even more enticing for those whose campsite culinary skills are less than adequate—or if a run for that extra six-pack is needed. As its name implies, the Beaver Meadows Recreation Area is home to many beaver. They can be seen along Salmon Creek and in some of the feeder streams to the lake, working on their dams. There are many opportunities for wildlife viewing. The area has loads of hiking trails for those who wish to explore the area on foot.

The ride begins on the north shore of the lake and immediately crosses the dam breast and bridge over the spillway. A wooden staircase leads to the forks of the Salmon Creek Loop, where a left turn winds through needle-bedded pine forest. The trail appears to end abruptly in a clearing, but it breaks from the singletrack, crosses a small stream, and passes an abandoned powder house. This old tin structure once housed the dynamite used in blasting local oil and gas wells. Snowmobile trails lead past quiet ponds and over a small swamp via the sketchy boardwalk. Casual riding on fire and Forest Service roads rolls around to a mellow finish at the trailhead.

(Note: The ride crosses the Marienville ATV trail system, which is open to mountain bikes. This ride can be extended by linking the ATV trail and Forest Service roads to bring you back to the trailhead. Marienville ATV trail maps can be found at the Marienville Ranger Station, 3 miles north of Marienville on State Pennsylvania 66.)

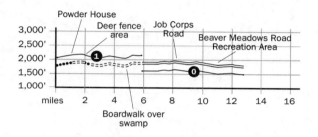

THE RIDE

0.0 From the parking lot, ride back out the entrance road toward the dam. Turn left at the dam, ride across it over the spillway bridge, and climb the wooden stairs. At the trail sign, take Salmon Creek Loop to the left, through the pine forest.

0.8 Continue straight through an open area, cross a small stream and swampy area, and pick up the trail in the form of an old logging road. Do <u>not</u> follow the singletrack trail to the right!

1.1 Turn left at the T intersection onto snowmobile Trail 11 and follow the orange blazes. Note the abandoned powder house on your left; at one time it stored dynamite for use in drilling oil and gas wells.

1.3 Pass Forest Road 178A on the left.

1.9 Turn hard right onto the grassy singletrack. You missed the turn if you hit the deer-fenced habitat restoration area.

2.3 Turn left at T intersection.

2.5 Enter a large meadow and ride directly across it, staying to the left of the lake. Many waterfowl live on this lake, so a slow and quiet approach may yield some impressive views. The trail resumes on the opposite side.

3.1 Turn left at T intersection onto FR 521.

3.5 Pass the motorcross trail on your left and then pass around a gate. Continue to follow the orange blazes marking the snowmobile trail.

4.2 Cross the Marienville ATV Trail and continue straight.

4.3 Follow the orange blazes left, drop over the hill, and merge with the Marienville ATV Trail.

4.7 Ride the boardwalk over the swamp. The craftsmanship is a bit sketchy, so beware of loose boards, nails, holes, and slime!

Beaver Meadows

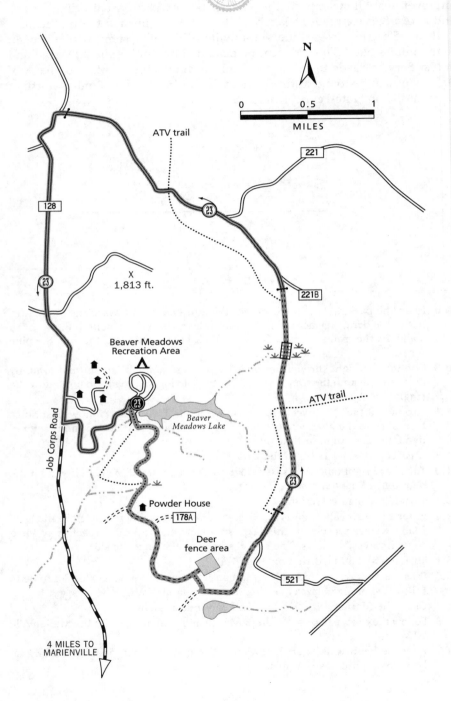

N

0   0.5   1
MILES

ATV trail

221

128

23

X
1,813 ft.

221B

Beaver Meadows
Recreation Area

ATV trail

Job Corps Road

23

Beaver
Meadows Lake

Powder House
178A

Deer
fence area

521

4 MILES TO
MARIENVILLE

6.1 Pass around a gate. Turn left at the fork onto FR 221B, leaving the Marienville ATV Trail.

6.7 Turn left onto FR 221.

8.3 Pass around a gate and turn left onto Job Corps Road, following signs for snowmobile Trail 9. This road is traveled heavily on weekends, so be cautious.

11.1 Turn left into Beaver Meadows Recreation Area.

12.2 Trailhead.

Lower Buzzard Swamp

Location:	5 miles southeast of Marienville.
Distance:	3.5-mile loop.
Time:	30 minutes to 1 hour.
Tread:	The entire loop is hardpacked dirt road with a wonderfully flat, well-drained, smooth surface for easy riding.
Aerobic level:	Easy. The entire route is generally flat and requires little in the way of aerobic energy. The perfect beginner or family ride.
Technical difficulty:	0. There are no technical challenges along this route which is great for entry-level riders. The ultrasmooth surface allows for a faster ride than would be found on a typical mountain bike trail.
Highlights:	Outstanding wildlife viewing and photography, great fishing, nonmotorized boating, scenic views, great outdoor family ride.
Land status:	Allegheny National Forest.
Maps:	USGS Marienville East; Allegheny National Forest Buzzard Swamp Trail map.

Access: From Marienville, take Pennsylvania Highway 2005 south and follow the signs for Loleta Campground. After 1 mile, turn left onto Forest Road 157. Follow FR 157 for approximately 2.5 miles to the dead-end. Park in the open lot area on your left; this is the trailhead.

Notes on the trail: The perfect family ride with great outdoor wildlife viewing opportunities awaits at Buzzard Swamp. The swamp is host to over twenty different species of waterfowl that migrate along the Atlantic flyway, most of which can be seen in the spring. During the fall migration, you might see ducks, geese, herons, egrets, and other raptors, including bald eagles.

Lower Buzzard Swamp

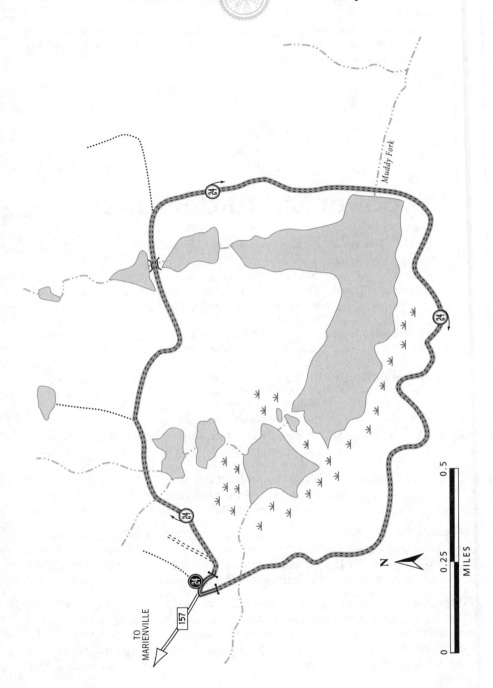

Muddy Fork

24

24

24

24

157

TO
MARIENVILLE

N

0   0.25   0.5
MILES

The ride takes you around the four largest ponds in the swamp and circles the restricted propagation area. This special section of marsh and swamp land is home to important waterfowl vegetation and also provides an uninterrupted habitat for nesting birds. This small, 40-acre tract is restricted to human traffic but offers the best chances of observing wildlife in the swamp. Binoculars are a must.

Largemouth and smallmouth bass, catfish, perch, crappie, and bluegills inhabit all the ponds, and the forest service allows nonmotorized boating. For families setting out for an afternoon trek, be aware that this ride runs mainly through vast, open fields offering little in the way of sun or wind protection; plan accordingly.

Beginning at the Forest Service bulletin board, the ride heads due east on the gated service road. You may notice signs of porcupine, which like to eat aluminum Forest Service signs. Soon the trail crosses the two upper ponds on a grated spillway bridge, one of the two places that offers trailside fishing. As the trail bends and turns right, the vastness of the fields is almost breathtaking. On the dam of the largest pond, the second trailside fishing spot, the trail begins to wind slowly up along the propagation area. Take your time and pedal slowly, for all kinds of creatures are hidden in the vegetation. Patience and sharp eyes will be your best chance at finding these creatures in their natural habitat. Pass a final gate and you're back at the trailhead. It's such a great ride you may even want to do it backward.

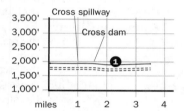

THE RIDE

0.0 From the trail sign at the parking area, ride out to your right, pass around a gated service road, and keep right at the Y.

1.0 Cross over the spillway bridge between the ponds. What a great place to fish and such a killer open view!

1.1 The trail turns right and follows along the dirt road. Keep the ponds in sight on your right.

1.6 Ride across the largest pond's dam, the second-best place for fishing.

3.5 Pass around the gate and finish back at the trailhead.

Upper Buzzard Swamp

Location:	5 miles southeast of Marienville.
Distance:	8.4-mile loop.
Time:	1 to 2 hours.
Tread:	Everything from singletrack and doubletrack to grassy service road and forest service dirt road. The stretch between miles 6.3 and 7.3 can become wet and swampy. Avoid this area after any rainfall or snowmelt.
Aerobic level:	Easy +. The trails run on a relatively flat grade with the exception of the last mile, which offers a short but moderate climb. The climb can be avoided by bypassing the hill and returning directly to the trailhead.
Technical difficulty:	1 +. Grass makes going a bit slower but is faster than the possibly waterlogged section between miles 6.3 and 7.3. The singletrack section adds a bit of spice to the end of the ride with a mild, rolling, rocky ramble.
Highlights:	Sweet singletrack with a taste of technical, wide open flat stretches; wildlife galore; awesome fishing; great photography opportunities.
Land status:	Allegheny National Forest.
Maps:	USGS Marienville East; National Forest Buzzard Swamp trail map.

Access: From Marienville, take Pennsylvania Highway 2005 south and follow the signs for Loleta Campground. After 1 mile, turn left onto Forest Road 157. Follow FR 157 for approximately 2.5 miles to the dead-end. Park in the open lot area on your left; this is the trailhead.

Notes on the trail: The Buzzard Swamp is a unique place designed and constructed mainly by the hands of men. The 15 man-made ponds were built in a joint partnership between the USDA Forest Service and the Pennsylvania Game Commission. The ponds and wetlands draw an abundance of wildlife. Bear, deer, porcupine, beaver, coyote, turtles, osprey, and the occasional bald eagle are common to this area. The ponds are full of life below the surface as well. Each has a variety of bass, perch, catfish, sunfish, and crappies. So why not bring along a rod? You're bound to get lucky at Buzzard Swamp!

Beginning at the Forest Service bulletin board, the trail heads due east around a gate. (You may notice the gnawed aluminum signs—evidence of

Upper Buzzard Swamp

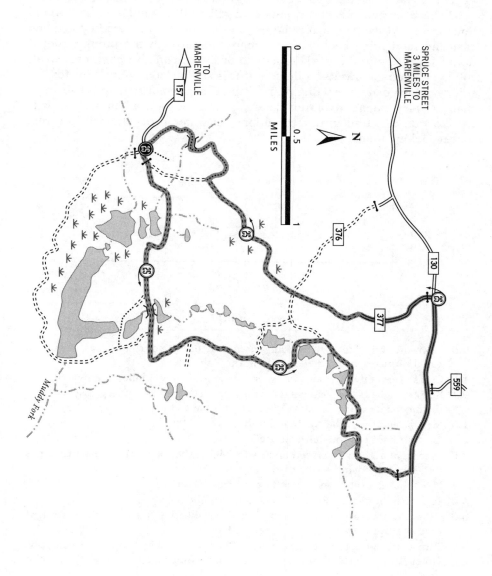

ravenous porcupines. Porcupines have a strange appetite for aluminum, so watch where you lay down that aluminum-framed bike.) A flat stretch opens out into a massive clearing, with views toward the lower ponds, and turns up a mild grade past the upper ponds to Forest Road 130. A fast cruise on FR 130 leads to an even faster descent down gated FR 377 and into the lowland doubletrack. If it's wet, avoid the tire-swallowing terror ahead by heading east and navigating back, using a map. Up through the bumpy, rooted doubletrack, the trail turns sharply and pushes up an abrupt climb. Sweet, rolling singletrack awaits to finish out this stellar loop. Watch out for the bridge, which can be real dicey on damp days. The entire map is shown so that you may extend, avoid, or delete sections of the trail as needed. It is best to ride this trail in dry conditions, as water turns the soil into real wheel-sucking muck.

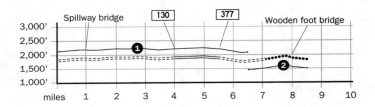

THE RIDE

0.0 From the trail sign at the parking area, ride out to your right, pass around a gated service road, and keep right at the Y.

1.0 Cross over spillway bridge between the ponds. What a killer open view!

1.1 Keep straight as the road bends to the right. The trail becomes grassy and less distinct as it continues along the edge of the woods.

1.5 Keep straight past the righthand trail.

2.2 Keep straight past the lefthand trail.

2.8 Turn right at the T intersection. Keep straight at the slight right fork that is not a trail but the dam service road.

4.1 Pass around a gate and turn left onto Forest Road 130.

5.4 Turn left onto Forest Road 377 and pass around a gate.

6.3 Cross the four-way intersection with Forest Road 376 and continue straight onto the doubletrack, or bail left if it's too wet.

7.3 Turn hard right at the T intersection. The trail cuts back and climbs sharply. Note: Turning left will bring you out to the trailhead, approximately 0.4 mile away.

8.0 Cross the wooden footbridge; it's slippery when wet.

8.4 Trailhead.

Kelly Pines Powerhouse

Location:	7 miles east of Marienville.
Distance:	6.3-mile loop.
Time:	1 hour.
Tread:	The first 4 miles are on dirt fire road. The descent down the last 2 miles is a mix of old woods road and doubletrack.
Aerobic level:	Easy. The beginning has some small, gradual hill climbing, but the rewards of the ridge top and downhill are well worth the little bit of effort to get there.
Technical difficulty:	1+. The only real technical negotiation is the deep water bars on the descent. However, the aggressive rider will find the water bars quite kind as they will have you logging those "frequent flier miles."
Highlights:	Historical relics; unique geologic features; all the classic elements of a perfect ride, including an uphill section, a flat section, and fast downhill.
Land status:	Allegheny National Forest.
Maps:	USGS Marienville East, Halton.

Access: From the center of Marienville, head east on Spruce Street. Once out of town, Spruce Street turns into Forest Road 130. At the 5-mile mark you will come to a four-way intersection. Turn left onto FR 131. Two more miles down the road is the Kelly Pines Campground. Turn right into the campground and park in the field on your left. This is the trailhead.

Notes on the trail: This beautiful ride leaves from one of the more spectacular campgrounds in Pennsylvania. Majestic white pine and hemlock trees grow in this peaceful spot as Wolf Run quietly meanders through. Kelly Pines Campground makes a wonderful base camp when riding this region. Only 7 miles from town, this little-known spot was once a managed Forest Service campground, and you can still see the old steel deposit box over by the creek. It doesn't boast a lot of camping sites, but the best part about them is that they're free. There are pit toilets, but no potable water; you will have to filter that from the stream.

The first half of the ride slowly climbs through lush mixed hardwood forests to an area with many unique gritstone boulders on either side of the road. These huge blocks are the remains of glacial action that took place quite some time ago, and they make for an incredible playground. Covered

Kelly Pines Powerhouse

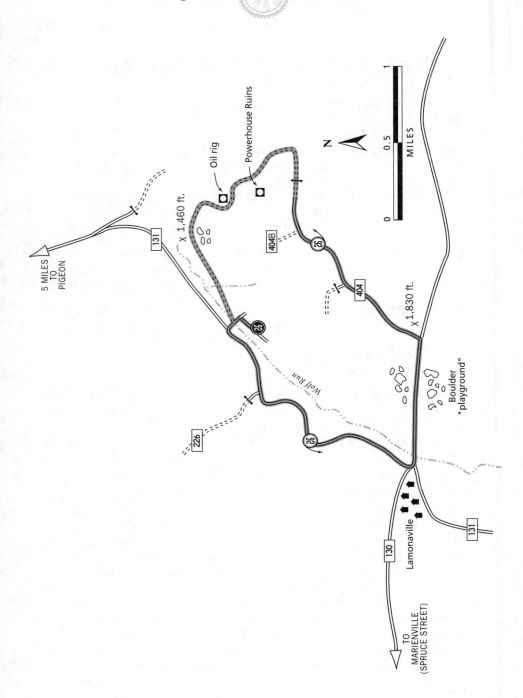

Oil rig

Powerhouse Ruins

X 1,460 ft.

131

5 MILES TO PIGEON

404B

26

404

X 1,830 ft.

26

Wolf Run

26

226

Boulder "playground"

Lamonaville

130

131

TO MARIENVILLE (SPRUCE STREET)

N

0   0.5   1

MILES

with many species of lichen and mosses, they are also a haven to many critters, including the eastern timber rattlesnake. The route begins to level out as you cruise across the flat top to the gated descent trail. The descent brings you to an abandoned oil powerhouse and an area that once contained many close-surface deposits of oil. The powerhouse's unique set of wheels and gears provided power to the rod-driven oil rigs. The engine turned the cogs, which spun the off-center cams. Rods were connected from the cam to the rig and operated in a push-pull fashion. The tripod rod supports are scattered throughout the woods. Holes in the cams show the wear of this once busy rig that still sits in the woods, approximately 300 yards back up the trail. Many historic relics can be found here, including the huge canvas drive belt, tinware, steel bars, and cables, as well as stone foundations and rotting wood-framed walls. Although nature is reclaiming the site, the huge steel beast will be around long after we are gone.

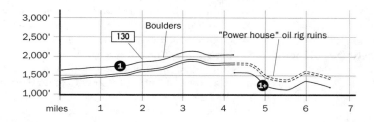

THE RIDE

0.0 From the campground, ride out to Forest Road 131. Turn left onto FR 131, and begin the climb back along the road you just drove in on.

2.1 Yes, you have been here before! Turn left at the four-way intersection onto FR 130.

2.6 Notice the incredible gritstone boulders in the woods on the right. (If you have some time, check out these awesome formations. If you like to climb, there is some fine bouldering on some of the faces not cloaked in thick moss. These rocks have been known to harbor a few friendly snakes, so just be mindful where you put your hands.)

2.9 The climbing is over! Turn left onto FR 404.

3.7 Pass a gated logging road on the left.

4.2 Pass FR 404B on the left.

4.3 Ride around the gate and notice the orange blazed diamonds. It's all downhill now!

5.1 Historic stop. On your left you will notice the old powerhouse sitting up on the hill. You can still retrace the rods that once extended from the powerhouse to the actual well heads.

5.3 Pass a road on your left and an old functioning oil rig on your right.

5.5 Pass some more massive boulders above you on the hill.

6.3 Back at Kelly Pines Campground and the trailhead.

Willow Creek ATV Trail

Location:	11 miles west of Bradford.
Distance:	10.2-mile loop.
Time:	1 to 2 hours.
Tread:	The tread varies from sand fire road to hardpack loam and loose, rocky doubletrack. Conditions change often due to the rain and amount of ATV traffic.
Aerobic level:	Moderate. The ride circles a rounded mountain top with many short climbs and descents. Some sections will require a little energy and, at times, you may wish you were the one riding the motorized couch! Does sucking two-cycle exhaust count as aerobic difficulty?!
Technical difficulty:	3. There are sections of large, loose rocks that can be tough to negotiate. Loose soil fluffed up from spinning tires and big mud holes filled with stale beer can test a rider's agility as can the possibility of being buzzed by the occasional motorized maniac.
Highlights:	Fast rolling doubletrack; quiet woodlands trail; mud holes and burly berms.
Land status:	Allegheny National Forest.
Maps:	USGS Stickney; Allegheny National Forest Willow Creek ATV Trail map.

Access: From Bradford take Pennsylvania Highway 346 west. After approximately 10 miles, turn left onto Forest Road 137. Drive approximately 2.5 miles down FR 137 to the parking lot and trailhead for the Willow Creek ATV Trail on the left.

Notes on the trail: A great ride, considering it was designed for ATVs. The Willow Creek Trail runs one way, which makes it relatively safe for all riders. The ride remains in the woods for the most part and is filled with numerous tight turns, bends, steep climbs, descents, and berms. The aggressive rider will really enjoy the berms as they allow you to rail the corners with speed without eating bark. The trail has been well marked with yellow diamond blazes on the trees, so it's hard to get lost.

The trail is a designated ATV trail and ATV users have the right-of-way. Mountain bikes are allowed here but you must always yield to any motorized rider. Your best bet may be a weekday ride. It really is a nice ride, you just have to take it for what it's worth.

From the trailhead you can see the exit and entrance to the trail on either side of the Forest Service bulletin board. Head right and you soon encounter

Willow Creek ATV Trail

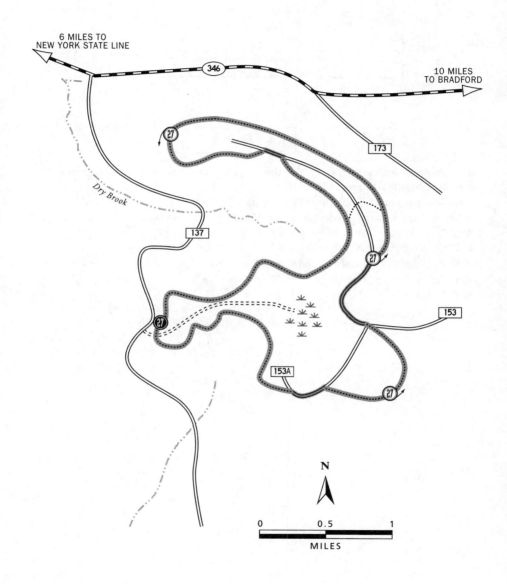

small rollers and twisty turns through the dense hardwoods. More wood-land trail takes you out along Forest Road 153 and then along the Dry Brook drainage. Another short cruise along FR 153 will have you back in the woods negotiating tricky climbs and the final flat pitch to the trailhead.

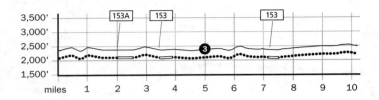

THE RIDE

0.0 The trail begins to the right of the covered Forest Service bulletin board.

2.0 Turn right onto Forest Road 153A.

2.5 Trail turns right, back into the woods.

3.3 Trail dumps out onto Forest Road 153; turn left.

3.8 Trail reenters the woods on the right.

4.4 Keep right at the fork in the trail.

7.3 Trail dumps out onto FR 153; turn right.

7.5 Trail reenters the woods on the right.

10.2 Trailhead.

Brush Hollow

Location: 10 miles north of Ridgeway.

Distance: 6.4-mile loop.

Time: 30 minutes to 1 hour.

Tread: Mainly grassy doubletrack, which passes through some swampy ground. There may be a few sections of singletrack, depending on when the forest service mows back the trail.

Aerobic level: Easy +. There are a few climbs, but nothing the beginning rider can't handle.

Technical difficulty: 1. Aside from crossing some boglike areas and a few bumps, this ride is void of any real technical challenges.

Highlights: Quiet woodlands, abundant wildlife, vista, haunted trail?!

Land status: Allegheny National Forest.

Maps: USGS James City; Allegheny National Forest Brush Hollow Ski Area Map.

Access: From Ridgeway, take Pennsylvania Highway 948 north for approximately 10 miles. The trailhead parking lot will be on the right and is well marked by forest service signs.

Notes on the trail: A great ride for the novice mountain biker with loads of scenery and a deep-woods feel. Located only 10 miles out of Ridgeway, it's close to civilization yet affords an experience of being far away from all its stresses. Brush Hollow is part of the many tracts of land managed by the national forest, and it's loaded with wildlife, including grouse, turkey, and deer. The area was originally designed for cross country skiing and has been deemed appropriate for mountain bike use as well. The ride is leisurely, tranquil and supposedly haunted!

Local legend claims that there was a logging camp built high in this hollow around mile mark 2.5. At this camp there was a dispute between two loggers and one night one of the men was murdered. The other fella was found guilty and hanged for the incident. Folks believe that the spirit of the murdered logger still roams the upper parts of this hollow in a state of unrest. If you're not afraid of ghosts, a full-moon ride may be a good test of the local lore!

The ride runs entirely on old logging grades, beginning with a flat cruise up alongside Big Mill Creek. After crossing a few well-built footbridges, the

Brush Hollow

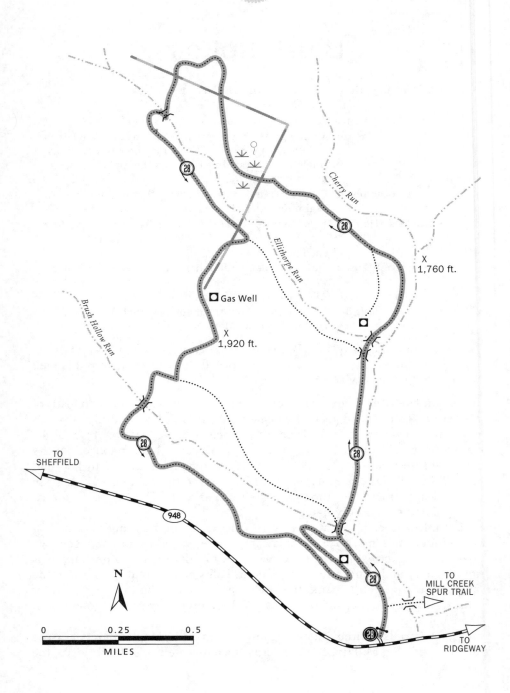

Cherry Run

X
1,760 ft.

Ellithorpe Run

☐ Gas Well

X
1,920 ft.

Brush Hollow Run

TO
SHEFFIELD

948

TO
MILL CREEK
SPUR TRAIL

TO
RIDGEWAY

N

0   0.25   0.5
MILES

trail breaks away from the valley and ascends up through Cherry Run Hollow. Passing boglike areas, you may get the feeling someone is watching you—could it be the ghost of the logger? Another bridge crossing the Ellithorpe Run leads up through a slightly technical section before coming out into a clearing with gas well heads. Squeeze through the metal poles and wind around into Brush Hollow, where a scenic vista awaits among tall cherry trees. A quick drop from the vista adds a bit of spice to the tail end of the ride as you roll out along Big Mill Creek to the trailhead.

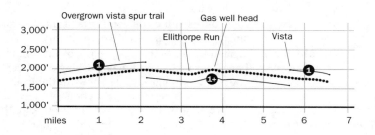

THE RIDE

0.0 The trail begins at the end of the parking lot, heading north.

0.1 Pass the Mill Creek Trail Spur on your right. Continue straight.

0.4 Cross over a wooden footbridge and pass signs for the Challenger and Brushy Gap Loops.

1.0 After crossing two wooden footbridges, you will pass another spur trail for the Brushy Gap Loop; keep right.

1.5 A spur trail to the left leads to an overgrown vista. Keep straight at this intersection and continue to climb the hill.

3.0 After slogging through the upper springs and boglike areas, cross the wooden footbridge over Ellithorpe Run, which leads to drier terrain.

3.6 Turn right at the fork in the trail.

3.8 Continue straight across an open clearing with a gas well head. At the far side pick up the trail where it is marked by two steel signposts. Don't worry about the pole spacing, your bars should just make it through.

4.2 Turn right at T intersection and climb back up Brush Hollow.

4.4 Cross wooden footbridge over Brush Hollow Run.

5.7 Small vista amid tall cherries, overlooking the Big Mill Creek drainage.

6.0 Turn right at T intersection.

6.4 Trailhead.

Minister Creek

Location: 25 miles south of Warren.
Distance: 6.3-mile loop.
Time: 1.5 to 2 hours.
Tread: Most of the route runs on some of the most beautiful singletrack in northwest Pennsylvania.
Aerobic level: Strenuous. The technical sections and rolling terrain have your heart and lungs working overtime while your mind struggles to be one with the trail. There is also a short, steep portage section up the cliff that will require a bit of strength and finesse to gain the vista.
Technical difficulty: 5. Unless you're a proficient rider, you might as well put on hiking shoes. As for the hammerheads, this ride is a perfect blend of short, fast singletrack mingled with gnarly boulder sections, sketchy stream crossings, and an incredible abundance of natural jumps.
Highlights: Rock climbing, rock canyon, huge boulders, crawfish laden streams, lung-buster climbs, screamer downhills, loads of natural jumps.
Land status: Allegheny National Forest.
Maps: USGS Cherry Grove, Mayberg; Allegheny National Forest Minister Creek Trail map.

Access: From Warren, take U.S. Highway 6 southwest to Sheffield. In Sheffield turn right onto Pennsylvania Highway 666 and follow it for approximately 15 miles. At a sharp left-hand bend in the road you will see the small Minister Creek Campground on the right. The trailhead parking lot is opposite the campground, on the left side of Pennsylvania 666.

Notes on the trail: "Technical" best describes this incredible Allegheny Mountain trail. This trail is made up of the perfect combination of fast, twisty singletrack and rounded, technical boulders. The setting is like none other, with every turn in the trail showing yet another unique natural feature. At the heart of Allegheny National Forest, Minister Creek is an area that has remained untouched for some time. Beautiful hemlocks, oaks, maples, and cherries fill the woods as you cross the lacework of feeder streams to Minister Creek.

The ride begins down on Pennsylvania 666, an eerie route number indeed, and takes an abrupt climb to the rockpile overlook. Riding first on old woods road, then on singletrack, you are increasingly challenged as you

Minister Creek

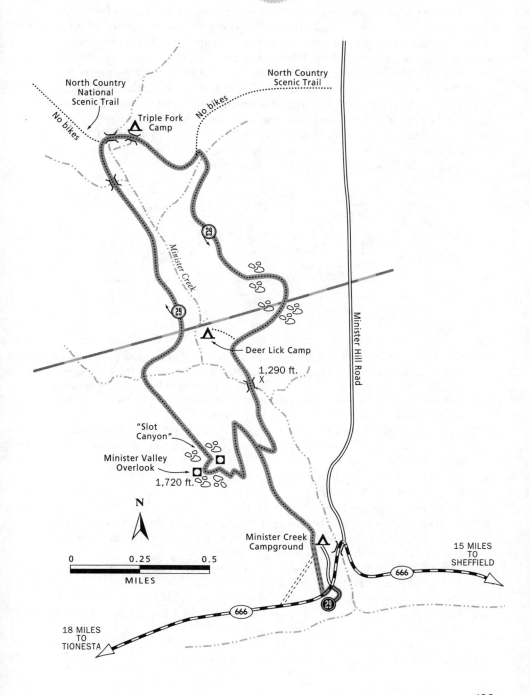

North Country
National
Scenic Trail

No bikes

North Country
Scenic Trail

No bikes

Triple Fork
Camp

29

Minister Creek

29

Deer Lick Camp

1,290 ft.
X

"Slot
Canyon"

Minister Valley
Overlook

1,720 ft.

Minister Hill Road

N

0   0.25   0.5
MILES

Minister Creek
Campground

666

29

15 MILES
TO
SHEFFIELD

666

18 MILES
TO
TIONESTA

approach the summit. A short but demanding portage up through the rocks will have you peering out over the Minister Valley below. Descending off the cliff, the trail passes through a most unique rock canyon, probably caused by huge rock blocks splitting out and away from the Pottstown formation. Once through the canyon, the trail rolls along the west side of Minister Creek, crossing a bunch of feeder streams and bridges. The northernmost and halfway point is the short traverse along the North Country National Scenic Trail. Riders should dismount and hike this small 0.3-mile section until the ride breaks away from the NCS Trail. From here the ride takes a general downhill trend with plenty of natural jumps and technical sections that wind down along the east side and eventually cross Minister Creek. A short, demanding climb up a series of switchbacks will have all but the most pumped riders bike-hiking up the hill. The exit ride is a scream out the singletrack and down the grassy old woods road.

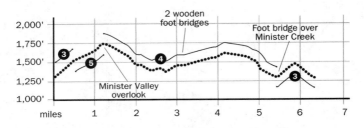

THE RIDE

0.0 From the trailhead parking area, cross Pennsylvania Highway 666 (unless you're really superstitious!) and pick up the trail a bit to the left of the campground entrance road. Begin a killer hill climb up the old woods road! The trail will merge right with the grass road, then shortly cross over a dirt berm as it becomes singletrack into the woods.

0.5 Keep left at the trail marker, heading up to the Minister Valley Overlook.

1.2 Shoulder the bike and hike up the rock stairs, through the boulders.

1.3 Minister Valley Overlook.

1.4 Pass through the unique rock canyon.

1.8 Cross over a feeder stream.

2.9 Cross over a wooden footbridge.

3.2 Keeping right, cross 2 footbridges and pass the North Country National Scenic Trail sign. Please dismount and enjoy a short hike as you are now on a short section of the North Country National Scenic Trail.

3.6 Turn right at T intersection, noting the trail sign for Minister Creek.

4.7 Pass a righthand trail to Deer Lick camping area.

5.4 Cross the wooden footbridge. This pool is a great soaking spot!

5.5 Turn right at fork, climbing the switchbacks up the killer hill (going straight will take you along the creek to a campground).

5.7 Turn left at T intersection. Had enough air yet? Big water-bar descent ahead!

6.3 Carefully cross Pennsylvania 666, back to the trailhead.

30

Thundershower Surprise

Location: 20 miles north of Kane.
Distance: 11.9-mile loop.
Time: 2 to 3 hours.
Tread: The first 3 miles are on nice hardpack doubletrack and fire road; the next 4 miles are on grass covered cross-country ski trails; and the remaining 5 miles are fire road and sweet doubletrack.
Aerobic level: Moderate. The route is moderate, mainly due to the initial hill climb. The grassy trails require a bit of pedaling as well, due to their rolling nature and the slow tread surface.
Technical difficulty: 2. The descent holds the only technical section and can be controlled by your speed. The water bars on the descent have 5-inch steel pipes across them, which makes them awkward to jump at high speed.
Highlights: Remains of an old oil and gas well, ghost town, hidden secret descent.
Land status: Allegheny National Forest.
Maps: USGS Westline.

Access: From Kane, take U.S. Highway 6 east for 10 miles, to U.S. Highway 219. Turn left onto U.S. Highway 219 and drive 6 miles to Pennsylvania Road 3006. Turn left onto Pennsylvania Road 3006; Westline is about 4 miles down the road. The Westline Inn, at the end of the paved road, is the trailhead parking lot. Note: PA Road 3006 turns into FS 321 at Westline.

Notes on the trail: There is a lot of oil history in these parts, and this ride highlights, yet another abandoned oil field and ghost town along its course. But let's start with the climb up the beautiful Thundershower Run on perfect grade. This beautifully wooded hollow is home to an array of wildlife, so animals are seen crossing the fire road quite often. The folks at the Westline Inn run a fine establishment with Bed and Breakfast accommodations, and they serve a mean lunch and dinner too. Not only do they have brewed beverages on tap, but they claim to rent a few mountain bikes as well.

The ride runs up and down the mountain, covering a variety of tread surfaces. Atop the hill you'll find a vast array of cross-country ski trails to explore. Remains of the days of old, barely visible above the monstrous hay-scented ferns, draw the curious in for a closer look. Old well heads, a tin shack, and some rusted pipes are all that remain of this once busy ridge-top drilling operation. The descent is quite wild and well worth the climb.

Thundershower Surprise

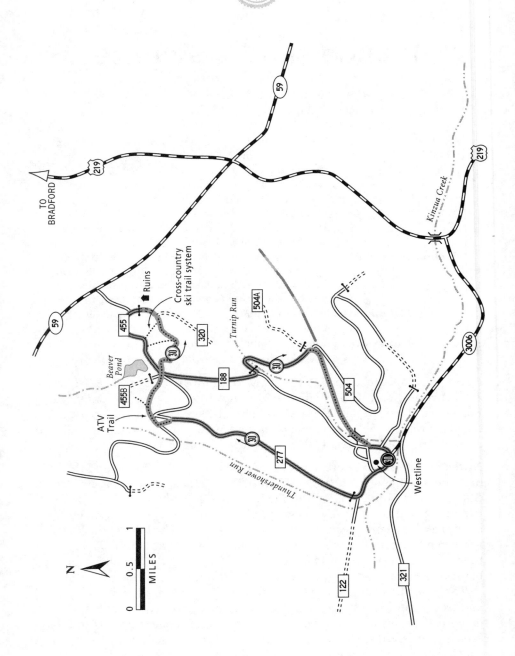

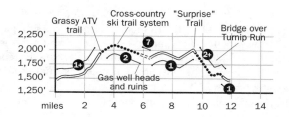

THE RIDE

0.0 Standing at the phone booth, with the Westline Inn to your back, turn right, heading west. The row of mailboxes on your left is an indication that you are on the correct road. You will soon come to a stop sign. Turn left at the stop sign. This is Forest Road 122 (but may not be marked as such.)

0.6 Turn right onto Forest Road 277. Ride around the gate and begin the nice, mellow climb along Thundershower Run.

1.1 Pass gated road on your right. You may begin to notice the plastic blue diamond blazes on the trees.

3.1 The trail turns left onto a small, grassy, ATV-type trail.

3.2 Cross Forest Road 455 and continue to follow the blue blazes into the grassy clearing. The trail becomes faint as it forks to the right approximately 0.1 mile off the road. Pay close attention to the blazes and continue to follow them up and to the right.

3.8 The trail dumps out at an intersection of roads. There is also a sign listing all the cross-country trails that lie ahead. Ignore all roads down to your right. To your immediate left is gated Forest Road 455B: **do not** take this road. The road in front of you is FR 455; turn left. Approximately 0.2 mile ahead on your right will be the beginning of the cross-country ski trail system.

4.1 Look for the truck-blocking boulders and the two signposts reading "Boo Boo's Delight" and "Thundershower." Turn right, riding past the boulders, on the Thundershower Trail.

4.3 You will come to a large clearing (and an old log skidder station); continue to ride straight across this clearing and pick up the sign for "Ledges."

5.0 You will come to a junction of ski trails. Follow the Inside Out Trail to your right.

5.3 Cross an old pipeline cut.

5.6 Turn left onto Forest Road 320. About 0.2 mile down FR 320 you will notice an old well driller's tin shed up in the woods on the right. Traces of old pipelines and well heads are hidden among the ferns. Further down on both sides of the road, you will notice old concrete footings from of buildings that stood long ago. It's hard to imagine that this quiet, peaceful spot was once bustling with the workings of the oil and gas wells.

6.1 Turn left on FR 455.

6.2 Pass gated road on your left.

7.2 Now that you have finished the upper loop of the ride, it's time to head down off the mountain. Keep left at the fork, which is now FR 188.

8.4 Lay on the brakes! Turn left on Forest Road 504; don't miss it!

9.9 Pass gated FR 504A on your left. Immediately after passing gated FR 504A, turn right onto the pipeline, heading up over a berm and into the woods. This is the surprise secret hidden trail, chock-full of waterbars. Except for the steel pipes across the troughs of the water bars, this ride is a flat-out bomber cruise!

11.4 Cross the sketchy bridge (if it hasn't washed out!) or ride the creek.

11.6 Take the grassy access road, which runs between a few folks' homes and camps. Turn left onto the paved road.

11.9 Back at the Westfield Inn. A fine brew would really round out this stellar ride!

Rimrock Ramble

Location:	16 miles east of Warren, or 17 miles west of Bradford.
Distance:	16.8-mile loop.
Time:	2 to 4 hours
Tread:	Technical singletrack in the first 2 miles gives way to wet and dry creekbeds for the next 4 miles; 3 more miles of technical singletrack lead to 3 miles of old logging roads.
Aerobic level:	Strenuous. The first half of the ride is all downhill but loaded with incredibly technical sections. The climb back out is hard-core gnarled rocky sections that give way to a relentless grind back up the mountain.
Technical difficulty:	4+. Right from the start, you encounter tight, twisty, rock-strewn singletrack. The climb back out will require you to sit tight in the saddle if you don't want your back end to spin out.
Highlights:	Lakeshore primitive campsites (walk, ride, or boat in only!), gnarly rocks, dense hemlock forest, beautiful lake vista, cold-air caves, rock climbing.
Land status:	Allegheny National Forest.
Maps:	USGS Corn Planter Bridge; Allegheny National Forest Morrison Hiking Trail map.

Access: From Warren head east on Pennsylvania Highway 59. Once you cross the Morrison Bridge over the Allegheny Reservoir, the trailhead lot is approximately 4 miles ahead on your right. The lot is well marked as the Forest Service Morrison access area.

Notes on the trail: "Heart-pounding" is about the only word that could sum up this ride. The first mile winds along the top of the ridge and is filled with fun, fast singletrack, and some nice-sized rocks. Once the trail dumps you out into Morrison Run, it starts to get nice—nice and scary! Your technical skills will be tried to the utmost as you pick, choose, and slam your way down this gnarly streambed. Water washes over your rims and grit packs into your brakes as you try to stave off the tenacious pull of gravity. The ability to choose a solid line down this valley will be your only redemption.

As the stream nears its destination, the trail will peel off right and begin a series of short but extremely steep climbs. A signpost with the trail name marks the tiny singletrack that leads down to the Morrison campground. This is a great spot to stop and soak in this beautiful lake.

The crank out of this valley is fun if you enjoy pain. You slowly traverse through huge blocks of gritstone. If you're into riding big formations, this section is definitely for you. The technical challenge gives way to a steep grind up old logging grades that run up the valley along the tranquil Campbell Run. Topping out on the ridge will give you the option of packing it in and heading home or cruising out to catch the vista and caves at Rimrock Overlook. The ride out to Rimrock is paved but involves more climbing. The ride back from the Rimrock Overlook Road heads back into the woods to meander along a newer logging road which has been designated as a cross-country ski trail. Quite an arduous adventure with a lot of nice trailside attractions.

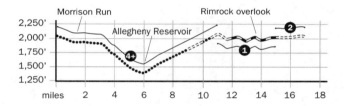

THE RIDE

0.0 The trail starts behind a covered forest service bulletin board. (Due to extremely poor signage, most folks do not know that the trail begins here.) You'll also find a beautiful wooden trail map on the backside of this covered board. Ride straight, following the blazes.

0.3 Turn left at the fork in the trail, following the Morrison Trail Loop. Wind along the ridge top along the rocky singletrack.

1.4 Cross a stream and a grass-covered fire road as the trail begins to drop.

1.8 Trail dumps into the Morrison Run drainage. Travel along here will be rough going but well worth the lessons it will teach you about technical riding. Watch for those wet, slippery rocks which are everywhere, and remember to take in the incredible scenery of this beautiful drainage.

3.8 Spur loop of Morrison trail breaks right. Go straight and continue to descend the drainage. Might be a good place to hold up and allow your brain and kidneys to settle into their respective places. Halfway down!

Rimrock Ramble

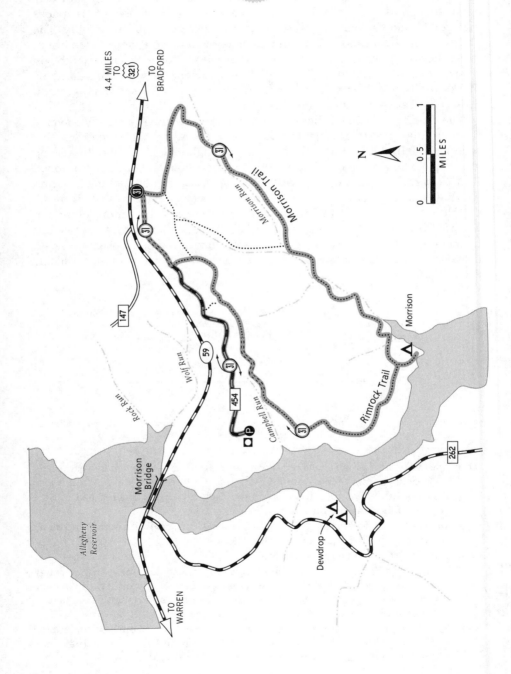

5.8 Trail sign for the Rimrock Trail. Take a left here to head to the lake. Spend a minute checking out the shore, and maybe even test the water if it's a hot and humid summer day. Travel back up the same trail and continue left on the Rimrock Trail. Just when you thought the rocks were gone, welcome to the death zone. There is a general line, but only the most honed rider will be able to send it clean.

9.1 Left onto grass fire road. You will soon pass a controlled-burn section of the woods, evident on both sides of the trail.

10.0 Pass a spur trail on your right, and keep going straight.

10.5 The trail forks. If you want to ride out to Rimrock Overlook, commit this point to memory and take the left fork. If you choose to head back to the trailhead, take the right fork and follow directions from mile 15.6.

10.6 Turn left onto Rimrock Overlook Road, Forest Road 454.

13.2 Rimrock Overlook. The actual overlook is located at the upper end of the parking lot. Just follow the paved path, or ride over the huge boulders. A few trails descend along the cliff face to the bottom. The southern end of the face has two cold-air caves that run back into the darkness. Headlamps are a must, as is a cool head through the tight passes. You'll find a few decent crack and face climbs here, toprope and leads as well. Return back down Rimrock Overlook Road.

15.5 Turn right up the grass logging road.

15.6 Turn left at the T (the point you were supposed to commit to memory) and follow the logging road along a relatively flat course.

16.8 Trailhead.

Endless Mountains

Also known as "God's Country," this area lies at the heart of the north-central mountainous region. Surrounded by the largest cluster of state forest lands, the region contains the most wild and remote tracts of land in Pennsylvania. Comprised of Susquehannock, Tiadaghton, Sproul, Tioga, and Elk State Forests, these woods offer the best in backcountry adventures. Within this region is the spectacular and impressive Pine Creek Gorge, also known as the "Grand Canyon of Pennsylvania." As you snake along Pine Creek, countless waterfalls, bald eagles, and river otters are just a few of the sights you'll find in this precipitous gorge. Miles of old logging railroad grades and mule skidder paths are all that remain from the once busy timber industry. These pathways have evolved into some of the finest backwoods singletrack in the state.

Commissioner Run

Location:	9 miles east of Coudersport.
Distance:	12.1-mile loop.
Time:	2 to 3 hours.
Tread:	Most of the ride follows incredible old woods roads that are hardpacked doubletrack. The rest of the ride is sweet singletrack.
Aerobic level:	Moderate. The ride starts out easy with a cruise and a seriously fun descent. The halfway point marks the climb back up to regain elevation, and although it's a long singletrack climb, it follows a mild grade.
Technical difficulty:	2. The old woods road descending Denton Hill and the climb up Commissioner Run are the only sections with any kind of technical terrain. . . the ride through the rest area is full of "land mines"—heed the warning of the "Dog Walk Area" sign!
Highlights:	Beautiful and remote mountain drainage, great wildlife viewing, the impressive Pennsylvania Lumber Museum.

Land status: Pennsylvania State Forest; Department of Conservation and Natural Resources.

Maps: USGS Brookland; DCNR Susquehannock State Forest map.

Access: From Coudersport, take U.S. Highway 6 east to Denton Hill, which is at the intersection with Billy Lewis Road. Continue for 0.5 mile on US 6 to the Susquehannock State Forest District Office. Turn right onto the paved road and park in the huge, gravel snowmobile parking lot on the right. This is the trailhead.

Notes on the trail: Not too easy but not real tough, the Commissioner Run is a great ride for most mountain bikers. It's in an ideal setting, surrounded by the Susquehannock State Forest, which offers more than 260,000 acres of woods to explore. Nearby is Lyman Run State Park, with a beautiful lake and campground. There is a sandy swimming beach, food concession, boating, fishing, and outstanding hiking in and around the park. The ride begins just west of the Denton Hill State Park ski area and the Pennsylvania Lumber Museum. Although Denton Hill offers little in the off-season, it's a great place to bomb if you're a bonsai downhiller, but there are no chairlifts to drag that 35-pound bike up the mountain.

The trail passes the Pennsylvania Lumber Museum, which is a must-see stop. The museum exhibits help explain the composition and condition of the forest from past to present. Many of the trails in these northern regions follow the old logging roads, paths, railroads, and slides, so the exhibits help you to better see and understand how they got there.

Beginning at the Susquehannock State Forest District Office—which is a great place to get a map and inquire about the local trail conditions—the trail rolls out toward the eastern sky on a smooth, well-maintained woods road. A few turns, one not so obvious, lead to the descent down Denton Hill's north face. The exciting 500-foot drop runs out across U.S. Highway 6, past the Lumber Museum, and through the minefield of dog droppings. Pedaling away from civilization, the singletrack meanders up Commissioner Run through the lush, moist drainage. Pulling out across the top, you cross many old, rotten culvert pipes as the trail reverts back to grassy woods road. A few links through the ridge-top cross-country ski trail system lead you back to the trailhead.

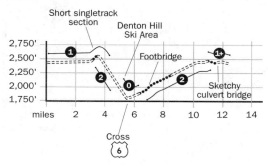

Commissioner Run

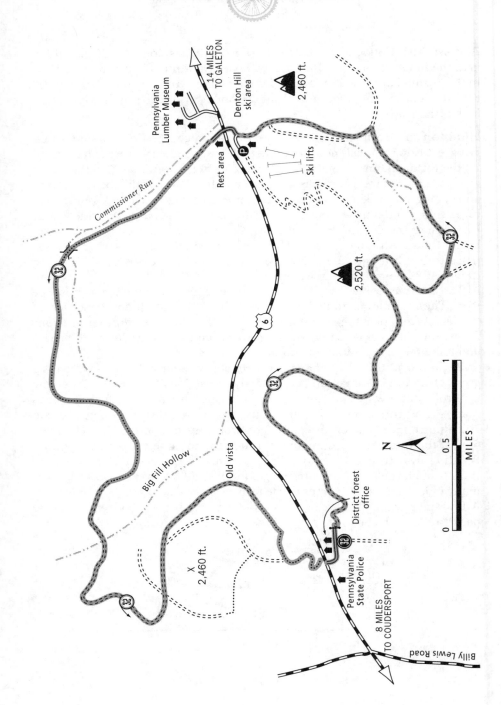

14 MILES TO GALETON

Pennsylvania Lumber Museum

Denton Hill ski area

2,460 ft.

Rest area

P

Ski lifts

Commissioner Run

32

32

6

2,520 ft.

32

Big Fill Hollow

Old vista

32

X 2,460 ft.

District forest office

32

Pennsylvania State Police

8 MILES TO COUDERSPORT

Billy Lewis Road

N

MILES
0   0.5   1

THE RIDE

0.0 From the trailhead lot, ride out to the paved road and turn right, passing the maintenance buildings on the left. Soon after, pass around a gate and continue on the doubletrack dirt road.

2.7 Pass a blue diamond with the number 5 printed on it.

3.2 Just before you reenter the woods, turn left onto the singletrack spur. There should be a brown post with a biker icon on it at this junction, but this is a real easy turn to miss.

3.4 Turn left at the T intersection onto the grassy woods road. Soon after the trail forks, keep right, following the blue diamond blazes. This trail skirts the drainage to its right.

4.6 Turn left at the T intersection, noting the brown post with the number 7 and biker icon on it.

4.9 Keep right at the fork, staying high above the seasonal creek.

5.4 Turn right as the trail spills out into the bottom of the ski area slopes. Continue to follow it to the gravel service road and follow that to the paved entrance road. After passing the restrooms on the left, turn right on the entrance road and ride out to U.S. Highway 6.

5.7 After carefully crossing US 6, continue straight into the rest area, passing a wooden trail sign for Commissioner Run on the left. The trail resumes at the end of the lot after passing around an old wooden gate. While riding through here, heed the "warning" sign stating "Dog Walk Area." Soon after, keep left at the faint fork. This trail is blazed with the tiniest blue diamonds.

7.0 Cross the footbridge over Commissioner Run.

10.4 Cross the four-way intersection onto the grassy woods road, noting the post with the number 23. Soon after, keep left at the fork on the Vista Loop marked by a wooden sign.

11.3 Pass post number 19 and reenter the woods on the singletrack.

11.6 Turn left at the T intersection in a small grassy clearing. As you make this turn, note the wooden sign that reads "To Route 6, Denton Hill Crossing."

11.8 Merge right onto the old logging road. The trail soon crosses left over a sketchy culvert pipe bridge and passes through the broken guardrail. Carefully cross US 6 to the Susquehannock State Forest District Office building, and take the entrance road to the trailhead.

12.1 Trailhead.

33

Potato City Singletrack

Location: 8 miles east of Coudersport.

Distance: 14.8-mile loop.

Time: 2.5 to 4 hours.

Tread: Rocky singletrack, old woods roads, forest roads, and ATV trail. The surfaces vary from loam, rock, grass, and sand to hardpacked dirt.

Aerobic level: Moderate. The first half of the ride runs the flat but demanding singletrack across the mountain plateau, and the finish climb is long and sustained.

Technical difficulty: 3 + . The technical challenges are in the first few miles of the ride, along the mountaintop singletrack. Slippery roots, lichen-covered rocks, and greasy logs are just a few of the fun obstacles along the way.

Highlights: Five long, hard miles of singletrack; mountaintop views; Pennsylvania Lumber Museum; trout fishing on Splash Dam Branch of Lyman Run; nearby Lyman Run State Park.

Land status: Pennsylvania State Forest, Department of Conservation and Natural Resources.

Maps: USGS Ayers Hill, Brookland, Cherry Springs, Sweden Valley; DCNR Bureau of Forestry: Susquehannock State Forest map, Susquehannock ATV trail map.

Access: From Coudersport, head west on U.S. Highway 6 for 8 miles, passing the village of Sweden Valley. Immediately after the four-way intersection with Billy Lewis Road and the Pennsylvania State Police Barracks, turn right into the Susquehannock District Forest entrance. Drive past the forest office on the left and pull into the large, gravel snowmobile parking area on the right. This lot is the trailhead.

Notes on the trail: Located in the Allegheny Highland Plateau, this route flows through rugged singletrack, rubbly ATV trail, and fast forest roads. The trail utilizes parts of the 35-mile Susquehannock All Terrain Vehicle Trail and a fresh-cut cross-country ski trail. The first few miles are the most challenging and offer a diverse array of surfaces including loam, rock, and grass. Unfortunately this stretch of singletrack takes many obscure turns and is very poorly marked. A watchful eye and good woods sense will help keep you in the forest and on the right path. If your route-finding skills are a bit rusty and you become frustrated with this poorly marked trail, have no worries. Billy Lewis Road parallels the singletrack and a short bushwhack will take you out to the road. Following Billy Lewis Road south, you can regain the trail again at the crossing of Sunken Branch Road (mile 5.2) with little alteration in trail log mileage.

From the trailhead the ride immediately slips into the woods on the singletrack cross-country ski trail. A brown pole with a biker-skier icon marks the trail's entrance, and subsequent icon signs are randomly nailed along the route. Rugged trail ensues for a tantalizing but tiring 5 miles to Sunken Branch Road. A mix of grassy pipeline and wide grassy singletrack descend to the dirt ATV trail where the rest of the ride plays out. With the flat, rough terrain behind, smooth and hilly roads lay ahead. A ridge climb leads to a bomber bonsai descent through Splash Dam Hollow and regains the ridge with 600 feet of vertical climbing. A view or two can be found along the ridge-top logging roads as they meander back to the trailhead.

Nearby attractions include the Pennsylvania Lumber Museum and Lyman Run State Park. The museum is chock-full of historical information from the industrious days of the timber men. Many of the rides in the region follow the well-worn paths of this era and a visit to the museum helps explain the history, destruction, and regeneration of this beautiful forest. With over 50 campsites and beautiful Lyman Lake, Lyman Run State Park makes a great base camp for the rides in this region. When you want to get away from it all, this is the place.

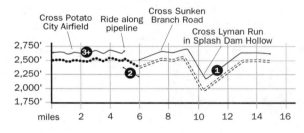

THE RIDE

0.0 Ride southwest out of the gravel lot, toward the overflow lot, and enter the woods on the left, riding the singletrack trail blazed with blue diamonds. The beginning of the trail is marked with a brown post with cross-country skier and mountain biker icons. This is a bit difficult to find at first, but the signs and trail will become apparent.

1.3 After crossing the gravel road, cross the open, grassy airstrip (Potato City Airport). The trail resumes a bit to the right on the opposite side and soon enters the woods and turns right along the electric deer fence.

1.7 Cross an old woods road with a blue diamond "3" marker.

3.0 Keep right at the fork. If you begin descending you missed the turn.

3.2 Turn right at the T intersection onto the grassy woods road.

3.6 The trail bends right and passes around a gate. Ride 30 yards along the old woods road and angle off left into a small clearing and onto the singletrack. It's definitely tricky here, but the trail can be found with a bit of persistence.

Potato City Singletrack

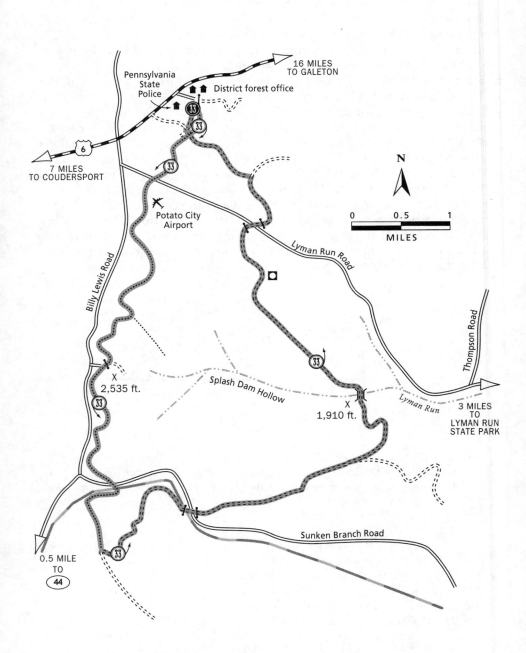

16 MILES
TO GALETON

Pennsylvania
State
Police

District forest office

33

33

6

7 MILES
TO COUDERSPORT

33

N

Potato City
Airport

Billy Lewis Road

Lyman Run Road

0   0.5   1

MILES

X
2,535 ft.

33

Splash Dam Hollow

X
1,910 ft.

Lyman Run

Thompson Road

33

3 MILES
TO
LYMAN RUN
STATE PARK

Sunken Branch Road

0.5 MILE
TO
44

33

5.2 The trail empties out onto Sunken Branch Road. Turn right and ride for 30 yards and turn left to resume the singletrack trail. Soon after, turn right at a T intersection, on the old pipeline.

5.9 The grassy trail terminates at the switchback of a dirt ATV trail. Turn left at the "elbow," climbing the ATV trail. Follow the orange diamond blazes.

7.6 The ATV trail bends left, crosses Sunken Branch Road and passes around two sets of gates.

9.3 Keep left at the fork, following the sign to Denton Hill Summit.

12.3 Views from the logging road at the forest cut.

13.0 Cross over Lyman Run Road, passing around two sets of gates.

13.4 Turn left at the spur trail, following the sign to Denton Hill Summit.

14.5 Keep right at the fork, following the sign to Denton Hill Summit.

14.8 Trailhead lot.

Middle Ridge Trail

Location:	10 miles west of Wellsboro above Asaph.
Distance:	8.1-mile loop.
Time:	1.5 to 2.5 hours.
Tread:	The climb follows smooth forest road, the ridge-top follows grassy old woods road, and the descent is a wide, burly singletrack, which becomes progressively rockier as the trail loses elevation and approaches the ford at the trailhead.
Aerobic level:	Moderate. The initial climb gains 800 feet over 3 miles but is on smooth forest road. The ride across Middle Ridge is a grunt in places. In the end gravity is your friend, as you plummet off the mountain into the chilly Asaph Run ford.
Technical difficulty:	3+. The technical hazards in the Asaph Wild Area include deep mud holes, rock gardens, and windfallen trees. The descent is a bit hairy, especially at speed, with loose stone and stout log jumps. An east coast rider's dream indeed!
Highlights:	The beautiful and remote Asaph Wild Area; stellar mountain singletrack; great wildlife viewing; close to the Grand Canyon of Pennsylvania, and Colton and Leonard Harrison State Parks.
Land status:	Pennsylvania State Forest. Department of Conservation and Natural Resources.
Maps:	USGS Asaph; DCNR Tioga State Forest map.

Middle Ridge Trail

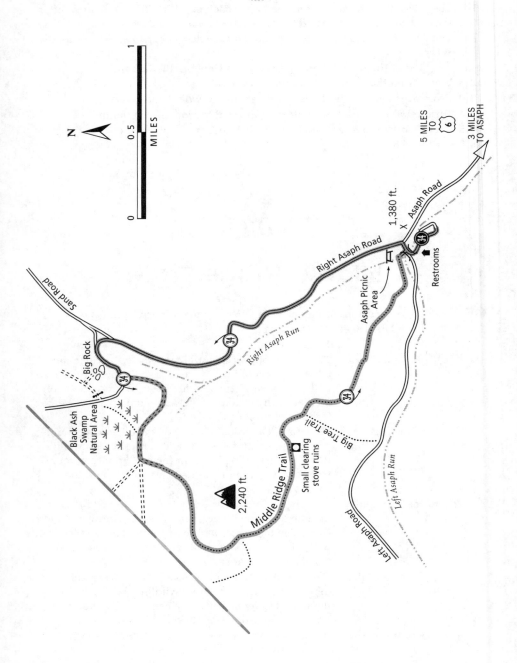

Access: From Wellsboro take U.S. Highway 6 west 10 miles to Ansonia. Immediately after crossing the bridge over Marsh Creek into Ansonia, turn right onto Asaph Road and follow it for 2.5 miles to the little village of Asaph. Turn left onto Asaph Road and continue driving 3 miles to the road fork at the Asaph picnic area. Park in the lot just across the bridge on the left fork (Left Asaph Road). This picnic area lot is the trailhead.

Notes on the trail: The ride centers on the Asaph Wild Area, with the key word being "wild." Over 2,000 acres of rugged mountain terrain comprise this beautiful forest tract, including the Black Ash Swamp Natural Area. The Black Ash Swamp harbors many unique wetland flora and mature stands of second-growth maple and cherry. Both ridge top and valley are alive with the sights and sounds of a deep forest, lending a rugged and solitary feel to the ride.

As the ride follows the Right Asaph Road, keep an eye out for wildlife in and along the woods. In midsummer this road is a salamander crossing and is covered with the redspotted newts. These unique salamanders—or Efts, as they may be called—are some of the most beautiful reptiles in Pennsylvania. Bright orange to salmon red in color with blackringed red spots, this terrestrial critter lives on the moist forest floor.

On the mountaintop, the ride dips into an old woods road just below the Black Ash Swamp and skirts its damp southern edge. An obscure spur leads out along the top of Middle Ridge, traversing some technical challenges and passing the site of an old homestead at a small clearing. The remains of an old cast-iron woodstove lie in a broken and scattered state. The moss-covered pieces now offer a home for many snakes. The ride soon passes the Big Tree Hollow Trail where the wide singletrack sheds some serious elevation. The drop can be quite gripping as there are a bunch of loose stones to stuff your wheel and log jumps that can toss you hard. The final move on the route is a cold ford across either branch of Asaph Run to the trailhead.

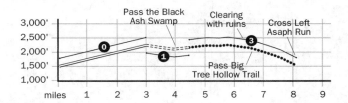

THE RIDE

0.0 From the trailhead lot, cross over the bridge and begin the long climb up Right Asaph Road.

2.7 Keep left at the fork with Sand Road, continuing to ride on Right Asaph Road.

3.0 Turn left onto a gated, grassy, old woods road.

Jammin' the downhill on the Middle Ridge Trail.

4.2 After passing a singletrack that comes in from Black Ash Swamp on the right, take notice of the blue blazes on the trees. Soon after, turn left on a old woods road spur, marked by a double set of blue blazes.

5.0 Keep left at the fork.

6.4 In a small clearing keep right at the fork, passing the ruins of an old cast iron stove.

6.6 Pass the Big Tree Hollow Trail on the right. It's marked by an engraved trail sign in the huge beech tree with an orange blaze.

8.1 Ford either branch of Asaph Run to the trailhead.

Asaph Classic

Location:	10 miles west of Wellsboro at Asaph.
Distance:	23.4-mile loop.
Time:	3 to 6 hours.
Tread:	Hard core singletrack, forest roads, old logging roads, grassy pipelines, and old woods roads.
Aerobic level:	Strenuous. This route climbs almost 3,000 feet, most of which takes place in the first half of the ride. The singletrack is demanding and the woods roads rugged.
Technical difficulty:	4. Some singletrack sections cover loose rocks and roots. A few of the old woods roads are being rapidly reclaimed by nature, presenting a myriad of stump-jumping and rock-hopping opportunities. The descents are no joke, as they, too, are technical screamers.
Highlights:	Rugged mountain riding with endless miles of classic singletrack and screamer downhills; historic Hessel Gessel mill stone quarry; USGS Fish Research Lab; close to the Grand Canyon of Pennsylvania and Colton and Leonard Harrison State Parks.
Land status:	Pennsylvania State Forest, Department of Conservation and Natural Resources.
Maps:	USGS Asaph, Keeneyville; DCNR Tioga State Forest Map.

Access: From Wellsboro take U.S. Highway 6 west 10 miles to Ansonia. Immediately after crossing the bridge over Marsh Creek into Ansonia, turn right onto Asaph Road and follow for 3 miles to a four-way intersection with Strait Run Road. Turn left on Strait Run Road and then take an immediate right into the USGS Biological Research Lab parking area. This lot is the trailhead.

Asaph Classic

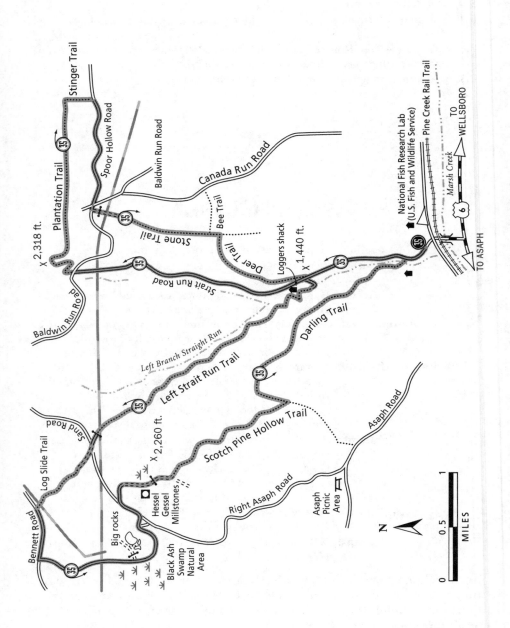

Notes on the trail: This is a must-do adventure for the hard core rider looking to log some serious mileage on fat singletrack. Surrounded by the geologic and industrial history of the area, the ride begins just north of Pine Creek at the USGS Fish Research Lab. This federal facility is open to the public. There are all kinds of aquatic experiments taking place for your viewing pleasure and tanks of some of the biggest fish I've ever seen, including trout that could bite your hand off and piles of prehistoric sturgeon.

Old logging grades, countless miles of singletrack, and the site of the Hessel Gessel mill stone quarry are a few of the features along this outstanding ride. Most of the ride follows a racecourse set up by the fellas from Country Ski and Sports in Wellsboro, appropriately named the Asaph Mountain Bike Classic. It's a classic indeed, and to be here and not ride this trail is like jetting to Moab and forgetting your bike; it's a definite crime.

The ride begins with a long, steep climb up Strait Run Road. At the intersection with Baldwin Run Road, it continues to climb into the woods on a technical and windy singletrack. The adrenaline kicks in as you shred the tight hardpacked singletrack to the infamous Stinger Trail. Commit hard to the wicked plunge on this heinously loose and sick trail as it rolls out to a placid forest road and reclimbs to the next singletrack. The old Stone Trail doubletrack is the lead-in to the next vicious descent, dropping a harrowing 800 feet in a mere mile. Of course this is only the beginning and you know you'll want more!

Climbing the rugged Left Strait Run Trail, you braid your way up through the stream to the wide climb to the top. You may wish you had bailed back at the road, but suck it up because your payment will come due. Cruising out on old logging and forest roads, you pass the old Hessel Gessel mill stone quarry site. Check out this neat site before cashing in your express ticket to the trailhead. Follow a wide, rugged singletrack on the Scotch Pine Hollow Trail to a sharp turn on the Darling Trail, and a darling it is with yet another 800-foot screamer off the mountain. At this point you'll have to pull a Flintstones special to stop your warped-wheel and brakepadless bike before the trailhead.

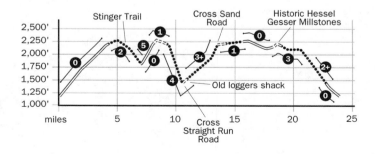

0.0 From the USGS Lab, turn right on Strait Run Road and begin the long slog.

4.1 At a T intersection with Baldwin Run Road, continue straight across on the unmarked singletrack, 30 yards left of the wooden road sign. Carefully follow the windy singletrack as it climbs and weaves for a bit before running a straight shot down the white-blazed forest boundary line, on the Plantation Trail.

6.3 The trail bends 90 degrees right and descends the wicked Stinger Trail. Take caution here as help is far away!

6.7 Turn right onto Spoor Hollow Road and check your shorts!

8.0 Keep left at the first fork, right at the second fork, and 20 yards later turn left onto the doubletrack Stone Trail, passing around the gate and noting the trail sign.

9.4 Turn right onto the Deer Trail, noting the trail sign. Hope you have it together; it's not a descent for squids.

10.6 Turn right on Strait Run Road, ride 50 yards, and turn hard left onto the old woods road, Left Strait Run Trail. The trail descends a bit before switchbacking hard right and climbing along the stream, crossing it many times.

11.1 Pass an old logger's shack on the right.

13.6 After crossing a grassy pipeline, pass around a gate and turn left on Sand Road. Soon after, turn right on the Log Slide Trail, noting the trail sign (mile 13.7).

15.0 Turn left onto Bennett Road, a dirt road.

15.5 Keep left at the fork in the road, onto Right Asaph Road.

17.3 Turn left at the T intersection onto Sand Road.

17.7 Turn right onto Hessel Gessel Road.

18.4 Pass the historical mill stone quarry site on the right and a bog on the left. To see the old mill stones, turn right on this singletrack and ride approximately 100 yards to the wooden sign and old mill stone quarry. Continue straight, passing around a gate on the doubletrack grassy woods road.

18.7 Turn 90 degrees left in a clearing onto the faint doubletrack that soon turns to singletrack. This is the Scotch Pine Hollow Trail.

20.2 Turn 120 degrees hard left where the unmarked and obscure Darling Trail branches off. This is a real easy turn to miss so keep your head up!

22.8 The kamikaze downhill empties out behind a cabin. Politely skirt the left edge of the yard and turn right onto Strait Run Road.

23.4 Collapse at the trailhead!

Bee Tree Trail

Location:	Colton Point State Park. 9 miles west of Wellsboro.
Distance:	18.2-mile loop.
Time:	2 to 5 hours.
Tread:	A great woodland mix of singletrack, old woods roads, and Forest Service roads linked with two minor sections of paved road.
Aerobic level:	Moderate. The ride climbs a total of almost 2,000 feet. The climbs overall are relatively mellow but long and sustained, and the flat singletrack sections require a bit of pedaling in places.
Technical difficulty:	2. The majority of the technical riding is along the Bee Tree Trail, which crosses a few small loose stone sections and some wind-fallen trees along this lengthy traverse.
Highlights:	The Grand Canyon of Pennsylvania with superior views; long descents and climbs; fishing and whitewater boating along Pine Creek; horseback rides; Colton Point State Park.
Land status:	Pennsylvania State Forest and Parks. Department of Conservation and Natural Resources.
Maps:	USGS Marshlands, Tiadaghton; DCNR Tioga State Forest map.

Access: From Wellsboro take U.S. Highway 6 west 10 miles to Ansonia. After crossing the bridge over Marsh Creek into Ansonia, turn left onto Colton Road at the Gulf gas station. Cross the bridge over Pine Creek and climb the long, twisty road 6.5 miles to Colton Point State Park at the rim of the canyon. Park in the first lot on the right next to the small playground, just opposite the small park office. This lot is the trailhead.

Notes on the trail: Fun descents, long climbs, and fine trail are just a few of the outstanding features of this ride. Located in the Tioga State Forest, the ride covers some of the historical logging grades and pathways of the timber era. The Grand Canyon is a natural feat of glacial deposition, which caused the sharp bend in the flow of the Pine Creek. The trailhead was named after Henry Colton, who was a supervising lumberman in the late 1800s. The park across the gorge was named after Leonard Harrison, who devoted his time and money to developing a public picnic and recreation area on the precipitous east rim lookout. He later gave the property to the state which is now maintained by the park service.

Bee Tree Trail

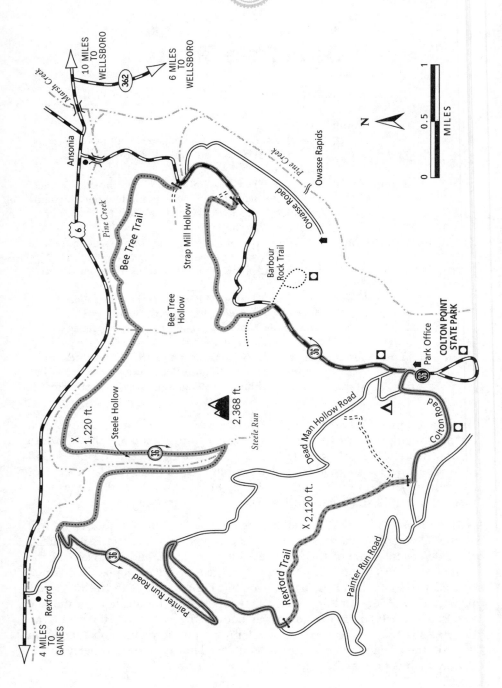

Sunset from the west rim of the Grand Canyon.

The ride begins on the West Rim of the Grand Canyon and heads back down toward Ansonia, dropping almost 900 feet on a mix of singletrack and paved road. Near the bottom the ride turns left and traverses the Bee Tree Trail out along the mountain. Climbing up Steele Hollow, the trail crosses the steep-cut drainage and meanders out to a paved road. After a short paved section, the trail turns hard left onto the dirt road and begins a moderately long and sustained climb up Painter Run Road. With over half the climb behind you, the route reaches its pinnacle on the Rexford Trail at an elevation of 2,125 feet. A great woods road descent follows, with a spectacular overlook at the Four Mile Vista and a smooth cruise along Colton Road to the trailhead.

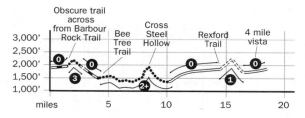

THE RIDE

0.0 From the trailhead lot, ride back down the paved Colton Road to the Barbour Rock Trail parking area.

1.5 At the Barbour Rock Trail parking area, turn left directly opposite the lot onto an obscure singletrack that follows an old overgrown woods road grade. It's a tough find at first but the trail opens up soon after, so scout hard and stick with it.

1.7 Keep right at the fork, following the red blazes and continuing to climb.

2.7 Keep right at the fork, continuing to descend. Soon after, pass around a gate then turn left onto Colton Road and continue to descend.

4.2 Turn left onto the Bee Tree Trail marked by the wooden sign. Fifteen yards into the trail, keep right at the fork as the trail climbs into the woods. Follow the faint blue circle blazes.

10.2 Turn left onto the paved road and ride for 200 yards before turning hard left onto the dirt road, Painter Run Road.

12.6 Turn right at the switchback and continue to climb on Painter Run Road.

14.7 Turn hard left onto the old woods road, the Rexford Trail, and pass around a gate.

16.7 Pass around a gate and turn left onto Colton Road.

17.7 Pass the spectacular Four Mile Vista.

18.2 Turn right into Colton Point State Park and the trailhead.

Wild Apple to Bake Oven

Location:	Colton Point State Park, 9 miles west of Wellsboro.
Distance:	11.1-mile loop.
Time:	1.5 to 3 hours.
Tread:	A high mountain mix of fun singletrack, old woods road, and forest roads.
Aerobic level:	Moderate. The ride rolls along the mountaintop, covering mild terrain and easy changes in elevation.
Technical difficulty:	2. The majority of the tread surfaces are smooth, hardpacked dirt with fun, fast lines. There are a few small but fun sections with surface roots and a handful of loose stones.
Highlights:	Mountaintop woodland riding; the impressive Four Mile Vista; the Grand Canyon of Pennsylvania with superior views; horseback riding, whitewater boating, and fishing; Colton Point State Park.
Land status:	Pennsylvania State Forest and Parks. Department of Conservation and Natural Resources.
Maps:	USGS: Tiadaghton, Marshlands. DCNR Pennsylvania State Forest: Tioga State Forest maps.

Wild Apple to Bake Oven

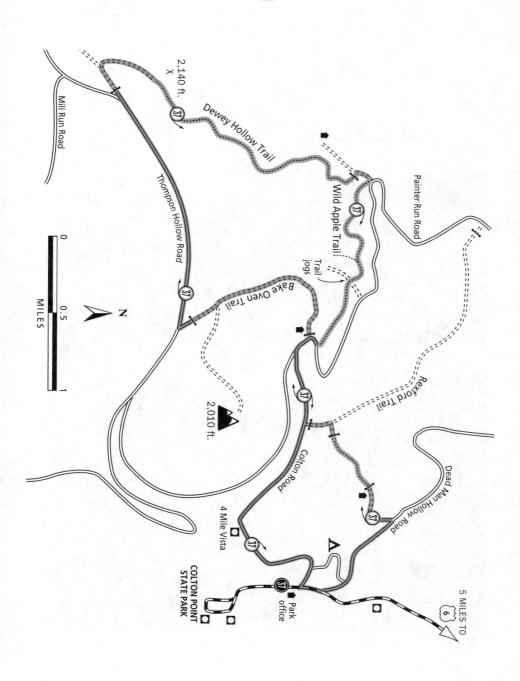

Mill Run Road

2,140 ft.
X

Dewey Hollow Trail

37

Thompson Hollow Road

Wild Apple Trail

37

Painter Run Road

Trail
jogs

Bake Oven Trail

37

N

MILES

0   0.5   1

2,010 ft.

Rexford Trail

37

Colton Road

37

Dead Man Hollow Road

4 Mile Vista

37

COLTON POINT
STATE PARK

Park
office

37

5 MILES TO
6

Sunset from the west rim of the Grand Canyon.

Access: From Wellsboro, take U.S. Highway 6 west 10 miles to Ansonia. After crossing the bridge over Marsh Creek into Ansonia, turn left onto Colton Road at the Gulf gas station. Cross the bridge over Pine Creek and climb the long, twisty road 6.5 miles to Colton Point State Park at the rim of the canyon. Park in the first lot on the right, next to the small playground, just opposite the small park office. This lot is the trailhead.

Notes on the trail: This is the finest ride on the West Rim of Pennsylvania's Grand Canyon. The trailhead alone is worth the trip as it sits precariously above the 1,000-foot-deep canyon. Turkey vultures, hawks, and the occasional bald eagle ride thermals up and down the natural chasm as river otters and fishermen try their luck in Pine Creek below.

Colton Point State Park, is named after Henry Colton, who was an important timber supervisor in this region. The Seneca Nation Indian Tribe, which inhabited the area prior to the settlement of the white man, named this area Tyoga, which means "the meeting of two rivers." In 1968 the Pine Creek Gorge was designated as a National Natural Landmark.

Leaving the rim, the ride warms up on the fast and smooth Deadman Hollow Road before turning off onto a woods road. The woods road soon yields to sweet singletrack before returning to another forest road link. Near a cabin, the Bake Oven Trail hides in the back of a property and gently climbs on an overgrown old woods road. You eventually ride out onto another forest road link to find the Dewey Hollow Trail, which begins as a broad grassy fire road and shrinks down to a wide, heavily forested singletrack. Watch for an obscure turn at the intersection of a four-wheel drive road and Painter Run Road, and then climb a steep but short singletrack to the Wild Apple Trail. This trail winds its way down through a mix of overgrown old woods roads and stellar singletrack to return to Painter Run Road. A mellow cruise back on Colton Road passes the impressive Four Mile Vista and returns to the West Rim trailhead.

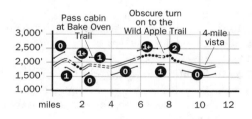

THE RIDE

0.0 From the trailhead lot, ride back down Colton Road and turn left onto Deadman Hollow Road, passing the organized group tent area on the left.

0.8 Turn left onto the gravel woods road and descend a bit.

1.2 Pass around a gate and continue straight on the divine singletrack.

2.0 Pass around a gate and turn left at the T intersection as you continue to descend. Soon after, turn right at the T intersection on Colton Road.

2.6 Continue straight as you merge onto Painter Lettrona Road (aka Painter Run Road). Soon after, turn left onto the dirt woods road, Bake Oven Trail, marked by the wooden trail sign. Pass around a gate and cross over a small wooden bridge toward the cabin. From the cabin, angle right to the corner of the woods to resume the trail as a wide singletrack in the forest (mile 2.7).

3.9 Pass around a gate and turn right on Thompson Hollow Road.

5.4 Turn right onto the gated, grassy old woods road, the Dewey Hollow Trail. Soon after, keep right at the fork as the woods road climbs up and to the right. The woods road will bend left, but keep right (straight) on the wide, grassy singletrack.

7.3 After passing around a gate, turn right onto the four-wheel drive road.

7.6 At the T intersection of the four-wheel-drive road and Painter Run Road, turn 160 degrees hard right onto the obscure singletrack that climbs up the steep hill.

8.0 In a small clearing the trail turns left at a T intersection and continues to descend.

8.3 Cross a four-way intersection as the trail takes a slight jog to the right and turns left. Get ready for big air on some burly water-bar jumps.

8.8 Turn right onto Painter Run Road, and soon after, keep left at the fork, continuing on Colton Road.

11.1 After passing Four Mile Vista on the right (mile 10.3), return to the trailhead.

The Grand Canyon

Location:	8 miles west of Wellsboro at the town of Ansonia.
Distance:	20.6 miles one way.
Time:	1 to 3 hours.
Tread:	Beautiful, hardpacked, cinder rail grade.
Aerobic level:	Easy. Riding the route from Ansonia south, there is a slight downslope, yet you will barely notice the change in elevation.
Technical difficulty:	0. Remember this is a rail-trail.
Highlights:	The impressive Pine Creek Gorge, rock cliffs, countless waterfalls, incredible wildlife viewing, rare species of Pennsylvania wildlife and plants, spring whitewater boating, rock climbing, ice climbing, scenic vistas, fishing, camping along the canyon rail-trail and at the two state parks on the rim.

The Grand Canyon

Asaph ●

Marsh Creek

Ansonia Trailhead Parking

38

Ansonia ●

6

287

6

Pine Creek

Wellsboro ●

6

Darling Run parking area

342

660

Darling Run

COLTON POINT
STATE PARK

4-Mile Run

287

LEONARD HARRISON
STATE PARK

Stowell Run

Campbell Run

Restrooms

Tiadaghton

Rail Island Run

Pine Island Run

Pine Creek

Clay Mine Run

Water Tank Run

● Morris

414

Stone Quarry Run

N

0   1   2

MILES

Blackwell

P

Rattlesnake Rock
Parking Area

Blackwell take-out
parking area

Restrooms

Rattlesnake Rock

287

414

Trout Run

Waterfalls along the Grand Canyon ride.

Land status: Pennsylvania State Forest, Department of
Conservation and Natural Resources.
Maps: USGS Tiadaghton, Cedar Run; DCNR Bureau of
Forestry: Tioga State Forest map.

Access: From Wellsboro, take U.S. Highway 6 west, to Ansonia. After passing signs for Leonard Harrison State Park and crossing the bridge over Marsh Creek, turn right onto Asaph Road. Travel down Asaph Road for 0.1 mile and park in the gravel lot on the right. This is the trailhead.

Notes on the trail: The Pine Creek Gorge, or the Grand Canyon of Pennsylvania, as it is more notably called, is truly a remarkable place. The gorge's history dates back to the ice age when retreating glaciers deposited a huge pile of silty moraine here. Pine Creek's flow originally traveled northeast but the glacier's dam sent the water south, carving out the Pine Creek Gorge. The 90-degree right-hand bend of Pine Creek at Ansonia is evidence of this theory.

The deepest part of the canyon is between the two state parks perched on opposite sides of the canyon's rim. Leonard Harrison and Colton Point State Parks stand 800 feet above the gorge. The canyons walls are filled with countless spectacular waterfalls that run best in the springtime. With the higher flow of water, the Pine Creek becomes an exciting whitewater rafting, canoe, or kayak trip. Some of Pennsylvania's most rare and beautiful wildlife can be found in the canyon. A pair of bald eagles continue to nest yearly in the gorge, and otters, successfully reintroduced to Pine Creek, are a welcome sight. Hawks, herons, osprey, wild turkey, and coyotes are just a few of the more common inhabitants here.

The ride begins in Ansonia, travels downstream along the abandoned rail grade, and meanders below lichen-covered cliffs and lush, forested hills. One special stop along the way is the series of waterfalls at Four-Mile Run. From here the Turkey Path climbs a series of steps up the east rim of the canyon to a vista at Leonard Harrison State Park. Further along is the village of Tiadaghton, which offers water, restrooms, and campsites. As the ride continues, the waterfalls become more impressive before the canyon rim sinks to the valley floor. Cross Pennsylvania Highway 414 carefully before riding the last 2 miles to Rattlesnake Rock via an old rail bridge.

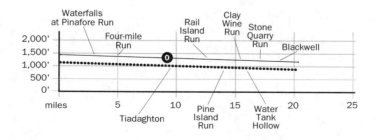

THE RIDE

0.0 At the Ansonia parking area, begin the rail-trail by heading south, passing around a set of gates, crossing an old bridge and riding under U.S. Highway 6. Note the separate paths for horses and cyclists.

1.1 Pass the Darling Run trailhead parking area. There are restrooms and water here.

1.5 Cross the bridge over Darling Run.

3.0 Pass the waterfalls at Pinafore Run.

3.3 Pass a concrete mile marker.

5.0 Cross the bridge over Four-Mile Run. A bike rack has been installed here for cyclists to lock their bikes to while exploring the incredible waterfalls on Four-Mile Run. The Turkey Path Trail begins here, and climbs 782 feet to the lookout vista on the east rim at Leonard Harrison State Park.

5.5 Pass Stowell Run and another concrete mile marker.

9.6 Pass around a set of gates and the small village of cabins at Tiadaghton. You'll find picnic tables, restrooms, and water here. Pass around another set of gates and the bridge over Campbell Run. From here, the rail-trail is reserved for cyclists only.

12.4 Pass the waterfalls at Rail Island Run.

14.0 Pass the rugged, forked canyon and waterfalls at Pine Island Run.

15.3 Pass a concrete mile marker and cross the bridge over Benjamin Hollow with its 50-foot high waterfall.

15.6 Pass the waterfalls at Clay Mine Run.

16.1 Cross the bridge at Water Tank Hollow. A great hiking trail leads up to the base of the tiered waterfalls.

17.3 Pass the waterfalls at Stone Quarry Run.

18.7 Pass around a gate and carefully cross over Pennsylvania Highway 414 at the town of Blackwell. There's food and lodging here as well as restrooms and water at the take-out parking area. The rail-trail continues on the other side after passing around another set of gates. Soon after, the trail crosses over an old rail bridge.

20.6 The southern terminus, Rattlesnake Rock access area. The actual Rattlesnake Rock is down at the sharp bend in Pine Creek. Restrooms and water located here. From here you will need to return back to Ansonia if other arrangements have not been made.

Big Trestle Trail

Location:	16 miles south of Galeton, 26 miles north of Renovo.
Distance:	15.4-mile loop.
Time:	2 to 4 hours.
Tread:	After 2 miles of dirt road, you find yourself on sweet singletrack for the next 5 miles. The last 7 miles are on rough forest and gas well roads.
Aerobic level:	Moderate to Strenuous. The initial 800-foot climb over a short 2 miles is a real grind, but soon you will be rolling along the ridge top. Easier hill climbs follow with plenty of rolling terrain along old rail grades and fire roads.
Technical difficulty:	3. Tricky sections await, from the initial climb on the Swartwood trail to the incredible singletrack along the North Link Trail, but don't let this hold you back from experiencing some of Pennsylvania's finest backcountry riding. The second half of the route follows easier terrain back to Ole Bull.
Highlights:	Some of Pennsylvania's finest backcountry mountain biking; remote and rarely traveled trails that give the rider a true wilderness experience; a midride spring; native trout streams; incredible scenery.
Land status:	Pennsylvania State Forest, Pennsylvania State Parks, Department of Conservation and Natural Resources.
Maps:	USGS Oleana; DCNR Bureau of Forestry: Susquehannock State Forest map.

Access: From Renovo, head north on Pennsylvania Highway 144 for approximately 26 miles to Ole Bull State Park. Turn left into Ole Bull State Park and then turn right at the ranger station. Park along the left side in the lot. The ride begins at the ranger station.

From Galeton, take Pennsylvania Highway 144 south for 16 miles. Ole Bull is on the right.

Notes on the trail: This is a wilderness excursion that takes you back into the most remote parts of Pennsylvania's woods. Thanks to the local logging history, there are miles of abandoned railroad grades that have remained intact but unmaintained for years. These narrow rail grades have since grown in, leaving us singletrack lovers with some of the finest trail in Pennsylvania. The origin of the park's name comes from Ole Bornemann, a famous Norwegian violinist who was touring the country in the mid 1800s and

Big Trestle Trail

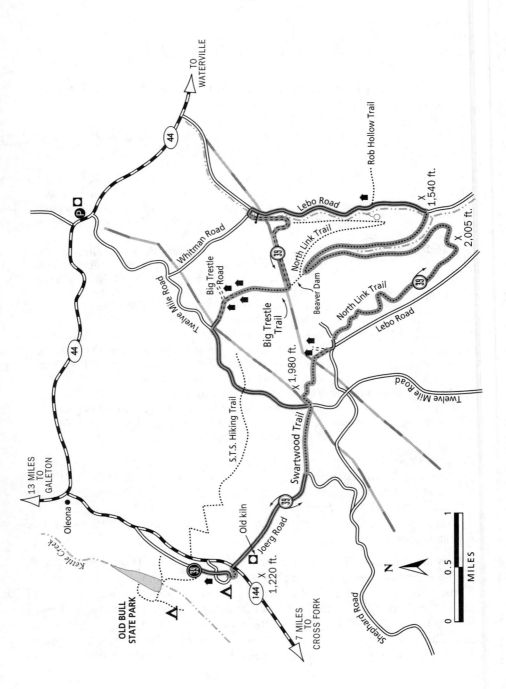

TO WATERVILLE

44

P

Whitman Road

Lebo Road

Rob Hollow Trail

X 1,540 ft.

North Link Trail

39

X 2,005 ft.

Twelve Mile Road

Big Trestle Road

Beaver Dam

North Link Trail

Lebo Road

39

Big Trestle Trail

X 1,980 ft.

Twelve Mile Road

44

S.T.S. Hiking Trail

Swartwood Trail

13 MILES TO GALETON

Oleona

Old kiln

39

Joerg Road

Kettle Creek

OLD BULL STATE PARK

39

X 1,220 ft.

144

7 MILES TO CROSS FORK

Shephard Road

N

MILES

0   0.5   1

attempted to settle a colony of Norwegian folks in the beautiful hills of Potter county.

Beginning at Ole Bull State Park, along the banks of the beautiful Kettle Creek, you embark on a strenuous 800-foot climb into the rolling ridges of the Susquehannock State Forest. Once atop the ridge, you travel a very short distance on a pipeline before testing your route-finding skills. An obscure singletrack lies hidden in the woods, near the old twin hemlocks on the pipeline edge. Once past this, the trail takes you deep into the Big Trestle drainage, where intense backcountry singletrack awaits along old railroad grades. The bumps throughout this section are not a freak of nature but the remains of the old railroad ties. Do not mistake this for a rail-trail though, as it is far from being that mellow. Tight, twisty, and mildly technical, this is what mountain biking truly is all about. A mild dirt road climb brings you to a gated dirt road where you travel along the pipeline. A steep descent takes you back to the north end of the Big Trestle Trail, which starts out on singletrack and changes to a four-wheel drive road. The run back across the ridge on dirt road brings you to the final long, steep descent back down to Ole Bull.

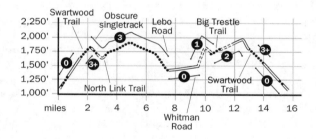

THE RIDE

0.0 From the ranger station, ride directly into the campground on the "Do not enter, exit only" signed road.

0.1 As the campground road bends right, break off across the field, staying along the left edge. You will soon pass over a small culvert pipe and a brown trail signpost marking the snowmobile and mountain bike trail. The trail forks shortly; keep left as you head out to Pennsylvania Highway 144.

0.3 Cross Pennsylvania 144 and begin the climb up Joerg Road. Note the old kiln on your right, complete with ironwork still intact. The roof has since collapsed, but the structure still stands as a icon of the industrious times of long ago.

1.6 As Joerg Road bends hard right, ride straight into the woods on the Swartwood Trail, and get ready to grunt out the final leg of the climb.

2.2 After passing over the summit, turn right on Twelve Mile Road. In approximately 60 yards, turn left on the open pipeline, marked by the snowmobile orange blazes and traffic signs.

2.3 This is the crux of the whole ride! Approximately 150 yards down the pipeline on the right is your next turn. Its only distinguishing features are a pair of huge hemlock trees growing along the pipeline edge and a very old and obscure dirt berm that will drop you down into the singletrack. The singletrack follows an old logging road that is quite wide in grade but is slowly becoming overgrown. These are all the clues I can give you—there are no trail markers so your route-finding skills and intuition will have to do the rest.

2.7 Cross a pipeline cut and continue straight. Note the single power line above.

2.9 Join left with a grass road, which then joins right with a dirt road. The road ends at Lebo Road; turn left onto Lebo Road.

3.0 Turn left onto a gravel and dirt access road. After approximately 150 yards turn right onto the North Link Trail (NLT). This point is marked by a small wooden NLT trail sign and blue blazes painted on the pines. This section runs through beautifully dense pines, and the tread is much like a washboard due to exposed roots.

3.4 The NLT turns 90 degrees right (note double blazes) onto the old rail grade. The washboard feeling continues a bit, but not from roots. The subtle, evenly spaced bumps you now feel are the remains of old rail ties from over 130 years ago.

5.1 Pass through a small, narrow, hand-cut gorge. This type of cut was usually accomplished by burning big fires on the rock and then quickly quenching the hot rock with cold spring water. This action caused the rock to split; then it could be broken down by hand and hauled away.

6.4 Turn right as the trail turns off and head down a tight singletrack into the drainage. After approximately 60 yards, turn right at the T intersection, onto another singletrack. Follow this incredible off-camber section through huge ferns and revel in the sights, smells and sounds of the wilderness mountain bike experience.

7.6 The trail dumps out onto Lebo Road. Turn left onto Lebo Road and start a mellow climb.

8.0 Pass the Rob Hollow Trail on the right. A bit further up the road you will pass a spring on the left and cabin on the right.

9.4 Turn left onto Whitman Road. Once across the small bridge turn left again onto a dirt access road, just before the cabin. You will soon pass a gate and begin to climb on the gas well access road.

10.1 Road bends hard left and passes a large gas well station. Descend a steep and fast gravel and dirt road.

10.7 Just past the bottom of the descent as you begin to climb again, the Big Trestle Trail cuts off to the right. Turn right onto the Big Trestle Trail and pass the huge dirt mound.

10.9 Pass two cabins as the singletrack becomes a rutted four-wheel-drive road.

11.4 After passing two more cabins, turn left onto Big Trestle Road.

11.7 Turn left onto Twelve Mile Road.

12.5 Pass the Susquehannock Trail System Hiking Trail on your right.

13.2 Turn right onto the Swartwood Trail and begin the steep, singletrack descent.

13.8 Dump out onto Joerg Road, continue to descend to the park.

15.1 Cross Pennsylvania 144. Continue back along the wooded trail, along the field and through the campground.

15.4 Trailhead.

Black Forest Shay Trail

Location:	36 miles north of Lock Haven or 24 miles south of Galeton, in the Tiadaghton State Forest.
Distance:	14.3-mile loop.
Time:	2 to 5 hours.
Tread:	This ride is a singletrack special! There are numerous wide sections of trail that follow the historic Sentiero di Shay rail grade. A few short links of dirt fire road finish out this backcountry classic.
Aerobic level:	Moderate. Except for the descent into the Big Dam Hollow, most of the ride is on a plateau. However, trail surface factors in a higher aerobic level rating.
Technical difficulty:	3 +. Logs, rocks, roots, and soft soils constantly force the rider to adapt to the changing trail conditions. The most difficult section is the tight, off-camber, and obscure singletrack that runs down into Big Dam Hollow. Competency in both technical riding and route-finding skills are needed.
Highlights:	Beautiful backcountry riding, historic old rail grades, remote hollows, great wildlife viewing.
Land status:	Pennsylvania State Forest, Department of Conservation and Natural Resources.
Maps:	USGS Lee Fire Tower, Slate Run; DCNR Bureau of Forestry: Tiadaghton State Forest map.

Access: From Lock Haven, take Pennsylvania Highway 664 north for 16 miles to Haneyville. At Haneyville continue north on Pennsylvania Highway 44 for approximately 15 miles to the Black Forest Inn restaurant. Turn around here and drive back south on Pennsylvania 44 for approximately 0.5 mile and park in a small lot hidden among tall pine trees. The lot can only handle about six cars. It has a wooden trail sign marked for the Sentiero di Shay and the Pine Tree Trails. This is the trailhead.

Notes on the trail: The Sentiero di Shay Trail is historically recognized for the achievements of the men and machines that logged these mountains. The Italian name translates as the "Path of Shay" and derives from the narrow-gauge railroad engines that ran the mountains in this region. The Shay locomotive was a special climbing engine that was able to run on steep, rough, mountain track. Throughout this ride, the old rail ties and cuts through the rock can still be felt and seen on the grades.

Black Forest Shay Trail

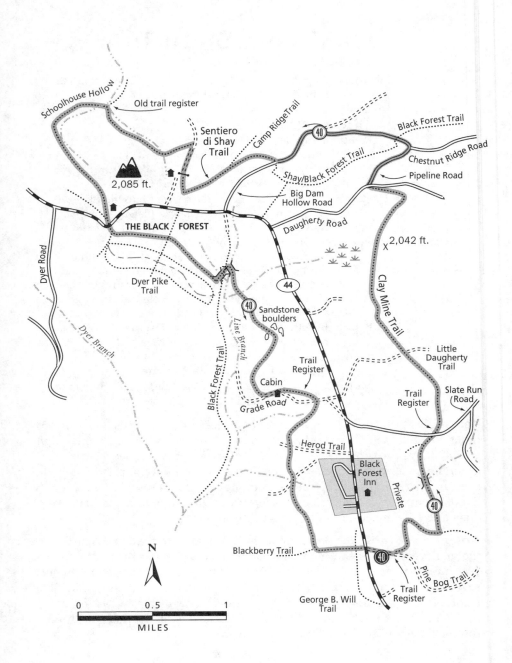

Schoolhouse Hollow

Old trail register

Sentiero di Shay Trail

Camp Ridge Trail

40

Black Forest Trail

Chestnut Ridge Road

Shay/Black Forest Trail

Pipeline Road

Big Dam Hollow Road

2,085 ft.

Daugherty Road

X 2,042 ft.

THE BLACK FOREST

Dyer Road

Dyer Pike Trail

Dyer Branch

Line Branch

44

40

Sandstone boulders

Clay Mine Trail

Little Daugherty Trail

Black Forest Trail

Trail Register

Cabin

Grade Road

Trail Register

Slate Run Road

Herod Trail

Black Forest Inn

Private

40

Blackberry Trail

40

George B. Will Trail

Trail Register

Pine Bog Trail

N

0   0.5   1

MILES

The ride begins on great singletrack that winds northward across the plateau, crossing a few fire and old woods roads. A rugged climb ensues after a short stint on the Pipeline Road, which winds its way out to the Big Dam Hollow descent. After passing the old green metal gate, the old woods road begins to fade into an obscure singletrack trail that crosses a stream. This drainage empties into another where the trail faintly crosses the stream and heads up a singletrack through the hollow. Once across Pennsylvania Highway 44, the ride enters the lush, cool, dank Black Forest on a section of the old rail grade. A mix of old logging roads and plenty more old rail grades winds back through the plateau. You'll also encounter unique features like a small city of sandstone rocks and high mountain swamps on the return trip. The Blackberry Trail is a sign that you're nearing the end as you reach the trailhead on Pennsylvania 44.

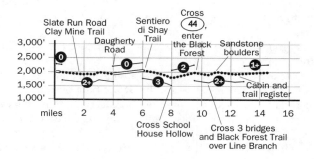

THE RIDE

0.0 From the trailhead, note the wooden sign for the Sentiero di Shay and Pine Bog Trails. Follow the blue circle blazes as they lead past a brown metal trail register box on the right.

0.2 Keep left at the fork, following the blue circle blazes, not the blue rectangle blazes.

1.2 Cross a small metal footbridge over a stream.

1.6 Pass a wooden trail sign for the Black Forest Inn on the left. Cross over Slate Run Road and continue on the trail, passing the wooden sign for Clay Mine Trail and Daugherty Road. As you enter the woods, note the trail register box mounted on the tree.

2.4 Cross an old woods road, Little Daugherty Trail.

4.2 Turn left onto Daugherty Road. Soon after, turn right at the T intersection onto Pipeline Road.

4.8 Pass Chestnut Ridge Road on the right; soon after, pass the Black Forest Trail on the left. Pipeline Road will merge with Big Dam Hollow Road.

6.3 Turn right at the four-way intersection on the Sentiero di Shay Trail.

7.0 Turn right at the T intersection onto the old woods road and pass around an old green metal gate. Note the cabin off to the left. As you descend Big Dam Hollow, the trail crosses the stream at mile 7.8.

8.2 The trail bends left, chasing the blazes up and across the Big Dam Hollow drainage. Note the old green wooden trail register. The porcupine, mice, and squirrels are slowly reclaiming the wooden box.

9.5 Turn right onto the cabin driveway (note the green and white cabin) passing a tall wooden post with "Schoolhouse Hollow Trail" engraved on it. Carefully cross Pennsylvania Highway 44. Once across the road, turn left at the fork marked "Sentiero di Shay and Dyer Pike Trail." This marks the beginning of the dark, cool 'Black Forest.'

10.0 Cross the Dyer Pike Trail.

10.5 Turn left at the T intersection, following the Shay trail. After crossing a small metal footbridge, keep right at the fork. Follow the blue blazes and the sign marked "High Water Route for the Black Forest Trail." Keep a watchful eye to the blazes as the trail bends sharply a few times in this section.

11.1 Pass a unique grouping of large sandstone boulders and merge right onto the old railroad grade. The bumps you feel are the remains of the old railroad ties

12.3 Pass a cabin and a trail register on the right and, soon after, cross a fire road, grade road.

13.0 Pass the Herod Trail and an old woods road. Note the wooden sign "Black Forest Inn .7 miles."

13.2 Cross a small stream and turn right onto a wide logging road. The trail reenters 60 yards up on the left—look carefully for the blue blazes.

13.9 Turn left at the T intersection onto the Blackberry Trail, noting the sign "High Water Route for the Black Forest Trail." Soon after, pass the right spur of the George B. Will Trail.

14.3 Cross the George B. Will Trail and carefully cross Pennsylvania 44 to the trailhead.

Pump Station to Shady Grove

Location:	36 miles north of Lock Haven or 24 miles south of Galeton, in the Tiadaghton State Forest.
Distance:	10.2-mile loop.
Time:	1 to 3 hours.
Tread:	Wide, grassy woods roads, hardpacked historic rail grade, fern-covered singletrack, and a short stint on paved road.
Aerobic level:	Easy. The route follows the historic rail grades, which run along the contours of the mountain. These hardpacked grades are very mellow with little gain in elevation.

Technical difficulty: 1+. The remains of the rotted timbers that once lined the rail grades have left a rippled surface in sections. There are a few small logs, roots, and rocks that are typical of most mountain bike trails.

Highlights: Historic old tram and logging railroad grades, spectacular scenery, remote woodland feeling, Pump Station Fire Tower, grand vistas.

Land status: Pennsylvania State Forest, Department of Conservation and Natural Resources.

Maps: USGS Slate Run; DCNR Bureau of Forestry: Tiadaghton State Forest map, Susquehannock State Forest map.

Access: From Lock Haven, take Pennsylvania Highway 664 north for 12 miles to Pennsylvania Highway 44 at Haneyville. Follow Pennsylvania 44 north for 13.5 miles and turn right onto Manor Fork Road (a dirt forest road located at a stand of tall pines that line the road). Park 200 yards on the right in the small, marked recreation parking area. The recreation area lot is the trailhead. (Manor Fork Road is 1 mile south of the Black Forest Inn.)

Notes on the trail: This is an awesome woodland mountaintop ride that is perfect for the adventurous novice. The scenic beauty and multiple backcountry vistas alone are truly worth the trip, so don't forget the camera. The ride traces sections of the historical logging rail grades that lace the surrounding mountains.

The ride begins at the recreation area parking lot and turns immediately onto the Old Railroad Grade Trail. Enjoy the great vista looking down into the Pine Creek Valley through the Naval Run drainage. After carefully crossing Pennsylvania Highway 44, take the gated road, which leads to the Pump Station Fire Tower with endless views over the Allegheny Plateau. Finish this short loop and pass the trailhead lot, then work your way out to the Harrowed Trail. The flat Harrowed Trail, which is a continuation of the Old Railroad Grade Trail, meanders through beautiful stands of oak, white pine, hemlock, mountain laurel, and blueberry.

Head across Pennsylvania 44 for a loop that passes another awesome vista overlooking the headwater drainages of Young Womans Creek. Traverse through a rich high mountain bog on footbridges. Return following the old rail grade on the Harrowed Trail to Manor Fork Road, which leads to the trailhead.

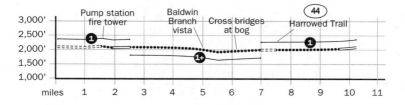

Pump Station to Shady Grove

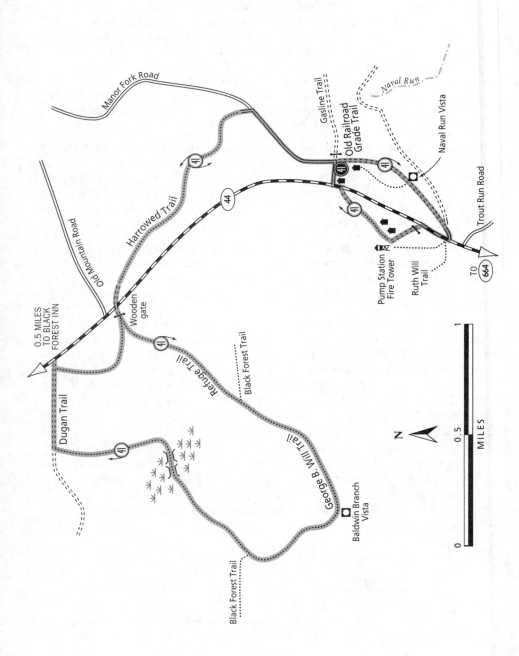

Manor Fork Road

Gasline Trail

Old Railroad Grade Trail

Naval Run

Naval Run Vista

Trout Run Road

Harrowed Trail

44

Old Mountain Road

Pump Station Fire Tower

Ruth Will Trail

TO 664

0.5 MILES TO BLACK FOREST INN

Wooden gate

Refuge Trail

Black Forest Trail

Dugan Trail

George B. Will Trail

Baldwin Branch Vista

Black Forest Trail

N

MILES

0   0.5   1

THE RIDE

0.0 From the trailhead lot, ride out and turn right onto Manor Fork Road. Approximately 40 yards after, turn right onto the Old Railroad Grade Trail marked by the wooden sign.

0.8 Pass the awesome vista on the left, over Pine Creek Gorge.

1.1 Turn right onto Pennsylvania Highway 44.

1.3 Turn left onto the gated dirt access road.

1.4 Reach the Pump Station Fire Tower. From the fire tower, turn right, passing the left side of the left most cabin (Camp Two Buck) following the blue blazes.

1.7 Turn left onto Pennsylvania 44, and soon after turn right onto Manor Fork Road (dirt). Follow the road as it passes the trailhead parking area and bends left.

2.4 Turn left onto the Harrowed Trail, marked by a wooden sign opposite the trail entrance, and enjoy this shady, flat, old rail grade.

3.4 Cross over the George B. Will Trail.

3.6 Carefully cross Pennsylvania 44 and continue on the Refuge Trail, passing around a wooden gate.

4.3 Pass a trail spur to the left. Continue straight following the blue and orange blazes.

5.0 Pass an incredible vista looking out over the headwater drainages of Young Womans Creek.

5.5 Keep right at the fork, staying on the George B. Will Trail and following the blue blazes. This intersection is marked by a wooden trail sign and also marks the High Water Route for the Black Forest Trail.

Backcountry beauty along the Shady Grove Trail.

The grand view over Young Womans Creek drainage, from the Pump Station Fire Tower.

6.3 Cross two small metal bridges in a bog.

7.1 Turn right onto the Dugan Trail (old woods road).

7.5 Just before you come out onto Pennsylvania 44, turn right at the four-way intersection onto the old rail grade.

8.4 Carefully cross Pennsylvania State Highway 44 and continue across on the Harrowed Trail.

9.7 Merge right onto Manor Fork Road.

10.2 Back at the trailhead.

Ruth Will Trail

Location: 36 miles north of Lock Haven or 24 miles south of Galeton, in the Tiadaghton State Forest.

Distance: 4.6 mile loop.

Time: 30 minutes to 1 hour.

Tread: The ride follows the historic pathways of the old narrow-gauge railroads, which have hardpacked, grassy, and sometimes bumpy surfaces.

Aerobic level: Easy. The ride runs along the plateau so there are no major changes in elevation. The most physically demanding section will probably be the mild climb back up to the trailhead.

Technical difficulty: 3. The few bumps and dips along the way are hardly difficult but worth mentioning nonetheless. The 1-mile stretch of tight, rocky singletrack along the Laurel Path at the beginning of the ride is a quite a challenge but can be easily skirted using the highway and the Old Railroad Grade Trail. The bypass lowers the technical difficulty to a 1.

Highlights: Historic stone railroad logging cabin, historic rail grades, beautiful high mountain scenery, remote mountain vistas, Pump Station Fire Tower, great wildlife viewing.

Land status: Pennsylvania State Forest, Department of Conservation and Natural Resources.

Maps: USGS Slate Run; DCNR Bureau of Forestry: Tiadaghton State Forest map, Susquehannock State Forest maps.

Access: From Lock Haven, take Pennsylvania Highway 664 north for 20 miles to Haneyville. At Haneyville, continue north on Pennsylvania 44 for

Ruth Will Trail

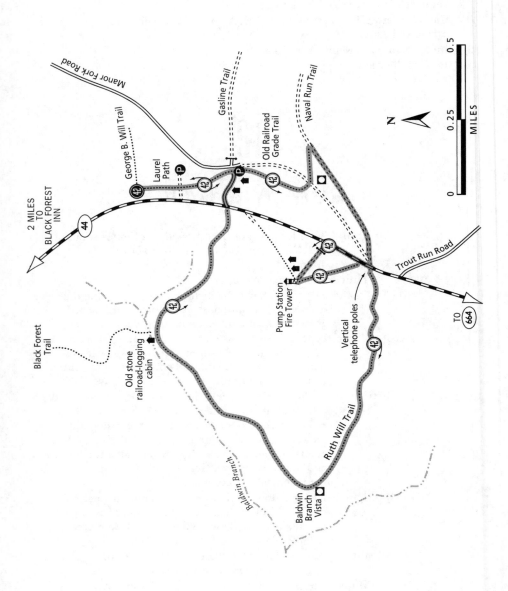

Manor Fork Road

Gasline Trail

Old Railroad Grade Trail

Naval Run Trail

George B. Will Trail

Laurel Path

2 MILES TO BLACK FOREST INN

44

Trout Run Road

TO 664

Pump Station Fire Tower

Vertical telephone poles

Black Forest Trail

Old stone railroad-logging cabin

Baldwin Branch

Baldwin Branch Vista

Ruth Will Trail

N

MILES

0   0.25   0.5

approximately 16 miles to the large pull-off parking area on the right marked by a large wooden sign for the George B. Will Trail. If you pass the Black Forest Inn restaurant, you missed the trailhead.

Notes on the trail: Filled with awesome natural and historical stops, the ride loops around the plateau on some mild terrain. The views from the mountain into the deep backcountry gorges are impressive.

From the trailhead, the trail immediately jumps onto the sweet singletrack of the Laurel Path. From the recreation parking lot on Manor Fork Road, the Laurel Path resumes in the upper corner of the small lot and progressively becomes rockier. You can bypass this section by taking the marked Old Railroad Grade Trail. Gaze out over the first vista, over the Naval Run drainage and out toward the mountains across the Pine Creek Gorge. A short singletrack section leads to Naval Run Trail and terminates on Pennsylvania 44. Take a short ride along Pennsylvania Highway 44, then turn off onto the Pump Station Fire Tower Road. Views from the tower are quite impressive, especially looking west over the Young Womans Creek headwaters area. A secret singletrack descends to the Ruth Will Ski Trail, which is really an old railroad grade that wraps around the mountain. The backcountry vista at Baldwin Branch lends a greater perspective to the ruggedness of these high-country drainages. Passing by the ancient railroad logging cabin, one can only imagine what it was like to live here back then. The final leg is a retracing of the Laurel Path, this time riding it downhill to the trailhead through all the rough stuff.

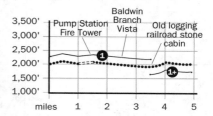

THE RIDE

0.0 Find the singletrack trail, located at the southern end of the trailhead lot. Ride up onto the marked Laurel Path singletrack.

0.4 Turn right onto Manor Fork Road, ride for 50 yards, and turn left into the small gravel parking area. Resume the Laurel Path at the southern end of the small parking lot marked by the wooden sign. (To avoid this section, take the Old Railroad Grade Trail that begins left of the parking area and rejoins the trail at the Naval Run vista.)

0.9 Turn left onto the Old Railroad Grade Trail and gaze out over Naval Run and the Pine Creek Gorge. Ride the Old Railroad Grade Trail for 20 yards and turn right onto the singletrack trail that is marked by a small wooden sign) saying "To Naval Run Trail." After the short, steep descent, turn right onto the doubletrack Naval Run Trail.

1.3 Turn right onto Pennsylvania Highway 44, staying on the road's edge.

1.5 Turn left, crossing Pennsylvania 44, and continue up a gated forest road to the Pump Station fire tower. After checking out the tower, turn left (mile 1.6) onto the somewhat obscure, blue-blazed singletrack. It's short but it's secret and it's sweet.

The old stone railroad cabin along the Ruth Will Trail.

1.8 Turn right onto Pennsylvania State Highway 44 briefly then turn right onto the Ruth Will Ski Trail, passing around a set of vertical telephone poles that act as a gate.

2.8 Pass the Baldwin Branch Vista, which looks out over Pennsylvania's finest backcountry.

3.5 After passing the Black Forest Trail on the left, pass the rustic, stone railroad-logging cabin on the left. Check out the old narrow-gauge rails used for the roof beams. From here, the Black Forest Trail also breaks off left again. Continue straight, climbing the grade and following the blue blazes.

4.1 Cross Pennsylvania 44 and continue straight on Manor Fork Road.

4.2 Turn left onto the Laurel Path singletrack, opposite the Old Railroad Grade Trail, retracing the route back to the trailhead. The singletrack may be a bit hard to find, but you've been here before so it shouldn't take too long.

4.6 Return to the trailhead.

Tamarack Tower

Location:	9 miles north of Renovo.
Distance:	12-mile loop.
Time:	1.5 to 2.5 hours.
Tread:	Most of the ride follows rocky ATV trail and heavily wooded singletrack. There are a few sections of gated forest and pipeline roads that link the ride together.
Aerobic level:	Moderate. The ride is constantly changing elevation. Hill climbs lead to descents and so the circle goes, for 12 incredible miles. Endurance and stamina are helpful in dealing with the constantly changing topography.
Technical difficulty:	3. The ATV trails are rugged in places with many areas of exposed rock. The climb up to the tower and the descent are classic woodland singletrack trails with a few fallen logs and hidden rocks.
Highlights:	Tamarack Fire Tower, views, bermed ATV trails, sweet hidden singletrack, stream crossings.
Land status:	Pennsylvania State Forest. Department of Conservation and Natural Resources.
Maps:	USGS Hammersly Fork, Tamarack, Keating, Renovo West; DCNR Pennsylvania State Forest: Sproul State Forest map, Sproul ATV Trail map.

Access: From Renovo, take Pennsylvania Highway 144 north for 5 miles to Big Basin Road, a dirt forest road. Follow Big Basin Road for 3 miles, passing

Tamarack Tower

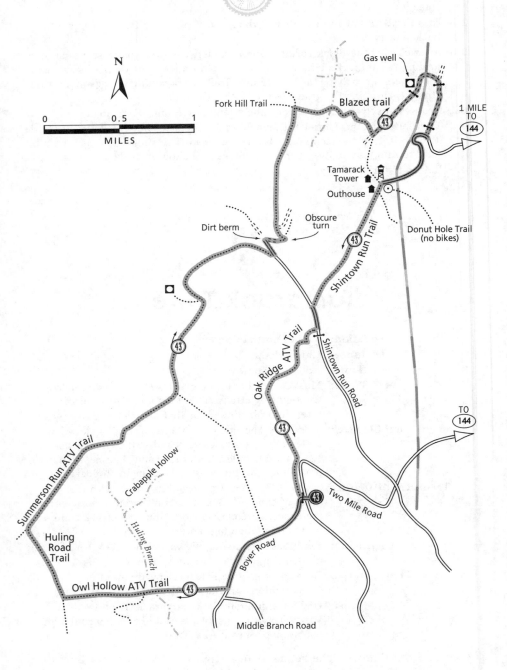

N

0   0.5   1
MILES

Gas well

Fork Hill Trail

Blazed trail

43

1 MILE TO 144

Tamarack Tower

Outhouse

43

Shintown Run Trail

Donut Hole Trail (no bikes)

Obscure turn

Dirt berm

43

Oak Ridge ATV Trail

Shintown Run Road

TO 144

43

Summerson Run ATV Trail

Crabapple Hollow

Huling Branch

43

Two Mile Road

Huling Road Trail

Boyer Road

Owl Hollow ATV Trail

43

Middle Branch Road

Oh, the luxuries of woodland riding. Jay getting more mileage from his map along the Tamarak Tower Trail.

a sharp left-hand bend in the road, to the small ATV trailhead pull-out on the left. This small parking area is opposite the gated Boyer Road.

Notes on the trail: The Tamarack area is rugged and beautiful. The Tamarack Swamp Natural Area as well as some of the state's largest, shallow natural gas fields are located here, in the northern corner of the Sproul State Forest. A large compressor station that pumps gas through interstate pipelines from massive underground wells is also located here. Gas is stored in underground reservoirs, which is one of the safest and most effective ways to store this nonrenewable resource. These subterranean caverns hold an excess supply of gas that is used throughout the winter months not only by Pennsylvanians but many others in neighboring states. The pipelines are great for mountain biking but at times can be downright confusing. A sense of adventure and good navigational skills are needed.

Along sections of the ride you will pass numbered ATV trail signs, which relate to the Sproul ATV Trail map. With the ATV map, you'll find countless trails to explore west of this ride on the old mountaintop strip mine. Without the map, it's a nightmarish maze of access roads. If you plan on launching any expeditions into this semi-charted territory, I highly recommend getting an ATV map and practicing your compass skills.

The ride begins in the ATV trail network on the smooth Boyer Road. After a bit of a warm-up, you're off into the woods on the ATV trails. Snaking out to the vista over Tamarack, the trail descends to the first crux of the ride. Using keen woods sense and the explicit written directions, pick your way through some adventurous terrain to the second highpoint, atop the Tamarack Fire Tower. From here the views are endless. Now, I hope you're pumped to pull off the second crux of finding the secret trail "behind" the outhouse (a little backcountry humor). After the sweet descent off the mountain, more ATV trails lead back to the trailhead in style.

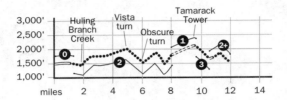

THE RIDE

0.0 Ride around the gate onto the smooth, hardpacked Boyer Road.

1.0 Just before a road intersection, turn right onto the grassy woods road, noting the wooden trail sign that reads "Owl Hollow Trail".

1.7 Cross the Huling Branch stream, then pass a left-hand spur trail and climb the steep hill.

2.0 Turn right at the T intersection onto the Huling Road trail. Note the ATV trail marker number 2.

2.6 The ATV trail bends right. Note the post marked "Summerson Trail."

4.1 Pass ATV trail marker number 1 and a 4 x 4 post marked "Summerson Trail."

4.9 Pass the left-hand spur of the Vista Trail on the rocky knob. Riding out to this worthy view is an 0.8-mile round-trip not included in the mileage log. The impressive lookout peers out over the Tamarack Swamp Natural Area and the adjacent Natural Gas Compression Station.

5.9 Turn left on Shintown Run Road and ride on for 0.2 mile to the end of the dirt road. At the end of the road, turn right onto an obscure, overgrown old woods road with a faint singletrack line cutting the middle. This trail will cross a dirt berm and follow a dry creek for 0.1 mile before turning 90 degrees left it then climbs a loose dirt trail 100 yards up the steep but short hill. Once atop the hill, turn left onto the faint, narrow, grassy woods road, and continue to climb. This is one of the cruxes, so follow with a keen sense of direction.

7.2 Turn right at the intersection onto the blazed singletrack trail.

7.9 After crossing a small stream and climbing a steep hill, leave the blazed trail and turn left onto the narrow, grassy old woods road.

8.4 Pass around a gate and a natural gas well head on the left as the trail turns to dirt pipeline access road. Follow it as it climbs, bending right and crossing a pipeline.

8.6 Turn right at the T intersection and pass around a green, metal gate.

8.8 Turn right at the T intersection and climb Tamarack Tower Road.

View from Tamarak Tower, Tamarak Tower Trail.

9.4 Pass around a gate and ride up to the Tamarack Tower. From here the trail resumes 30 yards left of the outhouse, on an overgrown, grassy old woods road. The outhouse is to the left of the stone cabin; finding this trail is the second crux. The trail will soon fork. Keep right and descend the singletrack sweetness.

10.5 Turn left on Shintown Road. Soon after turn right onto the ATV trail, 70 yards before the gate on Shintown Road.

11.7 Turn right, following the Oak Ridge ATV Trail as it parallels Big Basin Road.

12.0 Return to the trailhead.

Ridge and Valley Province

Centered around Happy Valley, home of the Nittany Lions, these rides take you on the ridge and valley folds of the central mountains. The Rothrock, Bald Eagle, and lower Moshannon State Forests harbor some of the finest, nationally renowned native trout streams as well as mysterious limestone caves and caverns. A few old logging railroads mixed in with some stellar singletrack make for some intense riding in this little-known mecca for outdoor adventurers. Fire tower vistas, cool mountain streams and high mountain bogs are just some of the hidden highlights of the area.

44

Cowbell Hollow

Location: R. B. Winter State Park, 18 miles west of Lewisburg.

Distance: 28.1-mile loop.

Time: 4 to 6 hours.

Tread: Outstanding woodland singletrack, rocky old woods road, and a few dirt forest roads.

Aerobic level: Strenuous. The ride gains a significant amount of elevation and covers some extremely demanding terrain. The trail demands endurance, finesse, and technical skill.

Technical difficulty: 4. Stout quads and burly biceps are helpful as you must negotiate all types of technical challenges, including big logs, loose rocks, slick roots, and steep descents.

Highlights: Classic ridge and valley technical riding, remote woodland trails, Cooper Mill Vista, state park amenities, which include swimming and fishing in the spring-fed lake, camping, nature trails, and an awesome environmental education center for learning more about the flora and fauna of Pennsylvania.

Land status: Pennsylvania State Parks and State Forest, Department of Conservation and Natural Resources.

Maps: USGS Williamsport SE, Mifflinburg, Hartleton, Carroll; DCNR Bureau of Forestry: Bald Eagle State Forest, Bald Eagle Mountain Bike Trail maps.

Access: From Lewisburg, take Pennsylvania Highway 192 west for approximately 18 miles to R. B. Winter State Park. As the road passes the park's lake on the right, travel for 0.5 mile and take a hard right on McCall Dam road. Immediately after this intersection, keep right at the fork, following Sand Mountain Road to the mountain bike trailhead parking area. Turn right into the large lot, and note the large wooden sign board stating "Mountain Bike Trailhead," complete with cryptic map. This is the trailhead.

Notes on the trail: It's trails like these that breed hard-core riders. Located in the heart of the 200,000-acre Bald Eagle State Forest, this ride winds its way over ridge and valley, offering hundreds of feet of vertical climbing. The forest tract received its name from the famous American Indian Chief Bald Eagle, of the Munsee tribe. Woapalanne, as he was known among his people, led war parties from the "Nest" (formerly named Bald Eagles Nest but now known as Milesburg) against settlements in the West Branch of the Susquehanna Valley.

The ride begins at R. B. Winter State Park and climbs into the northeastern section of forest. After a series of forest roads, the first singletrack runs parallel to White Deer Creek. Slick roots sprawl out across the trail like the arms of an angry octopus and moss-covered rocks line the trail like soft green turtles. Passing by the tranquil McCall Dam picnic area, the ride climbs on some fast fire road before entering the singletrack Stony Hollow Trail. Then you're back out on forest roads that lead to the 3-mile classic Cowbell Hollow Trail. Tight, twisty trail gives way to a steep, boulder-strewn drainage requiring a cool head and tight grip. As the trail empties out at a cabin, take care to skirt the property edge, crossing the stream on the driveway bridge.

At the halfway point, the ride climbs Nittany Mountain and runs out along the technical Top Mountain Trail, which is 5 miles of unrelenting, rocky old woods road. A forest road links the final stretch of technical terrain on the Bake Oven Trail to finish with a well-deserved bomber downhill to the trailhead.

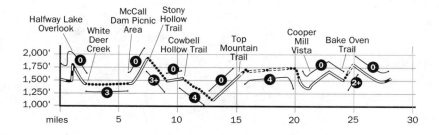

Cowbell Hollow

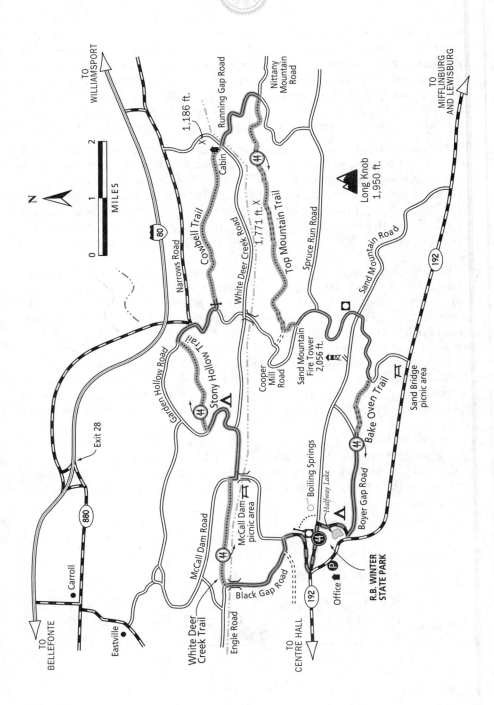

THE RIDE

0.0 From the trailhead lot, turn left onto Sand Mountain Road.

0.7 Take a hard right onto the paved McCall Dam Road and climb the hill.

1.2 Pass the well-earned overlook of Halfway Lake and Brush Valley.

1.7 Turn left onto Black Gap Road.

3.3 After crossing a small bridge over White Deer Creek, turn right onto the White Deer Creek singletrack trail marked by the wooden trail sign.

5.4 After crossing through the stream (on foot please), turn right onto McCall Dam Road. Ride for 100 yards and turn left onto White Deer Creek Road. The McCall Dam picnic area on the right is a great place to take a break.

6.2 Turn left on Garden Hollow Road and climb the hill.

6.8 Pass the Duncan Trail and state forest campsite on the right.

7.6 Turn right onto the Stony Hollow singletrack trail, which is marked by wooden sign.

9.3 Turn right onto Garden Hollow Trail, noting Interstate 80 to the left.

9.8 Keep right at the fork and climb Cooper Mill Road.

10.4 Turn left onto the Cowbell Hollow Trail, pass around a gate, and continue on the old woods road. The trail soon turns to singletrack sweetness after the clearing.

13.4 The trail dumps out at the Stauffer's cabin. Politely ride around the perimeter of the property to the dirt driveway and then ride the driveway out across the bridge to the forest road. Turn right onto White Deer Creek Road and begin to climb.

13.8 Turn left onto Running Gap Road and climb Nittany Mountain.

15.6 At the crest of the ridge, turn right onto the Top Mountain Trail. This old woods road is opposite the intersection with Nittany Mountain Road, which is marked by a wooden trail sign.

20.5 Keep left at a fork marked by a grassy campsite clearing, and ride over a dirt berm descending on a wide, grassy singletrack trail. This wide singletrack trail leaves the obvious old woods road that swings right.

20.8 Turn left onto Cooper Mill Road, continuing to descend.

22.7 Pass Cooper Mill Vista.

22.9 Cross the four-way intersection with Sand Mountain Road and begin to descend.

23.9 Turn right onto the (partly obscured) old woods road spur, the Bake Oven Trail.

25.3 Turn left at the T intersection onto Boyer Gap Road.

27.2 Turn right at the T intersection onto the paved park road.

28.1 Follow the paved road as it bends left to the trailhead lot.

Remember: Gravity is your friend; the author logging some air-time in the Endless Mountains.

Boiling Springs

Location:	R. B. Winter State Park, 18 miles west of Lewisburg.
Distance:	13.3-mile loop.
Time:	1 to 3 hours.
Tread:	Grassy woods road, forest fire road, and a dash of bumpy singletrack.
Aerobic level:	Easy. Except for the short beginning climb, the ride changes little in elevation. This makes for a great novice ride through some truly mountainous country.
Technical difficulty:	2. There is a short section of singletrack along the Black Gap Trail that is a bit rocky and descends along a dank, mossy drainage. The old woods road that makes up the McCall Field Trail is a well-worn four-wheel-drive road that has some slippery roots, rocks, and mud holes.
Highlights:	The fascinating Boiling Springs, impressive park vista, great wildlife viewing, and all the state park amenities, which include swimming and fishing in the spring-fed lake, camping, nature trails, and an awesome environmental education center.
Land status:	Pennsylvania State Parks, Department of Conservation and Natural Resources.
Maps:	USGS: Logantown, Woodward, Hartleton, Carroll. DCNR Bureau of Forestry: Bald Eagle State Forest, Bald Eagle Mountain Bike Trail maps.

Access: From Lewisburg, take Pennsylvania Highway 192 west for approximately 18 miles to R. B. Winter State Park. As the road passes the park's lake on the right, travel for 0.5 mile and take a hard right on McCall Dam road. Immediately after this intersection, keep right at the fork, following Sand Mountain Road to the mountain bike trailhead parking area. Turn right into the large lot, and note the large wooden sign board stating "Mountain Bike Trailhead," complete with obscure map. This is the trailhead.

Notes on the trail: The sheer beauty of this region alone is reason enough to ride here, not to mention the great trail network within the Bald Eagle State Forest. The trailhead serves as a great base camp and is perfect for those humid midsummer rides because of the spring-fed lake. The park has a newly constructed environmental education center that is a real asset.

The ride begins with a steep but short climb up to the rewarding vista out over Halfway Lake and Brush Valley. The ride then meanders on forest and

Boiling Springs

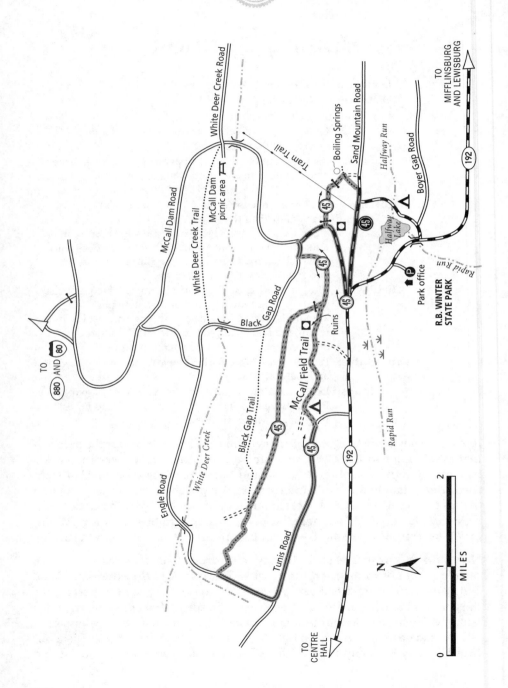

woods roads through regrowth timber stands where it's quite common to see our state bird—the ruffed grouse—and the plentiful white-tailed deer. Turkey, squirrel, and chipmunks abound where the Black Gap singletrack trail spurs off from the wide grassy road. A short, fun, and challenging run leads to the fire roads that link to the next section of trail. As you head back into the woods on the well-worn McCall Field Trail, you pass the ruins of an old cabin, complete with outhouse.

The final leg descends sharply to the trailhead, passing Boiling Springs. This fascinating geologic feature is an upwelling of spring water from the bedrock aquifer in a sand bed. The pressure of the water passing through the sand causes the sand to roll and "boil." The smaller "Little Bubbler" is another sand spring that can be found on the west end of the beach. It still boils as it feeds frigid water to Halfway Lake. A flat cruise along Sand Mountain Road terminates the ride at the trailhead.

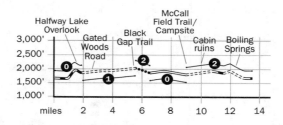

THE RIDE

0.0 From the trailhead lot, head out to Sand Mountain Road and turn left.

0.7 Take a hard right onto the paved McCall Dam Road and climb the hill.

1.2 Pass the well-earned overlook of Halfway Lake and Brush Valley.

1.7 Turn left onto Black Gap Road. Soon after (mile 1.9), turn left up the dirt doubletrack woods road which is the McCall Field Trail.

2.5 Keep right at the fork and pass around the gate on the grassy woods road.

5.5 Turn left onto the slightly-obscure singletrack (Black Gap Trail) which starts out a bit rocky. This turn is somewhat easy to miss, so keep your head up.

6.4 Turn left onto Engle Road. Soon after turn left at the T intersection onto Tunis Road.

8.9 Turn left onto McCall Field Trail (bumpy old woods road). Soon the road comes to a clearing at a camping area. Keep right following the wide trail back into the woods on the old four-wheel drive road.

9.9 Pass the old cabin ruins on the left, complete with old well and outhouse.

10.7 Merge right onto the wide grassy woods road—deja vu.

11.4 Turn right on Black Gap Road and soon after, turn right at the T intersection on McCall Dam Road.

11.6 Turn left onto the gated woods road marked by a sign saying "Boiling Springs and Sand Mountain Trails."

12.1 Ride under the power line, pass the Old Tram Trail on the left, and begin descending after passing another gate.

12.4 Pass Boiling Springs on the left. The spring is 100 yards down the foot trail and enclosed in a wire-mesh structure. Soon after, at a wooden sign, stay on the Boiling Springs Trail as it breaks off right.

12.8 Turn right onto Sand Mountain Road.

13.3 Turn left into the trailhead lot.

Tunnel Mountain Trail

Location:	Poe Paddy Recreation Area, 24 miles east of State College.
Distance:	22.6-mile loop.
Time:	3 to 5 hours.
Tread:	Gnarly, rocky singletrack and rutted old woods road linked with fast and smooth forest roads, ATV trails, and cinder-covered old railroad grade.
Aerobic level:	Strenuous. The ride gains significant elevation and traverses through many tough technical sections. The climbs are sustained and the singletrack sections are downright brutal.
Technical difficulty:	4. Not all of the ride covers extreme terrain, but when it drops into singletrack, buckle up cause it's gonna get rough.
Highlights:	Outstanding views from Penns View on Poe Mountain, two historic railroad tunnels, rock climbing, historic railroad grade, tubing at the oxbow on Penns Creek, world class trout fishing on the famous Penns Creek, Poe Paddy and Poe Valley State Park amenities, which include swimming, fishing, boat rentals, camping, and food concessions.
Land status:	Pennsylvania State Parks and State Forest, Department of Conservation and Natural Resources.
Maps:	USGS Coburn, Weikert, Spring Mills; DCNR Bureau of Forestry: Bald Eagle State Forest map.

Access: From State College, head east on U.S. Highway 322 to Boalsburg. At Boalsburg turn left on Pennsylvania Highway 45 and head north. After passing the small town of Springs Mills, drive for approximately 4 miles and turn right onto Paradise Road. Follow Paradise Road for 2 miles, crossing Georges Valley Road. Continue straight, crossing over Penns Creek, then continue on Millheim Pike. Millheim Pike climbs Poe Mountain, turns to dirt forest road, and passes a large wooden state forest sign on the right. At the T intersection, turn right to continue on Millheim Pike. At the bottom of the hill, turn left at the T intersection onto the paved Poe Valley Road. Continue on for 5 miles, passing Poe Valley State Park on the right, to Poe Paddy Recreation Area. At the T intersection, turn left on Poe Paddy Road and park in either of the two lots, just before the small wooden bridge. The recreation area is the trailhead.

Notes on the trail: As with many of the trails and roadways in Pennsylvania, this historic route follows part of an old Native American foot trail called the Penns Creek Indian Path. As Penns Valley was settled and the timber industry grew, a railroad was built in 1879 along Penns Creek to link other smaller mountain valley timber railroads. The trailhead is the site of Poe Mills, a prosperous but typically short-lived timber town that ran its course from around 1880 to the mid-1890s.

After crossing the old iron bridge and riding through a dank tunnel, the ride warms up on the old railroad grade. With a few miles of scenic railroad grade behind, the ride embarks on increasingly more difficult terrain as it climbs Old Mingle road. After bombing down the backside of the mountain, the road dead-ends at Penns Creek and follows some truly harrowing hoodoo singletrack along the creek. Past the old railroad bridge abutments, the trail gives way to the old railroad grade.

Following another old iron span over Penns Creek, the railroad grade leads to the dark, dank, and somewhat dangerous Tunnel Mountain tunnel. Let your eyes adjust to the darkness so that you don't ride over any rock that has fallen from the ceiling. Outside the tunnel, flat terrain follows along paved and dirt road to the strenuous singletrack that climbs the hill adjacent to the state forest sign. A few tricky turns lead to the impressive Penns View atop Poe Mountain. The best is yet to come, with a downright brutal singletrack descent straight off the mountain. Loose rock and frightening drop-offs run the length of this narrow, laurel-choked trail. A bit of bushwhacking keeps you honest, as does the ford on Big Poe Creek, before returning your wretched bones to the trailhead.

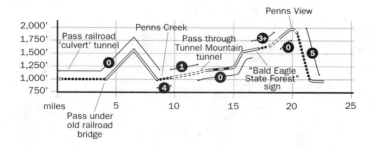

Tunnel Mountain Trail

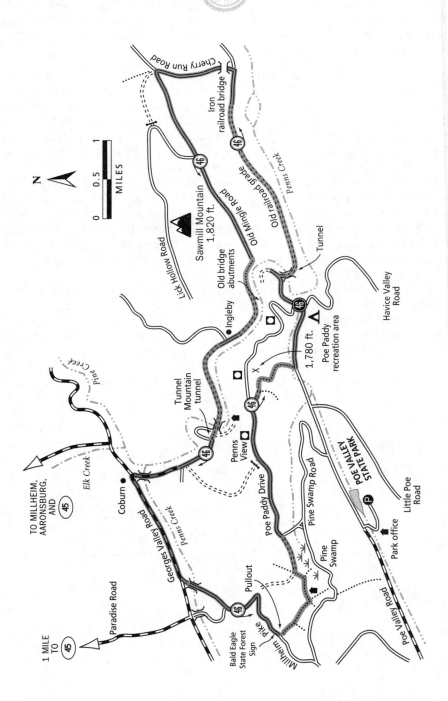

THE RIDE

0.0 From the recreation area, leave the lot, cross the small wooden bridge over Big Poe Creek, and continue on.

0.5 Take a hard right onto the dirt road, which soon turns to wide singletrack and crosses the old railroad bridge over Penns Creek.

0.8 Pass through the cool tunnel, which begins as a large culvert, and continue on the old railroad grade.

3.2 Merge right onto the dirt road.

4.0 Turn left onto Cherry Run Road, soon passing under a large iron railroad bridge.

5.3 Turn left and climb Old Mingle Road. Pass Lick Hollow Road at mile 6.8.

8.6 After a sweet descent, the road dead-ends at Penns Creek. Head straight on the singletrack that continues just to the water's edge and turn right onto the rocky singletrack that parallels the creek.

9.2 Pass the old railroad bridge abutments on the left.

10.0 Merge onto the road and pass through the village of Ingleby.

10.3 Turn left onto the road, keeping close to the creek.

10.5 Pass a cable gate, staying on the cinder railroad bed that bears to the right. Soon after, pass an old railroad mile marker (mile 10.8).

12.1 Cross another old railroad bridge and continue straight as the trail passes through the Tunnel Mountain tunnel. It's real dark in there, so take care to not ride into any of the huge rocks that have fallen from the ceiling. Once through the tunnel, turn left on the dirt road.

13.2 Keep right as the road forks.

13.7 Cross a green iron bridge into the town of Coburn. Turn left at the T intersection onto Georges Valley Road.

14.9 Turn left at the fork, crossing Penns Creek on a paved spur road, which merges left with Millheim Pike.

16.7 After passing the large wooden Bald Eagle State Forest sign on the right and the vehicle pullout on the left, turn left up the steep, wide singletrack trail, just past the telephone pole.

17.3 After passing a right-hand spur trail, turn left at a four-way intersection onto the ATV trail. Soon after, keep left at the trail fork.

17.9 Turn right at the four-way intersection onto the old woods road.

18.7 Turn left onto Poe Paddy Drive.

20.1 Pass the stunning Penns View.

20.5 Turn right onto the overgrown old woods road. Soon the woods road passes a right-hand spur trail and begins to narrow down to a tight blue-blazed singletrack that practically falls off the mountain.

21.6 The trail fades, and the blue blazes turn right. Continue by bushwhacking straight, crossing Big Poe Creek, and turning left on Poe Valley Road.

22.6 Arrive at the trailhead.

Little Flat Fire Tower

Location: 8 miles south of State College.

Distance: 7-mile loop.

Time: 1 to 2 hours.

Tread: Forest roads, way-technical rocky singletrack, slippery footbridges, and old woods road.

Aerobic level: Moderate to strenuous. The ride climbs over 1,100 feet in a mere 7 miles and covers some serious technical terrain.

Technical difficulty: 5. There are two super-steep descents down rugged, loose singletrack that will crumple your bike and body. The climb up the old Shingletown Trail is quite technical as well, with fallen logs and loose sandstone rocks.

Highlights: Little Flat Fire Tower and views, the hidden three bridges, Central Pennsylvania's best singletrack descent, great wildlife viewing, close to Happy Valley (home of the Nittany Lions).

Land status: Pennsylvania State Parks and State Forest, Department of Conservation and Natural Resources.

Maps: USGS State College, McAlevys Fort, Barrville, Centre Hall; DCNR Bureau of Forestry: Rothrock State Forest Map.

Access: From State College, head east on U.S. Highway 322 (business), passing through the town of Boalsburg. As the business route merges with the bypass route, stay on US 322 for approximately 1.5 miles to Tussey Mountain Ski Area. Turn right onto Bear Meadows Road, which soon passes Tussey Mountain Ski Area, and continue on this road as it changes to a dirt surface. After crossing two bridges, park in the small lot on the left at the fork in the road. Note the old millhouse foundation located at the trailhead pull-out.

Notes on the trail: Located on the northern edge of the Rothrock State Forest, the route covers some of the finest trail in the forest, which holds many secrets of its own. Legend has it that the Delaware Indian tribe built stone steps on the north face of Tussey Mountain to cross over this long ridge from Stone Creek to Spruce Creek. Appropriately named "Indian Steps," this unique trail can be found west of Pennsylvania Highway 26 on the state forest road named Kepler Road.

Beginning at the trailhead, one may notice the old mill ruins at the parking pull-out and across the way at the old dam and waterwheel foundation.

Little Flat Fire Tower

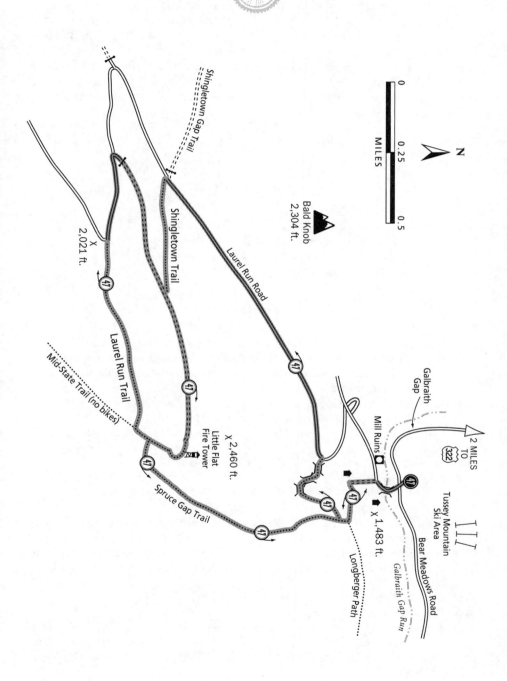

Shingletown Gap Trail

Shingletown Trail

X 2,021 ft.

Laurel Run Trail

Mid-State Trail (no bikes)

Laurel Run Road

Bald Knob
2,304 ft.

Little Flat
Fire Tower

X 2,460 ft.

Spruce Gap Trail

Longberger Path

Galbraith Gap

Mill Ruins

X 1,483 ft.

2 MILES
TO
322

Tussey Mountain
Ski Area

Bear Meadows Road

Galbraith Gap Run

0
0.25
0.5

MILES

N

Climbing up onto Little Flat Mountain, you are rewarded with outstanding views from the fire tower and some of the best gnarly downhill singletrack in the region. The first loop literally drops off the backside of the mountain down the rugged Laurel Run Trail. A moderate climb to regain the summit unveils the trail of all trails. It's time to get gripped as you drop over 800 feet in a mere 0.8 mile off the north face. This trail walks a fine line between an adrenaline rush and death. If you make it to the bottom alive you will have surely cheated the wrath of the reaper. Retracing some familiar trail, the ride coasts down to the old mill ruins at the trailhead. Sick and twisted...yes, a ride you want to miss...not in a million years.

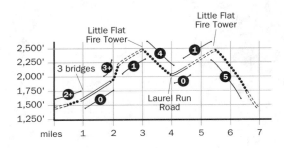

THE RIDE

0.0 From the trailhead, follow the right fork, which is Laurel Run Road.

0.2 Turn left up the gravel woods road. Follow this road to the cabin, cross the stream on the left to the blue-blazed singletrack trail that begins on the other side (Longberger Path).

0.5 Turn right onto the Spruce Gap singletrack trail. Soon after, keep right at the fork, riding the tight, rocky, and steep-sided singletrack trail.

0.8 Carefully cross three technically challenging bridges; they can be slick, especially when wet.

1.0 Turn left onto Laurel Run Road and climb the hill.

1.8 Take a hard left onto the somewhat obscure Shingletown Trail and climb the rugged singletrack. This trail is found opposite the gated woods road.

2.3 Turn left onto the fire tower access road.

2.9 Reach Little Flat Fire Tower. At the tower turn right, following the rocky singletrack into the woods.

3.1 After passing the Spruce Gap Trail on the left, turn right onto the Laurel Run Trail. Get ready for a rugged and hairy descent with steep drop-offs and loose blocks.

3.9 Turn right onto Laurel Run Road and climb the hill.

4.3 Take a hard right onto the gated fire tower access road.

5.5 Back at the Little Flat Fire Tower, reenter the woods again on the rocky singletrack to the right of the tower. Soon after, turn left onto the Spruce Gap Trail, also known as the "Edge." You'll soon find out how this wicked trail got its nickname.

6.6 Turn left at the T intersection onto the Longberger Path singletrack. From here the trail retraces the route back to the trailhead by crossing the stream, turning right on the gravel road at the cabin, and then right again onto Laurel Run Road.

7.0 Trailhead.

Rattlesnake Mountain

Location:	Black Moshannon State Park, 17 miles southeast of exit 21 on Interstate 80, 9 miles east of Philipsburg.
Distance:	16.3-mile loop.
Time:	2 to 4 hours.
Tread:	Rocky four-wheel-drive road, singletrack, old woods road, fast dirt forest road, and a short sprint on paved highway.
Aerobic level:	Moderate. The ride covers some elevation but it's gained on easy terrain. The singletrack and old woods terrain require you to muscle your way through technical obstacles.
Technical difficulty:	3. Technical challenges vary from rocky drainages, fallen logs, and grassy snowmobile trails to muddy and rutted four-wheel-drive roads. Watch out for snakebites.
Highlights:	Rattlesnake Mountain fire tower, high mountain bog and wetlands, mountain spring, state park amenities, include swimming, camping, shower house, cabin rentals, hiking, concessions boat rentals, and nonpowered boating.
Land status:	Pennsylvania State Parks and State Forest, Department of Conservation and Natural Resources.
Maps:	USGS Black Moshannon; DCNR Bureau of Forestry: Moshannon State Forest map.

Access: From exit 21 on Interstate 80, follow Pennsylvania Highway 53 south to U.S. Highway 322 east to Philipsburg. Once through the town of Philipsburg, turn left onto Pennsylvania Highway 504 east and drive 9 miles to Black Moshannon State Park. After crossing the bridge across the lake, turn left onto Black Moshannon Road, and then turn right into the large beach parking area. This parking lot is the trailhead.

Notes on the trail: Native Americans who roamed through this forest of virgin white pine and hemlock forest named the stream "Moss-hanne," which

Rattlesnake Mountain

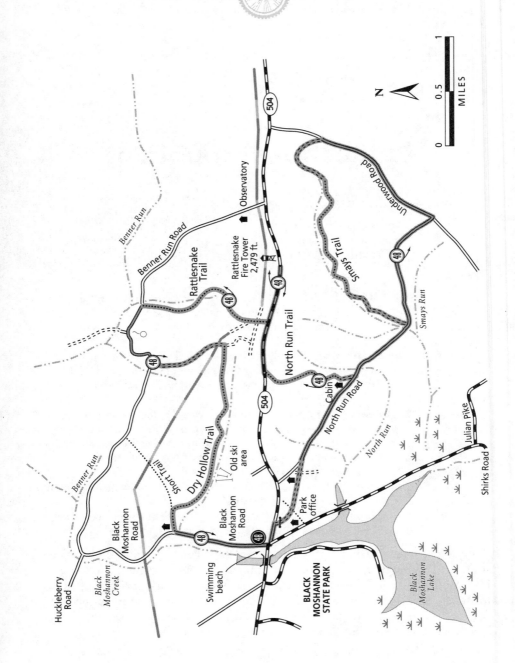

N

MILES

0   0.5   1

504

Observatory

Benner Run

Benner Run Road

Rattlesnake Trail

Rattlesnake Fire Tower 2,479 ft.

48

48

48

North Run Trail

Smays Trail

Underwood Road

48

Smays Run

Cabin

48

North Run Road

North Run

504

Dry Hollow Trail

Short Trail

Old ski area

Benner Run

Black Moshannon Road

Black Moshannon Road

Park office

Julian Pike

Huckleberry Road

Black Moshannon Creek

48

48

Swimming beach

BLACK MOSHANNON STATE PARK

Black Moshannon Lake

Shirks Road

translates as Moose Stream. It was the white pine that brought industry to this quiet woodlands, and at one time over 3 million board feet of logs were stored in the lake, some reaching 6 feet in diameter. Conrad Weiser, who visited the area in 1737, stated, "The woods are so thick, that for a mile at a time we could not find a place the size of a hand, where the sunshine would penetrate, even on the clearest day." Between 1860 and 1920 most of the monolithic white pine and hemlock trees were felled by axe and cross-cut saw. The valuable softwood was used for many things, from ship masts to fine furniture.

The ride begins at the lakeshore and slowly winds its way past a few key side trails to the Smays Run Trail. This old four-wheel-drive road descends off the mountain back to a familiar forest road, where a steep singletrack trail climbs back to the paved road. Cruising out along the paved road, make a mental note of the pipeline side-trail before reaching the ride's high point at the Rattlesnake Fire Tower. The tower sits atop the Allegheny Front mountain range and has views to the south of Bald Eagle Mountain and to the east of Bear Knob. Returning back to the pipeline, the route winds its way down to Benner Run on the Rattlesnake Trail along a seasonal drainage. Keep a sharp eye out—this trail did not receive its name by accident.

A short ride along the forest road takes you past an awesome mountain spring before returning back to the trees on a faint, old woods road. This somewhat rocky trail crosses a pipeline and turns right, following the Dry Hollow Trail. The Dry Hollow Trail braids its way between the banks of this seasonal stream. Along this stretch, you pass an old abandoned ski area on the left. After merging with the Short Trail, the ride chases the Black Moshannon Creek back to the trailhead.

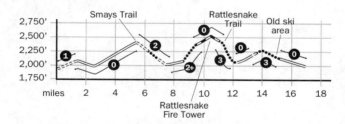

THE RIDE

0.0 From the trailhead lot, ride out to Pennsylvania Highway 504 and turn left. Once on the road immediately turn right onto the gated old woods road.

0.3 Keep right at the fork, staying on the main old woods road. Soon after, cross a four-way intersection and continue straight.

1.0 After passing a cabin, cross a dirt driveway and merge right with North Run Road.

2.0 Pass the North Run Trail (doubletrack road) on the left and make a mental note for later in the ride (mile 8.3).

2.6 Pass the Smays Trail on the left.

Trying not to "get bit," Rattlesnake Mountain.

3.8 Turn left on Underwood Road at the T intersection.

5.2 Turn left on the Smays Trail, a grassy four-wheel drive road.

7.6 Turn right at the T intersection onto North Run Road.

8.3 Turn right onto the North Run Trail, which begins as a dirt doubletrack. The trail will turn to singletrack after passing a cabin on the left, and then you'll begin a steep climb.

9.3 Turn right on Pennsylvania 504.

9.8 Pass a pipeline trail-cut in the clearing on the left and make a mental note for later in the ride (mile 10.9).

10.4 Turn left, and pass around the gate on the dirt road to the Rattlesnake Fire Tower. From here, return back down Pennsylvania 504 to the pipeline trail-cut in the clearing.

10.9 Turn right onto the pipeline trail and cross a four-way intersection. Soon after, keep right at the fork and descend the Rattlesnake Trail.

11.4 The Rattlesnake Trail bends left, following the orange diamond blazes along the rocky drainage.

12.2 Turn left onto Benner Run Road.

12.7 Pass a spring on the left.

13.1 Turn left onto the old woods road at the right-hand bend in the road.

13.6 Cross a four-way intersection with the pipeline and soon after (0.2 mile) turn right onto the Dry Hollow trail marked by the wooden sign. At mile 14.5 the trail passes an old ski area on the left, now abandoned by the park.

15.3 The Dry Hollow Trail merges left with the Short Trail. After passing a cabin, turn left onto Black Moshannon Road.

16.3 Return to the trailhead lot on the left.

Valleys of the Susquehanna

Covering both sides of the beautiful, lower Susquehanna River, these rides take you through the Michaux, Tuscarora and Buchanan State Forests, state game lands, and state and county parks. The rocky and rugged Michaux State Forest where rough trail and steep terrain abound is a haven for hammerheads. The York County parks offer a variety of trail from the mild to the wild, with some spectacular views of the countryside. The Buchanan and Tuscarora State forests shelter some hidden gems tucked in the folds of their sandstone mountains. Riding the second highest ridable point, Blue Knob is a must for adrenaline junkies and those who derive pleasure from pain.

Deep Hollow

Location:	Blue Knob State Park, 20 miles north of Bedford.
Distance:	9.8-mile loop.
Time:	2 to 4 hours.
Tread:	A rugged mountain mix of technical, rocky singletrack, smooth dirt, and gravel doubletrack with some paved sections.
Aerobic level:	Strenuous. With the highest vertical gain (1,635 feet) in Pennsylvania, the ride scales the mountain direct from the valley floor with few breaks in the sustained climb. Once near the top, a technical singletrack draws your last bit of energy as the ride finally tops out on the summit of Pennsylvania's second highest peak. The descent requires a lot of physical and mental stamina to remain in control through the varied terrain and heinous pull of gravity. This is the beast of the east!
Technical difficulty:	3+. The ride follows a mountaintop technical trail with capstone blocks that present a burly challenge, especially after slogging up 1,400 feet. The descent presents its greatest challenge as gravity draws you

through loose sections of talus and log strewn singletrack. A cool head and sharp reflexes are critical to keep the rubber side down.

Highlights: Second highest point and highest vertical climb (1,635 vertical feet) in Pennsylvania, rugged mountain trails, spectacular scenery, high mountain vistas, stellar jumps, gnarly singletrack, technical rock-hopping, woodland "ghost town," and state park amenities that include swimming pool, campground, interpretive nature trail, hiking trails, trout fishing on Bobs Creek.

Land status: Pennsylvania State Parks, Department of Conservation and Natural Resources.

Maps: USGS Blue Knob; DCNR Pennsylvania State Parks: Blue Knob State Park map.

Access: From the Pennsylvania Turnpike (Interstate 76), exit at Bedford (exit 11). Take U.S. Highway 220 north to Pennsylvania Highway 869 at the town of Osterburg. Head west for about 6 miles on Pennsylvania 869 to Pavia. At Pavia, follow the signs to Blue Knob State Park. Immediately after entering the park, turn right to park your vehicle at the park office. This small park office lot is the trailhead.

Notes on the trail: This is one of those rides that breaks a heart monitor. It's the ultimate vertical challenge in the state and climbs to the very top of the second highest point in the state. Due to the steep rise and topography, the average temperatures on the mountain are a bit cooler than in the low-lying valleys. The quartzite-capped mountain is situated on the very edge of the Allegheny Front, where it offers commanding views of the shorter Ridge and Valley formations to the east. Only 41 feet shorter that the highest point in Pennsylvania, it is quite a formidable challenge, comparable to that of Mount Davis, Pennsylvania's highest point at 3,213 feet.

Beginning at the park office, the ride follows Whysong Road as it winds and switchbacks up 800 feet to the Willow Springs picnic area. Ducking into the woods, the route embarks on another short but arduous ascent to a less steep, grassy, old woods road. If the sheer pull of gravity hasn't torn you from the mountain, then the technical singletrack section out across to the vista will surely finish you off. A bit more climbing leads to the summit, where a brief celebration may be in order.

Now comes the kind stuff. Although you may have been cursing gravity on the way up, the laws of physics are now in your favor. Some of the finest downhill singletrack lies hidden before you in the forested face below; keep it together on the descent—a mistake here could end in a visit to the hospital. Rolling, technical trail weaves down the south face past the "ghost town" and exits just above the trailhead. Enjoy the ride; it's one of Pennsylvania's finest!

Deep Hollow

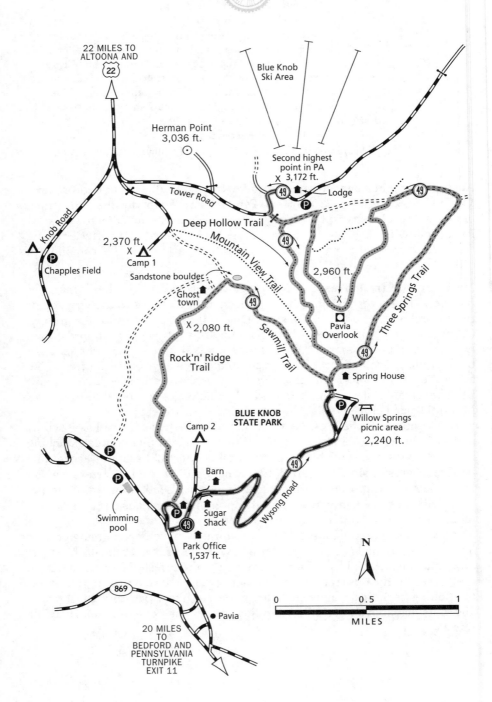

22 MILES TO
ALTOONA AND
22

Blue Knob
Ski Area

Herman Point
3,036 ft.

Second highest
point in PA
X 3,172 ft.

Tower Road

Lodge
49
P

Knob Road

Deep Hollow Trail

Mountain View Trail

49

2,370 ft.
X
Camp 1

P
Chapples Field

Sandstone boulder

Ghost
town

2,960 ft.

X

49

X 2,080 ft.

Pavia
Overlook

Three Springs Trail

Sawmill Trail

49

Rock'n' Ridge
Trail

Spring House

BLUE KNOB
STATE PARK

P

Willow Springs
picnic area
2,240 ft.

Camp 2

49

Barn

Swimming
pool

P

P

P
49

Sugar
Shack

Wysong Road

N

Park Office
1,537 ft.

869

Pavia

0   0.5   1

MILES

20 MILES
TO
BEDFORD AND
PENNSYLVANIA
TURNPIKE
EXIT 11

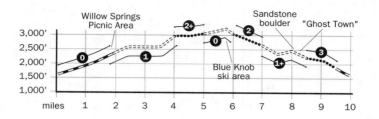

THE RIDE

0.0 From the park office lot, climb Whysong Road to the Willow Springs picnic area. Keep right at the road fork, cross the metal grate bridge, and passed the "Sugar Shack" on the right.

1.6 Keep left at the fork of the paved road and pass the "Do not enter" sign.

1.9 As the paved road bends right, turn left off the paved road onto the dirt road marked by the large, white posts stating "Three Springs and Sawmill Trails."

2.1 After passing around the gate, turn right on the Three Springs trail, climbing the steep, loose, washed out woods road.

2.3 Pass the Mountain View Trail on the left and a spring house on the right.

3.4 The trail bends left; stay on the gravel doubletrack.

3.9 Turn left onto the double-blazed red slash singletrack trail marked by a small wooden sign stating "Lookouts." This is a rugged part of the Mountain View Trail.

4.1 Turn left at the trail spur, continuing to follow the double red blazes. Note: *This turn is extremely easy to miss due to the technical riding prior to the turn.*

4.6 Pass the beautiful Pavia Overlook at an elevation of 2,960 feet.

4.9 Pass the blue-blazed Connector Trail.

5.1 Turn left onto the doubletrack gravel road.

5.4 Pass around the gate and turn right onto Tower Road.

5.6 Turn left just before the summit lodge of Blue Knob ski area. Ride through the employee parking area and out to the chairlifts atop the summit knob. Note the sign stating "The highest skiable point in Pennsylvania at an elevation of 3,172." Return back to the gate at mile 5.4.

6.0 After passing around the gate and riding 0.1 mile, turn right into a small grassy clearing. Immediately after, turn left onto the Deep Hollow Trail, which is marked by a small wooden sign. Get ready to hang it out as you descend 700 feet in a mere 0.7 mile on killer bermed singletrack. Watch for the sleepers on the other side of the numerous jumps.

6.7 Turn left onto the Mountain View Trail at the T intersection.

7.0 Turn right at the T intersection onto the Three Springs Trail, and bomb the dirt doubletrack. The gravitational force is a bit strong here and that's a good thing.

7.3 Turn right at the T intersection onto the Sawmill Trail.

8.1 Turn left on the spur trail at the massive sandstone boulder (Rock'n Ridge Trail).

8.2 Pass the ghost town of cabins and a right-hand spur trail. Follow the blue blazes.

9.6 Turn right on the paved road.

9.8 Turn left at the T intersection, and pass the gate to the trailhead.

Blue Knob

Location:	Blue Knob State Park, 20 miles north of Bedford.
Distance:	9.3-mile loop.
Time:	2 to 3 hours.
Tread:	Grassy woods road, old woods road, hardpacked and rocky singletrack, dirt doubletrack.
Aerobic level:	Moderate. As the trail traverses across the south face, it climbs the steep but stepped southeast shoulder. Technical riding below the summit will demand power, as will the awesome descent off the mountain.
Technical difficulty:	3. Sandstone and quartzite rock sections abound but speed and finesse will help pull you through. There are wet and moss-covered rock areas, which are quite slippery. The singletrack descent on Deep Hollow Trail is slightly off-camber and varies from talus-covered to hardpacked sections.
Highlights:	Second highest point in Pennsylvania (3,172 feet), rugged mountain trails, spectacular scenery, high mountain vistas, state park amenities that include swimming pool, campground, interpretive nature trail, hiking trails, trout fishing on Bobs Creek.
Land status:	Pennsylvania State Parks, Department of Conservation and Natural Resources.
Maps:	USGS Blue Knob; DCNR Pennsylvania State Parks, Blue Knob State Park map.

Access: From the Pennsylvania Turnpike (Interstate 76), take exit 11 at Bedford. Follow U.S. Highway 220 north to Pennsylvania Highway 869 at the town of Osterburg. Head west for about 6 miles on Pennsylvania 869 to Pavia. At Pavia, follow the signs to Blue Knob State Park. Climb the paved road 2.5 miles up through the park, pass the park office on the right, and park in the Chappel Fields grass parking area on the right. This trailhead lot is opposite the paved entrance to the campground.

Notes on the trail: This is a truly rugged ride on the second highest rideable and geologic point in Pennsylvania. Blue Knob State Park, which stretches in elevation from 1,537 feet at the valley floor to 3,172 feet at the summit of the ski area, is one of the very few state parks that you can ride in. You'll find a campground, swimming pool, trout stream, and some of the better riding in the southwestern part of the state.

Blue Knob

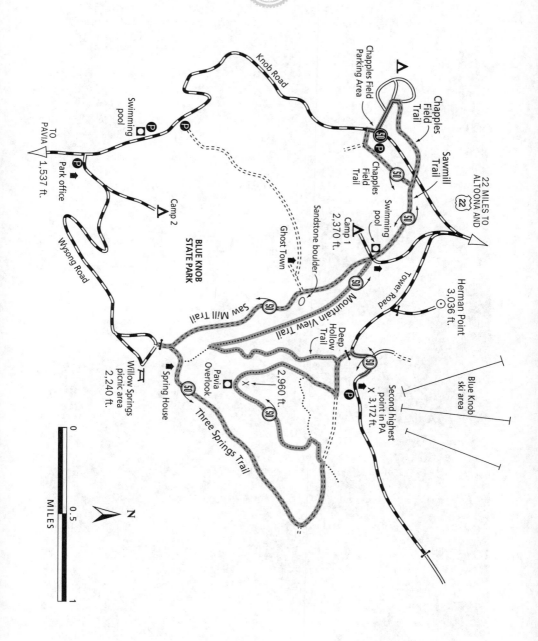

Foolin' the brain into thinking the fall-line is your friend, Blue Knob.

The ride begins at the Chappel Fields parking area, adjacent to the campground entrance road, and traverses the south face on old woods road. At the southeast shoulder, a sharp rise leads toward the summit. Along the way a beautiful singletrack diversion leads out to a spectacular overlook to the neighboring peaks and the valleys below. On the summit you are rewarded with more views looking north. The return trip is just as exciting, as you descend a killer singletrack trail and traverse back across the mountain on a technical, rocky, old woods road. The final section is a short loop out and around the campground that finishes at the trailhead.

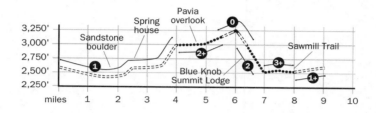

THE RIDE

0.0 From the Chapples Field parking area sign, turn left on Knob Road. After 0.1 mile, turn left at a cluster of trees onto the Chapples Field Trail. This trail is marked by a large, white, wooden post stating the trail name. After descending the short downhill, turn left at the T intersection.

0.5 The trail exits the woods near Knob Road. Keep along the right side of the woods, then reenter the woods on the Sawmill Trail, marked by another white post.

1.0 Cross over a paved road and continue straight on the Sawmill Trail. Note the Mountain View Trail to the left and the swimming pool down on the right.

1.5 Pass the massive sandstone boulder on the left and a right-hand spur trail.

2.3 Turn left at the Three Springs Trail and ascend the steep, washed-out hill. As the hill mellows out, you'll pass the Mountain View Trail on the left and a wooden spring house.

3.6 The trail bends left, continuing to climb on the grass and gravel woods road.

4.1 Turn left onto the singletrack that climbs the bank. The trail is marked by a small wooden sign that reads "Lookouts" and is blazed with double red slashes. This is another section of the Mountain View Trail. Shortly after (0.2 mile), turn left at the obscure fork, staying on the double red blazed trail. It's really easy to miss this turn!

4.8 Check out the grand view atop the Pavia Overlook at an elevation of 2,560 feet.

5.3 Turn left onto the gravel doubletrack road.

5.6 After passing around a gate, turn right onto Tower Road.

5.9 Ride up toward the summit lodge, turn left into the employee parking lot, and ride out to the summit knob at the convergence of chairlifts. Check out the sign stating "Highest skiable point in Pennsylvania, 3,172 feet." Return back to the gate at mile 5.6.

6.2 Soon after passing around the gate, turn right into a small, grassy clearing. Then turn left onto the obscure but marked Deep Hollow Trail. Watch out for 'sleepers' on the other sides of the numerous berm jumps.

6.9 After the great descent, turn hard right at the T intersection onto the rocky Mountain View Trail.

8.0 Cross the paved road and continue on the dirt doubletrack Saw Mill Trail.

8.5 Cross over Knob Road and resume riding on the wide, grassy Chapples Field Trail, marked by another wooden post.

9.1 Turn left onto the gravel road at the campground and keep left as the road turns to pavement.

9.3 Exit the campground and cross Knob Road to the trailhead.

Pigeon Hills

Location: Shawnee State Park, 8 miles west of Bedford.

Distance: 7.2-mile loop.

Time: 1 to 2 hours.

Tread: An even amount of dirt singletrack, dirt doubletrack, and grassy woods roads.

Aerobic level: Moderate. Undulating terrain is in your face every pedal stroke of the way with short, steep climbs and rippin' downhills. The climbs keep you shifting gears and the downhills never seem to give you quite enough recovery time.

Technical difficulty: 1 +. Typical spots of loose gravel and a few roots are interspersed throughout the ride. The steep nature of the short hills will require additional technical skill on both the ascent and descent. Staying tight in the saddle will prevent spinning out and help you clean the steep climbs. Sending a good line on the downhills will keep you from logging frequent-flier miles and add to the momentum to climb the next rise.

Highlights: Classic roller-coaster style ride, state park amenities that include swimming beach, bike and boat rental, hiking trails, food concessions, camping, fishing, and great wildlife viewing opportunities.

Land status: Pennsylvania State Parks, Department of Conservation and Natural Resources.

Maps: USGS Bedford, Schellsburg; DCNR Pennsylvania State Parks, Shawnee State Park map.

Access: From the Pennsylvania Turnpike, take exit 11 at Bedford. Follow U.S. Highway 30 west for approximately 6.5 miles. Turn left into Shawnee State Park, marked by the large wooden sign. Turn right at the T intersection and follow the paved park road around to the first parking area on the left. Turn left into this parking area, which is the trailhead. (If while traveling on US 30 you arrive at the town of Schellsburg, you have missed the park entrance by 1 mile.)

Notes on the trail: The Pigeon Hills highlight this ride, which is in beautiful Shawnee State Park. The park offers many amenities and is an awesome location for mountain biking. Swimming, food, and a spot to camp are all a rider needs to enjoy an outstanding weekend in the woods. Better yet, the park rents bikes and boats for those who do not have their own. The lake has some of the finest warm-water fishing around, and there are a few trails open to foot travel only worth exploring. The unique topography of this hilly location presents a great challenge to the novice rider. Woodlands, fields, and wetlands abound with wildlife, although I can't recall seeing any pigeons!

The ride begins with a short, stout climb up the Field Trail, which mellows out as it passes through a field into wooded forest. A great downhill follows as the ride crosses the paved park entrance road and climbs again, paralleling U.S. Highway 30. A wicked but fun drop leads to the Pigeon Hills Trail where the roller-coaster of climbs and descents begin. The final stretch of off-road bliss is a rocky, old woods road that switchbacks down to the lake and passes the sewage treatment plant and dam. As you head back to the trailhead on the scenic Lake Shore Trail, keep a keen eye out for wildlife along the water's edge.

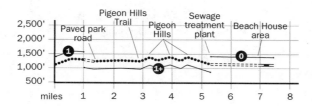

THE RIDE

0.0 From the lot, head out the entrance. Directly across from the entrance is a wide, grassy trail that climbs the hill. You'll see the sign for the Field Trail—begin here.

0.5 Continue straight at the three-way intersection, following the marked Field Trail into the woods.

1.2 Turn right at the fork and descend some sweet downhill. At the bottom of the hill, cross diagonally left, over the paved road, and continue on the marked Field Trail.

Pigeon Hills

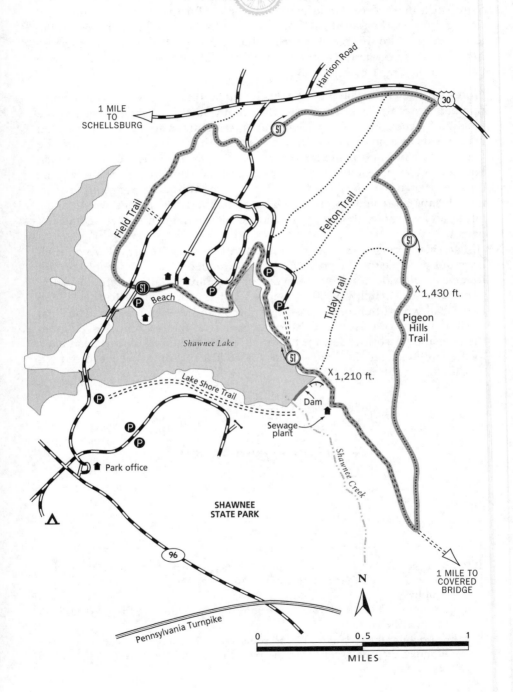

Harrison Road

1 MILE
TO
SCHELLSBURG

30

51

Field Trail

Felton Trail

Tidy Trail

51

X 1,430 ft.

Pigeon
Hills
Trail

Beach

Shawnee Lake

51

X 1,210 ft.

Lake Shore Trail

Dam

Sewage
plant

Park office

Shawnee Creek

SHAWNEE
STATE PARK

96

1 MILE TO
COVERED
BRIDGE

N

Pennsylvania Turnpike

0   0.5   1

MILES

2.1 The trail passes close to U.S. Highway 30 and passes the Felton Trail on the right. Continue straight on the Field Trail.

2.8 Keep left at the fork, climbing the Pigeon Hills Trail.

4.6 The trail switchbacks hard right and continues to descend on loose stone.

5.3 The dirt trail turns to gravel as it passes a sewage treatment plant on the left.

5.6 Turn left at the fork onto the marked, cinder Lake Shore Trail.

6.9 The cinder path changes to paved road as the trail passes the lower beach. Keep left at the road fork soon to come.

7.2 Return to the trailhead.

Hidden Tunnel Trail

Location:	Buchanan State Forest, 8 miles northeast of Breezewood.
Distance:	9.7-mile loop.
Time:	1 to 3 hours.
Tread:	The ride is mostly wide singletrack and ATV-style trails. The tread surface varies from grassy to rocky. A small section of fire road and some asphalt climbing are mixed in and break up the rugged sections of the ride.
Aerobic level:	Moderate. The initial climb up the west face of Sideling Hill is quite demanding but relatively short in length. The traverse out along Sciotha Trail is a bit more challenging. A final, short climb will land you on Summit Road, and from there the rest is a downhill scream.
Technical difficulty:	3. The initial climb covers sections of loose, rocky terrain and the Sciotha Trail traverse is somewhat rugged in many places. The descent route down the Prop Trail has some bike-launching rocks mixed in with sections of loose, sandy soils. The rest of the ride follows easier terrain on more mellow ground.
Highlights:	Historic sandstone aqueduct, abandoned Sideling Hill Pennsylvania Turnpike Tunnel, incredible woods trail riding, kamikaze descent.
Land status:	Pennsylvania State Forest, Department of Conservation and Natural Resources.
Maps:	USGS Wells Tannery, Hustontown; DCNR Bureau of Forestry: Buchanan State Forest map.

Hidden Tunnel Trail

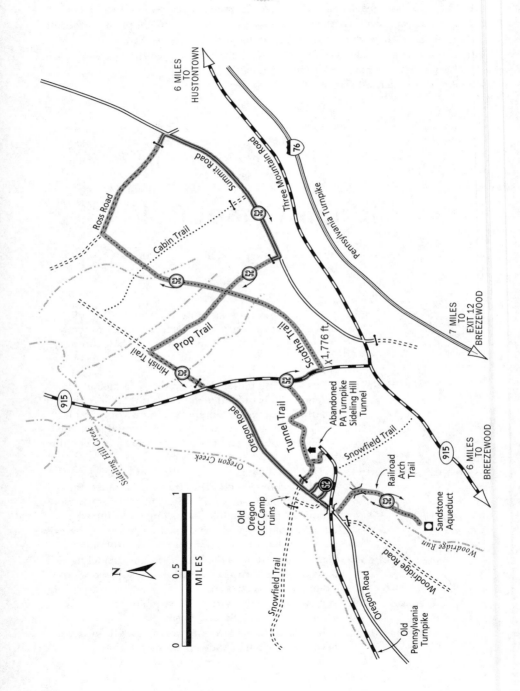

6 MILES TO HUSTONTOWN

Three Mountain Road

76

Pennsylvania Turnpike

7 MILES TO EXIT 12 BREEZEWOOD

Ross Road

Summit Road

Cabin Trail

Prop Trail

Hinish Trail

Sciotha Trail

X 1,776 ft

915

Sideling Hill Creek

Oregon Creek

Oregon Road

Tunnel Trail

Abandoned PA Turnpike Sideling Hill Tunnel

Snowfield Trail

Railroad Arch Trail

915

6 MILES TO BREEZEWOOD

Old Oregon CCC Camp ruins

Sandstone Aqueduct

Woodridge Run

Woodridge Road

Snowfield Trail

Oregon Road

Old Pennsylvania Turnpike

N

MILES

0   0.5   1

Access: From the Breezewood exit of the Pennsylvania Turnpike, take U.S. Highway 30 east for 4 miles to Pennsylvania Highway 915. Turn left onto Pennsylvania 915 and head northwest for 2 miles; then head left again at a left-hand intersection. Follow Pennsylvania 915 for another mile as it descends the hill. Then take the first left turn onto Oregon Road (dirt Forest Service road). Travel another mile and park at the old cabin on the left marked by the large wooden sign saying the "CCC Oregon Camp." This is the trailhead.

Notes on the trail: The ride derives its name from the two tunnels discovered along the route that are both now abandoned. The route first takes you to the sandstone aqueduct built in 1904 by several hundred skilled Italian stone masons, who carved the native sandstone blocks. This 180-foot tunnel was to serve as an aqueduct for Woodridge Run. The old railroad grade on the huge berm to the south was supposed to span Woodridge Run, hence the aqueduct. The ride then takes you to the second tunnel, which is a massive cavern that was originally cut in the early 1900s by the South Penn Railroad and later used by the Pennsylvania Turnpike Commission. It now lies dormant, as does the ribbon of buckled asphalt that wanders from its dank opening.

After a bit of backtracking, you climb the southwest face of Sideling Hill on an ATV-style trail. A short climb on the paved (Pennsylvania Highway 915) road leads to the exciting and challenging traverse of the Sciotha Trail. Rolling and rugged in nature, this beautifully maintained network of trails includes some of the finest in the state. Once you reach Prop Trail, get ready

The cold house ruins along the Hidden Tunnel Trail.

The ancient sandstone aqueduct in the Woodridge Hollow, Hidden Tunnel Trail.

for a bomber, kamikaze descent and big air as the trail unleashes off the ridge. Watch for loose soil and rock in the turns as this trail can be quite hairy at speed!

The final run is out across the sandy Hinish Trail. Crossing Pennsylvania Highway 915 onto Oregon Road should look familiar as the ride rolls gently back to the trailhead. You'll see many stone structures and ruins at the old Civilian Conservation Corps site. Foundations, chimneys, and a cold house provide reminders of the men and boys who worked in the forest during the Great Depression.

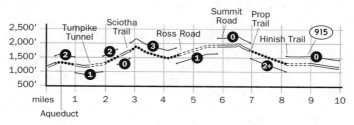

THE RIDE

0.0 From the Oregon Camp, turn left onto Oregon Road.

0.4 After passing under the old Pennsylvania Turnpike concrete bridge, turn left onto the Railroad Arch Trail marked by the wooden sign.

0.7 Arrive at the unique, sandstone aqueduct built in 1904. Note the huge earthen mound on the left. This was supposed to support the old railroad grade that never spanned the Woodridge Run. Return from here to the Oregon Camp trailhead.

1.4 Once at the Oregon Camp, ride 50 yards and turn right onto the gated, gravel road on the right, just past the cabin. Ride through the field and pass another gate. Note an old green building on the left.

1.7 Come out to the old Pennsylvania Turnpike and stare down into the ominous mouth of the Sideling Hill Tunnel. Return back to the gate and turn right onto an obscure old woods road (mile 1.9). This trail will bend right before turning left at the old highway wire fence and climbing Sideling Hill.

2.5 Turn right onto Pennsylvania Highway 915.

2.8 Turn left onto Sciotha Trail, marked by the wooden sign.

3.4 Cross the four-way intersection with the Prop Trail.

4.1 Cross the four-way intersection with the Cabin Trail.

4.7 Turn right onto Ross Road, a grassy, old woods road, and begin to climb.

5.6 Turn right onto Summit Road after passing around a gate.

6.5 Pass the Cabin Trail on the right.

7.0 Turn right onto the Prop Trail, passing around an old wooden gate. Get ready for a mile-long bomber descent!

7.6 Pass the four-way intersection with Sciotha Trail.

8.2 Turn left onto the Hinish Trail, which is a dirt fire road.

8.7 Cross Pennsylvania 915 and continue on Oregon Road.

9.7 Back at the Oregon Camp trailhead.

Roaring Run

Location:	Buchanan State Forest, 5 miles east of Breezewood.
Distance:	12.4-mile loop.
Time:	2 to 4 hours.
Tread:	A combination of beautiful, grassy woods road and rugged singletrack trail comprise the majority of the ride. Small sections of fire road play a vital role in linking singletrack sections to complete the ride.
Aerobic level:	Moderate to strenuous. After the initial 1200-foot vertical descent into the valley, the trail becomes more challenging. The first short climb leads to the Peck Trail descent. Once across Roaring Run, the ride then gains the summit ridge with 900 vertical feet of climbing 2.5 miles.
Technical difficulty:	3 +. From the summit, the trail progressively becomes more difficult as it changes from wide, grassy road to tight, rocky, rhododendron-choked singletrack. The route ascends the ridge on a bumpy four-wheel-drive road only to plummet back down the rugged Peck Trail. The final slog follows mild old woods road.
Highlights:	Beautifully remote mountain drainage trail, towering rhododendron and hemlocks, numerous springs, impressive vistas, classic technical mountain riding, Sideling Hill Fire Tower, tons of side trails to explore.
Land status:	Pennsylvania State Forest, Department of Conservation and Natural Resources.
Maps:	USGS Breezewood, Wells Tannery; DCNR Bureau of Forestry: Buchanan State Forest map.

Access: From the Breezewood exit of the Pennsylvania Turnpike, take U.S. Highway 30 east for 4 miles to Pennsylvania Highway 915. Pass the intersection with Pennsylvania 915 and travel for another 0.5 miles to the Sideling Hill picnic area, located on the right side of the road. Park in the picnic area, which is the trailhead.

Notes on the trail: "Classic" is an understatement in describing this ride. From the Sideling Hill picnic area, you embark on a tenacious descent down into the depths of Roaring Run drainage. A visit to the Cliff Trail Vista is a short side trip that is worthy of a photo or two. The view east over the farms and fields of Allens Valley is quite impressive. The trail progress from mellow to maddening as the wide grassy woods road tapers down into the lush, damp, dark hollow on rocky singletrack. Towering rhododendrons encase the trail and stout stands of hemlock penetrate the thick shrub layer. The sounds of the cascading creek fill the air as small birds dart in and out of the evergreen tunnel.

After the ride bellies out near the valley bottom, you'll ascend a four-wheel-drive road that weaves up the east face of the ridge. The Peck Trail awaits with a beautifully rugged descent down tight, woodland singletrack. At the base of the descent, the trail fords Roaring Run. Due to fluctuations in water levels this can be a cold, wet encounter, so plan accordingly. The ford isn't necessarily dangerous or deep, just fast and cold.

The final leg climbs the spine on the Bald Hill Trail, a somewhat arduous grind up 900 feet to the summit in a mere 2.5 miles. A low gear will pull you through this section and land you on the summit. From here, enjoy the southerly vista at the base of the Sideling Hill Fire Tower. A short cruise on flat terrain will finish the ride at the Sideling Hill picnic area trailhead.

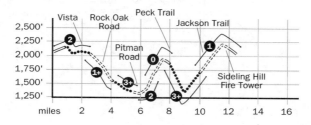

THE RIDE

0.0 From the picnic area, ride east to Bark Road and turn right.

0.6 Keep right at the fork, following the sign for the fire tower.

0.8 You have now arrived at the Sideling Hill Fire Tower at an elevation of 2,310 feet. From the tower turn left onto the Cliff Trail.

1.1 Turn right at the T intersection onto the old woods road. Soon after, keep left at the fork, staying on the Cliff Trail. Note the three signs marked "Roaring Run," "Sideling Hill Loop" and "Cliff Trail;" you will be returning back to this intersection shortly.

1.9 After crossing Bark Road, ride for 150 yards to the impressive vista at the end of Cliff Trail. You can see now how the trail got its name—be careful above the broken cliff bands. Return back down Cliff Trail to the forked intersection.

2.5 Turn left at the fork and descend on the Roaring Run Trail. You should notice the faint light blue blazes on the trees as the trail descends the mountain.

3.7 Turn right at the fork with Rock Oak Road (old woods road), continuing on the Roaring Run Trail. Soon after, pass the Deer Hill Trail at a four-way intersection.

4.3 Pass the Jackson Trail on the left. At the small clearing, keep right at the fork, following the faint blue blazes. Soon after, the Jackson Trail splits off right (mile 4.5).

4.8 Ford Roaring Run.

5.2 Ford Roaring Run and soon after cross over the Peck Trail.

5.8 Turn left at the T intersection onto Roaring Run Road (an old woods road).

Roaring Run

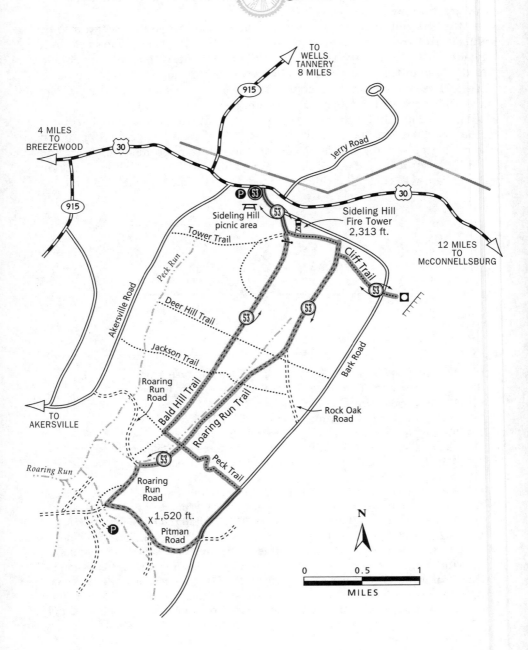

TO
WELLS
TANNERY
8 MILES

915

4 MILES
TO
BREEZEWOOD

30

915

P 53

Sideling Hill
picnic area

53

Sideling Hill
Fire Tower
2,313 ft.

Jerry Road

30

12 MILES
TO
McCONNELLSBURG

Tower Trail

Cliff Trail

53

Peck Run

Akersville Road

Deer Hill Trail

53

53

Jackson Trail

Bark Road

Roaring
Run
Road

Bald Hill Trail

Roaring Run Trail

Rock Oak
Road

TO
AKERSVILLE

53

Peck Trail

Roaring Run

Roaring
Run
Road

X 1,520 ft.

Pitman
Road

N

0   0.5   1

MILES

The serene beauty along Roaring Run.

6.3 Keep left at an indistinct fork and immediately after, turn hard left onto Pitman Road (four-wheel-drive road) and begin to climb.

6.9 Keep left at the fork, staying on the main four-wheel drive road.

7.5 After the tough climb, turn left onto Bark Road.

8.1 Turn left onto the Peck Trail and get ready for a killer descent.

9.0 Cross the Roaring Run Trail and ford Roaring Run. The trail, although obscure, ascends directly up the hill and becomes very apparent at the crest of the ridge.

9.3 Turn right at the four-way intersection onto the rocky Bald Hill Trail.

10.1 Cross the Jackson Trail as the rocky trail becomes a wide, grassy woods road.

10.4 Cross the Deer Hill Trail.

11.6 Pass around a gate, ride past the Sideling Hill Fire Tower and out to Bark Road. Soon merge left with Bark Road (mile 11.8).

12.4 Turn left into the Sideling Hill picnic area trailhead.

Big Springs To Bear Pond

Location:	Big Springs State Park, 14 miles northeast of Willow Hill.
Distance:	19.4-mile loop.
Time:	3 to 6 hours.
Tread:	A true mountain bike mix covering singletrack, doubletrack, and fire roads.
Aerobic level:	Strenuous. The route covers over 2,500 vertical feet and runs from deep valley to the high ridge top. When you thought the tuff stuff was behind you, a grueling grind across the rocky, rail-grade trail ends at the trailhead.
Technical difficulty:	3 +. There are gnarly sections of loose, grapefruit-sized rocks on steep drops. The final 3-mile leg along the Big Springs Run may prove to be the most challenging, due to a continuous stretch of burly rocks. You can avoid this section, however.
Highlights:	Tuscarora sandstone technical sections, the historical Path Valley railroad tunnel, restrooms and beautifully wooded picnic area, classic ridge and valley riding.
Land status:	Pennsylvania State Forest, Department of Conservation and Natural Resources.
Maps:	USGS Blairs Mill, Blain, Doylesburg, Newburg; DCNR Bureau of Forestry: Tuscarora State Forest map.

Access: From exit 14 of the Pennsylvania Turnpike, take Pennsylvania Highway 75 northeast to Doylesburg (approximately 9 miles). After passing through Doylesburg, turn right onto Pennsylvania 274, following it northeast for 4 miles over the Rising Mountains. As the road descends to the valley floor, look for the large wooden sign for Big Springs State Park on the right. Turn right onto Hemlock Road (dirt Forest Service road) just before the Big Springs State Park picnic area and park in the lot on the left, 100 yards down Hemlock Road. This parking area is the trailhead.

Notes on the trail: The unique natural and man-made features found along the route combined with the outstanding riding terrain make this ride truly stellar. Beginning in the valley at Big Springs State Park, the ride runs out on incredible singletrack trail to the old Path Valley railroad tunnel. This classic example of old-school tunneling stands as a reminder of the hard work and labor involved in running railroads through the Pennsylvania moun-

Big Springs To Bear Pond

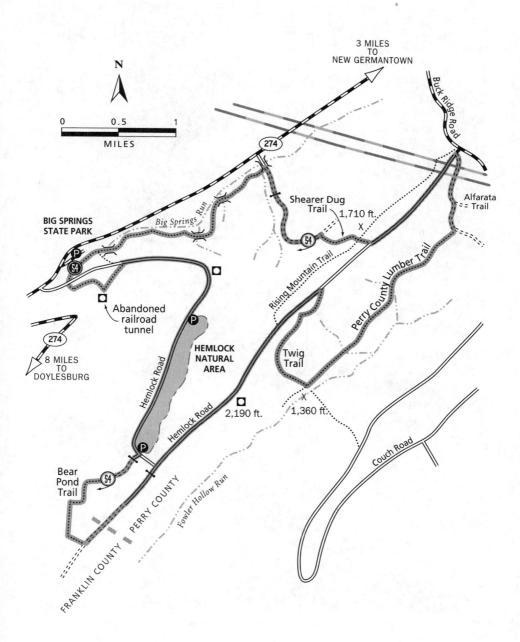

N

0   0.5   1
MILES

3 MILES
TO
NEW GERMANTOWN

Buck Ridge Road

274

BIG SPRINGS
STATE PARK

Big Springs Run

Shearer Dug
Trail   1,710 ft.
X

Alfarata
Trail

54

P

54

Abandoned
railroad
tunnel

Rising Mountain Trail

Perry County Lumber Trail

P

HEMLOCK
NATURAL
AREA

Twig
Trail

274

8 MILES
TO
DOYLESBURG

Hemlock Road

Hemlock Road

2,190 ft.

X
1,360 ft.

Couch Road

P

54

Bear
Pond
Trail

PERRY COUNTY

Fowler Hollow Run

FRANKLIN COUNTY

The old, raised Path Valley Railroad Grade on the Big Springs to Bear Pond Trail.

tains. The unfinished tunnel is not that deep, about 300 feet, and the roof is somewhat unstable, so please stay behind the wooden fence.

As the trail exits onto Hemlock Road, the arduous climb begins with 3.5 miles of well-groomed fire road that climb along the impressive Hemlocks Natural Area. This narrow tract of upper mountain valley contains virgin and first-growth stands of our state tree. The top of Bear Pond Trail is a great finish to the climb as the route runs up the spine of the ridge. The Twig Trail awaits with some sketchy, loose singletrack down onto the old Perry Lumber Company Trail. At one time narrow-gauge trains raged through this valley, hauling tons of lumber taken from the surrounding hillsides. What remains is a sweet doubletrack trail worthy of the most discriminating rider.

The ride continues on up to the ridge again before dropping off the north face on the Shearer Dug Trail. A short section of steep, gnarly singletrack runs out into smooth, doubletrack logging road. The final leg is a tough 3 miles of rocky, arm-pumping, kidney-jarring trail that runs along Big Spring Run. If the old rail grade doesn't rupture your bladder, it'll definitely realign your spine. An option out of this section is to ride the road back from the descent. To do this, continue straight at mile 16.4 and then turn left onto the paved road, which leads back to the Big Springs State Park trailhead. The mileage is approximately the same on either route.

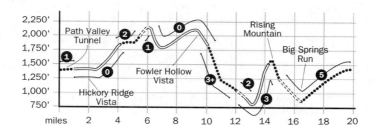

THE RIDE

0.0 From the trailhead lot, cross straight over Hemlock Road and begin on the Tunnel Trail, marked by the wooden sign.

0.5 The trail passes the old railroad tunnel. Take a minute to check out this rough-hewn feature in the mountain that was obviously abandoned not far into the project. Continue on the trail, which follows faint blue blazes.

0.7 Turn right onto Hemlock Road and begin the climb.

1.9 Pass the Hickory Ridge Vista.

2.6 Pass the beginning of the Hemlocks Natural Area, marked by the large trail sign on the left. As you ascend the road, peer down into this lush and beautiful stand of virgin hemlock trees that shades the climb from the sun on a hot day.

4.3 Opposite a small parking area marked by the large Hemlocks Natural Area sign, turn right onto the Bear Pond Trail, marked by the wooden sign.

5.4 Turn left onto the dirt fire road.

6.2 Pass the Perry/Franklin county line marker on the right.

6.8 Pass around a gate and turn right onto Hemlock Road.

9.6 Pass the Fowler Hollow Vista on the right.

10.0 At a huge wooden sign saying the "Amberson Ridge Limited Access Buck Hunting Area," turn right onto the Twig Trail, also marked by a wooden sign.

10.8 Turn left at the four-way intersection onto the Perry Lumber Company trail. This section of trail follows orange triangle blazes.

11.7 Turn left onto the fire road.

12.9 Merge left onto another fire road (the Alfarata Trail). Note the Perry Lumber Company wooden trail sign at this intersection.

13.2 Turn left at the T intersection onto Hemlock Road. Note the pipeline cut in front of the intersection and another sign for the "Amberson Ridge Limited Access Buck Hunting Area."

14.5 Turn right onto the Shearer-Dug Trail. Take this short bike-hike up to the crest of the ridge, where the trail soon crosses over the Rising Mountain Trail and descends.

15.3 Turn left at the T intersection onto the old woods road, following the rocky descent.

16.4 After passing around a gate, turn left onto the trail marked by the brown hiker sign. This left turn is just before the small, concrete bridge over Big Springs Run. Follow the orange blazes along Big Springs Run. To bail on the heinous miles of rock that lie ahead, continue straight to Pennsylvania Highway exit 274 and turn left. Follow Pennsylvania 274 to Big Springs State Park.

18.9 Cross over a wooden footbridge and pass a left-hand trail spur. Note the small wooden sign saying the end of the railroad grade.

19.1 Pass a stone pavilion on your right and continue to follow the orange and blue blazes on the trees.

19.4 After passing a unique, rock-lined walkway at a four-way intersection, you arrive at the trailhead.

Grave Ridge to Rocky Pass

Location: Michaux State Forest, 20 miles south of Carlisle, adjacent to Pine Grove Furnace State Park.

Distance: 18.1-mile loop.

Time: 2 to 4 hours.

Tread: The entire ride follows the Michaux State Forest ATV trail system. The trails are a combination of a smooth dirt fire road and extremely rugged ATV doubletrack.

Aerobic level: Strenuous. The route drops in and out of two separate ridge systems with steep, loose climbing. The flats are littered with rocks of all sizes, requiring you to constantly pedal through burly technical sections. Even the downhills take their toll as you death-grip the bars and brakes for dear life.

Technical difficulty: 5. Rocks of all sizes cover almost the entire ride; many are loose and hard-edged.

Highlights: The most technical ride in Pennsylvania, the infamous Grave Ridge Trail; beautiful hemlock and laurel forest, cool stream crossing, shared ATV trails, historic Pine Grove Furnace State Park nearby with swimming at two separate lakes, restrooms, concessions, boat and bike rental, rock climbing atop Pole Steeple.

Land status: Pennsylvania State Forest, Department of Conservation and Recreation.

Maps: USGS Arendtsville, Dickinson; DCNR Bureau of Forestry: Michaux State Forest map, Michaux State Forest ATV Trail map.

Access: From Carlisle, take U.S. Highway 81 south. Look for signs to Pine Grove Furnace State Park and take exit 11, to Pennsylvania Highway 233 south. Follow Pennsylvania 233 until it reaches a T intersection at the park office. Turn right, continuing on 233 south for 0.1 mile, and then turn left onto Bendersville Road. Follow Bendersville Road for 2.5 miles to the Michaux ATV and snowmobile parking area on the right. As you enter the lot, park on the left side. Piney Mountain Road will be directly in front of you. This lot is the trailhead.

Notes on the trail: The infamous Grave Ridge Trail, in the heart of the Michaux State Forest, is a trail to be reckoned with. Eighteen miles of some of the most technical singletrack in the state make up this stout route. The entire ride runs on the Michaux State Forest ATV trail system,

Grave Ridge to Rocky Pass

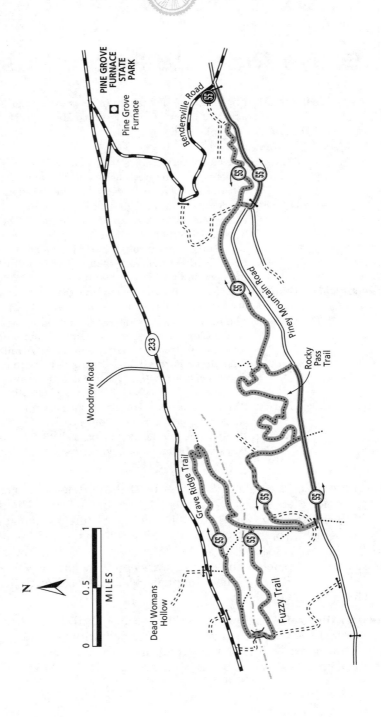

which is frequently traveled by four-wheelers. Due to the technical difficulty of most trails, you won't likely find the ATV riders screaming past you at insane speeds, but puttering by as they negotiate the burly obstacles on the trail. Michaux is a well-kept secret in the south-central region and rarely do you have to compete for trail space. Maybe it's the heinous terrain that keeps most people away. It's not unfamiliar to all though—this is home to a group of local, dedicated riders who have worked with the state to plan and maintain trails throughout the state forest. Michaux Off-Road Enthusiasts (MORE) is a driving force in keeping the trails accessible and in good shape.

The ride begins immediately on very difficult terrain, climbing through a few miles of rocky doubletrack. After a short break on the fire road, you're soon hurling head first into the rocky depths of the valley. A tough climb out and another steep descent leads to the infamous Grave Ridge. Another quick climb leads to the "gravestone" spine of the ridge, where riding a clean line is a must. With the ridge behind you, a beautiful valley drainage ride, complete with creek crossing, rolls into the next arduous climb to Piney Mountain Road. Dropping back into the woods, the trail passes the rock garden at Rocky Pass and then reclimbs the valley to the technical doubletrack along Piney Mountain Road. The last mile rolls along the flat expanse of Piney Mountain Road, allowing your rattled body to compose itself somewhat before collapsing at the trailhead.

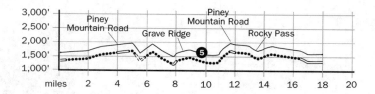

THE RIDE

0.0 From the parking lot, cross over at one of the ATV cuts in the wood row and turn right onto Piney Mountain Ridge Road.

0.3 Turn right at the right-hand woods road spur and then after 50 yards, turn left onto a tight doubletrack/singletrack (may be marked as trail 43).

1.4 Cross a woods road and continue straight (may be marked as trail 39). Soon after the trail forks, turn right at the next fork and continue to climb the hill.

3.5 Turn left at the T intersection.

4.0 Turn left at the fork, then turn right onto Piney Mountain Ridge Road.

4.7 Turn right onto the trail spur and descend the steep, rocky ATV trail.

5.1 Turn left at the T intersection onto the wide woods road.

The impressive quartzite cliffs of Pole Steeple, Pine Grove Furnace State Park.

5.8 Turn right at the fork, and climb the steep, narrow, technical singletrack (may be marked as trail 18).

6.2 Turn right at the T intersection (may be marked as trail 13). Soon the trail forks; keep right and continue to descend. As the trail bends left, note the obscure trail on the right at the bend. The return route will ascend that trail at mile 11.0.

7.7 Turn right at the T intersection onto the easy woods road.

7.9 After crossing a wooden bridge, turn right onto the trail spur.

8.2 Keep left at the trail fork.

8.5 Keep right at the trail fork (may be marked as trail 11).

8.8 Keep left at the trail fork. Welcome to the Grave Ridge Trail!

9.9 Turn hard right at the T intersection, descending off Grave Ridge. The trail will bend hard left, then hard right in the bottom of the valley. Do not follow the unmarked mud-hole trail to the left.

10.8 Cross a small stream in the heart of a beautiful rhododendron and hemlock woodland.

11.0 As the trail climbs out of the valley, keep right at an indistinct fork, then merge left with the ATV trail and continue to climb. This should look remotely familiar if you remembered that point back at mile 6.2 at the bend in the trail.

11.4 Pass around a gate and turn left onto Piney Mountain Ridge Road.

12.1 Turn left onto the trail spur and in approximately 100 yards turn hard right onto the right-hand trail (may be marked as trail 21).

13.3 Turn left onto Rocky Pass Trail (may be marked as trail 24).

13.8 Keep right at the trail fork (may be marked as trail 27). Welcome to the Rock Garden!

14.3 Turn right at the T intersection (may be marked as trail 28) and continue to climb.

14.6 Turn left at the left-hand trail spur (may be marked as trail 29).

16.6 After passing a left-hand trail spur, turn right onto the woods road (may be marked as trail 39).

16.8 Come to a four-way intersection, turn left and pass around a gate, this is Piney Mountain Ridge Road.

18.1 Turn left into the parking lot and trailhead.

Three Mile Trail

Location: 20 miles south of Carlisle.

Distance: 10.6-mile loop.

Time: 1 to 2 hours.

Tread: Beginning on state forest ATV trail, you climb onto and traverse Grave Ridge. Plates of rock stick out like the back of a stegosaurus and loose, gnarly boulders abound. The next 2 miles have a beautiful singletrack line that turns to a fire road climb. The Three Mile Trail is the crux, with a burly mix of rocks and roots, with the final descent on an old woods road.

Aerobic level: Strenuous. The ride is loaded with demanding climbs and mind-bending enduro singletrack. The technical sections require as much energy as the ride itself and are utterly relentless.

Technical difficulty: 4 + . This is full-on Michaux, the beast of the east. Grave Ridge's tombstone-like rocks are just waiting to grind up that carbon-fiber bike and its $150 derailleur. Likewise, the Three Mile Trail bares its wretched teeth looking for a taste of hapless mountain bikers. Be forewarned!

Highlights: Some of the most technical riding in Pennsylvania, enduro bike singletrack, the infamous Grave Ridge, 920-foot climb, scenic Pine Grove Furnace State Park nearby with swimming, concessions, boat and bike rental, rock climbing.

Land status: Pennsylvania State Forest, Department of Conservation and Recreation.

Maps: USGS Arendtsville, Caledonia Park, Dickinson, Walnut Bottom; DCNR Bureau of Forestry: Michaux State Forest map.

Access: From Carlisle take U.S. Highway 81 south. Look for signs to Pine Grove Furnace State Park and take exit 11, to Pennsylvania Highway 233 south. Follow Pennsylvania 233 until it comes to a T intersection at the park office. Turn right and continue on Pennsylvania 233 south for 4 miles, passing Michaux and Woodrow Roads on the right. Pull off at Dead Womans Hollow Road on the right and park on either side of the gate or along the edge of the road (do not block the gate!). Dead Womans Hollow Road is marked with a wooden sign, which is located 100 yards from the road, beyond the gate. This is the trailhead.

Notes on the trail: If you've got a taste for technical challenges, welcome to Flavor Country! Technical riding at its best for the hard-core, singletrack, hammerhead rider. With over 4 miles of some of the burliest riding in Pennsylvania, you'll be thankful that it's only a 10-mile loop. The location is prime mountain bike country, and folks flock from all around to test their mettle in the beautiful Michaux State Forest.

"Unforgiving" and "relentless" are the best words to describe this classic route. From the trailhead, you immediately climb the super-steep "Chainbreak" hill, which has claimed many a chain. Gasping for air, you confront Grave Ridge with its heinous spine of rock. As its name implies, Grave Ridge is a ridge-top trail that is littered with rocks resembling tombstones. If you look close enough you may find the names of a few riders who didn't survive this section scrawled on the stones! A few prayers and some dialed riding may be your only hope to pass over Grave Ridge.

After abruptly exiting off Grave Ridge, take a quick right turn and follow a hidden singletrack across a bridge and up through young woods to Woodrow Road. A steady grind up Woodrow will surprise you with a false summit that continues to climb out to Ridge Road, passing the famous Appalachian Trail. Woodrow Road joins Ridge Road at a bizarre intersection—where a short left turn onto Ridge Road will quickly spur off onto Three Mile Trail. This section—cut out by enduro riders—is where the trail gets tough and technical all over again. Three long, hard, and demanding miles await as the trail slowly climbs parallel to Ridge Road. Monster rocks, burly berms, and loose wash require all your technical skills to survive. If you love pain and are slightly deranged, you should make it through. The ride drops out onto a few fire roads before the final descent down Dead Womans Hollow Trail. Deceivingly mellow at first, Dead Womans Hollow soon turns to a rippin' downhill where speeds of 40 mph aren't uncommon. The surface is sketchy in places but my theory is "the faster you go, the faster you go." Just don't bail though, or they may have to rename it Dead Biker Hollow!

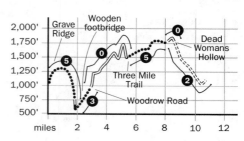

THE RIDE

0.0 From the trailhead, cross Pennsylvania Highway 233 diagonally right and pass around a gate.

0.1 Soon you will pass a four-way intersection. Keep straight as you climb "Chainbreak" hill. The ATV trail may be marked "10 More Difficult."

0.2 Turn left, following the trail just below the rocky prominent point of Grave Ridge.

0.4 Turn left at the fork, following the sign for "Most Difficult" trail. This is Grave Ridge.

Three Mile Trail

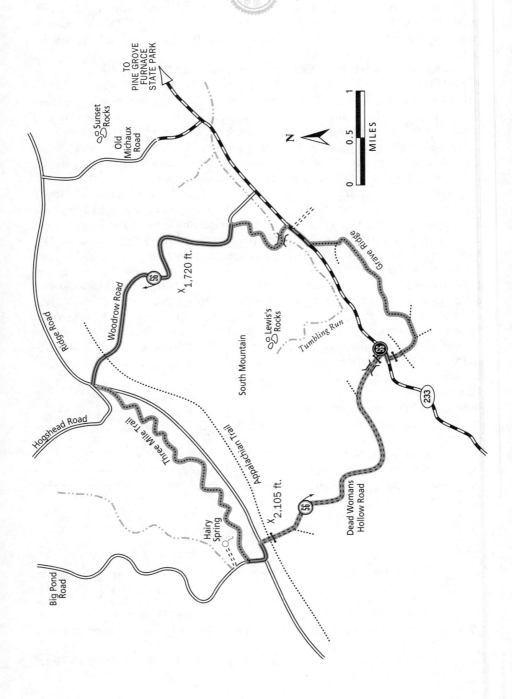

TO
PINE GROVE
FURNACE
STATE PARK

Sunset
Rocks

Old
Michaux
Road

N

MILES

0   0.5   1

X 1,720 ft.

Grave Ridge

Ridge Road

Woodrow Road

Lewis's
Rocks

South Mountain

Tumbling Run

233

Hogshead Road

Three Mile Trail

Appalachian Trail

X 2,105 ft.

Dead Womans
Hollow Road

Hairy
Spring

Big Pond
Road

1.4 The trail turns left, dropping down off the ridge. Take an immediate right onto the right-hand trail spur which empties out onto Pennsylvania 233. Turn right onto Pennsylvania 233 (mile 1.5).

1.6 Turn left at the small parking area, where you pass around the roadblocking boulders and regain the trail as an old woods road. It may be a bit obscure, but it's there and shortly turns to singletrack.

1.8 Cross a wooden footbridge; continue to climb on windy singletrack.

2.8 Turn left onto Woodrow Road and get ready to grind.

5.4 After passing the Appalachian Trail (note the sign on the left), turn hard left at the bizarre five-way intersection, onto Ridge Road. Travel for approximately 20 yards and turn right onto the obscure enduro singletrack. This trail quickly turns left and parallels Ridge Road.

8.2 Turn left onto Big Pond Road. Soon turn left again onto Ridge Road (mile 8.3).

8.4 Turn right onto Dead Womans Hollow Trail and pass around a gate. Keep straight at the fork, continuing to follow Dead Womans Hollow Trail, the blue blazes on the trees on the right.

10.6 After crossing a large wooden snowmobile bridge, pass around a gate to the trailhead.

Chimney Rocks

Location:	Mont Alto State Park, 14 miles southeast of Chambersburg
Distance:	15.8-mile loop.
Time:	2 to 3 hours.
Tread:	The majority of the ride is on state forest dirt roads. But 1.5 miles of sweet, switchbackin' singletrack drops off from the Chimney Rocks Vista and is peppered with smooth, rounded rocks—a nice break from the fast, flat, fire roads.
Aerobic level:	Moderate to strenuous. The ride involves a long, steady, 900-foot climb from the valley trailhead to the mountaintop fire tower. A rewarding downhill follows, with a more mellow climb back out of the valley. The finish is a bomber run back down to the trailhead.
Technical difficulty:	4. The real challenge is the 1.5 mile descent from Chimney Rocks, past the Hermitage Cabin and out to Swift Run Road, due to the amount of technical rock-hopping required in the rugged little valley below Climbing Rock.

Chimney Rocks

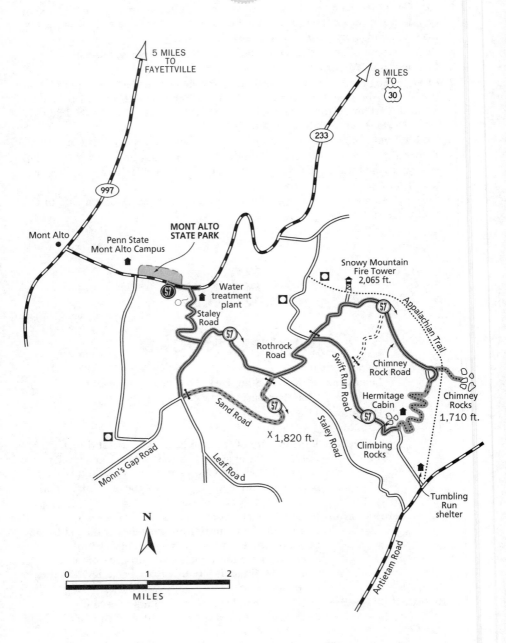

5 MILES
TO
FAYETTVILLE

8 MILES
TO
30

233

997

Mont Alto

Penn State
Mont Alto Campus

**MONT ALTO
STATE PARK**

Water
treatment
plant

Staley
Road

57

57

Rothrock
Road

Snowy Mountain
Fire Tower
2,065 ft.

Appalachian Trail

57

Chimney
Rock Road

Swift Run Road

Hermitage
Cabin

Chimney
Rocks
1,710 ft.

57

X 1,820 ft.

Sand Road

57

Staley
Road

Climbing
Rocks

Monn's Gap Road

Leaf Road

Tumbling
Run
shelter

N

Antietam Road

0   1   2

MILES

Highlights: Chimney Rocks and vista, Snowy Mountain Fire
Tower, Hermitage Cabin near the Appalachian Trail,
Climbing Rock outcrop, spring along the ride, scenic
woodland fire road riding.
Land status: Pennsylvania State Forest, Department of
Conservation and Recreation.
Maps: USGS Waynesboro, Iron Springs; DCNR Bureau of
Forestry: Michaux State Forest map.

Access: Interstate 81, take exit 6 (Chambersburg) to U.S. Highway 30 east.
Travel for 6 miles on US 30 to Pennsylvania Highway 997. Turn right onto
PA 997 (south) and travel for 4 miles to Mont Alto. At Mont Alto turn left
onto Pennsylvania Highway 233, traveling east for 1 mile to Mont Alto State
Park. Park in the lot directly across from the green bell-shaped pavilion,
which is at the trailhead.

Notes on the trail: The Michaux State Forest received its name from the
French botanist Andre Michaux, who explored this area extensively in the
late 1800s. With over 82,000 acres spanning three counties, Michaux offers
the outdoor enthusiast lots of places to explore. The trailhead is located
across from Pennsylvania's oldest tree nursery, which was started in 1902
and still produces 2 million trees annually.

The ride starts opposite the green, bell-shaped pavilion and begins a long
4.5-mile, 900-foot climb to the Snowy Mountain Fire Tower. Although the
tower is fenced, it still stands as a reminder of Pennsylvania forestry's days
of old. A short ridge road leads to the rugged and beautiful Chimney Rocks,
a formation of broken slabs that form interesting caves and climbing areas.
Enjoy the northeasterly view over the Waynesboro Reservoir and Green
Ridge. Then take an awesome switchback descent down into the Tumbling
Run drainage, past the Hermitage Cabin and Climbing Rocks. A moderate
climb and descent leads over Sand Ridge and swings down and around to
the trailhead.

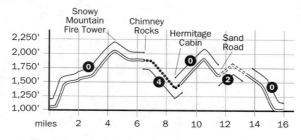

THE RIDE

0.0 From the trailhead lot, head out to Pennsylvnia Highway 233 and turn right.
Be careful along this section of road because there is no shoulder.
0.5 Turn right onto Staley Road, pass a water treatment plant on the left, and begin
the long climb. At mile 0.8 you will pass a spring on the right.

1.6 Keep left at the road fork, staying on Staley Road.

2.9 Turn left at the four-way intersection onto Rothrock Road and continue to climb.

3.9 Continue straight at a four-way intersection, pass around a gate, and continue to climb for just a bit more.

4.5 The road will fork. To visit the Snowy Mountain Fire Tower, turn left and travel for approximately 200 yards. To continue on the ride, turn right at the fork and continue out along Chimney Rock Road.

5.7 Cross over a pipeline.

6.5 Come to the end of Chimney Rock Road, identified by the circular loop in the road. You will notice two sets of blue blazes on the trees. Follow the blazes left (east) as they ascend a narrow, rocky singletrack trail to the Chimney Rocks formation. Once at the "Rocks" (mile 6.8), enjoy the impressive views overlooking the Waynesboro Reservoir and out onto Green Ridge. Return back down the blue-blazed trail to Chimney Rock Road, crossing the road and continuing to follow the blue blazes as they descend into the valley (mile 7.1).

8.1 After the fun switchbacks, the trail makes a hard right turn before crossing the creek at a trail sign. Follow the sign as it directs you toward the Hermitage Cabin and across two rustic footbridges. You encounter another wooden trail sign just below the Hermitage Cabin and then the blue blazed trail forks. Take the left fork, ride up in front of the cabin, and turn hard left as the trail climbs up and around to Climbing Rocks.

8.4 After pulling through a tough technical section, turn right onto Swift Run Road and begin the mellow fire road climb.

10.5 Turn left at the four-way intersection onto Rothrock Road and descend the hill.

11.5 Cross the four-way intersection onto Sand Road, soon passing around a gate.

13.4 After passing around another gate, turn right onto Leaf Road.

14.2 Turn left at the road fork, descending Staley Road.

15.3 Turn left onto Pennsylvnia 233, carefully riding along the road.

15.8 Turn left into the trailhead lot.

Rocky Ridge

Location: Rocky Ridge County Park, 3 miles northeast of York.

Distance: 7.7-mile loop.

Time: 1 to 2 hours.

Tread: The ride covers an array of trails, including rutted, rocky old woods roads, singletrack, doubletrack, and cinder-paved path.

Aerobic level: Moderate. The ride covers some moderate elevation gains as it figure-eights over the ridge's spine. The climbs are somewhat challenging and the descents are well-earned and downright rewarding.

Technical difficulty: 3+. The trails here as a whole are on the technical side. Certain sections are smooth and hardpacked while others are sporadically littered with stone and rock. Hence the name "Rocky Ridge."

Highlights: Multiple stream crossings, two incredible vistas, park amenities including restrooms, water, picnic pavilions, horseshoe pits, sand volleyball courts, and a fitness trail, camping nearby at Otter Creek and Pequea Campgrounds.

Land status: York County Parks.

Maps: USGS York Haven; York County Parks, Rocky Ridge County Park map.

Access: Rocky Ridge County Park is somewhat obscure and can be difficult to find, so follow the directions carefully. From York (in the heart of town where Interstate 83 passes through) take U.S. Highway 30 east to Pennsylvnia Highway 24, also known as Mount Zion Road. Turn left onto Mount Zion Road, head north, and drive for 1 mile to Deininger Road. Turn right onto Deininger Road (marked by a wooden park sign for Rocky Ridge County Park) and drive for 1 mile to the park entrance. Once at the park entrance, pass a parking lot on the left and travel for another mile to the back parking lot. As you enter this lot, the trail begins in the left (northwest) corner of the lot.

Notes on the trail: Rocky Ridge is a great place to get out and tear around on some technical trail, especially if you're in the York area. With the likes of Subway and Taco Bell almost within smelling distance, the riding here is almost too good to be true. The park's name reflects the abundance of moderate technical riding. I'm not one for urban mountain biking, but Rocky

Rocky Ridge

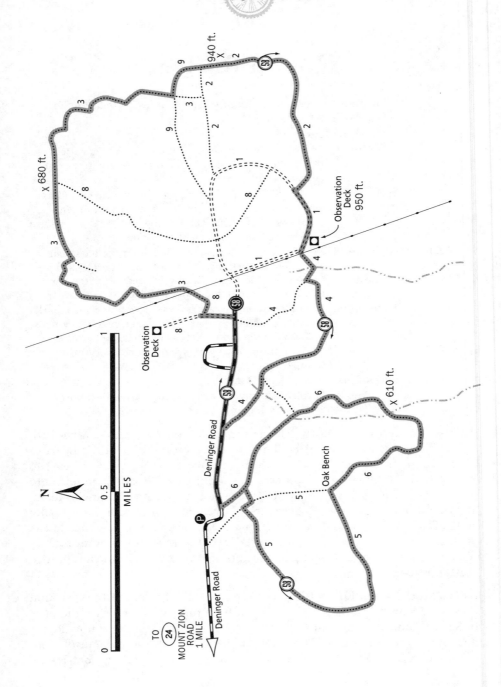

X 940 ft.

Observation Deck 950 ft.

X 680 ft.

Observation Deck

N

MILES

0   0.5   1

Deninger Road

X 610 ft.

Oak Bench

P

Deninger Road

TO 24 MOUNT ZION ROAD 1 MILE

Riders at Rocky Ridge.

Ridge offers a woodland riding experience even though it's surrounded by the comfortable urban amenities. The trails here are well marked.

The ride begins on the ridge at one of the highest points in the park and leads out to a beautiful vista looking north over the Susquehanna Valley. A gnarly, rocky, technical descent follows as the trail loses some elevation off the north face and runs the rocky valley below. A killer hill climb with burly rocks and soft soil brings you back to the top of the ridge. Take advantage of the second vista, this time looking south, out over the York Valley. Head back into the woods to a stream crossing and begin a rugged lower loop on the southwest face of the ridge. Two more stream crossings and a fun, moderate climb bring you back to the park entrance road and the trailhead.

York County Parks has a tight restriction on mountain biking and equestrian riding when the trails become saturated with water or unfit for use. Park rangers may issue fines to those in violation of restrictions. For information on trail conditions and closures, call the park's hot line at 717-840-7440.

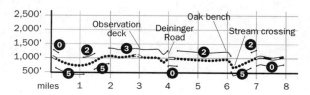

THE RIDE

0.0 From the parking area, head north past the restrooms on the left and take the cinder pathway toward the observation deck. A bit before the observation deck, the singletrack trail marked 8 begins on the right. Turn right onto trail 8. If you want to check out the view, do so and return to this point

0.7 After the killer technical descent, turn left at the T intersection onto trail 3.

1.0 Trail 8 splits off on the right, keep straight on trail 3.

1.7 After a heinous short climb, turn left at the four-way intersection onto trail 9. Soon after, the trail passes a right-hand trail spur, continue straight as trail 9 becomes trail 2.

2.8 Merge left onto the wide, cinder pathway marked trail 1.

2.9 Pass the southern observation deck. Check out the view over the York Valley. Immediately after passing the large power-line tower, turn left following the singletrack marked as trail 4 into the woods. After crossing a small stream, keep left at the fork on trail 4.

4.0 Turn left onto Deininger Road.

4.2 Turn left onto trail 6, just opposite the parking area. Soon after, turn right onto the trail spur marked 5.

4.5 Turn right at the T intersection, following trail 5 and then, 60 yards later, turn left at the next T intersection.

5.9 Turn right at the fork, following trail 6. Note the huge oak bench. Soon after, keep left at the fork and descend the steep, stepped trail.

Brad Trowbridge getting burly on the Rocky Ridge Vista.

6.4 Cross the stream.

6.6 Turn left onto the trail spur, ford the stream, and continue to follow trail 6. Continue straight on this trail, riding it out to Deininger Road.

7.0 Turn right onto Deininger Road.

7.7 Trailhead.

Lake Redman

Location:	William Kain County Park, 7 miles south of York.
Distance:	11-mile loop.
Time:	1 to 3 hours.
Tread:	The surfaces range from grassy woods roads to hardpacked singletrack. Wide open trails combined with some tight singletrack constitute great riding.
Aerobic level:	Easy to moderate. The Lake Redman area is hilly, but the climbs are on a comfortable grade and usually take place on wide-open grassy trails. The descents pass down through wooded singletrack.
Technical difficulty:	3. The only part of the ride that may present a technical challenge is the upper loop between miles 7 and 9.4, and that is easily bypassed. This would eliminate the technical downhill, which is rated at 3+.
Highlights:	Two beautiful lakes; lakeside riding, boating, and fishing; and all the amenities of the park including boat rentals, horseshoe pits, sand volleyball courts, and picnic pavilions; camping at nearby Otter Creek and Pequea Campgrounds.
Land status:	York County Parks.
Maps:	USGS York; York County Parks, William H. Kain County Park map.

Access: From York, take Interstate 83 south to exit 4. At the end of the exit ramp turn right onto Leader Heights Road and drive 1 mile to South George Street. Turn left onto South George Street and drive 2 miles to Church Street. Turn left onto Church Street and drive 0.5 mile to the Lake Redman parking area on the left. Park in the lower left-hand lot for ease in finding the trail.

Notes on the trail: William Kain County Park's 1,675 acres include two beautiful lakes, Lake William and Lake Redman. The lands surrounding

Lake Redman

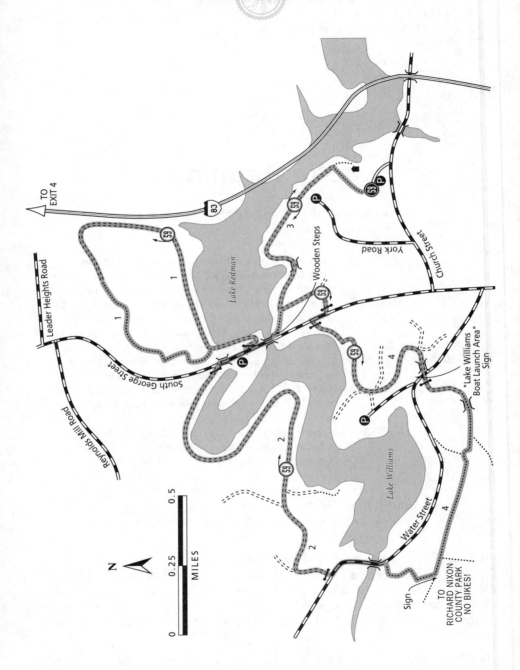

these two reservoirs offer an array of trails and numerous ways to link together a variety of loops. The trails here are well marked.

The ride begins at the popular Church Street entrance and immediately climbs a fun, dirt singletrack to a small vista. The trail continues along Lake Redman on wide grassy woods roads leading to the lower Lake William. A mixed variety of wide grassy roads, doubletrack and singletrack, follow as the route circles the contour of Lake William in a clockwise fashion. A final leg, and probably the most exciting section, runs a loop above the north shore of Lake Redman. The climb up an old woods road leads to the highest point on the ride before dropping onto the sweet, technical singletrack descent. Back out across the massive spillway, the trail takes a short hike up a steep set of stairs and returns back along Lake Redman on some familiar terrain to the trailhead.

York County Parks has a tight restriction on mountain biking and equestrian riding when the trails become saturated with water or unfit for use. Park rangers may issue fines to those in violation of restrictions. For information on trail conditions and closures, call the park's hot line at 717-840-7440.

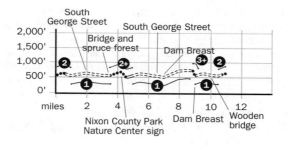

THE RIDE

0.0 From the lower parking area closest to the lake, look for the dirt trail in the left-hand corner of the parking lot. Ascend the trail. It will soon pass a small vista on the right and descend to the lake, merging left with another trail (trail 3).

0.3 Pass a gravel parking and picnic area on the left. Continue along the lake.

1.0 Cross a wooden bridge.

1.5 Keep left at the fork after climbing above the dam breast.

1.9 Turn right at the T intersection. Soon after, pass around a gate and turn right onto South George Street. Travel down South George Street for 150 yards, then turn left onto the gated old woods road and continue to descend.

2.2 Turn left at the T intersection.

2.6 Turn left at the T intersection, and immediately after, keep left at the fork on the trail marked 4. Soon after, keep right at another fork, staying on trail 4.

2.9 Turn right at the four-way intersection, staying on trail 4. Soon after, cross a bridge and turn right onto Water Street. Ride down Water Street for 100 yards and turn left onto a gated old woods road, opposite the large "Lake Williams Boat Launch Area" sign.

3.3 Cross a bridge over a stream in an enchanting spruce forest.

3.5 Keep right at the fork, following the trail 4 markers. Soon after, turn left at the T intersection and continue to climb.

4.2 Turn right onto the trail spur at the "Nixon County Park Nature Center" trail sign and descend the awesome singletrack.

4.5 Turn left onto Water Street, crossing the dam via the road bridge.

4.8 Turn right onto the gated old woods road and soon after keep right at the fork following trail 2.

5.1 Keep right at the fork, soon after turn left at the T intersection, and continue to follow trail 2.

6.7 Pass around a gate and turn right onto South George Street.

7.0 After crossing a bridge and passing the parking area on the right, turn left onto the gated, gravel road that climbs onto the dam breast. At the end of this gravel road, turn right at the T intersection and continue on the old woods road (mile 7.2). Note the singletrack trail down on the left at this intersection, this is where you will exit.

9.0 After a killer singletrack descent, turn right onto the gravel dam breast road and ride it back out to South George Street. Pass around the gate and turn left onto South George Street. Cross the bridge over the spillway, take an immediate left, and then hike up the wooden steps to gain the trail (mile 9.4). Once atop the trail, pass a right-hand trail and continue to follow trail 3. The trail should look familiar.

9.9 Cross the wooden bridge.

10.6 Keep right at the fork, climb the hill, and pass the small vista on the left.

11.0 After descending the short, steep trail, you're at the trailhead lot.

Spring Valley

Location: Spring Valley County Park, 15 miles south of York.

Distance: 6.5-mile loop.

Time: 30 minutes to 1.5 hours.

Tread: The ride runs mainly on singletrack trails that vary from smooth, hardpacked dirt to ridge-top rocky outcroppings. There are a few grassy old woods roads and gravel park roads that connect the trail network. Ridgeway Road is in bad shape and only half-paved.

Aerobic level: Moderate. The many hills offer short challenging climbs and great descents. Some flat, smooth terrain demands a bit of muscle at times to get through the tougher sections.

Technical difficulty: 2 + . The final leg along the East Branch of Codorus Creek presents the biggest challenge, as you dodge skunk cabbage around large rocks in a tight trail.

Highlights: Short and exciting ride, Fish for Fun pond, trout stream, camping nearby at the Otter Creek and Pequea Campgrounds, picnicking, gold panning?!

Land status: York County Parks.

Maps: USGS Glen Rock; York County Parks Spring Valley County Park map.

Access: From York take Interstate 83 south to exit 3. At the end of the exit ramp, turn left onto Pennsylvania Highway 216 and head northeast for 3 miles. As the road follows along Sneak Run, turn right onto the dirt and gravel road marked Line Road (it's opposite Erb Road and difficult to find). If you crossed the small bridge over the Codorus Creek, you just missed the turn. Travel down Line Road for 1 mile and park on the left at the Raccoon Pavilion parking area. This lot is the trailhead.

Notes on the trail: Spring Valley is the park farthest south in the York area, nestled in the rugged hills of the Lower Susquehanna Valley. The park boasts an array of amenities, including lots of open space, picnicking pavilions, a children's Fish for Fun pond, trout fishing, and a program in July where you can learn to pan for gold (Yes, real gold.) The East Branch of Codorus Creek that flows through the park is also heavily stocked with trout in the spring and is a hot spot during trout season.

The ride begins along the beautiful Codorus Creek and climbs abruptly into the hills. As the trail traverses the hilltops and valleys, it bridges

Spring Valley

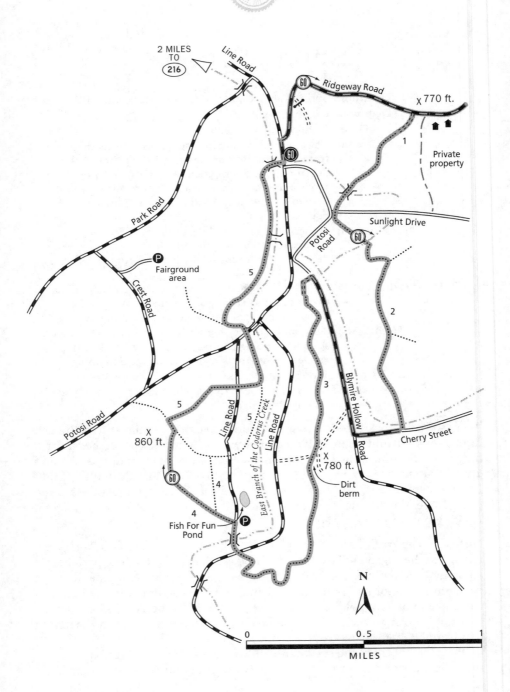

2 MILES TO 216

Line Road

Ridgeway Road

X 770 ft.

Private property

Park Road

Sunlight Drive

Fairground area

Potosi Road

Crest Road

5

2

Potosi Road

5

Line Road

5

Line Road

3

Blymire Hollow Road

Cherry Street

X 860 ft.

X 780 ft.

4

Dirt berm

East Branch of the Codorus Creek

4

Fish For Fun Pond

N

0   0.5   1

MILES

many streams and passes through young forests. Mild climbs and incredible descents are what's in store as the trail loops around the park in a clockwise fashion. Gravel roads link the sections of singletrack trails and offer a short reprieve from the hill climbing sessions. A spin by the Fish for Fun Pond leads to the final and most demanding of the climbs. With the climb behind you, roll out across the ridge as it empties down along the creek, and take the sweet, technical singletrack that leads back to the trailhead.

York County Parks has a tight restriction on mountain biking and equestrian riding when the trails become saturated with water or unfit for use. Park rangers may issue fines to those in violation of restrictions. For information on trail conditions and closures, call the park's hot line at 717-840-7440.

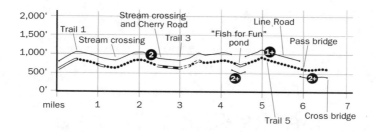

THE RIDE

0.0 From the trailhead parking area, turn right onto Line Road and then turn immediately right again onto Ridgeway Road climb the steep gravel road.

0.6 Turn right onto the obscure old woods road, marked by a vertical green fiberglass marker (may be marked as Trail 1). If you begin passing houses on the right, you missed the trail entrance. Some private property borders this section of woodlands and indicates the park boundary.

1.0 Cross a wide, wooden bridge and climb a short bit to an intersection of gravel roads. Continue straight across onto Potosi Road and ride for approximately 150 yards. At this point, turn left onto the trail spur marked by a green post with a 2 and descend the hill.

1.3 Cross a small stream and turn right at the T intersection.

1.7 Turn right at the fork.

2.3 After a nice descent, cross the stream and turn right at the T intersection onto Cherry Road. Soon after, you will come to another T intersection. Turn right again onto Blymire Hollow Road.

3.0 Turn left onto the old woods road spur marked by a green post with a 3 and climb the hill up into the singletrack.

3.8 Turn right onto the gravel old woods road. Keep right at the fork and cross over a dirt berm. Approximately 100 yards after the berm, turn left into the woods on the singletrack and descend the hill.

4.4 Turn left onto Line Road and then immediately, turn right at the next intersection (which is still Line Road) and cross a bridge. As the road climbs, it will pass the Fish for Fun Pond on the right and the large parking area. Just beyond this will be a left-hand trail spur marked by a green post with a 4, that climbs a steep hill. As it climbs the hill, trail 4 splits off to the right, you want to continue straight as the trail bend up left over the crest of the hill.

5.1 As the trail comes to a clearing, turn left at the T intersection onto the old woods road. In approximately 200 yards, turn right onto the trail marked by a green post with a 5, the trail passes through the pines.

5.5 Carefully cross Line Road and then soon after cross Potosi Road (mile 5.7).

5.8 Turn right at the fork and follow the technical singletrack along the creek. Watch for that skunk cabbage! Soon the trail passes a right-hand trail to a bridge. Continue straight.

6.5 Turn right as the trail crosses the brown, wooden bridge and finishes opposite the trailhead.

Devils Race Course

Location:	17 miles north of Harrisburg, 4 miles east of Dauphin.
Distance:	16.8-mile loop.
Time:	2 to 4 hours.
Tread:	Historic Stony Valley Railroad rail-trail, dirt woods roads, hardpacked doubletrack, and the gnarly Devils Race Course Trail, which is an extremely rocky, washed out old woods road.
Aerobic level:	Moderate to strenuous. The climb out of the Stony Valley up to Stony Mountain is sustained and steep. Once on top of the mountain, it's an easy cruise across the top and back down to the trailhead, making it well worth the initial effort.
Technical difficulty:	3. The 2-mile stretch of the Devil's Race Course presents the biggest challenge with its golf-ball to basketball-sized loose rocks.
Highlights:	The historic Stony Valley Railroad Grade, outstanding views atop the Stony Mountain Fire Tower, a shot at wagering your soul on the Devils Race Course, bomber descent.
Land status:	Pennsylvania Game Commission, SGL 211.
Maps:	USGS Enders, Grantville; Pennsylvania Game Commission SGL 211 map; DCNR Bureau of Forestry: Weiser State Forest maps.

Access: From Harrisburg, take U.S. Highway 322 west to Dauphin. As US 322 passes under a railroad bridge, just before the town of Dauphin, stay in the right lane and exit off of US 322 onto Pennsylvania Highway 225. Soon after, turn left at the T intersection onto Erie Street, then turn right onto Susquehanna Avenue. Travel for 4.5 miles on Susquehanna Avenue to the end of the paved road and a circle with mailboxes. Continue on the dirt road (Stony Creek Valley Road) that exits at the top of the circle, and drive another 2 miles to a gate and the large Pennsylvania State Game Lands parking area. This lot is the trailhead.

Notes on the trail: The Devils Race Course is gnarly indeed! Local legend claims that anyone passing through the Devil's course must wager their soul to race the Devil. If you should happen to lose, you might have a chance to redeem yourself on the bomber descent off the ridge; either way, it's a hellish encounter. Good luck!

The ride hits a few highlights of the area, the first being the historic Stony Valley Railroad. Built in the early 1850s to transport the plundered treasures of the surrounding mountains, the rail line had a lengthy lifespan. Coal and lumber were exported from the valley and, interestingly enough, wealthy tourists were later imported. The supposedly healing waters of Cold Spring drew many visitors, and a 200-room hotel was built to accommodate them. Eventually the Pennsylvania Game Commission purchased the lands and soon after converted the abandoned rail grade into one of the nation's first rail-trails.

From the trailhead, take the dirt road back toward Dauphin to start the arduous climb up the mountain. Four miles of sustained riding will have your heart pummeling your rib cage before the ride finally levels out atop the ridge. A side trip to the Stony Mountain Fire Tower will yield commanding views of the surrounding countryside. Watch out for military planes buzzing by.

The ride then follows beautiful doubletrack along the ridge, a good spot to see some wildlife. Now, here's the part you've been waiting for: the Devils Race Course. It's 2 miles of rocky, old four-wheel-drive road through lush, shady stands of hemlock, oak, and mountain laurel. The final bone is a fall-line drop off the ridge down a smooth woods road to the rail-trail, which leads back to the trailhead.

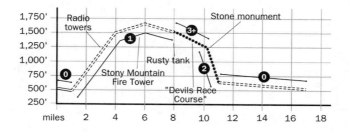

Devils Race Course

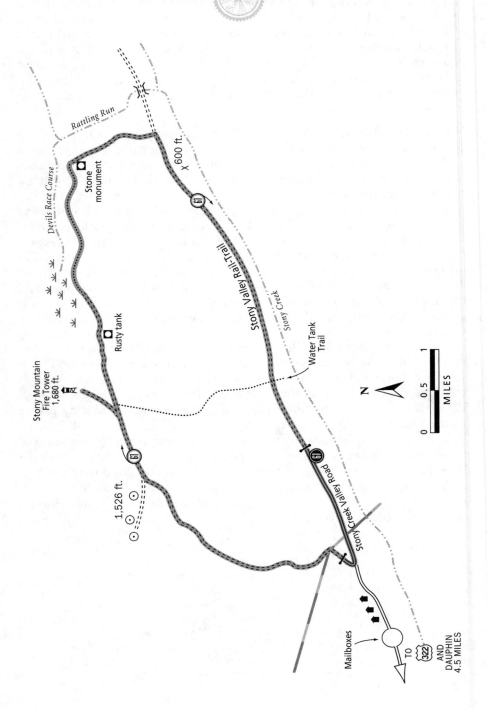

Rattling Run

Devils Race Course

Stone monument

X 600 ft.

61

Stony Valley Rail-Trail

Stony Creek

Rusty tank

Water Tank Trail

Stony Mountain Fire Tower 1,680 ft.

61

1,526 ft.

61

Stony Creek Valley Road

Mailboxes

TO 322 AND DAUPHIN 4.5 MILES

N

MILES

0   0.5   1

0.0 From the trailhead lot, ride back out the dirt road (Stony Creek Valley Road) you drove in on.

1.1 Turn right up the gated state game lands woods road. The road will soon bend left at a pipeline clearing, then continue to climb.

4.0 Pass a left-hand dirt woods road and a radio tower. The ride begins to level out.

5.3 Keep left at the fork to ride the spur trail out to the Stony Mountain Fire Tower.

5.9 Reach Stony Mountain Fire Tower. From here return the way you came to the intersection.

6.5 Turn left at the T intersection (the fork at mile 5.3) and continue on the sweet doubletrack along the ridge.

7.8 Pass a huge, rusty fuel tank on the right. The trail will soon turn into the Devils Race Course. Rumor has it that if the Devil beats you through his course, he takes your soul!

10.3 As the trail begins to mellow out, pass a large stone monument on the right with a plaque for the "Kabob Hiking Club." Get stoked for the killer descent—maybe you can redeem your soul!

11.2 Turn right at the T intersection onto the Stony Valley Rail-Trail.

16.8 Pass around the gate to the trailhead.

Stony Valley Rail-Trail

Location:	17 miles north of Harrisburg, 4 miles east of Dauphin.
Distance:	28.4 miles out and back.
Time:	2 to 6 hours.
Tread:	The entire ride follows the smooth, cinder-covered pathway of the old rail grade. One short section is on a hidden rail grade that has almost grown back into a singletrack trail.
Aerobic level:	Easy. The first half of the trip is uphill on the rail grade. The return trip is insignificantly easier as it follows the flow of Stony Creek into the Susquehanna River.
Technical difficulty:	0. The rail-trail is great for beginning riders, kid carts, hybrid mountain bikes, and even road bikes.
Highlights:	Historic stops along the way, including the ghost town of Rausch Gap (complete with foundation remains), old bridge trestle foundations, and the actual railroad grade; serene beauty; great trout fishing along the Stony Creek.

Stony Valley Rail-Trail

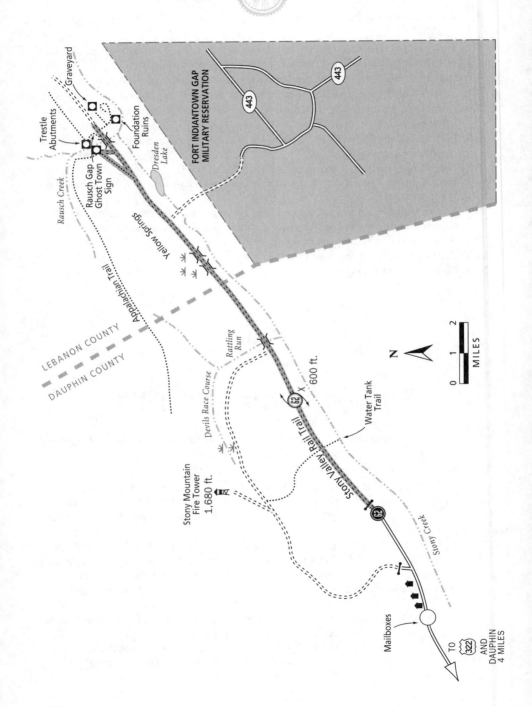

Graveyard

Trestle Abutments

Foundation Ruins

Rausch Gap Ghost Town Sign

Rausch Creek

Dresden Lake

FORT INDIANTOWN GAP MILITARY RESERVATION

443

443

Yellow Springs

Appalachian Trail

LEBANON COUNTY

DAUPHIN COUNTY

Rattling Run

Devils Race Course

Stony Valley Rail Trail

600 ft.

Water Tank Trail

Stony Mountain Fire Tower 1,680 ft.

Stony Creek

N

MILES

0   1   2

Mailboxes

TO 322 AND DAUPHIN 4 MILES

Land status: Pennsylvania Game Commission, SGL 211.

Maps: USGS Enders, Grantville; Pennsylvania Game Commission SGL 211 map; DCNR Bureau of Forestry: Weiser State Forest maps.

Access: From Harrisburg take U.S. Highway 322 west to Dauphin. As US 322 passes under a railroad bridge, just before the town of Dauphin, stay in the right lane and exit off US 322 onto Pennsylvania Highway 225. Soon after, turn left at the T intersection onto Erie Street, then turn right onto Susquehanna Avenue. Travel for 4.5 miles on Susquehanna Avenue to the end of the paved road and a circle with mailboxes. Continue on the dirt road (Stony Creek Valley Road) that exits at the top of the circle and drive another 2 miles to a gate and the large Pennsylvania state game lands parking area. This lot is the trailhead.

Notes on the trail: In addition to the historic Stony Valley Railroad, this ride also passes by the ruins of the old ghost town of Rausch Gap. Between 1828 and 1910, more than 1,000 people lived here. The town slowly disbanded over the next 50 years as the natural resources that sustained the town dwindled. By the mid 1940s the strip mines had proved unproductive and the last bit of lumber was felled from the ridge. The Pennsylvania Game Commission then purchased the lands and soon after converted the abandoned rail grade into one of the nation's first rail-trails.

The trail leaves from the game commission lot and heads up the Stony Creek Valley. Many side trails on the right offer places to drop a line and catch a trout or two. As the grade continues on, the woods envelop you and provide opportunities to see some wildlife. The turn-around point at Rausch Gap is a great place for exploration. A large wooden sign marks the site of the ghost town. Check out all the ruins, including the spooky cemetery of four gravestones dating back to 1854 and the old steps of the Cold Springs Hotel.

Rumor has it that a headless railroad worker stalks the old railroad bed at night, so you may want to head back before dark! The return trip detours to a colossal old stone rail trestle abutment over Rausch Creek. It then follows a beautiful narrow singletrack along another hidden old rail grade before dumping back out onto the Stony Valley Railroad. This section of trail is a bit more challenging and is not suitable for kid carts due to its narrow and somewhat bumpy nature. As an alternate route, return back on the rail-trail—the mileage is almost the same.

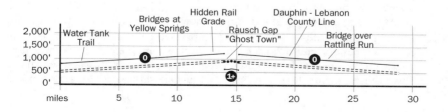

The fern-lined Stony Valley Rail-Trail.

THE RIDE

0.0 From the trailhead lot, ride around the gate onto the rail-trail.

1.8 Pass the Water Tank Trail.

5.6 Pass a left-hand old woods road spur.

6.0 Cross the bridge over Rattling Run.

8.9 Cross the county line between Dauphin and Lebanon Counties as marked by the wooden 4 x 4 post.

9.4 Cross a pair of bridges at Yellow Springs.

11.6 Pass a road on the right that winds its way down into Fort Indiantown Gap Military Reservation. Traveling down this road is not advised because of the shooting range further down.

13.1 Pass a trail spur on the left to the hidden rail grade. If you choose to ride the hidden rail grade on the return trip, this is where you will exit onto the Stony Valley Rail-Trail.

14.2 Cross a beautiful, arched stone bridge and arrive at the site of the Rausch Gap ghost town, marked by the large wooden sign. Once you're done exploring the area, return down the rail-trail for 0.1 mile to find the hidden rail grade. If you choose not to explore the hidden rail grade, then just return on the rail-trail.

14.3 Turn right on the old woods road, noting the white blazes, and follow the main route as it bends right to Rausch Creek. At this point the road ends at the creek by the huge stone trestle foundation on the right. Turn around and return back down the main route (note the dark, coal surface of the road) for approximately

200 yards and then turn right up a short trail to gain the hidden rail grade. You may notice the white blazes of the Appalachian Trail as it turns right on the hidden rail grade and climbs up Rausch Creek. Turn left on the hidden rail grade and ride out to the Stony Valley Rail-Trail on beautiful trail.

15.3 Merge right onto the Stony Valley Rail-Trail and continue back to the trailhead.

19.0 Cross a pair of bridges at Yellow Springs.

19.5 Cross the county line between Dauphin and Lebanon Counties as marked by the wooden 4 x 4 post.

22.4 Cross the bridge over Rattling Run.

26.2 Pass the Water Tank Trail.

28.4 Pass around the gate and return to the trailhead.

Coastal Piedmont and Dutch Country

Covering a broad region including Philadelphia, Lancaster, Reading, Easton, and Allentown, this area has many gems hidden in its urban centers. The small but steep Wissahickon Gorge offers some of the burliest singletrack around and lies right in the core of Philadelphia. Traveling west to the land of horse-drawn buggies, the northern Lancaster area has some fine woodland riding on state game lands. The Reading area boasts the fine impoundments and recreation areas at Blue Marsh Lake. Allentown unveils secrets like South Mountain, and Easton is the trailhead to a ride along one of the last free-flowing rivers in the United States.

Kelly's Run Pinnacle

Location:	18 miles southwest of Lancaster.
Distance:	7.4-mile loop.
Time:	1 to 2.5 hours.
Tread:	A mix of paved road, old woods roads, and some sweet singletrack.
Aerobic level:	Moderate to strenuous. The climbing here is sustained and tough. The flat sections along the ridges are fun and fast, and the downhills are your well-earned reward for slogging all those vertical miles.
Technical difficulty:	2. The only technical section is at the start of the ride along the singletrack on the Oliver Patton Trail. A mix of rocks and roots line the upper section of Kelly's Run.
Highlights:	Expansive vista over Lake Aldred; short steep climbs and descents; Kelly's Run Natural Area, which is listed as one of the most unique natural features in Pennsylvania; great camping at nearby Otter Creek and Pequea Campgrounds.
Land status:	Pennsylvania Power and Light.
Maps:	USGS Holtwood; Pennsylvania Power and Light: Kelly's Run Pinnacle Recreation Trail map.

The expansive view, looking north up the Susquehanna, from Kelly's Run Pinnacle.

Access: From Lancaster, take U.S. Highway 222 south to the town of Willow Street. At Willow Street, take Pennsylvania Highway 272 south 8.5 miles to the town of Buck. Turn right onto Pennsylvania Highway 372. Take Pennsylvania 372 for 5 miles to Bethesda, where you will turn right onto Holtwood Road (at a fork intersection). Travel for 0.5 mile, then turn right onto River Road. Travel 0.2 mile and turn left onto Street Road where you will find the Holtwood Recreation Area on the right. As you pull into the lot, turn right and park in the first parking area on the left; this will make finding the trail much easier.

Notes on the trail: Kelly's Run is a beautiful tract of land owned and operated by the Pennsylvania Power and Light utility company. Kelly's Run itself is a beautiful stream that tumbles down a series of small waterfalls through a deeply cut rock canyon. The ferns, mosses, and other flora that grow here are unique to this location, and the rugged nature of the canyon itself lends the feeling of a more wild and remote place.

The ride itself is steep and deep. Beginning on the ridge top, the trail winds through some of the beautiful singletrack behind the Holtwood Recreation Area. The singletrack soon gives way to open fields of doubletrack and the beginning of the long descent. An abandoned section of paved road descends to the riverbed where you cross an old iron rail bridge spanning Kelly's Run. Now begins the fun part—a tough 550-foot, 1-mile climb to the outstanding Pinnacle Vista. The terrain is a bit rocky and loose in sections, but a low gear and steady cadence will help you successfully reach the

Kelly's Run Pinnacle

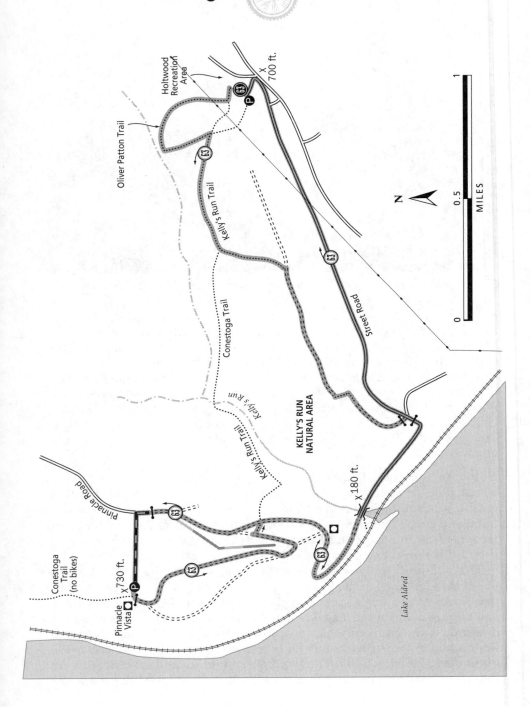

Holtwood Recreation Area

Oliver Patton Trail

X 700 ft.

P

63

Kelly's Run Trail

63

Conestoga Trail

Kelly's Run

KELLY'S RUN
NATURAL AREA

Kelly's Run Trail

Street Road

63

X 180 ft.

Pinnacle Road

63

63

63

Conestoga
Trail
(no bikes)

X 730 ft.

P

Pinnacle
Vista

Lake Aldred

N

MILES

0   0.5   1

summit. The vista is outstanding and impressive. Looking north up the Susquehanna River, the view extends out over Lake Aldred, contained by the Holtwood Dam. Enjoy the vista before the rad descent, knowing that you'll need to climb back up to the Holtwood Recreation Area.

The descent is well earned; it follows the old woods road back down to the old iron bridge. The climb back up begins on the abandoned paved road that leads into Street Road. This is the fastest and easiest way to the top, and the ride soon ends back at the trailhead at the Holtwood Recreation Area.

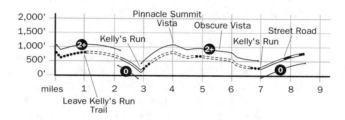

THE RIDE

0.0 From the left-most lot in the Holtwood parking area, ride toward the wood's edge and turn right, following the wood line. The trail is marked by a tall, wooden, 4 x 4 post indicating the Conestoga and Kelly's Run Trails. Turn left at this marker into the woods. After approximately 200 yards, turn right onto the yellow-blazed trail (Oliver Patton Trail) and soon pass under a power line.

0.6 Turn right at the four-way intersection onto the Conestoga and Kelly's Run Trails.

1.1 Turn left at the fork onto the obscure, red-blazed trail.

1.4 Turn right onto the old woods road. This trail runs out along the ridge between two farm fields. Note the wooden, blue-blazed posts that mark the woods road as it runs between the fields. At the end of the field the trail will turn left, following the wood line for 150 yards, and then reenter the woods in the lower corner. After a final descent the trail passes around a gate; turn right here and descend the paved pathway.

2.8 Cross the old iron bridge over Kelly's Run.

3.6 Along the arduous climb, a pipeline merges in from the left; continue to climb.

3.9 Pass around a gate and turn left onto Pinnacle Road.

4.1 Pinnacle Summit Vista. Enjoy the views looking northwest up the Susquehanna River. From here turn left, pass around a gate, keep left at the fork, and descend the hill.

4.5 Turn left at the T intersection onto the grassy old woods road. Soon after, turn left at the T intersection onto the grassy main road (note sign for buried cable.)

4.8 Turn right onto the obscure, white-blazed, singletrack trail and then take another right onto the rocky, old woods road.

5.8 Cross the old iron bridge over Kelly's Run.

6.3 Pass around the gate, keep left at the fork, and climb Street Road.

7.4 Arrive at the Holtwood trailhead.

Cornwall Fire Tower

Location: 8 miles east of Mount Gretna.

Distance: 9.7-mile loop.

Time: 2 to 3 hours.

Tread: The ride runs on a bit of paved and mostly gated dirt woods roads with a sweet, rocky singletrack finish.

Aerobic level: Easy. The long, mild ascent climbs 700 feet in over 7 miles of vertical terrain to the fire tower. The most demanding section will be the singletrack section as it drops from the ridge—but hey, it's all downhill!

Technical difficulty: 3. The difficulty rating refers exclusively to the singletrack downhill section off the hill. This 1.5-mile downhill section is a bit challenging, especially when wet. Loose and slick rocks give you plenty to contend with as the route drops a significant 500 feet off the hillside.

Highlights: Singletrack riding on the Horseshoe Trail, mellow woods road riding through forest and field, many wildlife viewing opportunities, the historic Cornwall Fire Tower.

Land status: Pennsylvania Game Commission.

Maps: USGS Lititz, Manheim; Pennsylvania Game Commission SGL 156 map.

Access: From the Pennsylvania Turnpike, take exit 20 (Lebanon and Lancaster) to Pennsylvania Highway 72 (Lebanon Road) north for 2.3 miles to U.S. Highway 322. At this junction, take US 322 east for 7 miles to the intersection with Pump Station Road. At this intersection is a large gravel parking area on the left. Pull in and park here. This lot is the trailhead. If you drive up over the Pennsylvania Turnpike, you missed the trailhead.

Notes on the trail: The Cornwall area is rich in history, and this ride is near the hills that were once run by prospect miners. Just a few miles north of the trailhead is the Cornwall Iron Furnace Historic Site where the local iron ore was mined. An impressive furnace structure and a huge, water-filled strip mine pit still remain.

The ride begins at the large parking area at Pump Station Road. From there it crosses U.S. Highway 322 and continues for a mile on the macadam. Turn off on the game commission lands. Miles of grassy and dirt woods roads lie ahead. First the road winds below the hill, but it soon turns and climbs the spine to the old Cornwall Fire Tower. Although there are no

Cornwall Fire Tower

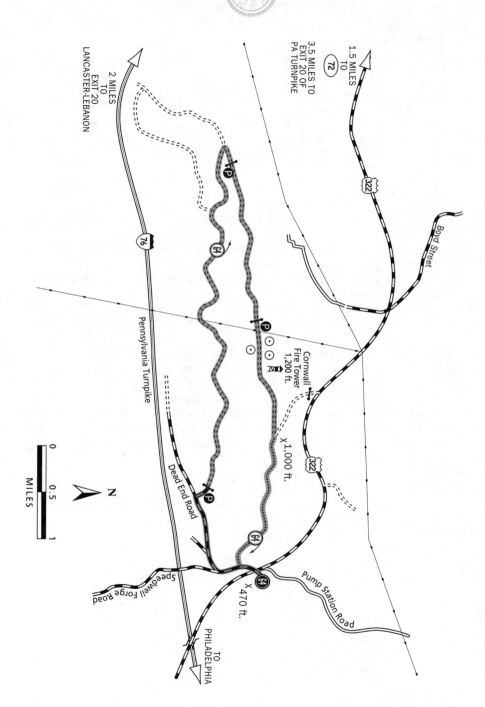

1.5 MILES TO 72

3.5 MILES TO EXIT 20 OF PA TURNPIKE

2 MILES TO EXIT 20 LANCASTER-LEBANON

76

64

322

Boyd Street

Pennsylvania Turnpike

P

Cornwall Fire Tower 1,200 ft.

X 1,000 ft.

322

Dead End Road

P

64

Speedwell Forge Road

X 470 ft.

64

Pump Station Road

TO PHILADELPHIA

0   0.5   1

MILES

N

views atop the hill, the tower marks the end of the climb. From here it's mostly downhill. A short roll out across two small knobs on the beautiful singletrack of the Horseshoe Trail will then lead to the rocky descent. A final bit of bushwhacking on the lower section runs out to Pump Station Road and the trailhead.

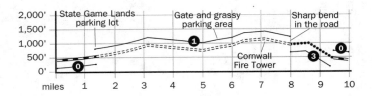

THE RIDE

0.0 From the parking area at Pump Station Road, carefully cross U.S. Highway 322 and continue on the paved Pump Station Road.

0.4 Turn right at the T intersection onto Speedwell Forge Road. Soon after, turn right onto paved Dead End Road.

1.2 Turn right into the game commission parking lot. Follow the lot to the back where the ride passes around a gate and slowly begins to climb on a grassy woods road.

5.1 Turn right at the T intersection and continue to climb at a stronger rate.

5.3 Pass around a gate and a large grassy parking area on the right.

6.8 Pass around another gate and pass through the radio tower zone.

7.2 Pass the Cornwall Fire Tower on the right at an elevation of 1,200 feet. At this point you should begin noticing the yellow blazes on the trees lining the road.

7.9 At a sharp left bend in the road, turn right into the small parking area. Follow the yellow blazes past the game commission sign and head into the woods on the singletrack.

9.4 Turn left onto Pump Station Road.

9.7 Carefully cross US 322 to the trailhead.

Governor Dick to Dinosaur Rock

Location: Mount Gretna.

Distance: 10.7-mile loop.

Time: 2 to 3 hours.

Tread: A potpourri of grassy woods roads, old rail grades, and singletrack. Most of the surfaces are smooth and fast, with only small sections of bumpy terrain.

Aerobic level: Easy to moderate. The ride does involve some climbing and is moderate in length.

Technical difficulty: 2. There are a few sections of small rocks interspersed throughout the ride as well as a section of singletrack along the Sunday Farm Trail that has some exposed roots, small downed trees, and soft trail. The rest of the ride follows beautiful old rail grades and hardpacked service roads.

Highlights: The Governor Dick observation tower and the colossal Dinosaur Rock ice age formation; great wildlife viewing.

Land status: Pennsylvania Game Commission, the Donegal School District.

Maps: USGS Elizabethtown, Manheim. Pennsylvania Game Commission, SGL 145 map.

Access: From the Pennsylvania Turnpike, take exit 20 (Lebanon and Lancaster), to Pennsylvania Highway 72 (Lebanon Road.) Go north for 2.3 miles to Pennsylvania Highway 117. At this junction, take Pennsylvania 117 southwest to Mount Gretna. In the quaint and eclectic town of Mount Gretna, turn left onto Pinch Road and climb the steep hill out of town. Near the crest of the hill is a large parking area on the left marked by a large boulder and sign board. Turn left and park in the wooded, gravel parking area. The sign board at the parking area saying "Governor Dick Wild Area" is the trailhead.

Notes on the trail: A definite must-do ride, not only for its variety of sweet trails but also for some of the coolest natural and man-made formations around. The beautiful little town of Mount Gretna in itself is quite an experience. Located in the heart of the Amish Country, this unique hillside village has a certain aura about it that just needs to be experienced first-hand. The history behind the name of the hill is interesting as well. It's named after a black woodchopper and charcoal burner who worked exclusively on this mountain felling and burning trees. His name was Dick, but

Governor Dick to Dinosaur Rock

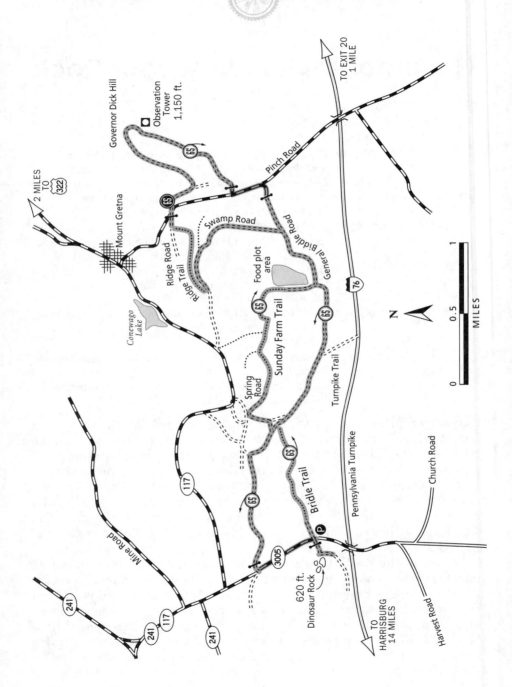

his friends nicknamed him Governor . . . and upon his death the hill was named for him. The ride begins above town on the grounds of the Governor Dick Wild Area. Atop the hill is a unique observation tower. Looking somewhat like a grain silo, this 65-foot-tall concrete tower is open to those who want to savor the 360-degree view of the surrounding Dutch Country.

The parking area is where the old narrow-gauge railroad crosses Pinch Road. From here the ride climbs the hill, linking various rail grades and old access roads to the open summit. The descent begins with a roll along the game lands out to the infamous Dinosaur Rock. This 50-foot-high balancing act of nature is quite an impressive sight. Left here from the last ice age, these precarious rocks have the uncanny texture and profile of a dinosaur. Considered terminal moraine, this field of glacier-polished stone is a great place to ride trials. The trail loops back, combining singletrack with woods roads and a bit of route-finding along grassy clearings to the trailhead. A prehistoric ride indeed!

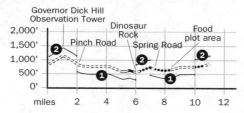

THE RIDE

0.0 From the trailhead, with Pinch Road to your back, take the gated road to the right (the old narrow gauge rail grade).

0.3 Turn left at the trail spur and climb the gritty access road.

1.2 Arrive at the summit observation tower. Check out the tower and its staggered ladder approach. The ride continues past the tower on the wide, gravel woods road, which will soon descend the hill in a most heinous way.

1.9 Pass around a gate and turn left onto Pinch Road.

2.1 Turn right into the state game land parking lot. Continue through the lot and pass through the gate onto the gravel woods road (General Biddle Road).

3.0 Keep left at the fork with the Sunday Farm Trail, staying on the main roadway. Make a mental note of this intersection, as you will return here again.

4.3 Keep left at the forked intersection.

5.1 Pass around the gate and ride through the lot out to Pennsylvania Road 3005. Turn left onto Pennsylvania 3005.

5.8 Turn right, just past the huge boulders, onto the gated Dinosaur Rock Trail.

5.9 Stare in amazement at the Dinosaur Rock formation. Enjoy the scenery and return back out to Pennsylvania 3005. Turn left onto Pennsylvania 3005 and after 100 yards turn right into the state game lands parking lot. Ride to the end of the lot to the Bridle Trail marked by a wooden trail sign. Enter the woods here on a singletrack trail (mile 6.1).

The infamous Dinosaur Rock.

6.9 Turn left at the T intersection and then, 100 yards later, turn right onto the grassy woods road. Soon after, this grassy woods road forks; keep left at the fork (mile 7.0).

7.2 Turn hard right onto the wide singletrack right-hand trail (Spring Road). This turn is 50 yards before a T intersection of the grassy woods roads.

7.7 Keep right at an indistinct fork.

7.9 Continue straight past a left-hand spur of the Sunday Farm Trail.

8.3 Come to the grassy clearing (food plot area), turn right here, and follow the edge of the wood line.

8.5 Turn left at the T intersection onto the dirt road (General Biddle Road).

9.0 Turn left at the trail spur onto the dirt, hardpacked Swamp Road.

9.9 After passing a right-hand spur trail, turn hard right onto the second singletrack (Ridge Trail) and begin a slow, wide singletrack climb.

10.5 Turn right at the T intersection onto Ridge Road.

10.7 Pass around a gate and carefully cross Pinch Road to the trailhead.

Roadkill Hill

Location: 5 miles northwest of Reading.

Distance: 7-mile loop.

Time: 30 minutes to 1.5 hours.

Tread: Most of the ride follows beautiful, lakeside, hardpacked, clay singletrack. Short areas of grassy doubletrack, gravel road, and paved road are interspersed throughout. Typical small areas of loose stones and a slick wooden bridge round out the terrain.

Aerobic level: Moderate to strenuous. The first half is relatively flat and fast, while the second half is quite a bit more challenging with a killer climb up Blue Marsh Ski Area, which is a real lung-buster.

Technical difficulty: 3 + . The Blue Marsh Ski Area climb is burly and the descent down the backside of the ski area is steep and sharply switchbacked. Roadkill Hill has a stout drop on a 50-degree slope with no run-out.

Highlights: Killer hill climb, sharp, sketchy, switchback descent, Roadkill Hill; Blue Marsh Lake with swimming area; fishing and powerboating, major bonus!

Land status: US Army Corps of Engineers.

Maps: USGS Bernville; US Army Corps of Engineers: Blue Marsh Lake Multi Purpose Trail map.

Roadkill Hill

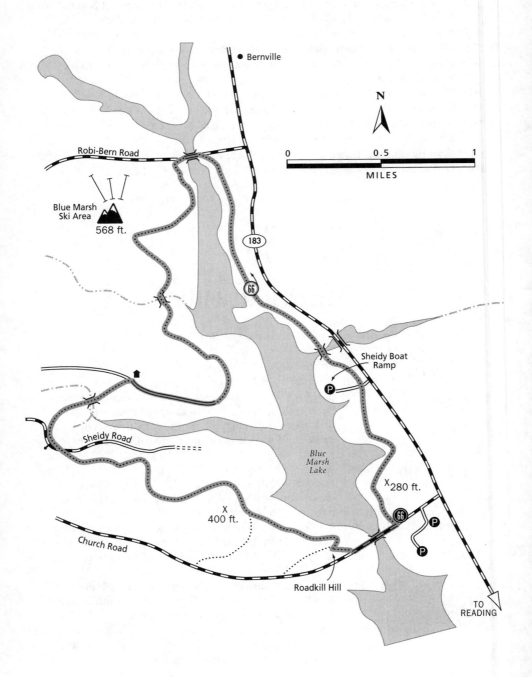

Bernville

N

0   0.5   1
MILES

Robi-Bern Road

Blue Marsh
Ski Area
568 ft.

183

66

Sheidy Boat
Ramp

P

Sheidy Road

Blue
Marsh
Lake

X 280 ft.

X
400 ft.

66

P

Church Road

P

Roadkill Hill

TO
READING

Access: From Reading, take Pennsylvania Highway 183 north to Bernville. After crossing the Mount Pleasant bridge, travel for 1.2 miles to Church Road. Turn left onto Church Road and park in the gravel parking lot on the right, just before the bridge. This is the trailhead.

Notes on the trail: This is a great ride when you're looking to blow off some steam but don't have a lot of time. The lake offers a swimming beach, and if you have a boat of any kind, Blue Marsh is the place to bring it. From power-boat waterskiing to still-water canoeing, this is a boater's paradise. Weekends, though, can be a boaters nightmare—bring a canoe or kayak and paddle the quiet upper reaches of the lake.

The ride leaves the lot and works its way along the east edge of the lake on flat, fast singletrack. The Robi-Bern Road bridge is about the midway mark, and by then you should be warmed up to take on the killer hill climb ahead. A small dip down to the lake level keeps you honest as the trail begins an arduous ascent to the summit. The consistent degree of steepness will have you sitting hard in the saddle as you struggle to clear the top. With your lungs on overtime, you can probably feel your heart beat through your bike's top-tube. The backside offers the welcome pull of gravity as it sends you down into a sharp switchback and over a slick bridge.

Gradual climbing through fields and woods leads to the finale, Roadkill Hill! Kick back in the saddle and blast down the hill; just watch for vehicles obscured by the hill on the left. As the name infers, if you aren't careful at the bottom of this descent, you may become some fine dining for the vultures or, possibly, a new hood ornament. If Roadkill Hill is beyond your nerve, you can continue straight along the top of the road cut and exit at a lower point.

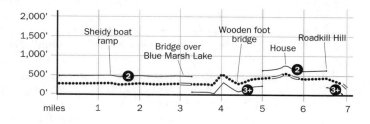

THE RIDE

0.0 The trail begins in the left corner of the lot, close to the bridge.

1.2 Cross the access road to Sheidy Boat Ramp, continue straight across the grassy field, looking for the brown fiberglass IMBA marker to regain the trail.

1.5 Cross a wooden bridge.

3.0 Turn left onto Robi-Bern Road. Cross the road bridge, noting Blue Marsh Ski Hill up above. After crossing the bridge and as the guardrail ends, hook a left around the guardrail to regain the trail back into the woods.

3.4 Turn left at the fork and descend down along the lake. Begin the killer grind!

4.3 Cross the stream via the wooden bridge.

5.5 Trail turns hard left into woods, across from a house. Turn left onto Sheidy Road (paved), pass around a gate, and follow the trail markers.

6.1 Turn left at the fork.

6.7 Turn left down Roadkill Hill, which is what you'll be if you run it out to the asphalt! Seriously, watch for cars along Church Road. Turn left onto Church Road and cross the road bridge.

7.0 Trailhead.

Blue Marsh Lake Loop

Location:	5 miles north-west of Reading.
Distance:	29.2-mile loop.
Time:	3 to 6 hours.
Tread:	Most of the ride follows beautiful, lakeside, hardpacked, clay singletrack. There are short areas of grassy doubletrack, gravel road and paved road interspersed throughout. Typical small areas of loose stones and a few slick wooden bridges round out the terrain.
Aerobic level:	Strenuous. This ride follows the contours of Blue Marsh Lake, with countless short climbs and descents. The hills are abrupt and demanding and usually hit you when you least expect it. The downhills are real rippers and get some serious adrenaline flowing.
Technical difficulty:	3. The most demanding section is a hill climb near the summit of Blue Marsh Ski Area, which is seriously sustained and steep.
Highlights:	Open rolling fields; tight, twisty singletrack; bridges; short, powerful hill climbs; Blue Marsh Lake with swimming area, fishing, and powerboating.
Land status:	US Army Corps of Engineers.
Maps:	USGS Bernville, Sinking Springs; Blue Marsh Lake Multi-Purpose Trail map.

Access: From Reading, head west on U.S. Highway 422. After passing the junction of U.S. Highway 222 and the town of Sinking Spring (approximately 1.5 miles), turn right onto Green Valley Road. Green Valley Road dead-ends into Brownsville Road; turn right onto Brownsville Road. Travel for 0.7 mile and turn left into the State Hill Boat Ramp parking area. The parking area is the trailhead.

Notes on the trail: Blue Marsh Lake, an oasis tucked away in the Reading area, was constructed by the Army Corps of Engineers in the late 1970s. The massive lake is open for boating and swimming and is great place to end the ride on a warm summer day. The trail is a mult-iuse trail, which means that you will be sharing it with hikers and equestrians as well. As IMBA rules state, cyclists must yield to both of these groups. The singletrack sections contain many blind turns, so please keep your speed in check, mainly because the trail is often ridden in both directions. The trail is generally marked with thin brown fiberglass posts, which have either a hiker and/or triangular IMBA symbol with a directional arrow. On the western side of the lake you will encounter a separate loop trail system. Follow the guide-book directions carefully through this section, so you don't stray from the intended ride. The countless bridges you will cross along the way are ex-tremely dangerous when wet. Locals tell heinous stories of riders decking out on the bridges at crazy speeds; use your head, or you'll be on it.

You will pass through diverse ecosystems as you wind through open field edges and pass through cool, wooded forests. The general topography is a fun mix of hills and rolling sections, making for a fast ride on the hardpack surface. After a good rain this trail becomes very muddy due to its clay base, so plan your trip accordingly. Finally, the views atop some of the climbs are quite grand and well worth the effort to get to them.

(A shorter loop may be made by crossing the Church Road bridge at mile 11.6 and continuing on with the directions from mile 19.0. By cutting out the upper loop you will be avoiding the killer climb as well as Roadkill Hill. You may find this necessary if you need a bail-out point. This shorter loop is approximately 22 miles.)

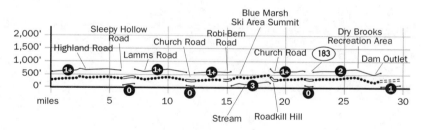

THE RIDE

0.0 From the trailhead, head northwest up through the grassy field pass the trailhead information pavilion and follow the singletrack into the woods.

0.1 Keep right at the trail fork, with the lake in view on your right. Soon after, merge with a gravel road and cross a wooden footbridge.

0.5 Keep right at the trail fork.

1.2 Cross a bridge and keep right at the trail fork. Soon after, cross another bridge and keep right at the trail fork.

2.3 Cross Sterners Hill Road and in 0.5 mile cross a bridge.

3.2 Cross a paved road.

Blue Marsh Lake Loop

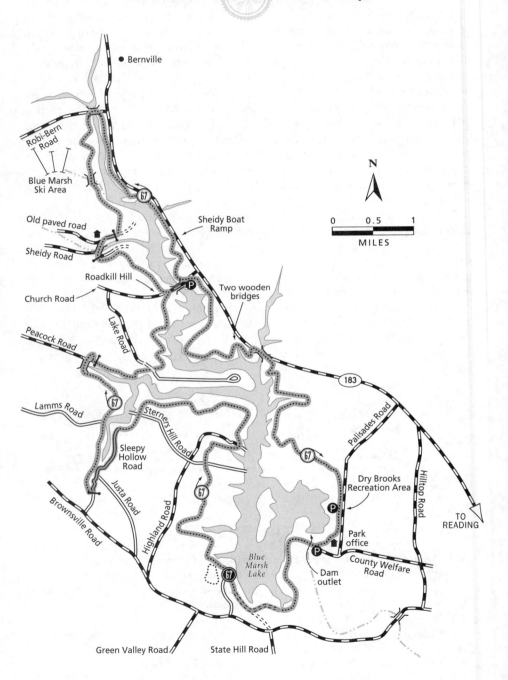

Bernville

Robi-Bern Road

Blue Marsh Ski Area

Old paved road

Sheidy Road

Roadkill Hill

Church Road

Peacock Road

Lake Road

Lamms Road

Sleepy Hollow Road

Justa Road

Brownsville Road

Highland Road

Sterners Hill Road

Sheidy Boat Ramp

Two wooden bridges

Palisades Road

Dry Brooks Recreation Area

Hilltop Road

TO READING

Park office

County Welfare Road

Dam outlet

Blue Marsh Lake

Green Valley Road

State Hill Road

N

0   0.5   1
MILES

67
183

4.7 Cross a wooden bridge.

5.6 Cross Sterners Hill Road again.

6.1 Turn left onto Sleepy Hollow Road. Follow the main road and watch for the hiker/IMBA icon markers along the road.

6.8 Pass Justa Road on left.

7.1 Pass around a gate and take an immediate right into woods. The trail soon crosses another wooden bridge.

7.8 Cross a bridge.

8.2 Cross Lamms Road.

9.0 Cross the bridge onto Peacock Road. Bear right and pass around a gate on the right. Turn left into the woods and after 0.2 mile head up a killer switchback.

9.8 Turn left up Lake Road, then turn right onto a grassy road. Soon after, turn left onto the blue and white diamond-blazed trail.

11.6 Turn right onto Church Road and note the gnarly downhill on your left across the road (Roadkill Hill). Cross the bridge, then turn left into the parking lot and regain the trail in the left corner of the lot as it heads back down toward the lake.

13.2 Cross the access road to Sheidy Boat Ramp. Continue straight across and into the grassy field, look for the IMBA marker to regain the trail. Soon you cross a bridge.

15.0 Turn left onto Robi-Bern Road. Cross the bridge. Note Blue Marsh Ski Area up above on the left—you will be climbing to its summit. As soon as the guardrail ends, take a hard left around it to regain the trail back down into the woods.

15.4 Turn left at the fork and descend along the lake to get the full brunt of the heinous hill climb.

16.3 Cross the stream.

17.5 Trail turns hard left into the woods, across from a house. Soon the trail crosses a bridge, turns left onto a paved road, and passes around a gate.

18.1 Turn left at the trail fork.

18.7 Turn left down Roadkill Hill, which is what you'll be if you run it out to the street! Turn left onto Church Road and cross the bridge again.

19.0 Pass a parking entrance on the right. The trail resumes about 100 yards further up on the right.

21.6 Cross over two wooden bridges.

22.0 Pass around guardrail, turn right onto Pennsylvania Highway 183, and cross the bridge. The trail ascends into the woods at mile 22.2. Note the Mount Pleasant sign.

23.5 Turn right at the Cornerhouse Road sign.

24.8 Turn left at the T intersection, following the direction for the "Main Hiking Trail."

25.9 Cross the paved road leading into Dry Brooks Recreation Area.

26.3 Cross the parking lot at the ranger station. Follow the signs southeast across the lot to the descending grass trail.

27.0 Turn right onto the paved road leading to the Stilling Basin parking area.

27.3 Cross the dam outlet.

28.2 Turn right at a T intersection, onto State Hill Road.

29.2 Trailhead.

French Creek

Location:	French Creek State Park, 15 miles southwest of Pottstown.
Distance:	18.5-mile loop.
Time:	2 to 4 hours.
Tread:	Washed-out trail with loose rocks, gravel, and dirt. A few sections run on old woods roads that are just as sketchy.
Aerobic level:	Moderate to strenuous. The ride rolls along with numerous dips and rises that will lift the heart rate. The ultratechnical sections will require extra endurance to ride them clean. The grind to the fire tower is tough, but if you stay low in the saddle and grunt it out, you can send it to the summit.
Technical difficulty:	4. Stones, rocks, boulders, blocks, babyheads, rimbenders, snakebiters—whatever you call them— French Creek is loaded with them. Notorious for its rough terrain, most of the trails encountered will be carpeted with all of the items listed above.
Highlights:	Technical singletrack, Hopewell Fire Tower, swimming pool, boating, fishing, disc golf, orienteering courses, camping, cabins, Hopewell Furnace National Historic Site.
Land status:	Pennsylvania State Park, Department of Conservation and Recreation.
Maps:	USGS Elverson; DCNR Pennsylvania State Parks: French Creek State Park map.

Access: From Pottstown, take Pennsylvania Highway 100 south to Pennsylvania Highway 23 in Bucktown. Turn right onto Pennsylvania 23 (aka Ridge Road) and head west for 6.5 miles to Pennsylvania 345. Turn right onto Pennsylvania 345, head north to the south entrance for French Creek State Park. Turn left into the south entrance for French Creek State Park and then, at the T intersection, turn right onto Park Road. Follow Park Road for 0.3 mile, passing the park office and first parking area. Turn into the second parking area on the right near Hopewell Lake. This lot is the trailhead.

Notes on the trail: French Creek, the eastern Pennsylvania mecca for mountain bikers, is quite a rad park. One of only thirteen state parks that actually allows mountain bikes, French Creek has prided itself on offering a vast array of trails for off-road two-wheeled thrill seekers. Located adjacent to the federal lands of Hopewell Furnace National Historic Site, this 7,339-acre park is laced with prime mountain bike bliss.

Before setting out on the ride, grab a free copy of the park's map. On it you will see the trails closed to mountain bikes (few indeed), so don't be a Bevis if you intend to explore trails off the described route. Our mountain biking relationship with French Creek depends on our actions as a whole, including volunteer trail maintenance. Call the park at 610-582-9680 for details on trail crew work days. It's not only a great way to support our sport, it's also a great way to meet other cool riders.

The loop is long, fun, and doubles back on itself in places, so study the map and directions before setting out. The ride begins with a full dose of rocks and logs as it winds around the knob below the fire tower. A gradual climb passes through the boulder field and the RV campground. It then crosses over Pennsylvania Highway 345 to the eastside loop. The Miller Point Rock outcrop is a good stopping place along the way; it has some wicked old woods roads that whip around to Pennsylvania 345. Retrace the route back through the boulder field; then the trail drops off a gnarly downhill to Scotts Lake. Payment is due as moderate grades lead to the supersteep climb to the fire tower. Bomber singletrack finishes the ride and spews you out at Hopewell Lake.

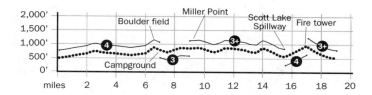

THE RIDE

0.0 From the parking area, head back down to Park Road and turn right.

0.4 Turn left onto the yellow-blazed Horseshoe Trail.

0.8 Keep left at the fork, staying on the yellow-blazed Horseshoe Trail. A trail will soon merge in from the right; keep straight.

1.2 Keep left at the fork, following the white and yellow blazes.

3.2 Pass the Ridge Trail (no bikes).

4.3 Cross the Fire Tower Road; pass a right-hand blue blazed trail; continue straight.

4.8 Turn left at the fork and follow the blue blazes (Boone Trail).

5.2 Cross Fire Tower Road.

5.6 Cross Fire Tower Road again and follow the gravel road, looking for the blue blazes. You'll pass a yellow-blazed trail on the left and the gravel road will switchback shortly.

6.1 The trail breaks from the gravel road and goes off into the woods; follow the blue blazes.

French Creek

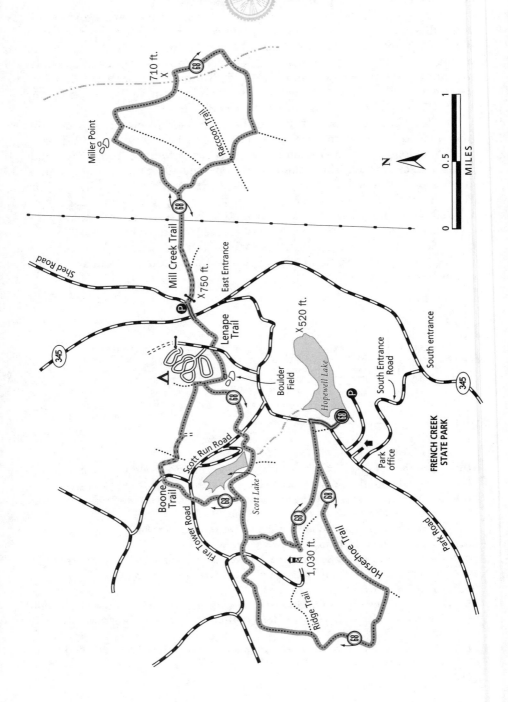

Miller Point

710 ft. X

68

Raccoon Trail

68

Shed Road

Mill Creek Trail

X 750 ft.

East Entrance

345

Lenape Trail

68

Boulder Field

Hopewell Lake

X 520 ft.

South Entrance Road

South entrance

345

Park office

Scott Run Road

Boone Trail

Fire Tower Road

68

Scott Lake

68

1,030 ft.

68

Ridge Trail

Horseshoe Trail

68

Park Road

FRENCH CREEK STATE PARK

N

0   0.5   1
MILES

6.5 Turn right at the T intersection, following the blue and green blazes. Pass the green trail as it spurs off right and ride through the boulder field.

6.9 Turn left following the green blazes (Lenape Trail) and cross the campground road.

7.3 Cross Pennsylvania Highway 345 and ride briefly along Shed Road. Take a quick right onto gated old woods road; you'll passing the mountain bike information bulletin board. Follow the white and red blazes on the Mill Creek Trail.

7.7 Pass a right-hand trail spur and pass under a power line.

8.5 Turn hard left at the trail spur; you can miss it easily, so look carefully.

9.2 Miller Point rock formation.

9.5 Turn left at the T intersection and descend to Mill Creek.

10.2 Pass red-blazed trail (Raccoon Trail) on the right.

11.6 Turn right at the fork at the bottom of the descent.

11.9 Pass the Raccoon Trail again; stay straight on the red and white blazes.

13.5 Turn left onto Shed Road, cross Pennsylvania 345, and ride up the green-blazed trail (Lenape Trail).

14.1 Cross over the paved campground road; follow the blue and green blazes back through the boulder field. Turn left soon after, descending the green-blazed Lenape Trail to Scott Run Road.

15.1 Cross Scott's Run Road.

15.3 Trail empties onto a paved road. Turn hard left, following the edge of the woods. Soon after turn right, cross the spillway bridge, and follow the yellow-blazed trail.

15.6 After riding up from the dam, turn right at the T intersection and stay on the yellow-blazed trail.

16.3 Turn left onto the blue and white-blazed trail, climbing to the fire tower. If you come to a paved road, you missed the left turn.

16.7 At the summit four-way intersection, turn right to check out the fire tower and stone ranger's cabin. Turn around and head back to the four-way intersection. Continue straight and follow the blue blazes as they descend off the hill.

18.0 Turn right and continue to descend on the blue-blazed trail.

18.3 Turn right on Park Road, then left up to the trailhead parking area.

18.5 Trailhead.

A bit haggard but still smiling after a "snake-bite."

Wicked Wissahickon Valley

Location: Fairmount Park, 5 miles east of Conshohocken.

Distance: 13.4-mile loop.

Time: 1 to 3 hours.

Tread: The majority of this ride follows wide singletrack generously covered with rocks and roots. Some sections feature twisty, hardpacked singletrack gravel pathways.

Aerobic level: Moderate to strenuous. Loaded with short, steep hill climbs, the trail becomes a rolling challenge that causes you to "ride the clutch" as you constantly shift gears.

Technical difficulty: 4. This place is loaded with technical challenges including loose sand, burly rocks, and scary-slick roots.

Highlights: Historic covered bridge, creek crossings, interesting geology, rock climbing at Livezey Rock, historic houses, statues, views, urban wilderness.

Land status: Philadelphia Parks System, Fairmount Park.

Maps: Fairmount Park Commission Wissahickon Multi-Use Trail map.

Access: From Conshohocken, at the corner of Ridge and Butler Pikes, head southeast on Ridge Avenue for 3 miles to Bells Mill Road. Turn left onto Bells Mill Road and follow it for 1 mile down into the valley. After passing a parking lot on the right and a stop sign, cross over the small stone bridge and turn left into the parking lot. This is the trailhead.

Notes on the trail: This is a stellar ride that offers some nice singletrack in the heart of the city. Proximity to the city has both advantages and disadvantages. Food, fuel, lodging, and nightlife are in abundance. Security can sometimes be a problem. Cars have often been broken into and even stolen from many of the trailhead lots. If you plan on riding here, hide anything that looks remotely tempting or, better yet, clean out the car and leave your valuables at home. Thieves have been known to break windows just for change or a CD sitting on a seat. On occasion lone riders have been stripped of their bikes. Ride in pairs for safety. The Fairmount Park Commission requires that riders obtain a park permit, which can be requested from the following address: Fairmount Park Commission, Memorial Hall, PO Box 21601, Philadelphia, PA 19131-0901, or call 215-685-0000. A small donation

Wicked Wissahickon Valley

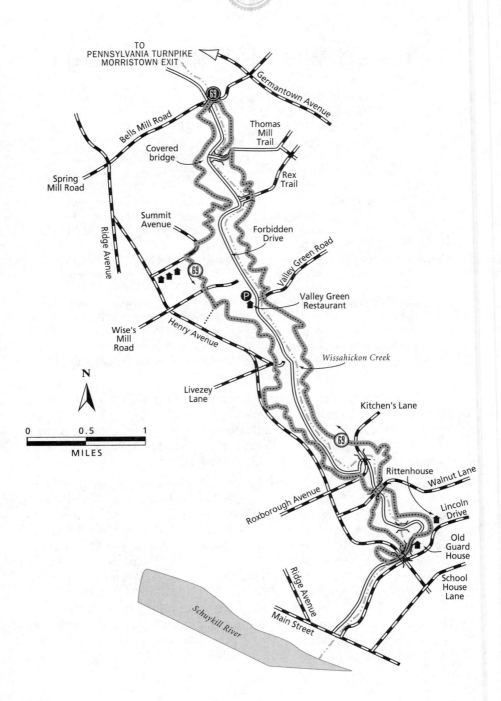

for this permit will help with trail maintenance and ensure that the area remains open for mountain biking.

This urban challenge is well worth riding and has some of the most technical lines in the region. The route runs along the narrow tract of Fairmount Park lands and the Wissahickon Creek. If you get turned around, just follow the Wissahickon upstream along Forbidden Drive to the trailhead. Evidence of the geologic history of Wissahickon Valley can be observed from the trail, and folded rock strata and garnet-peppered rock can be seen throughout the entire park. The infamous Livezey Rock is a popular spot for rock climbers who scale the 40-foot-high hunk of mica-schist. The tainted Wissahickon Creek is on the rebound: over time it's becoming a cleaner haven for aquatic critters and now offers the persistent fisherman some angling opportunities. Rhododendron grows here in abundance. In late June, its beautiful white blooms add a splash of brightness to the woodland landscape.

The ride begins with a rough hill climb up from the valley and rolls along the top ridge all the way to the Henry Avenue bridge. A quick drop will take you to the other side of the Wissahickon where the trail returns past the historic Rittenhouse. Singletrack snakes its way above the valley and challenges the rider with harder technical sections. The climb from Green Lane Road presents a formidable slog up the steep switchback, and the singletrack above that is littered with bone-breaking rocks. The trailhead may be a welcome sight for some whose ability and endurance have been pushed to the limit.

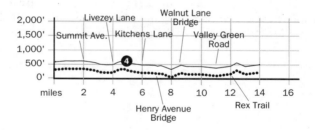

THE RIDE

0.0 From the lot, turn right onto Bells Mill Road and cross the stone bridge. Turn left onto the cinder pathway; this is Forbidden Drive. Travel on Forbidden Drive for approximately 100 yards, pass a trail map sign and split-rail fence, and turn right up the steep hill.

0.5 Trail forks; keep right and follow the yellow blazes.

0.9 Turn right at the trail spur. Keep left at the next fork.

1.4 Turn right at the T intersection, then turn right and cross the bridge.

1.9 Turn right at trail spur.

2.1 Exit onto Summit Avenue, turn left, and climb the hill.

2.3 Reenter the woods on the left on a faint singletrack. If you begin passing houses on the left, you missed the turn.

2.6 Cross Wise's Mill Road.

2.8 Turn left at the T intersection.

3.4 Continue straight at four-way intersection.

4.0 Cross Livezey Lane.

4.5 Turn hard right and cross two bridges.

5.3 Turn right at the T intersection and climb the hill. Once on top, turn left across the gravel trail.

6.0 Cross a path (Kitchens Lane.)

6.7 Turn right at the T intersection.

7.0 Pass under the infamous Henry Avenue bridge. As you walk down the dirt slope between the spans, you will note the obscure rock climbs in the arches. Soon, turn left at the T intersection and descend on a gravel and dirt path.

7.6 Lay on the brakes hard! Turn left at the T intersection; do not cross the bridge onto Lincoln Drive!

7.9 Follow the cinder path straight, as it passes directly through the old guardhouse.

8.1 Turn left at the T intersection, up a gravel drive. Pass the historic Rittenhouse on your right. The trail now follows the orange blazes.

8.6 Pass under the Walnut Lane bridge.

10.1 Turn left onto the paved road. Reenter the woods 0.1 mile down on the right.

11.0 Cross over Valley Green Road.

12.1 Cross over the Rex Trail and begin climbing the switchbacks. About halfway up, the trail forks; keep right at the fork and continue to climb the steep switchbacks.

12.6 Turn left at the T intersection and head down the wide gravel and dirt road.

12.8 The trail sweeps right into the woods just before the small clearing. If you came out into the clearing at the covered bridge, you went too far.

13.4 Trailhead.

Pine Run Preamble

Location: Pennypack Park, 4 miles south of Huntingdon Valley in northeast Philadelphia.

Distance: 5.8-mile loop.

Time: 30 minutes to 1 hour.

Tread: Paved multi-use pathways and singletrack trail with wide, dirt, multi-use trails making up the majority of the ride.

Aerobic level: Easy to moderate. There are plenty of rolling hills and flat cruising sections. The climbs are short, mild, and easily overcome by the diligent novice, and the descents are always welcome.

Technical difficulty: 1+. Most of the route runs on relatively smooth multi-use, dirt trail, with the occasional section of exposed rocks. The surface is well worn, and obvious riding lines through the difficult sections are apparent.

Highlights: Great woodland trail riding, fishing, wildlife viewing, authentic Philly hot-dog stand.

Land status: Philadelphia Parks System, Pennypack Park, Fairmount Park Commission.

Maps: Friends of the Pennypack Park Multi-use Trail map.

Access: From Huntingdon Valley at the intersection of Pennsylvania Highways 232 and 63, travel southeast on Pennsylvania 63 (Philmont Avenue) for 0.5 mile to Red Lion Road. Turn right onto Red Lion Road and climb the hill to the traffic light. At the traffic light turn right onto Pine Road. At the next traffic light turn left onto Welsh Road (Pennsylvania 63) and then turn right onto Pine Road at the next traffic light (Pine Road takes a jog but continues on uninterrupted). Travel approximately 2 miles to another traffic light at Moredon Road. Pass through the intersection at Moredon Road and cross a concrete bridge. Once across the bridge, take an immediate left into the Pine Run parking lot. Pine Run parking lot is the trailhead.

Notes on the trail: Pennypack Park is an oasis in the northeastern section of Philadelphia, just on the border of Montgomery County. A paved multi-use trail runs the length of the park on the southwest side of Pennypack Creek. Many people come here to unwind and at times the trail can become quite crowded. Moms with strollers, fledgling young bike riders, and seniors all stroll along the peaceful path, so keep your speed in check and your bike under control. The park is also well known for its high deer and duck populations and it's quite common to come in close contact with these

Pine Run Preamble

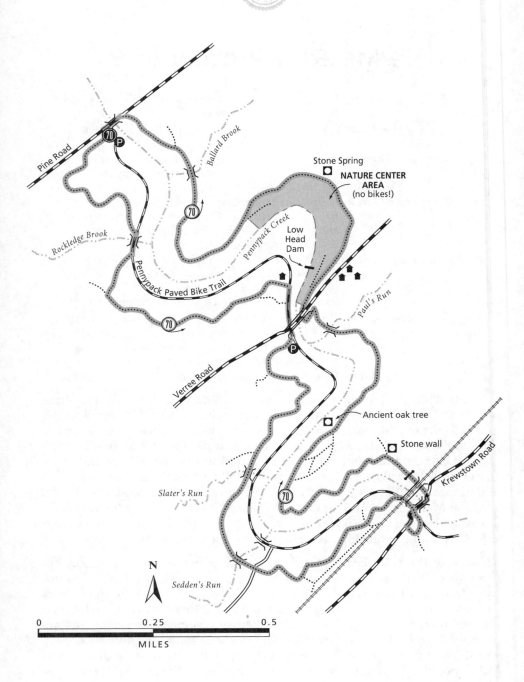

Stone Spring

NATURE CENTER AREA (no bikes!)

Pine Road

Ballard Brook

Rockledge Brook

Pennypack Creek

Low Head Dam

Pennypack Paved Bike Trail

Paul's Run

Verree Road

Ancient oak tree

Stone wall

Krewstown Road

Slater's Run

N

Sedden's Run

MILES

0   0.25   0.5

animals. Respect the wild animals by giving them space. Friends of the Pennypack Park is a great volunteer organization that works on trail projects and also offers a great trail map that may be helpful when riding in the park—see the appendix for an address.

From the trailhead, the ride sets out on wide singletrack for a short bit before dumping out on the paved path and crossing Rockledge Brook. The ride resumes on the other side with a nice section of wide dirt trail high above the creek. Further out, a quick descent will take you down under the massive Krewstown railroad bridge and up onto Krewstown Road. Careful crossing of the Krewstown bridge and road will have you riding back along the other side of Pennypack Creek. A windy and somewhat sandy trail awaits as the ride finds its course through a floodplain woodland. Ancient trees become pleasant obstacles as the trail weaves amid their towering trunks. After a final rocky crossing under the Verree Road bridge, you wind down the end of the ride, which loops back again to the Pine Run parking lot trailhead.

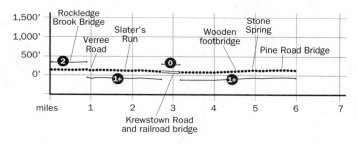

THE RIDE

0.0 From Pine Run parking lot, ride out toward Pine Road. Turn left just before you hit the road at a set of cut wooden telephone poles and climb the dirt trail.

0.4 Join paved trail and turn right, crossing the wooden bridge over Rockledge Brook. Bear right and climb up the wide dirt trail (which may be marked as a horse trail).

0.5 Once atop the hill turn left at the T intersection onto the wide dirt trail.

0.9 Turn left at the trail fork and descend the technical singletrack, passing the stone bathrooms. Turn right onto the paved trail and follow it left at the fork, under Verree Road.

1.0 Pass under the bridge and take an immediate right. (Be *very careful* crossing over the entrance of the parking area, as cars pull in from above on the right!) Resume riding on the dirt trail straight ahead.

1.1 After ascending the steep hill, keep left at the fork.

1.3 Keep straight at the right-hand trail.

1.8 Keep left at the trail fork and soon cross a wooden footbridge.

2.3 Keep left at the trail fork.

2.7 Turn left at the trail fork and go straight at next trail intersection. The trail descends to the paved trail; turn right onto the paved trail.

3.0 Cross under Krewstown railroad and road bridges. Once under the second bridge, turn right and climb the steep dirt trail. Turn right onto Krewstown Road, carefully ride across the bridge, and cross the road (lots of traffic, no shoulder!). Once across the bridge, turn left into the parking lot, continue straight past a steel gate, and go under the tall Krewstown railroad bridge.

3.2 Immediately after passing a small stone wall, turn left at the singletrack spur trail and descend the short, steep wash.

3.8 The trails begin dividing along this section; it's like trail a la carte! Ride any trail through this section (it's best to stay close to the creek); they all rejoin.

4.0 Pass a massive, old oak tree!

4.4 Cross a wooden footbridge. The trail forks and rejoins, choose either fork.

4.6 Cross another footbridge. The trail takes you to Verree Road and then turns left, dropping down sharply to pass under the Verree Road bridge.

4.7 Turn right at the trail fork and climb the wide dirt road. (Please stay off the nature center footpath!)

4.9 Pass an old stone spring on the right.

5.2 Keep left at the trail fork.

5.6 Turn left onto the Pine Run Road bridge and ride across on the sidewalk.

5.8 Turn left into the Pine Run parking lot trailhead.

The Edge

Location:	Pennypack Park, 4 miles south of Huntingdon Valley in northeast Philadelphia.
Distance:	9.1-mile loop.
Time:	1 to 2 hours.
Tread:	Half of the ride runs on relatively smooth multiuse dirt trail with occasional sections of exposed rocks. The other half covers tight, twisty singletrack, with surfaces ranging from deep sand along the creek bank to plates of pointed rock along the Mica-shist Cliff Trail.
Aerobic level:	Easy to moderate. There are lots of short, fun, rolling hills along this creekside ride.
Technical difficulty:	2 + . This ride encompasses two of the most technical lines in the park, the Edge Trail and the Mica-shist Cliff Trail. The Edge runs on a foot-wide trail, 30 feet above the Pennypack Creek. A fall here would mean a swim in the creek. The Mica-shist Cliff Trail drops off 50 feet through an outcropping of mica-schist. Fang-like plates of rock wait for the hapless mountain biker and shiny new frame!

Highlights:	Stream crossing, short 'n' scary technical lines, historic stone bridge circa 1793, great woodland trail riding, fishing, great wildlife viewing, authentic Philly hot-dog stand.
Land status:	Philadelphia Parks System, Pennypack Park, Fairmount Park Commission.
Maps:	USGS Frankford; Friends of the Pennypack Park Multiuse Trail map.

Access: From Huntingdon Valley at the intersection of Pennsylvania Highways 232 and 63, travel southeast on Pennsylvania 63 (Philmont Avenue) for 0.5 mile to Red Lion Road. Turn right onto Red Lion Road and climb the hill to the traffic light. At the traffic light turn right onto Pine Road. At the next traffic light turn left on Welsh Road (Pennsylvania 63) and then turn right onto Pine Road at the next traffic light (Pine Road takes a jog but continues on uninterrupted). Travel approximately 2 miles to the traffic light at Moredon Road. Pass through the intersection at Moredon Road and cross a concrete bridge. Once across the bridge, take an immediate left into the Pine Run parking lot, which is the trailhead.

Notes on the trail: The Pennypack Park is a great destination for riders in the Philadelphia vicinity and offers a variety of terrain in a small tract of land. The park is surrounded in rich history and includes the old Newtown Road Bridge, Verree House, Pennypack Environmental Center, Krewstown railroad bridge, and 200-year-old towering trees.

The ride begins at the Pine Road parking area and immediately jumps onto the singletrack. Wide dirt trails and rolling terrain ensue as the route crosses under Verree Road and down to the massive Krewstown railroad bridge. Once under this impressive structure, the trail continues on under Bustleton Avenue and leads to the "Edge." Careful riding will soon take you above the mighty mica-shist cliff and across Pennypack Creek, at the ride's midpoint.

A great return ride upstream passes over the historic Newtown Road Bridge and makes its way back to the Krewstown railroad bridge. The next section of singletrack, down along the floodplain, passes massive towering oaks and poplar trees. Some of the trees here must be 200 years old.

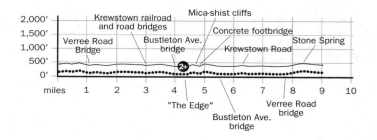

The Edge

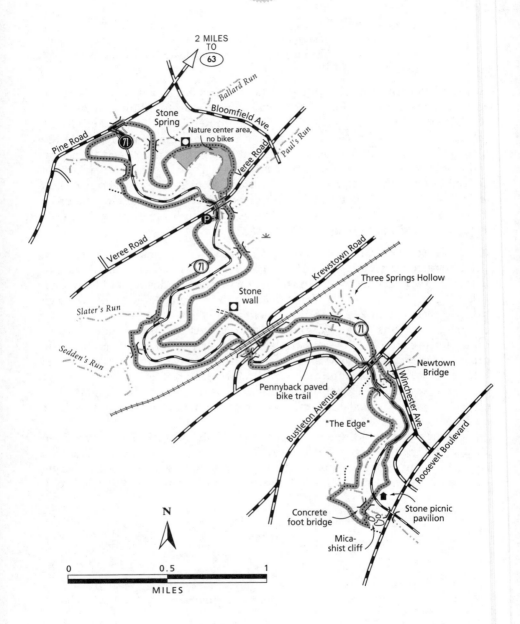

2 MILES TO 63

Ballard Run

Stone Spring

Bloomfield Ave.

Nature center area, no bikes

Pine Road

71

Veree Road

Paul's Run

P

Veree Road

71

Krewstown Road

Three Springs Hollow

Stone wall

71

Slater's Run

Sedden's Run

Newtown Bridge

Pennyback paved bike trail

Bustleton Avenue

Winchester Ave.

"The Edge"

Roosevelt Boulevard

N

Concrete foot bridge

Mica-shist cliff

Stone picnic pavilion

0   0.5   1

MILES

Continuing on, you pass by the Pennypack Environmental Center and the historic Verree House, built 76 years before the Declaration of Independence was signed. As you pass through the nature center grounds, be mindful to stay on the proper trail and keep a sharp eye alert for wildlife. A final stretch runs some great, wide singletrack to the Pine Road trailhead.

THE RIDE

0.0 From Pine Run parking lot, ride out toward Pine Road. Turn left just before you hit the road at a set of cut wooden telephone poles, and climb the dirt trail.

0.4 Join paved trail and turn right, crossing the wooden bridge over Rockledge Brook. Once across the bridge, bear right and climb up the wide dirt trail (which may be marked as a horse trail).

0.5 Once atop the hill, turn left at the T intersection onto the wide dirt trail.

0.9 Turn left at trail fork and descend the technical singletrack; pass the stone bathrooms. Turn right onto the paved trail and follow it left at the fork, under Verree Road.

1.0 Pass under the bridge and take an immediate right. (Be *very careful* crossing over the entrance of the parking area, as cars pull in from above on the right!) Resume riding on the dirt trail straight ahead.

1.1 After ascending the steep hill, keep left at the fork.

1.3 Continue straight past the right-hand trail.

1.8 Keep left at the trail fork and soon cross a wooden footbridge.

2.3 Keep left at the trail fork.

2.7 Turn left at the trail fork and go straight at next trail intersection. The trail descends to the paved trail; turn right onto the paved trail.

3.0 Cross under Krewstown railroad and road bridges. Once under the second bridge turn right and climb up the steep, dirt trail. Cross over another wide, dirt trail and continue climbing across the way.

3.1 Turn left at trail fork.

3.3 Keep right at the indistinct trail fork.

3.5 Pass a trail on the right; continue straight as the trail bends left.

3.7 Turn left at the T intersection onto the paved trail. Soon after, turn right at a T intersection. Cross under the Bustleton Avenue bridge and stay on the paved trail.

3.9 Just before you ride onto the wrought-iron, green painted bridge, the Edge Trail begins on your right. Turn right into the little chute as the trail parallels the stream. . . .Welcome to the Edge!

4.5 The trail meanders to the right, paralleling a feeder stream. Soon turn left and cross the stream. Once across the stream, turn right onto the dirt road, then turn hard left and climb up a wide, rocky dirt trail.

4.6 Turn hard left onto the tight singletrack (if you come to Roosevelt Boulevard you missed the turn). The trail divides above the mica-shist cliff. Keep on the high, right line for a more extreme descent; keep left for a mellow drop. Trails merge at the bottom.

One of the divine descents along the Edge Trail.

4.7 Turn left onto a rocky road, then take a quick right across the concrete footbridge. Cross over the paved path and continue straight, climbing the steep singletrack ahead. You will also pass a large, stone picnic pavilion on the right.

4.9 The trail descends and joins the paved trail heading right.

5.3 Turn right at the trail spur and drop down onto the wide, dirt trail. You will soon cross a small, arched stone bridge. This bridge is the old Newtown Road Bridge, built in 1793. It was later rebuilt in 1853.

5.5 Cross under the Bustleton Avenue bridge. The trail soon crosses a small footbridge.

6.1 Cross over Krewstown Road. This road crossing is very dangerous! The road bends hard here and impairs your line of sight, so cross carefully. Once across, ride through the parking area, pass around an old steel gate, and go under the massive, arched Krewstown railroad bridge.

6.3 The trail passes a small stone wall and turns left, descending down a steep chute to the creek.

6.9 Along this section of floodplain, the trail will branch many times. It is best to stay as close to the creek as possible, but all trails converge again. Soon after, the trail crosses two footbridges.

7.8 The trail takes you to Verree Road and then turns left, dropping down sharply to pass under the Verree Road bridge. Once past the bridge, turn right at the trail fork and climb the wide dirt road. (Please stay off the nature center footpath!) Above the trail is the Pennypack Nature Center and the Verree House, built circa 1700, which makes a great side trip.

8.1 Pass an old stone spring on the right.

8.7 Keep left at the trail fork.

9.1 Turn left onto the Pine Run Road bridge and ride across on the sidewalk. Finish the ride by turning left into the Pine Run parking lot trailhead.

Delaware Canal Path

Location:	Begins in Easton and ends in Yardley.
Distance:	45.5 miles one way.
Time:	3 to 7 hours.
Tread:	The surface is mainly hardpacked dirt with a few sporadic sections of grassy and paved trail.
Aerobic level:	Easy. The canal path is similar in grade to a rail-trail. Riding the trail as described here, will have you cruising downhill, dropping 165 feet in 45 miles. This drop is most evident at the locks where the trail shows a visual difference in grade.
Technical difficulty:	0. There are no technical difficulties along this trail, which makes it great for young families with tow-behind kid carriers and young riders.
Highlights:	National Heritage Trail, lots of food stops, riding along one of the last free-flowing rivers in the United States, incredibly scenic and easy ride, historic covered bridge.
Land status:	Pennsylvania State Park, Department of Conservation and Recreation.
Maps:	DCNR Pennsylvania State Parks: Delaware Canal State Park map.

Access: The ride can be accessed from either end of the trail but, for the purpose of this guide, it starts in Easton. To reach the trailhead from Easton, head south on Pennsylvania Highway 611. Once across the bridge spanning the Lehigh River, Pennsylvania 611 south turns hard left (note the colorful mural painted on the concrete retaining wall). Approximately 0.25 mile down on your left is the gravel parking lot for the trailhead. Look for a pair of steel railroad bridges at the lot. To get to the trailhead in Yardley, head east on Pennsylvania Highway 332 from Interstate 95. After crossing over Main Street, turn right onto Canal Street and park along here. If you cross over the canal bridge and dead-end into Pennsylvania Highway 32, you went too far.

Notes on the trail: Dedicated as a National Heritage Trail, the Delaware Canal Path is an outstanding reminder of our American history and heritage. The canal path was originally built in the early 1800s and much of it has been preserved since that time. All but a few of the existing structures are original to the canal, including the locks, stonework, aqueducts, spillways, and gatehouses. Some structures have been rebuilt to maintain their safety, but retain their original historic style. The canal played an important role in the industrial development of the Philadelphia area and neighboring cities. Mule-drawn barges would travel south bringing down hard Anthracite coal, while the return trips brought goods and supplies that served the growing communities of Northeastern Pennsylvania.

This is a one-way ride and can be tailored to your liking. At any time you can return to the trailhead. The trail surface, grade, history, and amenities make this an outstanding family mountain biking experience. The best time to ride this trail is at the fall foliage color peak, which seems to run about mid-October. There is no chance of getting lost on this ride and the scenery is quite beautiful. At times you will be very close to the Delaware River, one of the last free-flowing rivers in the United States; you can see and hear the power of this mighty body of water. At other times you will ride along quiet sections of the canal observing herons, turtles, and ducks. The ride is an educational adventure in both American and natural history.

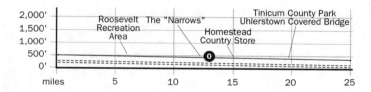

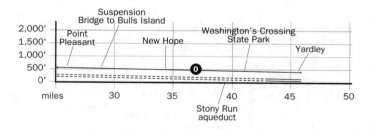

THE RIDE

0.0 From the lot, ride out to the fish ladder and check it out. A set of stairs takes you down to some viewing windows to spy on any aquatic creatures that might be using the ladder. From here, head down river (south) on the trail, under the steel railroad bridge.

5.0 Cross wooden bridge over concrete spill way. Soon after, you will cross over a low bridge on a stairway. On your left is the Raubsville Inn, a fine place to grab a sandwich.

5.9 Pass Locks 23 and 22, and pass a red footbridge. The Theodore Roosevelt Recreation and Conservation Area has restrooms, picnic area, mill house, and lock house.

Delaware Canal Path

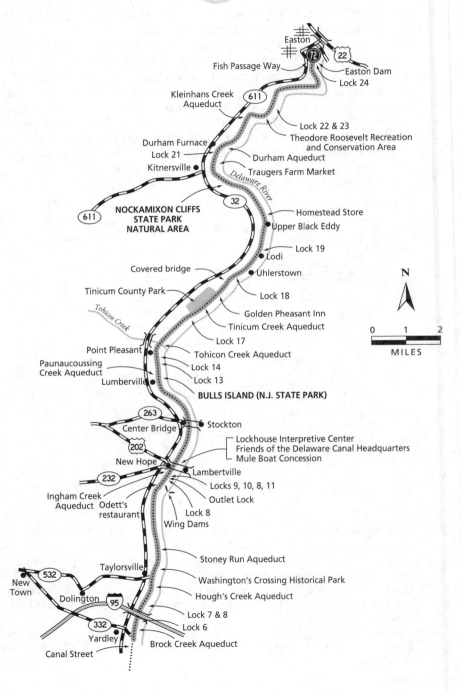

Easton
Fish Passage Way
Easton Dam
Lock 24
Kleinhans Creek Aqueduct
611
Lock 22 & 23
Theodore Roosevelt Recreation and Conservation Area
Durham Furnace
Lock 21
Durham Aqueduct
Kitnersville
Traugers Farm Market
Delaware River
32
NOCKAMIXON CLIFFS STATE PARK NATURAL AREA
611
Homestead Store
Upper Black Eddy
Lock 19
Lodi
Covered bridge
Uhlerstown
Tinicum County Park
Lock 18
Golden Pheasant Inn
Tohicon Creek
Tinicum Creek Aqueduct
Lock 17
Point Pleasant
Tohicon Creek Aqueduct
Paunaucoussing Creek Aqueduct
Lock 14
Lumberville
Lock 13
BULLS ISLAND (N.J. STATE PARK)
263
Center Bridge
Stockton
202
Lockhouse Interpretive Center
Friends of the Delaware Canal Headquarters
Mule Boat Concession
New Hope
232
Lambertville
Ingham Creek Aqueduct
Locks 9, 10, 8, 11
Odett's restaurant
Outlet Lock
Lock 8
Wing Dams
Stoney Run Aqueduct
Taylorsville
Washington's Crossing Historical Park
New Town
532
Hough's Creek Aqueduct
Dolington
95
Lock 7 & 8
332
Lock 6
Yardley
Brock Creek Aqueduct
Canal Street

N

0   1   2
MILES

7.0 Pass over Kleinhans Creek aqueduct.

9.8 Cross Durham aqueduct and pass Lock 21.

10.8 Pass under concrete road bridge; Traugers Farm Market is on your left.

11.9 Cross Gallows Run aqueduct as the trail draws closer to the river.

12.3 Pass Lock 20. There is a nice picnic spot here along the riverside.

15.6 After passing under Pennsylvania Highway 32 (on your left is the Manor House restaurant), you will pass under another bridge alongside the Homestead Country Store, which has some great ice cream. Soon after, you will pass a yellow house on your left.

17.0 Cross the paved road with caution. Pass Lodi State Park and Lock 19.

19.0 Pass the beautiful Uhlerstown Covered Bridge on the right. Shortly, you will pass Tinicum County Park on the left, which offers overnight camping.

21.9 After crossing under Pennsylvania 32 and passing the Golden Pheasant Inn, you cross over the wooden bridge on the Tinicum Creek Aqueduct.

24.2 Pass Locks 16 and 15.

26.4 Pass over the Tohicon Creek Aqueduct in Point Pleasant. Pass Locks 14 and 13.

28.1 Cross over the Paunaucoussing Creek aqueduct. Pass Lock 12 and go under the suspension footbridge to Bulls Island in New Jersey. Note the wing dam in the river.

34.7 You are now entering the quaint town of New Hope. On your right is the old train yard, which houses quite an array of old rail cars and locomotives. You will also pass under a bridge. Watch for mule dung! You will soon pass the Mule Barge Ride Ticket station. From here the canal path ends briefly, so continue to ride south on Pennsylvania 32. Pass Pennsylvania 232 on your right. *Danger! Watch for cars turning here!* Turn left into second lot entrance to Odett's restaurant.

Old locks and rail bridges, the Delaware Canal Path.

35.3 Once in Odetts lot, ride around the south end of the restaurant and pass around a wooden gate and lock bridge. Turn right onto the tow path and head south. From this point you may also notice the kayckers surfing the rapids at the wing dam in the river.

37.2 After passing some apartment buildings, you will need to pass over a paved road by going out around the guardrail. A gravel road soon turns left; stay along the canal.

39.5 Cross over the Stoney Run Aqueduct and under the bridge.

41.3 Cross under the Pennsylvania Highway 532 bridge at Washington's Crossing State Park.

42.4 Pass over on the Hough's Creek aqueduct.

44.0 After crossing the spillway, pass Lock 7 and cross under Interstate 95 bridge.

45.2 Canal path turns into North Edgewater Road (paved).

45.5 Cross over on the Brock Creek Aqueduct and cross under the PA 332 bridge. Once under the bridge, turn hard left and then left again onto PA 332, crossing the bridge. Trailhead parking is the first street on your left, which is Canal Street.

South Mountain

Location:	Emmaus, 1 mile south of Allentown.
Distance:	8.7-mile loop.
Time:	1.5 to 2.5 hours.
Tread:	The ride crawls past gnarly rock gardens and monolithic trials boulders, but there are also sections of soft, loamy, woodland singletrack, loose power line doubletrack, and grassy woods roads.
Aerobic level:	Moderate. The ride climbs all over the mountain and covers a few hundred feet of vertical elevation. The terrain is very demanding, requiring both brute force and ballet finesse.
Technical difficulty:	5. Welcome fellow hammerheads! Logs, rock gardens, burly boulders, steep drop-offs, slick roots, and tight bar-grabbing singletrack are just the beginning.
Highlights:	Tons of side trails to explore, some of the finest technical singletrack, great trials riding, roadside vista, a subterranean tunnel.
Land status:	Allentown Power Company and the Nature Conservancy.
Maps:	USGS Allentown East.

Access: From Allentown, head south on Pennsylvania Highway 309 and exit at Lehigh Street. Head west on Lehigh Street, which soon merges left onto Main Street (Emmaus Avenue). Drive along Main Street to Second Street. Turn left onto Second Street and, immediately after crossing the railroad tracks, turn left onto the paved road. Follow this road across Kunes Lane, parking in the gravel lot on the right next to the railroad tracks. This lot is the trailhead. Note the sign for the Emmaus Recycling-Compost Center.

Notes on the trail: If you get the hankerin' for some wicked terrain, South Mountain is a technical rider's dream. The network of trails resembles the web of a drunken spider, so giving directions here nearly impossible. To simplify things, I've linked the more prominent trails and included some of the fun highlights of the area. There is lots more to be found on South Mountain, and much of it is well hidden off the main trails. Pack some Power Bars and plan to spend the day exploring all the secret sweet-stuff this mountain has to offer.

The ride directions may seem complicated, but this outstanding ride is not to be missed. Beginning at the Emmaus Recycling-Compost Center, the singletrack slips into the woods, and you immediately confront some technical challenges. Logs and rocks litter the trail as it winds out to the singletrack switchbacks that ascend the mountain. From the switchbacks, the trail continues to climb out to the power line where more technical singletrack ensues. Slowly hammer your way down through tight, rocky singletrack to the power line, and then ride through the dank, wet tunnel under the highway. The trail ascends the mountain again on the east side. A loop up and around on some more stellar single and doubletrack returns you to the tunnel where the trail somewhat retraces itself. Don't forget to notice the views and the unique rock formations. After riding to the end of the power line, you roll along a beautiful singletrack along the north face of the mountain to the final, bomber descent. Romp over big logs and slick roots back to the trailhead lot.

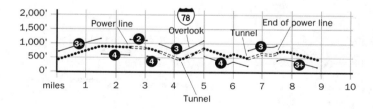

THE RIDE

0.0 From the trailhead, ride out to Kunes Lane and turn left, crossing the railroad tracks. Immediately after crossing the tracks, turn left and ride parallel to the tracks to the edge of the woods. Take the singletrack at the corner edge of the woods and pass over a dirt berm.

0.4 After passing a stick shelter, turn right at the T intersection. Soon after, turn left at the next T intersection.

South Mountain

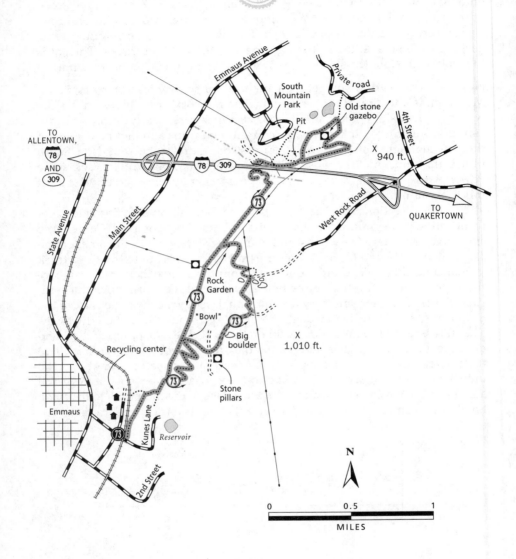

TO
ALLENTOWN,
78
AND
309

Emmaus Avenue

Private road

South
Mountain
Park

Pit

Old stone
gazebo

78 309

X
940 ft.

4th Street

73

West Rock Road

TO
QUAKERTOWN

State Avenue

Main Street

73

Rock
Garden

"Bowl"

73

Big
boulder

X
1,010 ft.

Recycling center

73

Stone
pillars

Emmaus

73

Kunes Lane

Reservoir

2nd Street

N

0   0.5   1

MILES

0.5 Keep left at a fork, cross the small stream, and keep right at the next fork. Climb the switchbacked trail.

0.8 Turn right at the four-way intersection, noting the large "bowl" depression.

1.1 Turn right at a T intersection and soon after, turn left at another T intersection, noting the stone pillars on the right (mile 1.2). After making the last turn, the trail will fork. Keep right at the fork and continue to climb.

1.7 After passing the huge boulder on the right (mile 1.5), turn left on the left-spur singletrack spur just before the power line and descend.

2.3 Turn right at the T intersection.

2.6 Keep right at the fork and soon exit out onto the power line road. Turn left on the power line road and continue to descend. Pass around a set of boulders and crossing over the gravel West Rock Road.

3.1 Keep left as the power line road forks. About 60 yards after the fork, turn left back into the wooded singletrack.

3.4 Grunt through the rock garden out to the power line, and turn right onto the power line doubletrack.

3.9 Follow the doubletrack as it leaves the power line and heads left into the woods. Soon, cross a stream and turn left at the T intersection.

4.2 As trail narrows down and parallels Pennsylvania Highway 309 and Interstate 78, cross over a caged riprap section and follow the singletrack as it curves around left and down to the tunnel. Pass through the tunnel and, once through, turn hard right and climb the rocky singletrack streambed.

4.5 Turn right onto the power line and climb the steep hill to the view over PA 309 and I-78. Continue to follow the singletrack as it becomes off-camber and eventually merges left with the power line.

The South Mountain secret.

5.1 At a small horseshoe-shaped turn-around on the power line, turn hard left onto an obscure singletrack that ducks back into the woods.

5.5 Turn right at a four-way intersection, pass an old stone gazebo structure, and merge left onto the downhill singletrack. At the bottom of the steep hill, turn left at the T intersection (mile 5.7).

6.0 After climbing the hill, turn left at the T intersection by a huge pit surrounded by boulders. Soon after, turn right at a T intersection and descend the off-camber singletrack and power line back to the tunnel. This section of trail should appear familiar.

6.5 Pass through the tunnel and follow the singletrack as it turns back to doubletrack. Turns right at the trail-spur, cross the stream, and return to the power line (mile 6.7). Soon, pass a power line trail on the left at mile 7.0.

7.5 Continue straight into the woods on a tight, rocky singletrack, as the wide, power line doubletrack ends. Note the vista at the power-line cut. Once in the woods, keep right at the fork.

7.9 Pass a right-hand spur at a dip and, about 40 yards later, keep right at a fork, merging onto the singletrack trail.

8.1 At the top of the switchbacks, near the large "bowl," turn right at the four-way intersection and descend the steep, straight singletrack. At the bottom of the hill, cross the stream. From here you retrace the route back to the trailhead.

8.3 Turn right at the spur trail and then turn left at the next spurtrail. Soon after, keep left at the fork and pass the shelter.

8.7 Ride out around the railroad tracks back to the trailhead.

Ironton Railroad

Location: Coplay, 5 miles north of Allentown.

Distance: 7.1-mile loop.

Time: 1 to 3 hours.

Tread: Cinder-covered railroad grade, grassy woods road, and a short stretch of paved trail.

Aerobic level: Easy. The ride is more hilly than most rail-trails but runs on an easy grade.

Technical difficulty: 0. The cinder covered railroad and the grassy woods roads are easy to negotiate by even novice riders on skinny tires.

Highlights: Tons of historic sites and buildings, old quarry, fish and view wildlife, playground, great family ride.

Land status: Whitehall Township Parks and Recreation.

Maps: USGS Cementon, Catasauqua.

Ironton Railroad

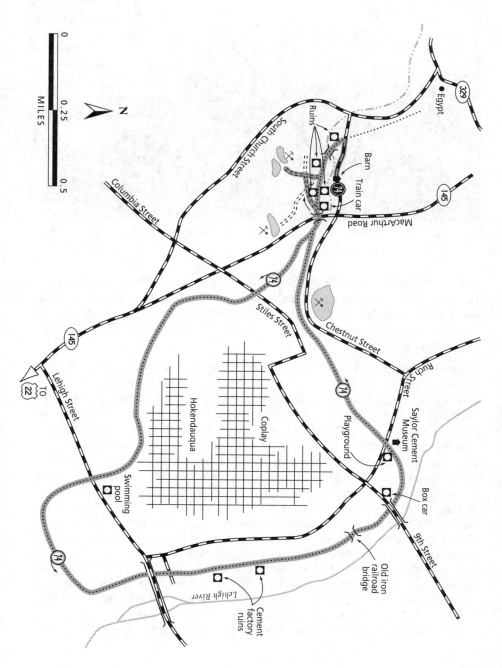

The Saylor Cement Museum stacks along the Ironton Railroad.

Access: From Allentown, take Pennsylvania Highway 145 north to Whitehall. At Whitehall continue for 3.5 miles on PA 145 (Macarthur Road) to Chestnut Street. Turn left on Chestnut Street and travel for approximately 0.3 mile to a big red barn. Turn left into the parking area at the barn; this lot is the trailhead.

Notes on the trail: The Ironton Railroad is heavily endowed with remains of historical structures. Iron caused the initial heavy industrial development of this region. Huge blast furnaces operated in the area and required massive amounts of coal, iron ore, and limestone. It was the Ironton Railroad, purchased from the Lehigh Valley Railroad by David Thomas, that supplied these raw materials to the Thomas Iron Works Company in the early 1880s. Not long after came the development of the cement industry. It was portland cement that brought fame and money to this small but growing area. Local quarries provided stone and the railroad transported other supplies.

Beginning at the barn, follow a short stint on the paved road before entering the rail-trail. Immediately you encounter the first historic building, complete with beautiful arches and a strange cement veneer. The ride continues onto the fork and passes many more structures and an old rail car. Following the right spur, you skirt many housing developments in Hokendauqua before heading north along the Lehigh River. Along the riverside stretch, you pass many more historic structures, including an old iron railroad bridge.

Heading back to the fork, you visit the impressive stacks at the Saylor Cement Museum and the Saylor Park playground. Back under Pennsylvania

Highway 145, the trail diverts from the rail grade and meanders out to the old quarry. This quiet and tranquil spot has a wooden overlook deck from which you can observe wildlife and great sunsets. The final leg retraces the railroad grade to the trailhead. Keep in mind that the trail crosses many roads, so please be careful at these junctions.

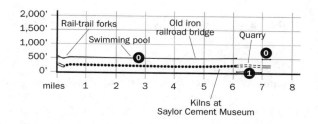

THE RIDE

0.0 From the trailhead lot at the barn, turn left onto Chestnut Street and ride the hill down to the rail-trail, which is marked by the bicycle sign. Turn left onto the rail-trail and soon after, pass the old building on the right (mile 0.2).

0.3 Cross a four-way intersection and head over the old railroad bridge. Look up into the woods on the right and left for more buildings and foundations.

0.6 After passing a neat old railroad car, cross over a wooden bridge, under Pennsylvania Highway 145 and keep right at the fork. Note the trail signboard with map.

1.2 Cross Stiles Street.

1.7 Cross Center Street and continue on paved rail-trail.

2.6 After passing a swimming pool club on the left, carefully cross the paved road as the trail descends and climbs sharply; return to cinder-paved trail.

3.8 After passing under a bridge, carefully cross another paved road, Lehigh Street.

4.1 Pass many more cement factory structures on the right.

4.7 Pass under the old iron railroad bridge.

5.0 Pass under the Ninth Street bridge and note the old railroad box car on the left.

5.4 Pass the stacks at Saylor Cement Museum and the Saylor Park. Soon after, the trail turns 90 degrees right, then turns left crossing Ruch Street.

6.2 The rail-trails merge, pass under PA 145 and cross the wooden bridge. Turn left onto the grassy woods road, just opposite the old rail car.

6.4 After passing many old structures and left-and-right-hand woods road spurs, turn left at the T intersection to the old quarry.

6.5 Check out the old quarry, which sprung a leak and is now a great haven for waterfowl and aquatic critters. Turn around and return straight down this gravel road to the rail-trail. At the rail-trail turn left (mile 6.7) and retrace the route to the trailhead.

7.1 After turning right on Chestnut Street, the ride finishes at the barn trailhead.

Homestead Trail

Location: Jacobsburg Environmental Education Center, 12 miles north of Easton.

Distance: 6.8-mile loop.

Time: 30 minutes to 1 hour.

Tread: A mix of cinder-coated singletrack, open grassy roads, woodland singletrack, paved and gravel roads.

Aerobic level: Easy. The ride travels to high and low points in the park, requiring short sections of easy climbing.

Technical difficulty: 1+. Jacobsburg is becoming increasingly soft as state officials try to smooth out the bumps on the trail. There are a few woodland sections blessed with rocks and roots. Some of these sections may be rated 3 to 4 but are very short in length and can easily be walked.

Highlights: Historic site of Jacobsburg, established 1740; historic buildings; Jacobsburg Environmental Education Center; fishing; creek crossings.

Land status: Pennsylvania State Park, Department of Conservation and Natural Resources.

Maps: DCNR Pennsylvania State Parks: Jacobsburg Environmental Education Center map.

Access: From Easton, take U.S. Highway 22 west to Pennsylvania Highway 33. Take PA 33 north and get off at the Belfast exit. At the bottom of the exit, turn right at the T intersection. At the stop sign, turn left onto Belfast Road and follow the signs for Jacobsburg Environmental Education Center. Turn left after crossing a small bridge into the parking lot. This lot is the trailhead.

Notes on the trail: The park's rich history dates back to the settlement of Jacobsburg in 1740. The preserved structures are listed on the National Register of Historic Places. The significance of the park's history dates back to the gun-making endeavors of William Henry. A gun factory and iron forge were built here and run by the Henrys. The factory produced firearms for all of our nation's early major conflicts, from the Revolutionary War to the Civil War. Firearms were also crafted and sold to John Jacob Astor's American Fur Company (one of the biggest business enterprises of the nineteenth century) and pioneers of the western frontier. The guns were known for their durability, accuracy, and low cost. The Jacobsburg Historical Society offers unique programs throughout the year, including classes in gun-making and blacksmithing.

Homestead Trail

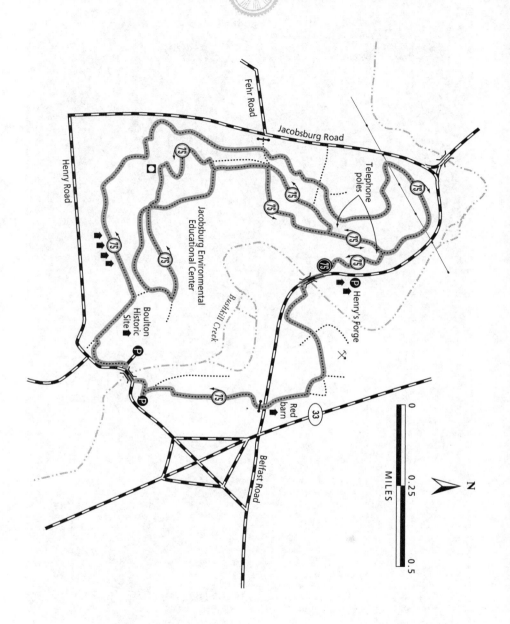

Sweet singletrack along Sober's Run, Jacobsburg State Park.

The Homestead Trail is an easy ride in the southeast section of the park. The route crisscrosses and doubles back over itself, so certain trails will seem familiar. Beginning at the trailhead, climb up and around the old quarry and head down to the Henry Road bridge on nice, wide, grassy trail. Once across the classic old bridge, you pass the historic Boulton Site and then climb again on the outer perimeter of the park. Rolling hills follow as the trail traces a huge, lazy "S" on a mix of wide grassy trails and singletrack back to the trailhead.

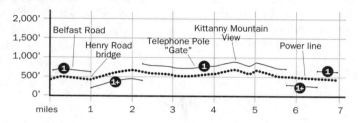

THE RIDE

0.0 From the trailhead lot, ride out to Belfast Road and turn right. Once across the road bridge, take an immediate left and climb the short singletrack as it turns right. The trail will soon bend hard left and continue to climb.

0.4 After crossing a gravel pathway, note the "Danger Quarry, Keep Out" sign on the left and turn right at the four-way intersection.

0.6 Turn left onto Belfast Road. After approximately 150 yards, turn right onto the red-blazed trail and pass around a gate.

1.0 Turn left at the T intersection. After 50 yards, turn hard right, then take an immediate left and travel down the singletrack to the steel bridge on Henry Road. Turn right onto Henry Road and cross the bridge. Once across the bridge, turn right up the gated gravel road and then turn left onto the singletrack trail, noting the equestrian signs. The trail soon crosses a gravel driveway and climbs a steep singletrack section.

1.4 Turn right at the T intersection at the top of the steep singletrack.

1.6 Turn left at the wide grassy trail spur and travel along behind a few houses.

2.5 Turn right at the T intersection and then in approximately 60 yards turn left, following the wide grassy trail.

2.8 After crossing another wide grassy trail, keep right at the fork.

3.2 Turn right at the T intersection, climbing the wide cinder singletrack.

3.6 After passing through a set of cut wooden telephone poles, turn right at the trail spur and follow the blue-blazed trail.

3.8 Turn right at the strange five-way intersection and immediately turn left onto the wide singletrack trail.

4.0 Turn right at the T intersection and then take an immediate left onto the wide grassy trail.

4.4 As the trails bends through a small wooded area, note the left-hand spur trail. Remember this junction for your return trip. Continue on the wide grassy trail as it climbs out to a beautiful northwesterly view over the Kittanny Mountains.

4.7 Turn left at the T intersection and soon after, turn left again at another T intersection. Climb the singletrack on the blue-blazed trail.

5.0 Turn right onto the wide grassy trail. After approximately 50 yards, turn right onto a blue-blazed trail (the point you committed to memory at mile 4.4).

5.2 Turn right again, keeping on the blue-blazed trail.

5.4 Turn hard right on the wide dirt and grass trail, soon passing through the cut wooden telephone poles.

6.2 The trail bends hard right under the power line and then turns left at the fork to descend the blue singletrack. The singletrack will come out at the bottom of the power line and pass through another set of cut wooden telephone poles. Follow the cinder singletrack.

6.8 Cross a very small, arched wooden bridge to the trailhead.

Jacobsburg Jive

Location:	Jacobsburg Environmental Education Center, 12 miles north of Easton.
Distance:	13.1-mile loop.
Time:	1 to 2 hours.
Tread:	A mix of cinder-coated singletrack, open grassy roads, woodland singletrack, paved and gravel roads, and creek crossings. During the summer these surfaces can become hardpacked and very fast.
Aerobic level:	Easy to moderate. The ride travels to the highest and lowest points in the park on easy terrain.
Technical difficulty:	2. Jacobsburg is becoming increasingly soft as the state attempts to smooth out the bumps on the trail. There are a few woodland sections blessed with rocks and roots. Some of these sections may be rated 3 to 4 but are very short in length and can easily be hiked through.
Highlights:	Historic site of Jacobsburg established 1740; environmental education center; fishing; creek crossings; fast singletrack.
Land status:	Pennsylvania State Park, Department of Conservation and Natural Resources.
Maps:	DCNR Pennsylvania State Parks: Jacobsburg Environmental Education Center State Park map.

Access: From Easton, take U.S. Highway 22 west to Pennsylvania Highway 33. Take PA 33 north and get off at the Belfast exit. At the bottom of the exit, turn right at the T intersection. At the stop sign, turn left onto Belfast Road and follow the signs for Jacobsburg Environmental Education Center. Turn left after crossing a small bridge into the parking lot. This lot is the trailhead.

Notes on the trail: Jacobsburg is one of the few state parks that allows mountain biking, and almost every trail is multi-use. This is good and bad. The good side is that mountain bikers have lots to shred on. The down side is that there are many other users out on the trail as well. Horses, hikers, and trail runners abound at Jacobsburg. With all the tight, twisty turns it would be easy to run someone down. Combine that with a really fast, hardpacked trail in summer and mountain bikers riding in all directions—well, you get the picture. Ride defensively and cautiously as there have been a few accidents that could have been avoided, and all involved a mountain bike.

The trail begins by looping the southeast part of the park on a mix of wide, grassy roads and singletrack sections. A short, steep descent leads to Bushkill Creek; then the trail slowly works its way up along Pennsylvania Highway 33. After crossing a triad of paved roads, the trail winds down along Sober's Run on some great woodland singletrack. Fording Sober's Run at the old bridge abutments can be sobering indeed, especially if its cold and the water's up.

The route then loops around the northwest part of the park before returning down along Sober's Run for a final wet crossing. Once across, the trail retraces some of the route back to the quarry, where the final descent ends at the trailhead. Plan accordingly for the fording of Sober's Run, as it can become the crux of the ride. The creek can reach depths of 3 feet and carry quite a current at the first ford. The second crossing is less intimidating but challenging nonetheless.

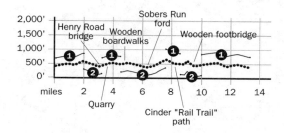

THE RIDE

0.0 Starting in the upper corner of the lot, you will see a small, curved wooden bridge. Cross the wooden bridge and head up the cinder-covered trail.

0.4 After passing through a set of cut wooden telephone poles, turn right at the fork under the power line. Keep left at the next fork and climb the hill. The trail will soon exit back to the power line, where you will turn right and follow the trail as it climbs around left.

Jacobsburg Jive

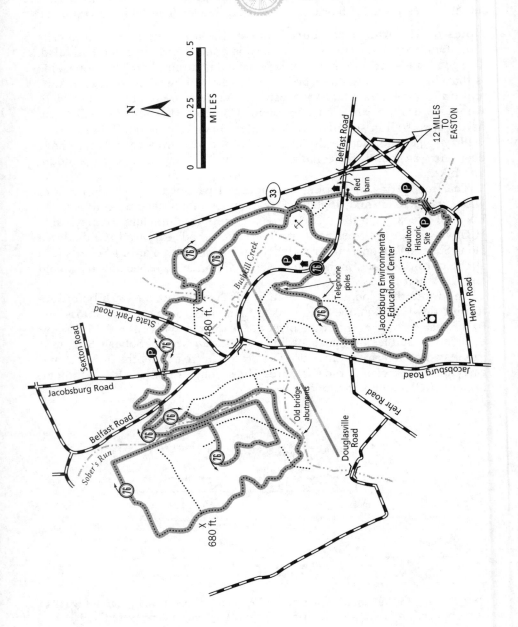

Henry's Forge historic site, Jacobsburg State Park.

1.1 Pass through another set of wooden telephone poles and turn right at the trail spur. Note the small blue-blazed sign in the ground.

1.4 Turn right at the strange five-way intersection and head for the gate. A bit before the gate turn left onto the grassy road.

2.4 Turn right at the T intersection. Soon after, turn left at the trail spur and descend the windy singletrack. The trail then crosses a gravel driveway and runs parallel to Henry Road.

2.8 Turn right at the T intersection onto the gravel road. Pass around a wooden gate, turn left onto Henry Road, and cross the steel bridge. Once across, turn left and follow the singletrack up into the woods.

2.9 Cross the path and small stream and turn left onto the wide cinder path. After approximately 50 yards, turn right up a wide grassy road.

3.2 After passing around a wooden gate, cross Belfast Road and resume the trail on the other side. Pass the red barn.

3.4 Keep right at the fork, pass around a wooden gate and cross a small wooden bridge. After crossing the bridge, turn left at the fork and pass a sign that says "Danger Quarry, Keep Out."

4.0 Turn left at the fork and follow the red blazes.

4.3 Turn left at the fork and cross the small wooden bridge. Once across the bridge, turn right on the trail marked with a yellow square and green arrow blaze.

4.8 Cross State Park Road and many wooden boardwalks. Trail crosses Jacobsburg Road and Belfast Road at miles 5.2 and 5.5, respectively.

5.7 Turn left at the four-way intersection and follow the green square and red arrow blaze.

5.9 Turn hard right at trail spur and head down along the stream.

6.3 Ford Sober's Run at the old bridge abutments. Once across, turn left on the wide grassy trail.

6.7 Pass over an old road grade (right-hand trail) and the old bridge abutments.

7.0 Turn left at the T intersection, then 30 yards later turn right, staying on the wide grassy road.

7.3 Turn left at the T intersection as the trail heads into the woods.

8.3 Turn right at the T intersection onto the flat, cinder rail-trail-like path.

8.8 Turn right at the trail spur and climb on the red and green blazed trail. Keep left at the fork and climb the most direct line across the water bars.

9.3 Turn left at the T intersection to descend, and then turn left again onto a flat rail-trail grade. Keep straight at the four-way intersection.

9.6 Turn left at the T intersection, noting the bridge ruins and the spot where you forded the creek. Cross over a small wooden bridge and continue on the singletrack upstream.

10.2 Turn right and ford Sober's Run again. Once across, bear left as the trail begins to climb. At the top of the hill, keep straight at the four-way intersection.

10.6 Cross Belfast Road, and then cross Jacobsburg and State Park Roads at miles 10.9 and 11.3, respectively.

11.6 Turn left at the T intersection and cross the small wooden bridge. Once across, turn left at the fork and soon pass a right-hand trail (same intersection as mile 4.3).

12.6 Cross a bridge, pass around a wooden gate and continue straight. As you pass a guardrail on the right, turn right at the four-way intersection and begin descending. The trail crosses a gravel path and soon bends hard right with an exit onto Belfast Road.

13.1 Turn right onto Belfast Road, cross the bridge, and turn left into the trailhead lot.

Lehigh Valley and Pocono Plateau

The Pocono Mountains offer an array of mountain biking opportunities. Wildlife, hunters, and Enduro riders have forged many sweet singletrack paths. The Delaware and Wyoming State Forests offer the majority of rides in the northern and western reaches of this region. From the perch atop the gaping chasm at World's End State Park to the turbulent boils of the Loyalsock Creek, this area is a little paradise for the outdoor lover. The Lehigh Gorge and all its grandeur flow through the town of Jim Thorpe, the most talked-about mountain bike mecca in Pennsylvania.

Bob's Option

Location:	Mauch Chunk Lake Park, 4 miles west of Jim Thorpe.
Distance:	8.2-mile loop.
Time:	1 to 2 hours.
Tread:	Historic Switchback Gravity Railroad Rail-Trail, old paved road, old woods road, rocky singletrack, and four-wheel drive road.
Aerobic level:	Easy to moderate. The ridge-top section of tough, technical riding will definitely demand mental and physical stamina. The climb up the ridge is quite mellow and, of course, the old rail grade is a real cruise.
Technical difficulty:	4. There is a solid 3-mile section of rough, loose, bone-breaking rocks up on the ridge. Aside from that the ride follows old rail grade and shoddy paved road.
Highlights:	Gnarly, rocky, singletrack downhill on the classic Bob's Option Trail; historic Switchback Gravity Railroad Rail-Trail.
Land status:	Mauch Chunk County Parks.
Maps:	USGS Nesquehoning, Lehighton.

Access: From Jim Thorpe, take Broadway Avenue (Pennsylvania Road 3012) west and climb out of town for 4 miles. Turn left into Mauch Chunk Lake

Bob's Option

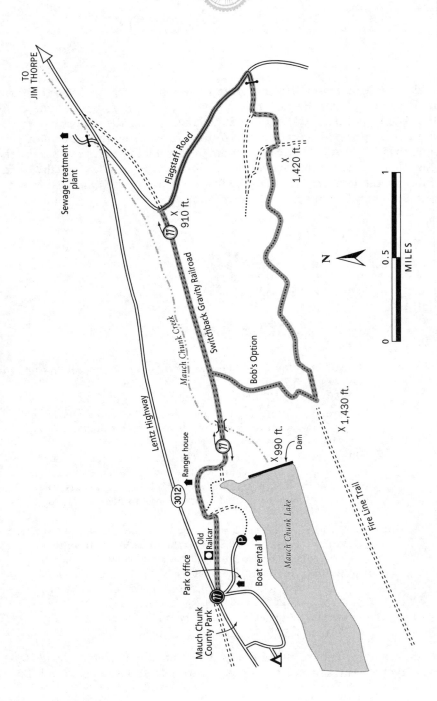

TO
JIM THORPE

Sewage treatment
plant

Flagstaff Road

X
910 ft.

X
1,420 ft.

Switchback Gravity Railroad

Mauch Chunk Creek

Bob's Option

Lentz Highway

Ranger house

X 990 ft.

Dam

X 1,430 ft.

Mauch Chunk Lake

Fire Line Trail

N

0   0.5   1

MILES

3012

Park office

Old
Railcar

P

Boat rental

Mauch Chunk County Park

Park and then left again at the road fork to park down by the boat launch area. The ride begins at the park entrance.

Notes on the trail: One of the many short but exciting classic mountain rides in the mountain biking mecca of Jim Thorpe. The route utilizes parts of the historic Switchback Gravity Railroad, which was started in 1827. This old rail grade originally transported coal from the town of Summit Hill down into Mauch Chunk, known more recently as Jim Thorpe. Mauch Chunk, meaning "Sleeping Bear," was the Lenni Lenape name given to the ridge northeast of town. Its profile depicts this image and is still called Bear Mountain. The coal was then loaded on barges at the Lehigh Canal and floated down the canal system along the Delaware River. Mauch Chunk Lake Park boasts an array of amenities, including fishing, swimming, nonmotorized boating, boat rentals, camping, food concessions, and restrooms with showers.

As for the ride itself, it's classic Jim Thorpe riding at its best. It begins at the lake and travels down the old Switchback Railroad. A moderate climb on the shambled Flagstaff Road will top out on the spine of Flagstaff Mountain. Rocky four-wheel drive road and singletrack await as the route continues to climb on a very slight grade. Just when the trail turns to smooth hardpacked dirt, it's back into the woods on the gnarly descent down Bob's Option. Keep your cool as the trail drops a heinous 400 vertical feet back down to the Switchback Railroad grade—a short but stout line for hammerhead junkies.

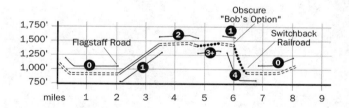

THE RIDE

0.0 The ride begins at the Mauch Chunk Lake Park entrance, where the Gravity Switchback Railroad grade crosses Pennsylvania Road 3012. At the entrance turn right onto the Switchback Railroad grade, passing the wooden sign and old rail car on your left.

0.4 Turn left in the grassy clearing as the route follows up and around the dugout for the dam breast. The ride passes behind the park ranger house and continues around, curving right and turning back into a cinder pathway (the dam cut into the original rail grade).

2.2 Turn right onto Flagstaff Road and climb the road.

3.6 Turn right onto the old woods road at the crest of the hill, note the old rusted gate.

A bike's-eye view of the chute on Bob's Option.

3.8 Turn left at the fork onto the rocky four-wheel-drive road.

4.2 Turn right at the T intersection. Soon after (mile 4.3) turn onto the left-hand spur trail.

5.7 At a small clearing, the trail exits the woods and turns right onto a smooth, hardpacked, grass and dirt ATV-type trail.

6.0 Turn right onto the obscure singletrack called Bob's Option. Let gravity be your friend and keep it dialed!

6.7 Turn left onto the Switchback Railroad grade. From here you will be retracing your route back to the trailhead.

7.5 Pass a left-hand trail at the clearing near the dam and continue straight, up and around the ranger house.

7.8 Turn right as the Switchback Railroad grade reenters the woods.

8.2 Trailhead.

Summit Hill

Location:	Mauch Chunk Lake Park, 4 miles west of Jim Thorpe.
Distance:	8.5-mile loop.
Time:	1 to 3 hours.
Tread:	Extreme technical, rocky singletrack, paved road, historic Switchback Gravity rail grade.
Aerobic level:	Moderate. The ascent up Pisgah Mountain is quite mellow and constitutes a substantial warm-up. It's the extreme rocky singletrack across the ridge that will demand muscle, stamina, and lots of finesse.
Technical difficulty:	4. The ascent up the ridge is quite mild, but the 2.5 miles of extreme rock that litters the backbone of the mountain makes the ride quite wild. A wicked descent down the Lung Buster Trail follows a deeply-cut rain channel with huge 2 to 3 foot drop-offs.
Highlights:	Extreme enduro downhill singletrack, the classic Lung Buster Trail, historic Switchback Gravity Railroad Rail-Trail.
Land status:	Mauch Chunk County Parks.
Maps:	USGS Nesquehoning, Lehighton.

Access: From Jim Thorpe, take Broadway Avenue (Pennsylvania Road 3012) west and climb out of town for 4 miles. Turn left into Mauch Chunk Lake Park and then left again at the road fork to park down by the boat launch area. The ride begins at the park entrance.

Summit Hill

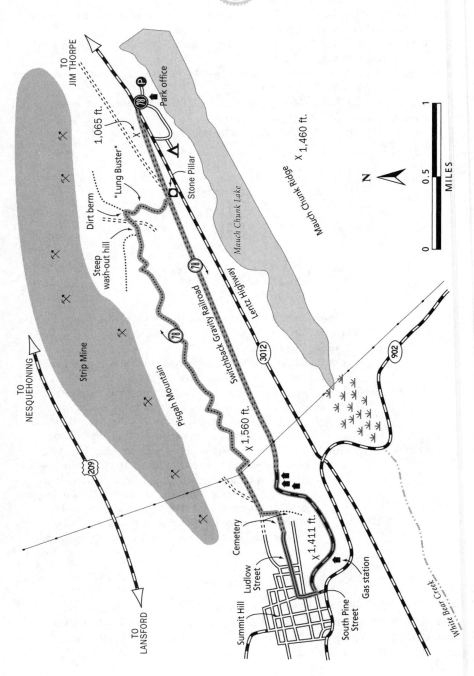

TO
JIM THORPE

Park office

1,065 ft.

"Lung Buster"

Dirt berm

Stone Pillar

Steep
wash-out hill

78

78

Switchback Gravity Railroad

Lentz Highway

Mauch Chunk Lake

Mauch Chunk Ridge   X 1,460 ft.

N

0   0.5   1

MILES

Strip Mine

Pisgah Mountain

X 1,560 ft.

3012

902

TO
NESQUEHONING

209

TO
LANSFORD

Cemetery

Ludlow
Street

Summit Hill

South Pine
Street

Gas station

X 1,411 ft.

White Bear Creek

Notes on the trail: Summit Hill was best known for its commanding position over the expansive acres of strip mines that lay on the northwest face of Mount Pisgah. Once a bustling mining town, Summit Hill has now settled into a more tranquil state. The ascent follows the historic Switchback Gravity Railroad Rail-Trail, right into the town of Summit Hill.

From the trailhead, the old Switchback Railroad is your link to Summit Hill. A few paved roads will loop around to the old cemetery where a few short singletracks and old woods roads take you to the power line. After a quick jaunt up the power line to its crest, hunt for the obscure singletrack, which is the trail to rock-bashing bliss. After a few miles of well-ridden enduro singletrack, you reach the finale—a 300-foot drop off Pisgah Mountain on the Lung Buster Trail (it lives up to its name when ridden in the opposite direction). The final mellow mile follows the Gravity Switchback in its intended direction, back to the trailhead.

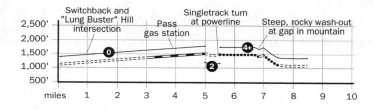

THE RIDE

0.0 The ride begins at the Mauch Chunk Lake Park entrance, where the Gravity Switchback Railroad grade crosses Pennsylvania Road 3012. From the entrance, carefully cross PA 3012 and turn left onto the Gravity Switchback Railroad Rail-Trail.

1.0 Just after passing the switchback on the right, notice the trail that forks off right, climbing the hill. This is the Lung Buster Hill and the route of descent off the ridge. Continue straight on the Switchback Gravity Railroad Rail-Trail.

2.8 Stay straight at the fork, continue out onto the paved road, and pass several houses on the left.

3.9 Pass the gas station on the left and turn right at the stop sign onto South Pine Street.

4.0 Turn right onto the second right-hand turn, Ludlow Street.

4.4 Continue straight as the paved road turns to gravel, then singletrack. At this point the trail passes graveyards on both sides.

4.6 Turn left at the T intersection.

4.8 Turn right at the T intersection onto the old woods road.

5.1 Turn right at the fork.

5.3 Turn right onto the power line and climb the loose, rocky hill. You will need to count the power line towers to find the obscure singletrack entrance.

The stripping's of Summit Hill. The barren wastes of an old strip mine.

5.4 At the crest of the hill, on a flat summit (great views both north and south), turn left 50 yards after passing the third power line tower, onto the obscure singletrack. Sometimes this location is marked by a stone cairn, but you can also look for another landmark, a rusted steel mattress frame with trees growing through it. Enter the burly enduro singletrack!

6.8 Pass a left-hand trail and climb (probably on foot) a steep, rocky washout.

6.9 Turn left at the T intersection on the wide, old woods road.

7.0 Turn right onto an obscure singletrack that drops down into the woods off the woods road and cross over a large dirt berm. After passing over the berm the trail enters a small clearing. Turn right at the T intersection (mile 7.1), following the singletrack trail into the woods. This is the head of the Lung Buster.

7.6 After a devilish descent, merge left onto the Switchback Gravity Railroad Rail-Trail.

8.5 Carefully cross PA 3012 to return the trailhead.

Switchback Gravity Railroad

Location:	2 miles west of Jim Thorpe.
Distance:	16.1 miles out and back.
Time:	1 to 4 hours.
Tread:	Cinder rail-trail with a few sections of scattered rocks and a short section of old woods road.
Aerobic level:	Easy. The trail ascends 500 vertical feet over 8 miles. The grade is consistent, as it was designed to keep the loaded coal cars headed downhill.
Technical difficulty:	1. The terrain is easy for the majority of the cinder-covered parts. The sections that cover old woods road are a bit loose and stony but easily ridden by novice riders.
Highlights:	A ride along the historic Switchback Gravity Railroad (circa 1827), old open mine shaft, incredible views of the Lehigh Gorge and Jim Thorpe; Mauch Chunk County Park amenities include camping, fishing, swimming, boating, food and boat concessions.
Land status:	Mauch Chunk County Parks.
Maps:	USGS Nesquehoning.

Access: From downtown Jim Thorpe, take Broadway Avenue west, climbing up out of town. As the road passes up through this hillside town, its name changes to Lentz Highway (Pennsylvania Road 3012). Approximately 2 miles from town, turn left onto Flagstaff Road. Travel for 200 yards on Flagstaff Road and park on the right near a cabled pathway. This area is the trailhead and the ride begins on the other side of the cable.

Notes on the trail: This outstanding, classic ride covers a huge section of the historic Switchback Gravity Railroad. Built in the early 1800s, this monumental system of gently sloping pathways was designed to haul coal from the massive anthracite mine on Summit Hill down to the Lehigh Canal. As the coal mine became depleted, the railroad saw little use and in 1872 it was converted to a popular tourist attraction (second only to Niagara Falls!)—a sight-seeing natural roller-coaster. After 60 years of service the attraction was sold for scrap, and all that remained was the coal-cinder pathway. Many years later it is a fine recreation trail, linking Jim Thorpe and Summit Hill to the overlook on Mount Pisgah.

Beginning from Flagstaff Road, the ride follows the grade along a babbling stream and passes through towering rhododendrons and hemlocks. The trail then snakes around the Mauch Chunk Lake, where the dam has

Switchback Gravity Railroad

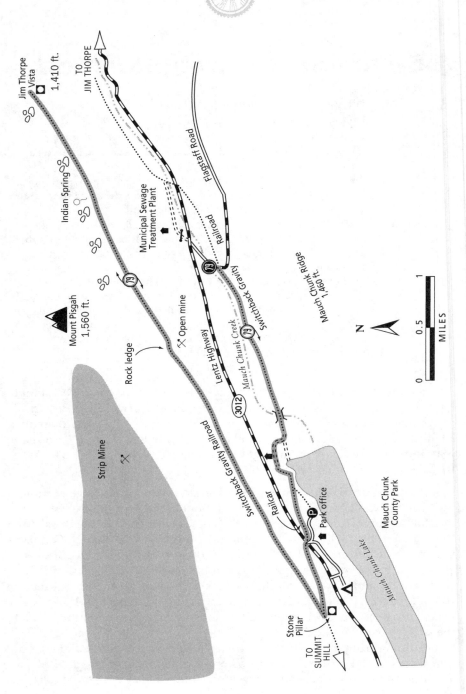

Jim Thorpe Vista
1,410 ft.

TO JIM THORPE

Indian Spring

Municipal Sewage Treatment Plant

Flagstaff Road

Railroad

79

Mount Pisgah
1,560 ft.

79

Open mine

Switchback Gravity

79

Mauch Chunk Ridge
1,460 ft.

Rock ledge

Lentz Highway

Mauch Chunk Creek

3012

Strip Mine

Switchback Gravity Railroad

Railcar

Park office

P

Mauch Chunk Lake

Mauch Chunk County Park

Stone Pillar

TO SUMMIT HILL

N

0   0.5   1
MILES

disrupted the original pathway, and soon passes a small interpretive site. After crossing Lentz Highway, the ride continues to the massive stone pillar where the trail switchbacks right and climbs Mount Pisgah. About halfway up the mountain the trail crosses a dangerous section over an old open mine shaft. This rock ledge crux is wide enough for you and your bike to safely walk across, but you will need to exercise extra caution. Pedal-pushing to the summit, you are rewarded with expansive views south over Jim Thorpe and into the Lehigh Gorge. The concrete abutment found here was part of the incline that pulled the empty coal cars back up the mountain to be refilled. Turn around at the summit and let the gravity railroad work for you, as it once did for coal cars and tourists.

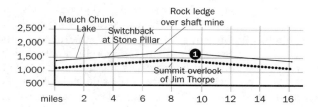

THE RIDE

0.0 From the trailhead pulloff on Flagstaff Road, cross the cable onto the Switchback Gravity Railroad and head west along the stream.

1.7 Come out to a grassy clearing below the Mauch Chunk Lake Dam. Turn left at the gravel road to check out the lake. On the dam top at mile 1.9, return back down the gravel road, turn left at the T intersection (mile 2.1), and ride up and around the lake.

2.4 As the dirt old woods road passes the park ranger house, it descends slightly. Turn right at the pathway, which is the Switchback Gravity Railroad.

2.8 After passing the Switchback Gravity Railroad interpretive display, carefully cross Lentz Highway diagonally at the Mauch Chunk Park entrance. Pass around a set of steel yellow poles and continue on the Switchback Gravity Railroad.

3.8 Turn hard right at the switchback marked by the massive stone pillar.

6.7 Carefully cross the rock ledge above the old open mine shaft. If you choose not to cross the ledge there are two options: Walk down the steep hill crossing the mouth of the mine and reclimb the steep hill on the other side, or return back down the trail to the trailhead.

8.2 On the summit! Enjoy the views southeast over Jim Thorpe and the Lehigh Gorge, and note the large concrete structure at the vista. Well, it's all downhill from here—retrace the route back to the trailhead.

16.1 Trailhead.

The American Standard

Location:	7 miles north of Jim Thorpe.
Distance:	25.4-mile loop.
Time:	3 to 6 hours.
Tread:	Classic east-coast trail riding with mixed hardpacked and rocky singletrack, old woods roads, enduro bike trail, and dirt access road.
Aerobic level:	Difficult. The ride follows the relatively flat top of Broad Mountain, but its rolling nature as it dips in and out of drainages and hollows and the tough technical nature of the ride make it very demanding.
Technical difficulty:	4+. The ride crosses many technical rock fields through endless miles of singletrack. But the rock gardens are short enough to be hiked through. You'll find fallen logs, low trees and limbs, body-snagging mountain laurel, tight tree passes, steep drop-offs, and loose terrain.
Highlights:	Endless miles of incredible technical east-coast singletrack, two impressive views of the Lehigh Gorge, technical rock gardens, spectacular side hike to Glen Onoko Falls, numerous stream crossings, great wildlife viewing.
Land status:	Pennsylvania Game Commission.
Maps:	USGS Weatherly; Pennsylvania Game Commission, SGL 141 map.

Access: From Jim Thorpe take U.S. Highway 209 south to Pennsylvania Highway 93. Turn right onto PA 93 and climb Broad Mountain. After approximately 3 miles the road crests the ridge and passes a truck pull-off on the left. Soon after, turn right into the state game lands parking area marked by the large wooden sign. This lot is the trailhead.

Notes on the trail: The ride, which derives its name from the porcelain urinal found at mile 7.9, is the finest ride on Broad Mountain. It covers some of the most twisty, technical, and tight singletrack on the mountain, with passes you can barely squeeze your bars through. A few rock gardens dot the trail, and although the ride changes little in elevation, the countless dips into the heads of the hollows begin to drain even the most burly of riders.

Galen Van Dine, who is the local pioneer of mountain biking in Jim Thorpe and whose legacy remains as the "Van Dine-asty," founded half of the ride. The ride was legally extended, mostly due to the efforts of Dean Leone, who hand-cut the critical links of singletrack trail. Good navigational skills are especially important when negotiating the singletrack between miles 10.7 and 13.5, which passes through intermittent rock gardens. One option is to ride the gravel road that parallels the singletrack, but just think of all that hidden sweet trail you'd be missing! There are also many optional bailout points along the way, including mile 13.5 and any of the old woods roads drawn on the map.

Beginning at the state game lands parking area, the ride immediately slips into the woods on singletrack sweetness and rolls along the Broad, using a few old woods roads to link the singletrack. The trail passes the rifle range and descends past the porcelain icon for which it's named. You reclimb on more rolling terrain to a rugged section of hard-to-follow trail. After crossing Pennsylvania Highway 93, the ride cruises on more singletrack bliss before turning out to two spectacular overlooks of the Lehigh Gorge. The final leg has you splashing your way through two stream crossings to the trailhead.

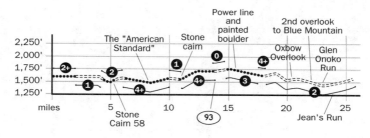

THE RIDE

0.0 From the trailhead lot, turn left onto Pennsylvania Highway 93 and carefully cross it to the truck pull-out. At the end of the truck pull-out there is an obvious singletrack trail that enters the woods. Turn right onto the singletrack and, once in the woods, keep right at the fork.

1.1 Cross over a four-way intersection at an old woods road and continue on the singletrack.

1.8 Turn right at the four-way intersection onto the grassy, doubletrack old woods road.

2.1 Turn left at the T intersection onto the grassy, doubletrack old woods road.

2.4 Turn left again at the four-way intersection onto the grassy, doubletrack old woods road that soon becomes rutted and muddy.

4.0 Turn left at the T intersection, onto the grassy, doubletrack old woods road that soon narrows down to an ATV-style trail.

4.2 Turn right onto the singletrack trail spur—be careful not to miss this turn!

4.7 Cross over a rock-strewn stream, Deep Run.

5.5 Turn right at the T intersection, note the white-painted stone cairn (state game lands boundary marker) with the number "58" painted in red. This singletrack will turn to doubletrack in approximately 0.3 mile.

6.2 Turn hard left off the doubletrack onto the singletrack trail; this turn is easy to miss, so keep your head up!

The American Standard

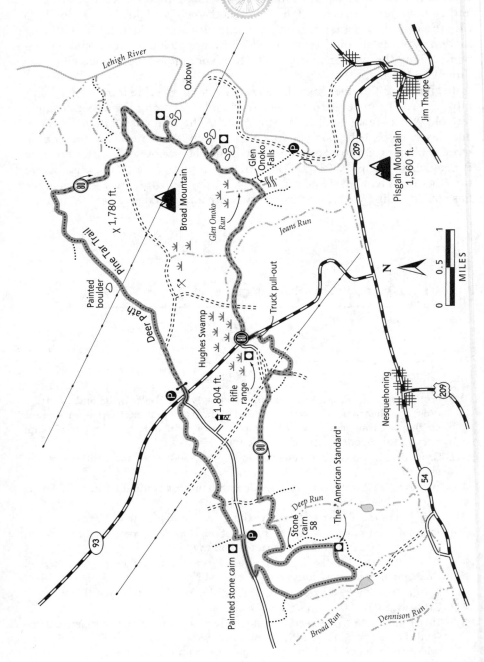

7.9 Keep right at the fork at the "American Standard" urinal.

9.2 Keep right at the singletrack fork.

9.7 The singletrack bends 90 degrees right as it continues a slow, gradual climb.

10.3 Turn left onto the grassy, doubletrack old woods road. Ride 150 yards and turn right onto the wide gravel road.

10.7 After passing an old woods road on the right, turn left onto the singletrack trail located directly across from a small grassy pull-out on the road. Soon after, pass a white-painted stone cairn (state game lands boundary marker); turn right onto the singletrack trail (mile 10.8). This trail will sporadically pass through rock gardens, where the trail is difficult to follow. When in doubt, head toward the right; the road is near. To avoid the technical and navigational difficulties, one option would be to stay on the wide, gravel road and ride it out to mile 13.5.

11.5 Cross a grassy, doubletrack old woods road.

12.4 Cross a grassy, doubletrack old woods road.

13.5 Turn left onto the dirt road. Ride it out to PA 93 (approximately 200 yards). Cross PA 93 diagonally right to the state game land parking area, pass around the gate, and continue on the grassy, doubletrack old woods road. If you've had enough riding, you can return to the trailhead from here by turning right on PA 93; the trailhead lot is 1 mile down the road.

14.4 At a slight right-hand bend in the road, turn left onto the singletrack over the small dirt berm. This is the Deer Path Trail.

15.7 Cross the four-way intersection at the power line, note the painted boulder on the left with the listing of trail names. This trail is now the Pine Tar Trail.

16.8 Turn right at the T intersection.

17.4 The trail bends 90 degrees right at an obscure intersection.

18.2 The singletrack trail exits the woods onto a grassy, doubletrack old woods road.

19.1 Keep straight at the four-way intersection.

20.6 After passing one left-hand woods road, turn left at the second woods road that turns back left and changes into wide singletrack. You will arrive at the Oxbow Overlook (mile 20.7) and the expansive views along the precipitous edge of the Lehigh Gorge. Return back to the main woods road and turn left to continue the ride (mile 20.8).

21.0 Turn right at the T intersection and soon after pass under the power line; continue straight across on the main old woods road.

21.8 Turn left at the T intersection to the second overlook from the rim of the gorge (mile 21.9), with Blue Mountain and the outskirts of Jim Thorpe visible in the distance. Return to the intersection and keep left (straight) to continue the ride (mile 22.0).

23.0 Cross Glen Onoko Run and immediately turn right at the four-way intersection and climb the sandy old woods road. If you wish to check out the Glen Onoko Falls, the foot trail starts 100 feet back from the stream crossing, on the downstream side. A short walk along this rugged trail will lead to the first in a series of steep, beautiful waterfalls. Be careful atop the falls; there have been a few fatalities.

24.2 Splash through the last stream crossing on Jeans Run.

24.9 Cross the four-way intersection and continue straight.

25.4 Trailhead lot.

Broad Mountain

Location:	7 miles north of Jim Thorpe.
Distance:	9.8-mile loop.
Time:	1 to 3 hours.
Tread:	Most of the ride follows dirt doubletrack, with some sections that are a bit rough with loose stone and sand.
Aerobic level:	Easy. The ride rolls around the big, flat top of Broad Mountain and takes an occasional dip into the tops of a few drainages.
Technical difficulty:	2. A few sections of loose rock and soft sand warrant a bit of caution. And there are three fun but challenging creek crossings.
Highlights:	Awesome wildlife viewing, two of the finest vistas in the state, great side trail hike to the spectacular Glen Onoko waterfalls.
Land status:	Pennsylvania Game Commission. SGL 141.
Maps:	USGS Weatherly; Pennsylvania Game Commission, SGL 141 map.

Access: From Jim Thorpe, take U.S. Highway 209 south to Pennsylvania Highway 93. Turn right onto PA 93 and climb Broad Mountain. After approximately 3 miles, the road crests the ridge and passes a truck pull-off on the left. Soon after, turn right into the state game lands parking area marked by the large wooden sign. This lot is the trailhead.

Notes on the trail: This ride tours through the state game lands located on Broad Mountain and skirts the precipitous edge of the Lehigh Gorge, offering outstanding views of the canyon. Don't forget your camera; you'll see loads of wildlife, including deer, turkey, grouse, and maybe even bear.

Beginning at the gated woods road, the ride cruises to a four-way intersection, skirts the lower end of the Hughes Swamp (great bear habitat), and crosses the stream. At the next turn, you pass an old open-pit quarry and continue on smooth doubletrack. The half-way point unveils the first gem, a stunning vista of the oxbow Bend in the Lehigh River. From here the views up and down the gorge are awesome, including the view of the Blue Mountain Ridge to the south. After a second vista, the ride spices up a bit as the clean, hardpacked lines fade to loose, stony, old woods road. If you have time for a side trip, check out the 0.5-mile walk to the Glen Onoko Falls (thefts have occurred here so take your bike with you or lock it up). Legend has it that Indian Princess Onoko threw herself from atop the falls because

Broad Mountain

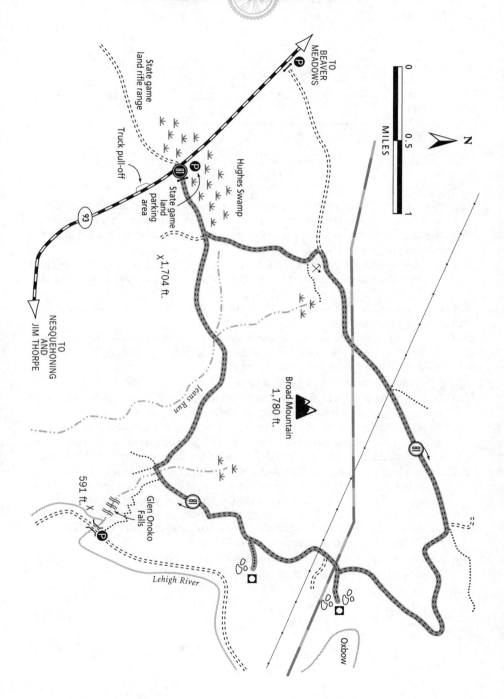

TO
BEAVER
MEADOWS

State game
land rifle range

Truck pull-off

93

TO
NESQUEHONING
AND
JIM THORPE

State game
land
parking
area

Hughes Swamp

x 1,704 ft.

Jeans Run

Broad Mountain
1,780 ft.

591 ft. x

Glen Onoko
Falls

Lehigh River

Oxbow

N

MILES

0   0.5   1

she could not marry the brave of her dreams. The ride ends with another great stream crossing and some smooth doubletrack lines that climb back to the trailhead.

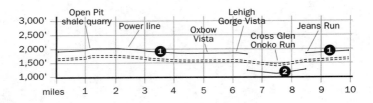

THE RIDE

0.0 From the trailhead lot, ride around the gate and onto the doubletrack grassy woods road. Heed the warning signs if you're riding during hunting season.

0.5 Turn left at the four-way intersection and soon cross a small stream that drains the Hughes Swamp to the west.

1.2 Pass around an open-pit shale quarry on the left. Soon after, turn right at the T intersection onto the gravel and dirt old woods road. The food plots on the left are great for viewing wildlife.

2.5 Cross under the powerline and continue straight on the main woods road.

3.5 Turn right at the intersection.

5.0 Turn left at the T intersection and head to the first overlook. The awesome Oxbow Overlook pans out over the deep Lehigh Gorge. Return back to the T intersection and keep left (straight) at mile 5.2.

5.3 Pass a half shot-up orange pipeline marker in the woods on the left.

5.5 Turn right at the T intersection and soon after (mile 5.7) pass under the power line and continue on the main old woods road.

6.2 Turn left at the T intersection and head to the second overlook. At mile 6.3 you are rewarded with another incredible view from the rim of the Lehigh Gorge. Blue Mountain is visible in the distance, as are the outskirts of Jim Thorpe.

7:4 Cross Glen Onoko Run and immediately turn right at the four-way intersection, climbing the sandy old woods road. If you wish to check out the Glen Onoko Falls, the foot trail starts 100 feet back from the stream crossing, on the downstream side. A short walk along this rugged trail will lead to the first in a series of steep, beautiful waterfalls. Be careful atop the falls, there have been a few fatalities, including Princess Onoko.

8.6 Splash through the last stream crossing on Jeans Run.

9.3 Cross the four-way intersection and continue straight.

9.8 Trailhead lot.

Lehigh Gorge

Location: Begins in White Haven and ends north of Jim Thorpe at the Glen Onoko access area.

Distance: 21.5 miles one way.

Time: 1.5 to 5 hours.

Tread: Smooth, cinder-covered rail-trail.

Aerobic level: Easy. The entire ride follows the downstream flow of the Lehigh River through the Lehigh Gorge on flat old railroad and canal grades.

Technical difficulty: 0. This is a great scenic, woodland ride for young riders, tow-behind kid carts, and mountain bikers who do better without the mountain.

Highlights: Incredible views from inside the Lehigh Gorge; cascading waterfalls; precipitous mountains; historic railroad tunnels, bridges, canals, and locks; cool riverside soaking spots; great wildlife viewing.

Land status: Pennsylvania State Parks, Department of Conservation and Natural Resources.

Maps: USGS Christmans, Hickory, Run, Lehighton, Weatherly, White Haven; DCNR Pennsylvania State Parks: Lehigh Gorge State Park recreation map.

Access: To get to the starting point from downtown Jim Thorpe, head south out of town on U.S. Highway 209 to the first light. Turn right at the light onto PA 903 and cross the bridge. Follow Pennsylvania Highway 903 through town to PA 534. At the town of Christmans, turn left onto Pennsylvania 534, heading north. Pass Tannery and go under Interstate 80, then turn left onto Pennsylvania 940 to White Haven. After crossing the bridge in White Haven, turn left into the Thriftway store parking lot. Drive through the lot and bear left to park at the state park access area. Another option is to hop a shuttle from Blue Mountain Sports, in Jim Thorpe, where the friendly and knowledgeable staff will set you up with a ride to the northern trailhead.

To leave a shuttle vehicle at the end of the ride, from downtown Jim Thorpe, head north on Pennsylvania 903, cross the Lehigh River, and head along Front Street (still PA 903). As PA 903 turns right, following North Street, continue straight on Coalport Road. Follow Coalport Road down the twisty turns, over the creek and turn left onto the partially paved Glen Onoko access area road. Follow the access road as it crosses over the Lehigh River again and park in the lot.

Lehigh Gorge

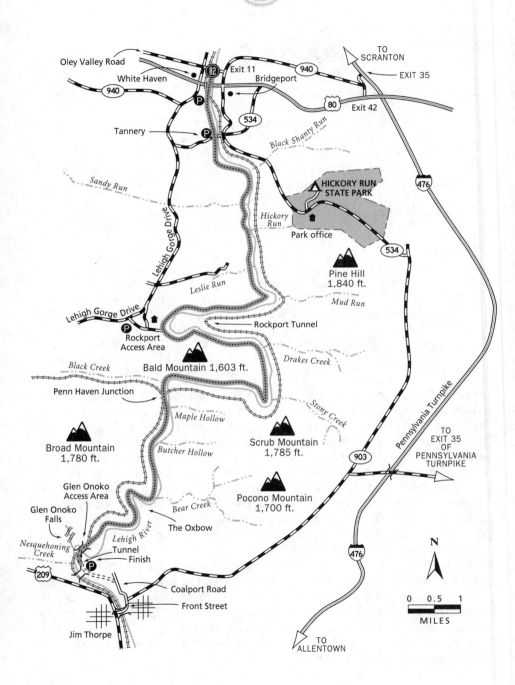

Notes on the trail: There aren't many finer things in life than a picnic-lunch ride down the Lehigh Gorge on a sunny day in the middle of the fall. The sky is clear, the river is flowing, the leaves are changing color, and you've got a full cooler headed south along the beautiful Lehigh River. Life just doesn't get any better than this.

Development in the Lehigh Gorge began in the early 1800s. Loggers felled the massive pines and moved them the cheapest and most efficient way, down the natural aquatic corridor of the river. The famous naturalist James Audubon even paid a visit to the area, although he left quickly, discouraged by the devastating and unsightly logging practices. The incredibly productive anthracite coal mine at Summit Hill (circa 1791) brought two major changes to the pristine beauty of the Lehigh Gorge: an influx of people and the canal system. The Upper Grand Section of the Lehigh Canal, named for its oversized and well-built locks and dams, was constructed between 1835 and 1838. It serviced coal barges down along the Lehigh River to the Delaware Canal; from there the coal was barged to Philadelphia.

The town of Tannery (Lehigh Tannery) was the site of the second largest tannery in the United States in the 1860s. A massive fire swept the valley in 1875, burning the mills, stockpiles, and remaining standing timber; it ended logging in the gorge for good. Tourism picked up at the turn of the twentieth century with the Wahnetah Hotel at Glen Onoko, which not only boasted hotel luxuries but the natural beauty of the Glen Onoko Falls. A few natural features are listed in the mileage log as points of reference along the trail.

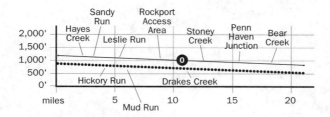

THE RIDE

0.0 At the state park access area, begin the ride on the cinder-covered pathway.

1.3 Cross a paved road and ride through the parking area, which is the Tannery access area; continue straight on the cinder-covered pathway.

2.5 Cross Hayes Creek.

3.2 Cross Sandy Run.

4.1 Cross Hickory Run.

5.3 Cross Leslie Run.

6.1 Cross Mud Run.

The waterfalls along Glen Onoko in the Lehigh Gorge.

8.9 Pass through the Rockport access area. Here you will find the park office and restrooms.

11.3 Cross Drakes Creek.

12.5 Cross Stony Creek.

15.5 Continue straight at the Penn Haven Junction. The trail now follows the left side of the railroad tracks.

18.2 Cross Bear Creek.

21.5 Arrive at the southern trailhead at the Glen Onoko access. Restrooms and the trailhead for the spectacular Glen Onoko Falls Trail are located here.

Pohopoco Tract

Location:	6 miles south of Blakeslee.
Distance:	7.3-mile loop.
Time:	1 to 2 hours.
Tread:	The ride follows a mixture of rocky ATV trails and grassy old woods roads.
Aerobic level:	Moderate. Although there are flat, grassy old woods roads throughout much of this ride, the route traverses the hilly terrain around Pimple Hill. The challenge comes when the hilly climbs combine with a bit of technical rocky trail riding, making for a substantial aerobic workout.
Technical difficulty:	3. The ride is somewhat rocky for long stretches at a time. The Pocono Plateau is notorious for its glacial deposits of rock, and the Pohopoco Tract is no exception. Although loose, the rocky sections are fairly easy to ride due to the volume of ATV traffic.
Highlights:	Pohopoco Fire Tower, Boulder Field, rocky ATV trails, vistas, countless miles of auxiliary trails to explore.
Land status:	Pennsylvania State Forest, Department of Conservation and Natural Resources.
Maps:	USGS Blakeslee, Pocono Pines; DCNR Bureau of Forestry: Delaware State Forest Map, Pohopoco ATV Trail map.

Access: From the intersection of Pennsylvania Highways 940 and 115 in Blakeslee, travel south on PA 115 for 6 miles to the entrance for the Pohopoco Tract of the Delaware State Forest, marked by a large brown and white "Pohopoco Tract" trailhead sign. Turn right at the trailhead sign and travel down the dirt road for 0.1 mile. Park in the huge gravel parking area on the

Pohopoco Tract

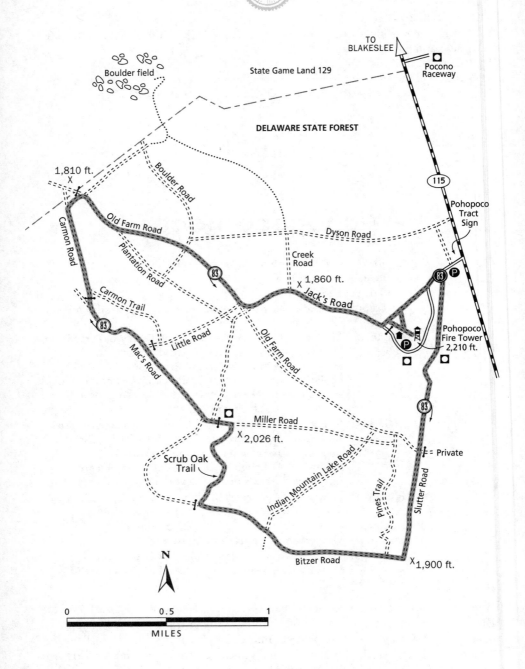

TO
BLAKESLEE

Pocono
Raceway

State Game Land 129

DELAWARE STATE FOREST

Boulder field

1,810 ft.

Boulder Road

Carmon Road

Old Farm Road

Plantation Road

Dyson Road

115

Pohopoco
Tract
Sign

Creek
Road

83

1,860 ft.

Jack's Road

Carmon Trail

83

Little Road

Old Farm Road

Pohopoco
Fire Tower
2,210 ft.

Mac's Road

83

Miller Road

2,026 ft.

Scrub Oak
Trail

Indian Mountain Lake Road

Pines Trail

Slutter Road

Private

83

Bitzer Road

1,900 ft.

N

0   0.5   1

MILES

left. The actual trailhead is located in the lower left corner of the lot, by the two huge boulders. You will know you're close to the trailhead lot when you pass the Pocono Raceway on the left.

Notes on the trail: This route is a great introductory ride to the a-"maze"-ing network of trails in this small section of state forest land. Pohopoco is a multi-use area with a vast network of trails that interlink. The area contains a few, highly visible remains of glacial deposition. You can take a short hike-a-bike side trip to one of these glacial boulder fields along the outskirts of this ride (see directions below). Kettle lakes and ponds, formed by the receding ice-age glaciers, are also found here. Another larger boulder field is in the nearby Hickory Run State Park. Although there is no mountain biking at Hickory Run, there is some great hiking and camping.

The ride runs parallel to Pennsylvania Highway 115 for the first 1.5 miles and passes a small vista along the way. It then follows a flat stretch before ascending a mellow, rocky grade to another stony vista. A beautiful downhill stretch along the grassy woods roads leads to the optional side trip out to the boulder field. A relatively flat expanse rolls to the final climb up the summit of Pimple Hill. Atop the hill, take in the grand views from the Pohopoco Fire Tower and then exit off the mountain on an exciting, rough, and rocky ATV trail.

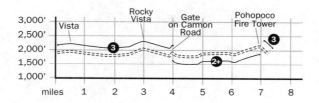

THE RIDE

0.0 From the trailhead lot, look for the entrance to the doubletrack ATV trail marked by the two huge boulders. Pass around the boulders and begin a mild, rocky climb.

0.4 Pass a small vista overlooking the expansive Pocono Plateau and the Pocono Raceway.

0.9 Pass a four-way intersection and continue straight on the Slutter Road Trail.

1.5 Turn right at the trail (Bitzer Road Trail).

2.2 Pass the Indian Mountain Lake Road Trail on the right and continue straight.

2.6 The trail bends right just before a gated road and begins a short, mellow climb.

3.0 Turn left at the T intersection onto the Miller Road Trail. Soon after (mile 3.1), the ride passes a rocky vista that looks out in a northern direction. Then ride around a gate.

3.2 Turn right at the T intersection onto the grassy old woods road (Mac's Road Trail).

The Pohopoco Fire Tower from the Pohopoco Tract.

3.7 Pass a right-hand trail and continue straight.

4.1 Keep right at the fork, climb a short but steep hill, and pass around a gate onto Carmon Road Trail.

4.7 The trail bends hard right and immediately comes to a four-way intersection. Turn right at the four-way intersection onto the Old Farm Road Trail. Note the "State Game Land 129" signs on the trees at this intersection. If you would like to explore the boulder field, ride straight at this intersection for 0.4 mile to the right bend in the old woods road. From here, dismount your bike and hike 0.3 mile on the blue-blazed trail, keeping left at all intersections, to the boulder field. Return back to the intersection at mile 4.7 to continue the ride. The side trip adds about 1.1 miles.

5.1 Keep left at a fork, staying on the Old Farm Road Trail.

5.4 Cross a four-way intersection with Dyson Road Trail and continue straight.

5.8 Turn left at a forking four-way intersection onto Jack's Road Trail. After approximately 100 yards, merge left at the T intersection to continue on Jack's Road Trail as it begins a moderate climb to the Pohopoco Fire Tower.

6.7 After passing around a gate, keep left at a fork and ride on the grassy old woods road. There will be a spur trail coming in from the left; make note of it as you will be returning back down that trail. The grassy old woods road crosses a gravel roadway, passes behind some transmission towers, and makes its way behind a large, white, forest service garage. The Pohopoco Fire Tower is just on the other side. Cross the gravel roadway and head behind the transmission towers, returning back to the grassy old woods road. Soon after, keep right at the trail fork and, a bit after that, turn right at the T intersection (mile 7.0) onto the rocky ATV trail.

7.3 Carefully cross over the Jack's Road Trail, and follow the ATV trail as it empties out into the trailhead lot.

Wolf Swamp

Location:	Big Pocono State Park, 4 miles west of Tannersville.
Distance:	11.7-mile loop.
Time:	1.5 to 3 hours.
Tread:	Old woods roads that vary from gravel and rock to grassy surfaces. A few sections of grassy field-edge riding and some rocky ATV-style trail.
Aerobic level:	Easy to moderate. The only difficult section of the ride is at the very end when a long, moderate climb regains the mountain shoulder trailhead.
Technical difficulty:	2 +. Most of the ride follows smooth, fast old woods roads. Even in the more difficult sections, smoother lines can be found to the outside edges of the roadway.
Highlights:	Wolf Swamp and surrounding glacial bogs and ponds with outstanding wildlife viewing; nice vista atop the "Knoll," Big Pocono State Park nearby with restrooms, picnic areas, and 360-degree views atop Camelback Mountain.
Land status:	Pennsylvania Game Commission. SGL 38.
Maps:	USGS Pocono Pines, Mount Pocono; Pennsylvania Game Commission, SGL 38 map.

Access: From exit 45 off Interstate 80 (Tannersville), head north on Pennsylvania Highway 715 for 0.2 mile and turn left onto Camelback Road. Keep left at the road fork and follow the signs to Camelback Ski Area. Pass the ski area and continue for 3 more miles. Park in the large, gravel state game lands parking lot on the right. This lot is the trailhead.

Notes on the trail: Wolf Swamp and the surrounding lakes are the result of the glacial ice sheets that came down into Pennsylvania. Receding ice, massive amounts of meltwater, and millions of years sculpted a landscape that includes many bogs, swamps, and kettle lakes. These same ice formations formed glacial bogs and deposited the various boulder fields throughout the region.

Big Pocono State Park is located just 0.4 mile away and offers incredible views from the summit of Camelback Mountain. On a clear day you can see the Catskill Mountains, over 80 miles to the northeast in New York, and the East High Point Mountains and Mount Tammany to the east in New Jersey. Binoculars and a camera are a definite must for this ride.

The ride begins atop the west shoulder of Camelback Mountain and slowly winds its way down to Wolf Swamp, passing the large painted boulder. A quiet approach may offer a glimpse of the local inhabitants, which include black bear, white-tailed deer, turkey, grouse, turtles, raptors, and waterfowl. From the swamp the ride climbs slightly to the Knoll, a rounded and somewhat exposed hill that rises abruptly from the surrounding plateau and offers some impressive views. As the ride meanders down along a smooth trail, it passes another bog on the right and makes its way to the food plot fields. A bit of navigation and careful attention to the directions are needed here, as the trail cuts across an open field and resumes in the woods. Following a bumpy downhill, the final leg ascends the long, stony ATV-style trail past the power line and out to the trailhead.

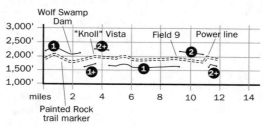

THE RIDE

0.0 From the state game lands parking area, pass around the gated woods road in the corner of the lot and pass under the power line.

0.5 After passing the radio towers, keep right at the fork and begin to descend.

1.3 Keep right at the fork and follow the painted stone directions to Wolf Swamp and Deep Lake.

1.6 Immediately after crossing the dam road at Wolf Swamp, turn left onto the grassy old woods road, riding up along the swamp. Look for wildlife in the swamp.

3.0 Continue straight at the four-way intersection, staying on the grassy woods road.

3.5 Keep left at the fork and continue to climb. The road will soon dead-end and pass a left-hand road. Continue straight at the dead-end on a singletrack trail that passes through small pines to the vista atop the Knoll. Return back through the pines and, once on the road, turn right onto the loose stone, old woods road; you'll soon pass a bog on the right.

4.5 Turn left at the four-way intersection.

4.9 Turn right at a four-way intersection and soon after turn left onto the left-hand road. From this left turn, begin counting the side roads, as it may help you find the turn at mile 7.6.

5.8 Pass a left-hand road. Pass consecutive left-hand roads at miles 6.1, 6.4, and 7.0. At miles 7.3 and 7.5 pass right-hand roads. (So, count five roads total before turning.)

7.6 Turn left at the left-spur road.

9.0 Turn right at the four-way intersection and soon pass around a gate into a large grassy field (Field 9). Ride across the field diagonally left (there may be a slight singletrack trail worn through this field) and resume on the old woods road.

Wolf Swamp

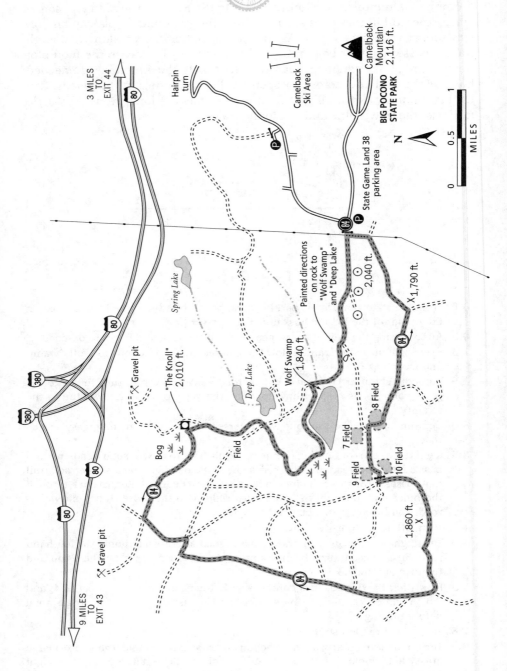

3 MILES TO EXIT 44

80

Hairpin turn

Camelback Ski Area

Camelback Mountain 2,116 ft.

BIG POCONO STATE PARK

State Game Land 38 parking area

N

0   0.5   1

MILES

P

Spring Lake

Painted directions on rock to "Wolf Swamp" and "Deep Lake"

2,040 ft.

X 1,790 ft.

84

80

380

380

Gravel pit

"The Knoll" 2,010 ft.

Deep Lake

Wolf Swamp 1,840 ft.

8 Field

Bog

Field

7 Field

80

84

9 Field

10 Field

1,860 ft. X

Gravel pit

84

9 MILES TO EXIT 43

80

9.6 Turn right onto the grassy woods road that leads to Field 8 (marked by a small white wooden sign). Follow the right edge of the field and resume on a narrow old woods road at the other end of the field.

10.1 Pass a right-hand road and continue straight.

10.7 Turn hard left at the fork and climb the rough, moderately-steep hill on ATV-style trail.

11.4 Turn left onto the trail that passes under the power line; soon after turn right at the four-way intersection onto the gravel road (mile 11.6).

11.7 Pass around the gate to the trailhead.

Bradys Lake

Location:	6 miles east of Blakeslee.
Distance:	5.3-mile loop.
Time:	30 minutes to 1 hour.
Tread:	Great, wide-open grassy old woods roads combined with a neat, hidden old railroad grade covered in cinders.
Aerobic level:	Easy. The ride runs atop the flat plateau of the Pocono Mountains on relatively flat old woods roads and the beautifully narrow old rail grade.
Technical difficulty:	1. Aside from the normal bumps and lumps commonly associated with old woods roads, there are no technical sections on this ride.
Highlights:	Short but secluded woodland ride, spectacular location on the shores of Bradys Lake, boating, fishing, foundation ruins, an ancient white pine tree, beautiful old rail grade, wildlife viewing including beaver, deer, and turkey.
Land status:	Pennsylvania Game Commission. SGL 127.
Maps:	USGS Thornhurst; DCNR Bureau of Forestry: Delaware State Forest map, Pennsylvania Game Commission SGL 127 map.

Access: From the intersection of Pennsylvania Highways 940 and 115 in Blakeslee, travel east on PA 940 for 6 miles. Along the way you'll pass the private community of Locust Lakes (mile 3.2) on the left and a two-story creek-stone house on the left. Just past the creek-stone house is a brown and white wooden sign marking the entrance road to Bradys Lake; turn left here onto the paved road. Travel down the road for 4 miles to the lake where it will dead-end into the parking area. This lot is the trailhead.

Bradys Lake

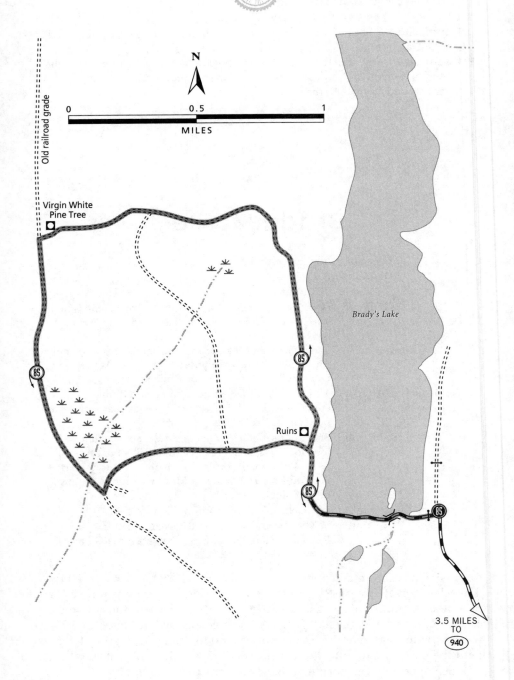

Old railroad grade

N

0   0.5   1

MILES

Virgin White
Pine Tree

85

85

Brady's Lake

Ruins

85

85

3.5 MILES
TO
940

Notes on the trail: The long drive to Bradys Lake alone will lend a sense of being deep in the woods. Once at the trailhead lot, the size of Bradys Lake seems endless as your eyes strain to reach the far shores of the lake. You'll find lots of wildlife here, both above and below the lake surface. You may spot hawks, waterfowl, and the occasional bald eagle, as well as white-tailed deer and a prolific flock of wild turkeys. The lake is stocked with fish and makes for some great shore and boat fishing. Bradys Lake is managed by the Pennsylvania Game Commission in conjunction with the Pennsylvania Fish Commission. Contact these two state agencies for regulations concerning hunting, fishing, and boating on and around the lake.

The ride begins at the lake parking area and heads across the dam and stone spillway. Soon the trail splits and the ride parallels the lake, passing a huge series of old stone foundations. After rolling through a mixture of open fields and hardwood forest, the ride leads past a magnificent white pine tree and out to the remote old rail grade. Look for traces of the old rail ties at the trail junction as the rail grade continues on a smooth course. A sharp left turn begins a return trip along the grassy old woods road that meanders among tall oaks, cherries, and various other assorted hardwood trees. A short pass over the dam will return you to the trailhead lot.

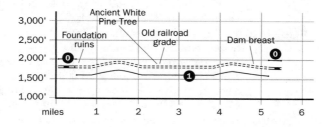

THE RIDE

0.0 From the parking area, head left of the wooden pilings on a gated paved road, travel out along the dam, and cross the spillway on a wooden bridge.

0.5 The road forks; keep right. Look off into the woods on the left for numerous stone building foundations.

2.1 Pass a left-hand old woods road. If you want a shorter ride, turn here. This road brings you to the intersection at mile 4.3.

2.6 After passing an ancient white pine tree, turn left at the four-way intersection. This is the old rail grade; at the trail junction observe the handful of rail ties still embedded in the cinders.

3.8 Turn hard left at the left-hand old woods road. Immediately after this intersection there will be another fork; keep left.

4.3 Pass the connecting old woods road on the left.

4.7 Keep right as the trail merges in from the left. The old woods road will bend along the lake and return back across the dam. If you haven't noticed already, there are a few beaver abodes down in the swamp, below the dam.

5.3 Pass around the gate to return to the trailhead.

High Knob to Pecks Pond

Location:	Pecks Pond, 26 miles north of East Stroudsburg.
Distance:	12.9-mile loop.
Time:	2 to 3 hours.
Tread:	Grassy woods roads, forest roads, singletrack, and a small section on paved road.
Aerobic level:	Moderate. The ride contains some significant climbing up to the High Knob lookout as well as consistent pedaling through the technical singletrack section around White Birch Swamp.
Technical difficulty:	2 + . The beginning grassy woods roads and the hidden singletrack section are the only technical sections on the ride. Watch for hidden stones and deep, grassy holes on the woods roads, and rocks and swampy water holes on the singletrack.
Highlights:	The glacially carved landscape of the area; numerous fishing and boating ponds; grand 360-degree views atop High Knob; views of the tornado destruction of 1998; close to Promised Land State Park and its amenities, which include swimming, boating, fishing, camping, food concession, and hiking trails.
Land status:	Pennsylvania State Forest. Department of Conservation and Natural Resources.
Maps:	USGS Pecks Pond; DCNR Pennsylvania State Forest: Delaware State Forest.

Access: From East Stroudsburg, take U.S. Highway 209 north for 3 miles to Marshalls Creek. At Marshalls Creek, turn left onto Pennsylvania Highway 402 and follow it north to Pecks Pond. After passing through the small village of Pecks Pond, continue for 2 miles to the Maple Run Road snowmobile parking area on the right. Because the locals shoot up the signs, the trailhead sign is typically taken down after the snow is gone.

Notes on the trail: It's hard to believe that this ride creeps along the same ground that was once covered by a 2,000-foot-thick ice-age formation. Evidence of all types of glacial activity can be seen around the area. Large embedded rocks have peculiar marks called glacial striations, from the mass of stones being ground together under the weight of thousands of feet of slow-moving ice. Potholes, or smooth depressions in the rock, were formed when whirlpools of glacial water and sand and gravel swirled around continuously in one place.

High Knob to Pecks Pond

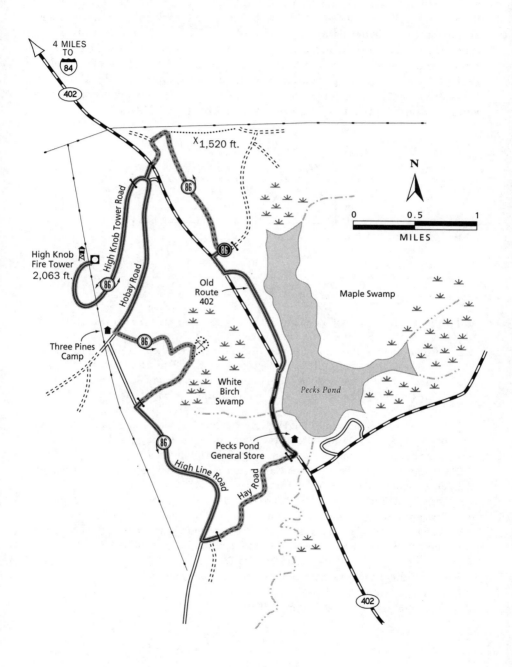

4 MILES TO 84

402

X 1,520 ft.

86

86

High Knob Tower Road

High Knob Fire Tower 2,063 ft.

86

Hobay Road

Old Route 402

Three Pines Camp

86

White Birch Swamp

Maple Swamp

Pecks Pond

N

0   0.5   1
MILES

86

Pecks Pond General Store

High Line Road

Hay Road

402

The ride begins at the snowmobile lot and follows the snowmobile trails out along the power line. From there a climb up the forest access road to the summit of High Knob rewards you with expansive views of the surrounding area, especially over Pecks Pond. A well-earned descent cruises out along flat forest road to the secret singletrack. The singletrack rolls out along rocks and around small ponds to the gravel pit near White Birch Swamp. From there the trail works around on forest and old woods roads, past the destruction of the 1998 tornado that ripped through the southwest corner of Pecks Pond. Shredded trees and newly barren landscape are bold reminders of nature's brute force. The final cruise follows along Pecks Pond on the old Pennsylvania Highway 402 before returning to the trailhead.

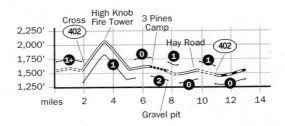

THE RIDE

0.0 From the trailhead lot, head north to the grassy woods road (snowmobile trail) that parallels Pennsylvania Highway 402.

1.2 Turn hard left at the T intersection under the power line and stay on the grassy woods road. Soon after, turn left again at another T intersection (mile 1.3).

1.5 Cross PA 402 to Hobay Road. Ride for 60 yards on Hobay Road, then turn right at the four-way intersection. Soon, pass around a gate and climb on High Knob Tower Road.

3.4 At the tower on the summit of High Knob, enjoy the views, especially southeast over Pecks Pond. From here, return back down to Hobay Road.

5.3 After passing around the gate, turn right on Hobay Road.

6.8 Just opposite the Three Pines Camp sign is an obscure singletrack. Turn left onto this hidden treasure of a trail.

7.6 Turn right onto the grassy woods road at the clearing with the shale pit quarry.

8.3 Pass around a gate and turn left onto High Line Road.

9.6 Turn left onto the old woods road, Hay Road, noting the orange diamond blaze. Soon after, keep left at the fork and pass around a gate (mile 9.7).

10.7 Pass around the gate and turn left onto PA 402.

11.3 Keep right at the fork onto Old PA 402 and pass the quaint cabins.

12.5 Turn right onto PA 402.

12.9 Turn right into the Maple Run trailhead.

Maple Run Ramble

Location:	Pecks Pond, 26 miles north of East Stroudsburg.
Distance:	6.4-mile loop.
Time:	30 minutes to 1.5 hours.
Tread:	The entire ride follows wide dirt and grass snowmobile trails.
Aerobic level:	Easy. Smooth terrain and easy grades make this an outstanding mild ride for novices and families.
Technical difficulty:	1. A section or two of bumpy grass road, loose dirt, or an occasional rock, all of which is easily ridden or skirted around.
Highlights:	The glacially carved landscape of the area; numerous fishing and boating ponds; wildlife viewing in the Maple Run Swamp; close to Promised Land State Park and its amenities, which include swimming, boating, fishing, camping, food concession, and hiking trails.
Land status:	Pennsylvania State Forest. Department of Conservation and Natural Resources.
Maps:	USGS Pecks Pond; DCNR Pennsylvania State Forest: Delaware State Forest.

Access: From East Stroudsburg, take U.S. Highway 209 north for 3 miles to Marshalls Creek. At Marshalls Creek, turn left onto Pennsylvania Highway 402, following it north to Pecks Pond. After passing through the small village of Pecks Pond, continue for 2 miles to the Maple Run Road snowmobile parking area on the right. Because the locals shoot up the signs, the trailhead sign is typically taken down after the snow is gone.

Notes on the trail: This awesome loop is geared just right for the novice rider or adventurous family looking to share some quality time in a beautiful woodland setting. The region got its makeover about 21,000 years ago when the continental glacier grated over the face of the earth. Many scars from the 2,000-foot-thick sheet of ice remain on the landscape today, including ponds, swamps, and peat bogs.

Beginning the ride at the snowmobile parking area, a fun descent follows around the northern end of Pecks Pond. The ride flattens out near a burned area, where a campfire recently got out of hand. Local wildlife often congregates in this regrowth area, so it's not uncommon to see deer, turkey, or possibly a hawk here. Leaving the northeastern corner of the lake, the route rolls back into the woods, following the well-maintained snowmobile trails. After passing one cabin and the remains of another, the roads lead out

Maple Run Ramble

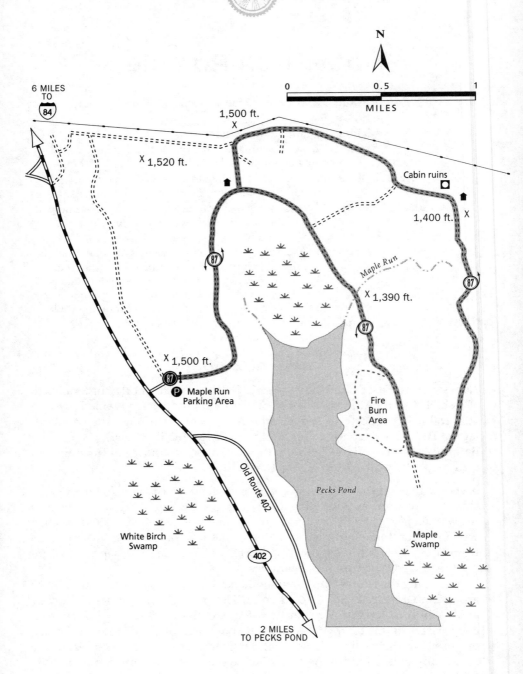

under the power line. Along this stretch it's possible to flush a few ruffed grouse in the brush alongside the wide power line trail. After leaving the power-line, the trail doubles back on itself and climbs the long, mellow hill back to the parking area.

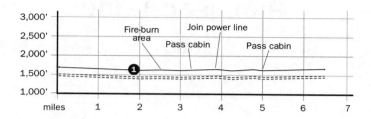

THE RIDE

0.0 From the trailhead lot, head east on the gated woods road that you see as you enter the trailhead lot.

1.4 Keep right at the fork.

1.9 Pass a left-hand trail.

2.6 Turn left at the trail spur, following the wide dirt and grass road. The clearing on the right is the result of an untended campfire that burned down these expansive wetlands.

3.3 As the road bends left, notice the cabin on the right and, soon after, notice the remains of a cabin foundation.

3.7 Keep right at the fork. Soon after, the road bends left and runs parallel to the power line (mile 3.9).

4.5 Pass a left-hand trail.

4.7 Turn left at the spur road, leaving the power line. Immediately after, keep right at the fork.

5.0 Turn right at the T intersection (deja vu), noting the small white cabin hidden on the right. From here you will retrace the route back to the trailhead.

6.4 Pass around the gate to return to the trailhead lot.

Promised Land

Location:	Promised Land State Park, 20 miles east of Scranton.
Distance:	18.1-mile loop.
Time:	2 to 4 hours.
Tread:	Rocky singletrack, old woods roads, and some paved trail.
Aerobic level:	Moderate to difficult. The ride follows subtle changes in elevation but covers some difficult and demanding terrain.
Technical difficulty:	3. The route covers a bit of technical terrain interspersed throughout the ride. Some of the old woods roads and singletrack sections are rock-strewn for lengthy sections, making for a rough ride.
Highlights:	Great woodland riding with a technical edge; the unique Bruce Lake Natural Area; views of the tornado destruction of 1998; state park amenities, which include camping, hiking, fishing, boating, swimming, environmental education programs, rental cabins, equestrian trails, and, food concessions.
Land status:	Pennsylvania State Park and State Forest, Department of Conservation and Natural Resources.
Maps:	USGS Newfoundland, Promised Land; DCNR Pennsylvania State Parks: Promised Land State Park map.

Access: From Scranton, take Interstate 84 east to exit 7, Pennsylvania Highway 390. Turn right onto PA 390 and head south for 3.5 miles, to Promised Land State Park. Turn left into the main parking area (day use area) above the beach and park in this upper lot. This lot is the trailhead.

Notes on the trail: Local legend has it that Shakers migrated to this area in hopes of finding good farmland. When they cleared the trees, however, they found the ground to be too rocky to farm. When the Shakers decided to abandon their efforts, they sarcastically named it the Promised Land. In 1902 the Commonwealth of Pennsylvania purchased the land, which by then was further damaged by erosion and fire. With the help of the Civilian Conservation Corps and nature's own rejuvenation, the land slowly returned to forest and was opened in 1905 as a recreational park.

   The Promised Land State Park is surrounded by the Delaware State Forest, which offers lots of mountain biking opportunities. Within the state forest is the beautiful 2,765-acre Bruce Lake Natural Area, which encompasses two lakes and an expansive wetlands with unique bog flora and a few resident black bear. Although this natural area is closed to riding, exploring it is well worth the hike.

The ride begins at the day use area. After crossing Pennsylvania Highway 390, the ride follows the Tree Tower Trail out to the park boundary and links up with the Bear Wallow Trail. Passing in and out of rhododendron tunnels and across sporadic rocky trail, the ride loops out through wet woodlands. On the return to the park lands, a section of paved trail leads to the second outer loop into the Delaware State Forest. Following old woods roads, the route skirts the tornado destruction of 1998, which leveled the forest. Back out onto the paved road, you'll see a cross section of the tornado devastation before crossing PA 390. The final links of dirt and paved road skirt Promised Land Lake, cross the spillway, and return to the trailhead.

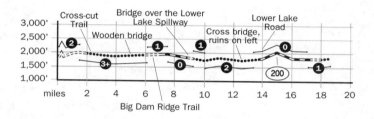

THE RIDE

0.0 Ride out to Pennsylvania Highway 390, turn right, and ride for 30 yards before turning left onto the Tree Tower Trail. Note the old furnace in the woods on the left.

0.2 Keep right at the fork, following the blue blazes past the large water tower.

0.4 Pass the Park Boundary Trail on the right.

0.6 Turn right at the T intersection onto the Bear Wallow Trail.

1.3 Cross the wooden bridge over Bear Wallow Creek.

1.5 Turn right at the fork and continue on the Bear Wallow Trail west.

2.1 Turn right on the Cross Cut Trail.

2.9 Cross a four-way intersection and continue on the Cross Cut Trail.

3.5 Turn left at the T intersection, just before the gate, onto the Klienhans Trail.

4.1 Turn left at the fork, following the blue blazes.

4.5 Turn left at the T intersection, staying on the Klienhans trail.

5.0 Cross the wooden bridge and, soon after, turn right at the four-way intersection onto the Cross Cut Trail.

6.0 Merge right onto the Bear Wallow Trail.

6.3 Turn left at the T intersection onto the Big Dam Ridge Trail.

7.1 Pass a right-hand trail (Big Dam Ridge Trail splits off) and continue straight on the Hemlock Trail.

7.6 Turn right onto the paved park campground road, note the large green water tower, and descend the hill.

Promised Land

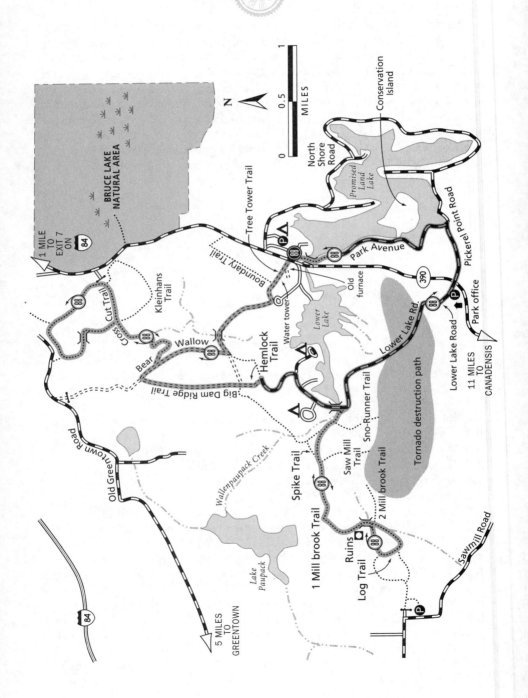

A Pennsylvania old woods road.

8.0 Turn right onto Lower Lake Road and continue to descend.

8.8 After crossing the spillway bridge, climb a bit before turning right into the park service maintenance entrance road. Ride the road for 40 yards and turn right onto the snowmobile trail marked by the wooden sign. Soon after, pass the Sno-Runner Trail.

9.2 Keep left at the fork on the Spike Trail.

9.5 Turn left at the T intersection on the 1 Mill Brook trail.

10.7 Keep straight at a four-way intersection on the 2 Mill Brook trail.

11.1 Continue straight at the fork on the Log Trail. Soon after turn right onto the 1 Mill Brook Trail.

11.5 Turn left at the four-way intersection and continue on the 1 Mill Brook Trail.

12.4 Cross the bridge again. Note the old stone ruins on the left.

13.0 Turn right at the four-way intersection and stay on the main old woods road.

13.8 Turn right onto Lower Lake Road.

15.1 Cross Pennsylvania Highway 390 and continue on Pickerel Point Road.

16.2 Turn left onto Park Avenue.

17.6 Keep right as the road bends left, riding on the gravel road that passes between many cabins and the lake. Ride the road to the parking lot where it crosses the spillway on a bridge.

18.1 Turn right to the trailhead lot.

Shanerburg Run

Location: Wyoming State Forest, 35 miles northeast of Williamsport.

Distance: 21.2-mile loop.

Time: 3 to 6 hours.

Tread: This ride has it all—from singletrack, doubletrack, old woods roads, and dirt forest service fire roads.

Aerobic level: Moderate to strenuous. The ride begins at the ridge top and slowly makes its way down off the mountain. At a ford on the Shanerburg Run, the trail then begins to ascend the ridge again. The total amount of vertical climbing is 1,350 feet.

Technical difficulty: 3. The beginning ridge-top ride has a few short rocky sections but nothing gonzo. The ride up and out of Shanerburg Run follows and crosses the creek several times, which is lined in places with exposed roots and creek-washed stones.

Highlights: Remote woodland ride; numerous stream crossings; beautiful flora and fauna; whitewater creek boating; trout fishing; Worlds End State Park amenities, which include swimming on the Loyalsock Creek, camping, restrooms, and seasonal concessions.

Land status: Pennsylvania State Forest, Department of Conservation and Natural Resources.

Maps: USGS Eagles Mere; DCNR Bureau of Forestry: Wyoming State Forest map, Bridle Trail map.

Access: From the park office at Worlds End State Park, exit the lot and travel south on Pennsylvania Highway 154. At approximately 0.5 mile, turn right onto Pennsylvania Road 3009, also known as Double Run Road. Climb Double Run Road for approximately 3 miles to a four-way intersection. The trailhead lot is 100 yards on the left, just past the four-way intersection with High Knob Road. Pull into the lot and park opposite the three-sided trail shelter. The actual trailhead is 100 yards further down into the lot on the right, marked by a large wooden sign (at times the forest service removes the signs for repair and maintenance).

Notes on the trail: This ride is not one to be missed; its location in the beautiful Wyoming State Forest lends a western flair with its rugged topography and stunning beauty.

Shanerburg Run

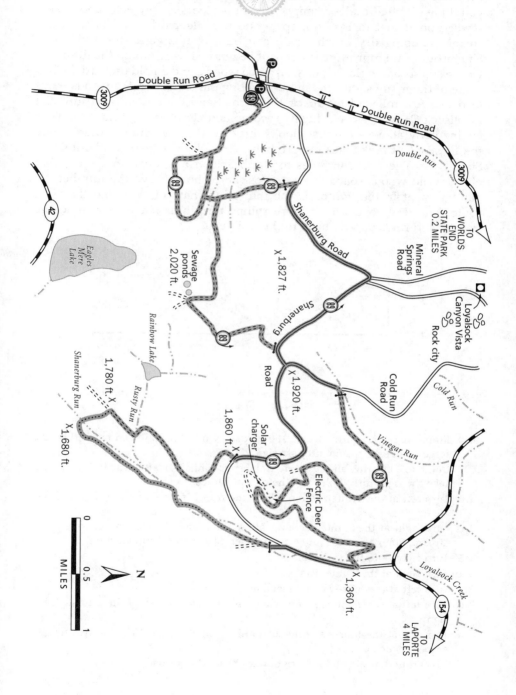

Double Run Road

3009

Double Run Road

Double Run

3009

TO WORLDS END STATE PARK 0.2 MILES

42

Eagles Mere Lake

Shanerburg Road

Mineral Springs Road

X 1,827 ft.

Sewage ponds 2,020 ft.

Loyalsock Canyon Vista

Rock city

Shanerburg Road

Rainbow Lake

Cold Run Road

Cold Run

X 1,920 ft.

1,780 ft. X

Shanerburg Run

Rusty Run

Vinegar Run

X 1,680 ft.

1,860 ft. X

Solar charger

Electric Deer Fence

X 1,360 ft.

Loyalsock Creek

154

TO LAPORTE 4 MILES

0   0.5   1

MILES

N

The ride begins atop the ridge where some rolling terrain leads to the fun, long descent and a hearty ford of Shanerburg Run. Along the way down you'll pass high-altitude swamps, forest management projects, and even a sewage pond that teems with spring peepers (leopard frogs) in the early spring. Keeping dry on this ride can be a challenge as the trail fords Shanerburg Run four more times as it begins a slow climb up the drainage. Dense stands of hemlock, moss-carpeted woods, and an old orchard are just some of the many sights encountered along the climb. Grassy woods roads lead to a few miles of hardpacked fire road and the option of visiting the Loyalsock Canyon Vista. A highly recommended side trip—if time and your aching body allows—the vista looks out over the precipitous gorge where the Loyalsock Creek takes a sharp bend through the canyon at Worlds End State Park. The ride continues to climb Shanerburg Road to a somewhat obscure old woods road. The gate post here should have the number "3" painted on it in red, which is the indication that you've found the right route. The trail covers a bit more rolling terrain as it passes around the swamp and finds its way back to the trailhead.

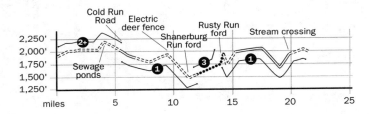

THE RIDE

0.0 From the parking area, travel 100 yards down to the trailhead marked by the large wooden cross-country ski sign.

0.7 Come to a clearing and turn left at the spur trail. Soon after, the trail will fork: take the right fork, following the orange blazes.

1.6 Turn left at the T intersection where the trail is marked by the "Horse Trail" sign.

2.0 Turn right at the T intersection, follow the orange blazes, and cross a small stream. Soon after this juncture, turn left at another T intersection.

2.5 Turn right onto the spur trail.

3.1 Turn right at the T intersection.

3.4 Turn left at the four-way intersection.

3.6 Turn left at the T intersection where the trail is marked by the "Horse Trail" sign.

4.0 Turn left at the four-way intersection in a big clearing. Note the two fenced sewage ponds on the right.

5.5 Pass around a gate and turn right onto Shanerburg Road.

The ford at Shanerburg Run.

5.7 Turn left onto Cold Run Road.

6.2 Turn right onto the gated old woods road. Note the yellow circle with red "X" blazes on the trees on the left.

7.9 Turn left at the T intersection, then ride 300 yards and turn right at the next T intersection.

8.6 Turn left on a trail marked by a wooden "Horse Trail" sign. Descend a short but sweet singletrack and then turn left onto the grassy old woods road at the T intersection.

9.5 After riding along the electric deer fence, turn left and descend the left-hand singletrack. It empties immediately out onto another grassy old woods road where you will turn left at a T intersection. Note the solar charger across from the entrance to the singletrack.

11.4 Ford the chilly Shanerburg Run and turn right onto Shanerburg Road.

12.2 Keep left at the fork, pass around a steel gate, and ford Shanerburg Run again. Soon after the trail forks again. Keep right at the fork, following the creek on the singletrack trail. Over the next mile you will ford the creek at least three more times.

13.9 After climbing a short but steep hill, turn right at the T intersection onto the old woods road. Soon after, turn right again at another T intersection and descend the grassy old woods road.

14.2 The trail turns hard left, fords Rusty Run, and begins to slowly climb.

15.5 Turn left onto Shanerburg Road.

17.4 Pass Cold Run Road on the right and continue straight.

Backcountry fords in the Wyoming State Forest.

18.8 Turn left at the strange T intersection (almost a four-way intersection) and continue to follow Shanerburg Road. For a great side trip, turn right here onto Mineral Springs Road and climb 1 mellow mile out to the incredible Loyalsock Canyon Vista. The trip is well worth the extra easy 2 miles.

19.6 Turn hard left (you can miss this one easily) onto the gated old woods road. The gate post may have a 6-inch, red "3" painted on it.

19.8 Cross over a small stream and pass a left-hand spur trail. Deja-vu . . . yes, you have been here before.

20.1 Keep right at the fork, following the orange and double green blazes. Soon after, the ride crosses a stream and passes a left-hand trail. Keep straight.

20.4 Turn right at the T intersection. After a short bit, the trail empties out into a clearing; turn right following the old woods road.

21.2 Trailhead.

Worlds End Trail

Location:	Above Worlds End State Park, 35 miles northeast of Williamsport.
Distance:	10.7-mile loop.
Time:	1 to 2 hours.
Tread:	Grassy old woods roads make up most of the ride. A few sections of fast, hardpacked fire roads and fun singletrack.
Aerobic level:	Easy-to-moderate. The rolling hills offer a few short, aerobic climbs and some fun freewheelin' descents. The ride's length and the slower surface of the grassy woods roads step up the level a bit. In dry conditions, though, it's a great, easy ride for all.
Technical difficulty:	2+. There is only one technical section, a 0.2-mile descent off the Scar Run Trail, which is rates a 3 but can easily be hiked.
Highlights:	Remote woodland ride; stream crossing; ruins of an old coal mining operation; beautiful flora and fauna; whitewater boating; trout fishing; Worlds End State Park amenities which include swimming on the Loyalsock Creek, camping, restrooms, and seasonal concessions.
Land status:	Pennsylvania State Forest, Department of Conservation and Natural Resources.
Maps:	USGS Eagles Mere; DCNR Bureau of Forestry: Wyoming State Forest map.

Worlds End Trail

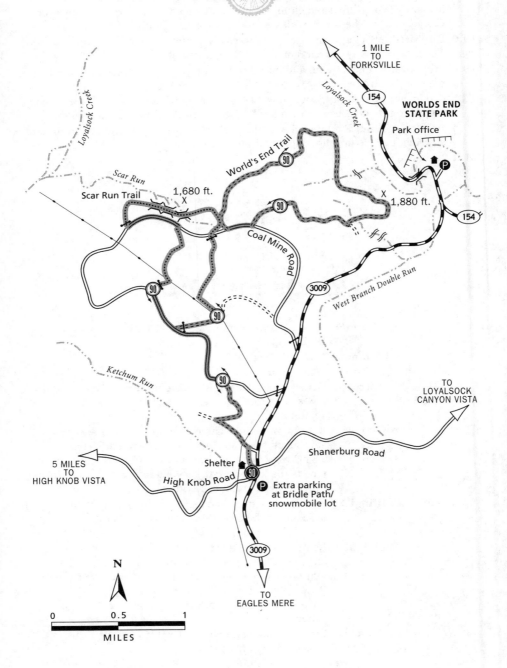

1 MILE
TO
FORKSVILLE

154

**WORLDS END
STATE PARK**

Park office

P

Loyalsock Creek

Loyalsock Creek

World's End Trail

90

Scar Run

Scar Run Trail

1,680 ft.
X

Coal Mine Road

90

X
1,880 ft.

154

90

3009

West Branch Double Run

90

90

Ketchum Run

TO
LOYALSOCK
CANYON VISTA

Shanerburg Road

5 MILES
TO
HIGH KNOB VISTA

Shelter

High Knob Road

90

P Extra parking
at Bridle Path/
snowmobile lot

3009

N

0   0.5   1

MILES

TO
EAGLES MERE

Access: From the park office at Worlds End State Park, exit the lot and travel south on Pennsylvania Highway 154. After approximately 0.5 mile, turn right onto Pennsylvania Road 3009, also known as Double Run Road. Climb Double Run Road for approximately 3 miles to a four-way intersection. The trailhead lot is on the right at the four-way intersection with High Knob Road. Pull into the lot and park near the three-sided trail shelter. This is the trailhead.

Notes on the trail: This ride follows the beautiful ridges atop Worlds End State Park. The park itself is in an S-shaped canyon of sheer beauty—"Sheer" in the sense that the mountain walls end in vertical cliffs that drop hundreds of feet right into the Loyalsock Creek. The first road through the gorge above the cliff bands, on the precipitous face of the mountain. Travelers along this high and exposed route thought they had come to the "end of the world"—to get a feel for this, travel up Mineral Springs Road for about 0.4 miles and look out over the edge as the road nears the top of the cliff.

As with most park and forest lands, this property was bought back from lumber companies and remains an outstanding point of interest in the Pennsylvania parks system. Nature has done its best to reclaim the land, and its success is evident in the fern carpeted trails and lush, young stands of hemlock.

The ride runs atop the ridge with little elevation gain. It takes you through beautiful and remote woodlands. It follows a series of circular green blazes, which at times may be paired with orange-red blazes. Beginning at the cross-country trailhead, the ride immediately dives into a short singletrack section before turning onto a system of old woods roads. The route then traverses across a wood lot surrounded by Coal Mine Road and leads to the old stone ruins of the coal mining operation. From here the ride sets out into remote territory, riding the ridge top out above the canyon and back to Coal Mine Road. Another short section of singletrack ensues traveling across a few old, slippery, oak bridges and back out to the road. A final traverse through thick hemlock woods leads to the old woods road that returns to the trailhead.

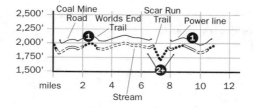

THE RIDE

0.0 From the shelter at the parking area, follow the parking lot past the Fern Rock Trail and out left almost onto Pennsylvania Road 3009 (also known as Double Run Road). Immediately on your left is a large wooden cross-country ski trail sign. Turn left here onto the trail blazed with green circles.

0.3 The horse bridle trail breaks off from here on the power line, marked by the icon sign and orange circle blazes. Continue straight on the green-blazed trail.

0.6 Turn hard right onto a spur trail. Continue to follow the green blazes.

1.2 Turn left onto Coal Mine Road, noting the large wooden cross-country ski trail sign across the road.

1.7 Turn hard right onto a gated old woods road at the large wooden cross-country ski trail sign.

2.1 Turn left at the four-way intersection and climb the beautiful fern-carpeted power line.

2.3 Turn right at the wooden "Ski Trail" sign and follow the trail into the woods.

2.8 Pass around a gate and cross Coal Mine Road, continuing straight across on the red-blazed trail (Worlds End Trail) through a beautiful pine forest and over three small wooden boardwalks. Here in the woods on the left are the stone wall remains of the coal mining attempts of long ago.

2.9 Turn left onto the grassy woods road and, after approximately 50 yards, turn right at the trail fork, following the green and red blazes on the old woods road. Remember this intersection, as you will be here again at mile 6.7.

5.1 The Worlds End Trail breaks off left and descends to the park. Keep right at the fork, continuing on the green-blazed trail, which follows the old woods road.

5.5 After crossing a small stream, turn right at the T intersection, following the cross-country ski trail signs.

6.5 Turn right onto Coal Mine Road.

6.7 Keep right at the fork. Pass a small, open parking area and go around a wooden gate. Soon the trail forks. Take the left fork and descend the green blazed trail (may be marked by a "More Difficult" ski trail sign). This is the Scar Run Trail.

7.7 Turn left onto Coal Mine Road after passing around a wooden gate and the Scar Run Trail sign.

8.1 Turn right onto the old woods road, continuing to follow the green-blazed ski trail.

8.5 The trail comes out to the power line and jogs a little. Turn left onto the power line, then take an immediate right as marked by the wooden "Ski Trail" signs. Soon (mile 8.6), turn left onto Coal Mine Road after passing around a wooden gate.

9.6 Turn right at the fork and take the old woods road back to the trailhead.

10.7 Return back to the trailhead.

High Knob Vista

Location:	Wyoming State Forest, 21 miles northeast of Montoursville.
Distance:	12.8-mile loop.
Time:	1.5 to 3 hours.
Tread:	Grassy old woods roads and forest service fire roads cover the first half of the ride, with paved road covering the middle 2 miles. A great mix of singletrack and old woods roads finish out the last 4 miles.
Aerobic level:	Strenuous. The initial climb is a full-on assault up the mountain, climbing 1,000 grueling feet from the trailhead in under 2.5 miles. The ride mellows out a bit from there, traveling along the rolling ridge top for a few miles before the final insane descent off the ridge.
Technical difficulty:	4+. The grassy woods roads are a bit slow and the paved roads are a nice break before heading back into the forest on old woods roads. The final leg is a well-earned descent down gnarly, washed-out singletrack and doubletrack trails.
Highlights:	High Knob Vista, grueling hill climb with killer technical descent, great wildlife viewing (plenty o' rattlesnakes), whitewater boating on the Loyalsock Creek, close to Worlds End State Park and its amenities.
Land status:	Pennsylvania State Forest, Department of Conservation and Natural Resources.
Maps:	USGS Hillsgrove; DCNR Bureau of Forestry: Wyoming State Forest map.

Access: From Williamsport, travel north on U.S. Highway 220 to Montoursville. At Montoursville, take Pennsylvania Highway 87 east for 21 miles to the Hillsgrove Forest Ranger Station marked by a hugh wooden forest service sign. Turn right at the wooden forest sign (may not be marked) onto Dry Run Road and travel 0.1 mile and park on the right, just before the ranger station, next to the picnic tables. The ranger station parking area is the trailhead. If you happen to drive into the small village of Hillsgrove, you missed the turn up Dry Run Road.

Notes on the trail: This ride is situated on the eastern flanks on the Endless Mountains. The initial climb is one of the steepest and most direct in

High Knob Vista

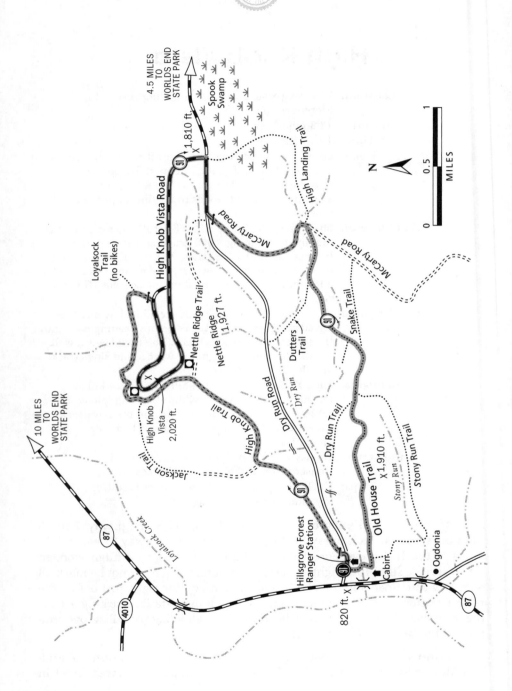

4.5 MILES TO WORLDS END STATE PARK

Spook Swamp

X 1,810 ft.

High Knob Vista Road

High Landing Trail

McCarty Road

McCarty Road

N

MILES

0   0.5   1

Loyalsock Trail (no bikes)

Nettle Ridge Trail

Nettle Ridge 1,927 ft.

Snake Trail

Dutters Trail

Dry Run Road

Dry Run

Dry Run Trail

High Knob Trail

High Knob Vista 2,020 ft.

Stony Run Trail

Old House Trail X 1,910 ft.

Stony Run

Jackson Trail

10 MILES TO WORLDS END STATE PARK

87

Loyalsock Creek

4010

Hillsgrove Forest Ranger Station

Cabin

Ogdonia

820 ft. X

87

the state and gives special meaning to the word "endless." It tackles 1,000 vertical feet in 2.3 miles. As long as you sit tight and keep the gears light, your heart may see you through another day. The ride mellows a bit as it skirts just below the vista, goes out on a wide loop, and returns to the summit of High Knob at 2,020 feet. A great mountain view looking west over Hillsgrove is a welcome sight. Now you can look forward to a few miles of fast, paved and dirt road downhill ahead.

The traverse leads to a southern ridge where old woods roads wind through remote rattlesnake country. The chances of actually seeing a snake are slim but more likely here than anywhere else in the area. Respect these beautiful creatures and remember that we are riding through their home. Old woods roads, single-and-doubletrack roll along the ridge top to the finale, a 900-foot, technical bomber downhill. Bone-crunching rocks and rutted, washed-out trail cover this rim-smoking descent—the word "snake-bite" here has a double meaning! Just when you thought your brake pads were going to melt, a wet ford of Dry Run quenches your wheels as you bonk at the trailhead. The entire ride follows orange circle blazes, so keep that in mind as you follow the route. The ford at Dry Run can be somewhat hairy if the water level is up; plan your ride accordingly.

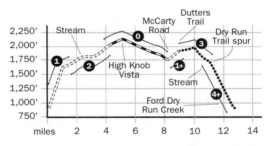

THE RIDE

0.0 From the parking area at the Hillsgrove Ranger Station, ride up Dry Run Road approximately 100 yards and turn left. Pass around the gate and climb the steep grassy old woods road.

1.3 With the steepest section of the climb behind you, turn right at the fork (marked by a wooden trail sign stating "High Knob Trail to Jackson Trail") and continue to climb.

2.1 The trail bears left at a fork and crosses a small stream.

2.3 Turn left at the fork marked by the wooden "Nettle Ridge Trail" sign.

2.6 Keep right at the fork, following the wooden sign marked "Horse Trail."

4.1 The Loyalsock Trail merges in from the left; soon after, the trail passes around a gate and turns right onto the paved High Knob Vista Road.

5.1 Reach High Knob Vista! Picnic tables and restrooms can be found here. The ride continues along High Knob Vista Road with panoramic southern views of the mountains. Continue down High Knob Vista Road.

The killer view atop High Knob Vista, Wyoming State Forest.

7.7 After a great descent, turn right onto Dry Run Road (dirt) and continue to descend.

8.1 Turn left onto McCarty Road (old woods road), pass around a gate, and keep right at a fork soon after.

9.3 At a sharp right-hand bend in the road, pass the High Landing Trail on your left. Almost directly across from the High Landing Trail is the Dutters Trail, marked by a wooden sign. Turn right onto the Dutters Trail, continuing to follow the orange blazes. Soon after, the ride crosses over the Loyalsock Trail.

10.0 Keep left at the trail fork and head toward the Stony Run Trail.

10.8 Cross a small stream and keep left at the fork, following the orange blazes. Soon after, pass a left-hand trail marked by the "Old House Trail" wooden sign.

11.3 Keep left at the fork, as the Dry Run Trail drops off to the right. The trail climbs a bit more, then runs the ridge for a short while before dropping down the insane descent.

12.6 Back in the valley, pass the left-hand Stony Run Trail. Soon after, follow the blazes as the trail bends hard-right near a cabin. Do not ride onto the private property around the cabin, and if you hear shooting, make your presence known loud and clear!

12.8 Ford Dry Run Creek and ride across the grass behind the ranger station 100 yards to the trailhead lot.

A Short Index of Rides

SPICY SINGLETRACKS

4   Sugarloaf Surprise
9   Roaring Run Ramble
21   Garocii Quarry Switchback Trail
29   Minister Creek
31   Rimrock Ramble
34   Middle Ridge Trail
35   Asaph Classic
39   Big Trestle Trail
44   Cowbell Hollow
47   Little Flat Fire Tower
48   Rattlesnake Mountain
56   Three Mile Trail
68   French Creek
69   Wicked Wissahickon Valley
73   South Mountain
77   Bob's Option
78   Summit Hill
80   The American Standard
91   High Knob Vista

KAMIKAZE DESCENTS

31   Rimrock Ramble
34   Middle Ridge Trail
35   Asaph Classic
39   Big Trestle Trail
44   Cowbell Hollow
46   Tunnel Mountain
47   Little Flat Fire Tower
49   Deep Hollow
50   Blue Knob
52   Hidden Tunnel Trail
56   Three Mile Trail
61   Devils Race Course
63   Kelly's Run Pinnacle
66   Roadkill Hill
67   Blue Marsh Lake Loop
77   Bob's Option
78   Summit Hill
86   High Knob to Pecks Pond
91   High Knob Vista

BEGINNER'S DELIGHT

2   Youghiogheny River Rail-Trail
3   Sugarloaf Surprise
11   Laurel Summit Loop
15   Ghost Town Trail
20   Little Toby Rail-Trail
24   Lower Buzzard Swamp
26   Kelly Pines Powerhouse
38   The Grand Canyon
41   Pump Station to Shady Grove
42   Ruth Will Trail
62   Stony Valley Rail-Trail
74   Ironton Railroad
79   Switchback Gravity Railroad
82   Lehigh Gorge
85   Bradys Lake
87   Maple Run Ramble

TECHNICAL TANTALIZERS

1   Moraine State Park
14   Wolf Rocks
18   Big Springs Draft
29   Minister Creek
31   Rimrock Ramble
33   Potato City Singletrack
34   Middle Ridge Trail
35   Asaph Classic
40   Black Forest Shay Trail
44   Cowbell Hollow
47   Little Flat Tire Tower
49   Deep Hollow
50   Blue Knob
53   Roaring Run
54   Big Springs to Bear Pond
55   Grave Ridge to Rocky Pass
56   Three Mile Trail
57   Chimney Rocks
58   Rocky Ridge
61   Devils Race Course
68   French Creek
69   Wicked Wissahickon Valley

Technical Tantalizers (cont.)

73 South Mountain
77 Bob's Option
78 Summit Hill
80 The American Standard
91 High Knob Vista

Aerobic Ascents

5 Laurel Hill Lung-Buster
22 Big Mill Creek
31 Rimrock Ramble
35 Asaph Classic
39 Big Trestle Trail
44 Cowbell Hollow
49 Deep Hollow
53 Roaring Run
56 Three Mile Trail
61 Devils Race Course
63 Kelly's Run Pinnacle
77 Bob's Option
86 High Knob to Pecks Pond
91 High Knob Vista

Enduro Epics

13 Taggart's Traverse
18 Big Springs Draft
19 Gore Vista
35 Asaph Classic
40 Black Forest Shay Trail
44 Cowbell Hollow
54 Big Springs to Bear Pond
67 Blue Marsh Lake Loop
80 The American Standard

Mellow Moderates

6 Mount Davis
7 Mountain View Trail
11 Laurel Summit Loop
12 Lower Beam Loop
16 Rockton Mountain
28 Brush Hollow
32 Commissioner Run
36 Bee Tree Trail
37 Wild Apple to Bake Oven
45 Boiling Springs
48 Rattlesnake Mountain
50 Blue Knob
51 Pigeon Hills
52 Hidden Tunnel Trail
59 Lake Redman
60 Spring Valley
64 Cornwall Fire Tower
65 Governor Dick to Dinosaur Rock
68 French Creek
69 Wicked Wissahickon Valley
70 Pine Run Preamble
71 The Edge
73 South Mountain
75 Homestead Trail
76 Jacobsburg Jive
81 Broad Mountain
83 Pohopoco Tract
84 Wolf Swamp
86 High Knob to Pecks Pond
88 Promised Land
90 Worlds End Trail

Griz Pic's 3-star Classics

5 Laurel Hill Lung-Buster
6 Mount Davis
13 Taggart's Traverse
19 Gore Vista
21 Garocii Quarry Switchback Trail
29 Minister Creek
35 Asaph Classic
37 Wild Apple to Bake Oven
42 Ruth Will Trail
44 Cowbell Hollow

47 Little Flat Fire Tower
49 Deep Hollow
52 Hidden Tunnel Trail
53 Roaring Run
55 Grave Ridge to Rocky Pass
61 Devils Race Course
67 Blue Marsh Lake Loop
69 Wicked Wissahickon Valley
73 South Mountain
74 Ironton Railroad
80 The American Standard
81 Broad Mountain
89 Shanerburg Run
91 High Knob Vista

SENSATIONAL SCENERY

5 Laurel Hill Lung-Buster
6 Mount Davis
19 Gore Vista
23 Beaver Meadows
24 Lower Buzzard Swamp
25 Upper Buzzard Swamp
31 Rimrock Ramble
38 The Grand Canyon
46 Tunnel Mountain Trail
47 Little Flat Fire Tower
48 Rattlesnake Mountain
49 Deep Hollow
50 Blue Knob
53 Roaring Run
54 Big Springs to Bear Pond
57 Chimney Rocks
58 Rocky Ridge
61 Devils Race Course
65 Governor Dick to Dinosaur Rock
79 Switchback Gravity Railroad
81 Broad Mountain
82 Lehigh Gorge
83 Pohopoco Tract
86 High Knob to Pecks Pond
91 High Knob Vista

HISTORICAL HIGHLIGHTS

6 Mount Davis
15 Ghost town Trail
21 Garocii Quarry Switchback trail
26 Kelly Pines Powerhouse
40 Black Forest Shay Trail
41 Pump Station to Shady Grove
46 Tunnel Mountain
52 Hidden Tunnel Trail
62 Stony Valley Rail-Trail
72 Delaware Canal
74 Ironton Railroad
78 Summit Hill
79 Switchback Gravity Railroad
82 Lehigh Gorge

NATURAL WONDERS

1 Moraine State Park
6 Mount Davis
14 Wolf Rocks
19 Gore Vista
29 Minister Creek
31 Rimrock Ramble
38 The Grand Canyon
45 Boiling Springs
53 Roaring Run
55 Grave Ridge to Rocky Pass
57 Chimney Rocks
61 Devils Race Course
65 Governor Dick to Dinosaur Rock
69 Wicked Wissahickon Valley
81 Broad Mountain
82 Lehigh Gorge
83 Pohopoco Tract
84 Wolf Swamp
86 High Knob to Pecks Pond
88 Promised Land
91 High Knob Vista

Appendix A: Land Management Contacts

State Parks	888-PA-PARKS	www.dcnr.state.pa.us
State Forests	717-783-7941	www.dcnr.state.pa.us
Game Commission	717-183-7507	www.pgc.state.pa.us
Fish and Boat Commission	717-657-4518	www.fish.state.pa.us

U.S. Army Corps of Engineers
Delaware Basin (eastern)

Blue Marsh Lake	215-656-6515	www.usace.army.mil
Susquehanna Basin (central)	410-962-2809	www.usace.army.mil
Ohio basin (western)	412-644-4130	www.usace.army.mil
Allegheny National Forest	814-723-5150	www.penn.com/~anf
National Park Service	215-597-7018	www.nps.gov
Pennsylvania Power and Light Company	717-284-2278	
York County Parks	717-840-7440	

(links to 24-hour trail hot line)

Appendix B: Maps and Guides

A.B. Patton Inc.	800-296-6277	fax: 215-345-8691
	e-mail: tpatton@pattonmaps.com	

A.B. Patton Inc. operates one of the largest map stores in the United States. They carry local maps, state maps, city maps, travel and outdoor guide books, laminated maps, wall maps, all USGS topo maps (Pennsylvania, New Jersey, and Delaware maps always in stock) and atlases, including the critical Pennsylvania Atlas and Gazetteer. If you need a map, Patton has got it for sure!

Pennsylvania Tourism Board	800-VISIT PA	www.state.pa.us/visit
Horse-Shoe Trail Club	215-887-1549	
Friends of Pennypack	215-934-PARK	
Fairmount Park Commission	215-685-0000	

Griz Guide to Mountain Biking: The original mountain bike guide to the central PA mountains. Contact Mtngriz@hotmail.com

Contact **Land Management Agencies** for the maps they offer.

Appendix C: Camping

State Parks
For camping or cabin reservations statewide call 888-PA-PARKS.
www.dcnr.state.pa.us

York-Harrisburg area
Pequea Creek Campground
86 Fox Hollow Road
Pequea, PA 17565
717-284-4587

Otter Creek Campground
1101 Furnace Road
Airville, PA 17302
717-862-3628

Allegheny National Forest
814-723-5150

Appendix D: Pennsylvania's Weather

Average temperature (degrees F)

Jan	Feb	Mar	Apr	May	Jun	Jul	Aug	Sep	Oct	Nov	Dec
26	28	40	49	60	67	75	70	65	52	43	31

Rainfall index (inches)

Jan	Feb	Mar	Apr	May	Jun	Jul	Aug	Sep	Oct	Nov	Dec
2.7	2.7	3.2	3.3	3.9	4.0	3.9	3.5	3.6	2.8	3.5	3.3

Glossary

ATV: All Terrain Vehicle; personal four-wheel-drive vehicles designed for off-road use, aka motorized couches.

Bail: A last ditch, usually unplanned, effort to avoid a catastrophic event by dismounting the bike. Usually graded on a scale of 1 to 10 by onlooking fellow riders. Remember pain is temporary, glory is forever!

Bonk: To become extremely fatigued resulting from a lack of water and food.

Bunny hop: A vertical cycling experience where the rider lifts the entire bike in the air while moving forward to clear trail obstacles.

Chocolate helmet: Taking a head-first endo into a pool of mud.

Clean: To ride without dabbing, usually in tough and technical sections.

Contour: A line or path of travel that traverses a level grade at a certain elevation. For example: "The trail follows the contour of the mountain before descending the hollow."

Dab: To touch any part of your body (voluntarily or not) to the ground while riding. If you dab on a ride (usually in the technical and tough sections) then you haven't ridden that part of the trail **clean.**

Deadfall: Rotten trees that have fallen on their own or in winds and now bless the trail with yet another obstacle. Usually havens for rattlers and other woodland critters.

Digger: A cut, gash, or other open wound incurred while riding on the trail. May require the use of first aid, duct tape, hard alcohol, or all of the above.

Doubletrack: An old road (logging, jeep, pipeline, or power-line access road) that is grassy, usually having two distinct, parallel dirt lines.

Endo: To crash by sailing straight over the front of the bike. Usually caused by stuffing your wheel in holes in rock gardens and poor timing while bunny-hopping logs. Also known as "going over the bars" and sometimes resulting in a **chocolate helmet.**

Enduro: Trails designed by cross-country off-road motorcycle riders. Tight, twisty, and technical in nature. Awesome east-coast riding.

Fall line: The gravitational line of pull. The line your bike and or your body follows when gravity takes control. Usually an out-of-body experience.

Granny gear: The combination of the lowest chain ring in the front and the largest in the rear. Used for climbing heinously steep grades. A gear that even granny can crank.

Hammerhead: A person who rides fast and hard all the time. Riders who thrive on giving blood and enjoying pain. Folks whose need for speed overcome their fear of death.

Line: The path of least resistance through a trail section. As the technical difficulty increases, a line becomes more difficult to find and ride.

Off-camber: Steep-sided mountainous singletrack that rises and drops off sharply on either side. Requires the rider to keep the inside (uphill) pedal up to avoid snagging it in the steep mountain face. May also require the rider to use body language to cant (lean) the bike to keep traction and avoid slipping off the trail.

Old woods road: Grassy and partially grown-in old logging and skidder roads. See also doubletrack.

Piton: To stuff the front wheel in a rock garden.

Quads: Referring to USGS 7.5-minute topographical maps. Can also refer to the thigh muscles. Both are important for riders traveling the backcountry.

Read the trail: Looking for the easiest line in a certain section of trail. Usually refers to trail sections of technical difficulty. Also very helpful when descending the same trail of ascent.

Singletrack: The trails normally associated with mountain biker dreams and maybe the number one reason why serious mountain bikers quit their jobs and leave their families. A narrow trail usually formed by enduro bikes, wildlife, hunters, hikers, or other mountain bikers.

Spur: A side trail of any type that splits, branches, or forks from the general route of travel.

Squid: A rider that has gotten in way too far over his or her head on a trail—a hazard and an obstacle to themselves and other competent riders.

Switchback: A trail of any type that zigzags up a precipitous slope with extremely tight turns. The trail can sometimes be off-camber, especially in the turns. Switchbacks offer a unique technical challenge

Trials: The art of balance and movement over extreme obstacles on a mountain bike. This includes boulders, massive logs, fallen riders, picnic tables, cars, and so on. A Zen-like experience performed by extreme riders.

Tread: Surface that appears on the actual trail (rocks, roots, dirt, sand, loam, clay, etc.).

Water bar: A log, timber, rock, dirt berm or other barrier used in diverting water off the trail to prevent erosion. These features are usually designed at an angle to the trail, are sometimes slippery, and may cause diggers when crossed improperly. Hammerheads love water bars because they typically form large jumps for big air.

Windfall: Trees that have succumbed to nature's wicked winds and are now trail obstacles, also called widow-makers.

About the Author

In my vast search for the most remote and wild places across our increasingly urbanized country, I had underestimated the beauty and mystery that lie right here beneath my feet. An explorer and mountain man at heart, I've found Pennsylvania to be an outdoor recreationist's paradise. From my paddling trips on the Middle Youghiogheny, epic rock and ice climbs at the Gap, backcountry rides in the Endless Mountains, to snowshoe backpack trips in the Alleghenies and hunting throughout the state, I've learned much from these outdoor experiences. I believe that the peace and respect I share with the natural world and the Great Spirit have enhanced my experiences in these woods. The wilderness continues to be my teacher, and I persist as its restless disciple. As a teacher of art and the environment, I've found this book to be an extension of who I am, sharing my knowledge and passion for the natural world. For now, Penn's Woods are my home; respect and enjoy all it has to offer. Namaste, Griz.

The author kicking it out on Galen's
old-school high-wheeler.

FALCONGUIDES ® Leading the Way™

FALCONGUIDES ® are available for where-to-go hiking, mountain biking, rock climbing, walking, scenic driving, fishing, rockhounding, paddling, birding, wildlife viewing, and camping. We also have FalconGuides® on essential outdoor skills and subjects and field identification. The following titles are currently available, but this list grows every year. For a free catalog with a complete list of titles, call FALCON® toll-free at 1-800-582-2665.

MOUNTAIN BIKING GUIDES

Mountain Biking Arizona
Mountain Biking Colorado
Mountain Biking Georgia
Mountain Biking Idaho
Mountain Biking New Mexico
Mountain Biking New York
Mountain Biking North Carolina
Mountain Biking Northern New England
Mountain Biking Oregon
Mountain Biking Pennsylvania
Mountain Biking South Carolina
Mountain Biking Southern California
Mountain Biking Southern New England
Mountain Biking Utah
Mountain Biking Washington
Mountain Biking Wisconsin
Mountain Biking Wyoming

LOCAL CYCLING SERIES

Mountain Biking Albuquerque
Mountain Biking Bend
Mountain Biking Boise
Mountain Biking Chequamegon
Mountain Biking Chico
Mountain Biking Colorado Springs
Mountain Biking Denver/Boulder
Mountain Biking Durango
Mountain Biking Flagstaff and Sedona
Mountain Biking Grand Junction & Fruita
Mountain Biking Helena
Mountain Biking Moab
Mountain Biking Phoenix
Mountain Biking Spokane and Coeur d'Alene
Mountain Biking the Twin Cities
Mountain Biking Utah's St. George/Cedar City Area
Mountain Biking the White Mountains (West)

■ *To order any of these books, check with your local bookseller or call The Globe Pequot Press® at **1-800-243-0495**. Visit us on the world wide web at:*
www.FalconGuide.com

FALCON®

FALCON GUIDES ® Leading the way™

FalconGuides® are available for where-to-go hiking, mountain biking, rock climbing, walking, scenic driving, fishing, rockhounding, paddling, birding, wildlife viewing, and camping. We also have FalconGuides on essential outdoor skills and subjects and field identification. The following titles are currently available, but this list grows every year. For a free catalog with a complete list of titles, call FALCON toll-free at 1-800-582-2665.

BIRDING GUIDES

Birding Georgia
Birding Illinois
Birding Minnesota
Birding Montana
Birding Northern California
Birding Texas
Birding Utah

PADDLING GUIDES

Paddling Minnesota
Paddling Montana
Paddling Okefenokee
Paddling Oregon
Paddling Yellowstone & Grand
    Teton National Parks

WALKING

Walking Colorado Springs
Walking Denver
Walking Portland
Walking Seattle
Walking St. Louis
Walking San Francisco
Walking Virginia Beach

CAMPING GUIDES

Camping Arizona
Camping California's
    National Forests
Camping Colorado
Camping Oregon
Camping Southern California
Camping Washington
Recreation Guide to Washington
    National Forests

FIELD GUIDES

Bitterroot: Montana State Flower
Canyon Country Wildflowers
Central Rocky Mountain
    Wildflowers
Chihuahuan Desert Wildflowers
Great Lakes Berry Book
New England Berry Book
Ozark Wildflowers
Pacific Northwest Berry Book
Plants of Arizona
Rare Plants of Colorado
Rocky Mountain Berry Book
Scats & Tracks of the Pacific
    Coast States
Scats & Tracks of the Rocky Mtns.
Sierra Nevada Wildflowers
Southern Rocky Mountain
    Wildflowers
Tallgrass Prairie Wildflowers
Western Trees

ROCKHOUNDING GUIDES

Rockhounding Arizona
Rockhounding California
Rockhounding Colorado
Rockhounding Montana
Rockhounding Nevada
Rockhounding New Mexico
Rockhounding Texas
Rockhounding Utah
Rockhounding Wyoming

HOW-TO GUIDES

Avalanche Aware
Backpacking Tips
Bear Aware
Desert Hiking Tips
Hiking with Dogs
Hiking with Kids
Mountain Lion Alert
Reading Weather
Route Finding
Using GPS
Wild Country Companion
Wilderness First Aid
Wilderness Survival

MORE GUIDEBOOKS

Backcountry Horseman's
    Guide to Washington
Family Fun in Montana
Family Fun in Yellowstone
Exploring Canyonlands & Arches
    National Parks
Exploring Hawaii's Parklands
Exploring Mount Helena
Exploring Southern California
    Beaches
Hiking Hot Springs of the Pacific
    Northwest
Touring Arizona Hot Springs
Touring California & Nevada
    Hot Springs
Touring Colorado Hot Springs
Touring Montana and Wyoming
    Hot Springs
Trail Riding Western Montana
Wilderness Directory
Wild Montana
Wild Utah
Wild Virginia

■ *To order any of these books, check with your local bookseller
or call The Globe Pequot Press® at 1-800-243-0495.
Visit us on the world wide web at:*
www.FalconGuide.com

FALCON®

FALCON GUIDES® Leading the Way™

HIKING GUIDES

Best Hikes Along the Continental Divide
Hiking Alaska
Hiking Arizona
Hiking Arizona's Cactus Country
Hiking the Beartooths
Hiking Big Bend National Park
Hiking the Bob Marshall Country
Hiking California
Hiking California's Desert Parks
Hiking Carlsbad Caverns
    and Guadalupe Mtns. National Parks
Hiking Colorado
Hiking Colorado, Vol. II
Hiking Colorado's Summits
Hiking Colorado's Weminuche Wilderness
Hiking the Columbia River Gorge
Hiking Florida
Hiking Georgia
Hiking Glacier & Waterton Lakes National Parks
Hiking Grand Canyon National Park
Hiking Grand Staircase-Escalante/Glen Canyon
Hiking Grand Teton National Park
Hiking Great Basin National Park
Hiking Hot Springs in the Pacific Northwest
Hiking Idaho
Hiking Indiana
Hiking Maine
Hiking Maryland and Delaware
Hiking Michigan
Hiking Minnesota
Hiking Montana
Hiking Mount Rainier National Park
Hiking Mount St. Helens
Hiking Nevada
Hiking New Hampshire
Hiking New Mexico
Hiking New Mexico's Gila Wilderness

Hiking New York
Hiking North Carolina
Hiking the North Cascades
Hiking Northern Arizona
Hiking Northern California
Hiking Olympic National Park
Hiking Oregon
Hiking Oregon's Eagle Cap Wilderness
Hiking Oregon's Mount Hood/Badger Creek
Hiking Oregon's Central Cascades
Hiking Pennsylvania
Hiking Ruins Seldom Seen
Hiking Shenandoah
Hiking the Sierra Nevada
Hiking South Carolina
Hiking South Dakota's Black Hills Country
Hiking Southern New England
Hiking Tennessee
Hiking Texas
Hiking Utah
Hiking Utah's Summits
Hiking Vermont
Hiking Virginia
Hiking Washington
Hiking Wisconsin
Hiking Wyoming
Hiking Wyoming's Cloud Peak Wilderness
Hiking Wyoming's Teton
    and Washakie Wilderness
Hiking Wyoming's Wind River Range
Hiking Yellowstone National Park
Hiking Yosemite National Park
Hiking Zion & Bryce Canyon National Parks
Wild Country Companion
Wild Montana
Wild Utah
Wild Virginia

- *To order any of these books, check with your local bookseller
or call The Globe Pequot Press® at **1-800-243-0495.**
Visit us on the world wide web at:*
www.FalconGuide.com

FALCON®

FALCON GUIDES ®Le

FALCON GUIDES ® are available for where-to-go hiking, mount
walking, scenic driving, fishing, rockhounding, paddling, birding,
camping. We also have FalconGuides® on essential outdoor skills and
identification. The following titles are currently available, but this list grov
For a free catalog with a complete list of titles, call FALCON® toll-free at 1-800-

SCENIC DRIVING GUIDES

Scenic Driving Alaska and the Yukon
Scenic Driving Arizona
Scenic Driving the Beartooth Highway
Scenic Driving California
Scenic Driving Colorado
Scenic Driving Florida
Scenic Driving Georgia
Scenic Driving Hawaii
Scenic Driving Idaho
Scenic Driving Indiana
Scenic Driving Kentucky
Scenic Driving Michigan
Scenic Driving Minnesota
Scenic Driving Montana
Scenic Driving New England
Scenic Driving New Mexico
Scenic Driving North Carolina
Scenic Driving Oregon
Scenic Driving the Ozarks
Scenic Driving Pennsylvania
Scenic Driving Texas
Scenic Driving Utah
Scenic Driving Virginia
Scenic Driving Washington
Scenic Driving Wisconsin
Scenic Driving Wyoming
Scenic Driving Yellowstone and
   the Grand Teton National Parks
Scenic Byways East & South
Scenic Byways Far West
Scenic Byways Rocky Mountains
Back Country Byways

HISTORIC TRAIL GUIDES

Traveling California's Gold Rush Country
Traveling the Lewis & Clark Trail
Traveling the Oregon Trail
Traveler's Guide to the Pony Express Trail

WILDLIFE VIEWING GUIDES

Alaska Wildlife Viewing Guide
Arizona Wildlife Viewing Guide
California Wildlife Viewing Guide
Colorado Wildlife Viewing Guide
Florida Wildlife Viewing Guide
Indiana Wildlife Vewing Guide
Iowa Wildlife Viewing Guide
Kentucky Wildlife Viewing Guide
Massachusetts Wildlife Viewing Guide
Montana Wildlife Viewing Guide
Nebraska Wildlife Viewing Guide
Nevada Wildlife Viewing Guide
New Hampshire Wildlife Viewing Guide
New Jersey Wildlife Viewing Guide
New Mexico Wildlife Viewing Guide
New York Wildlife Viewing Guide
North Carolina Wildlife Viewing Guide
North Dakota Wildlife Viewing Guide
Ohio Wildlife Viewing Guide
Oregon Wildlife Viewing Guide
Puerto Rico & the Virgin Islands
   Wildlife Viewing Guide
Tennessee Wildlife Viewing Guide
Texas Wildlife Viewing Guide
Utah Wildlife Viewing Guide
Vermont Wildlife Viewing Guide
Virginia Wildlife Viewing Guide
Washington Wildlife Viewing Guide
West Virginia Wildlife Viewing Guide
Wisconsin Wildlife Viewing Guide

■ *To order any of these books, check with your local bookseller
or call The Globe Pequot Press® at **1-800-243-0495**.
Visit us on the world wide web at:*
www.FalconGuide.com

FALCON®

FALCON GUIDES ® Leading the Way ™

HIKING GUIDES

Best Hikes Along the Continental Divide
Hiking Alaska
Hiking Arizona
Hiking Arizona's Cactus Country
Hiking the Beartooths
Hiking Big Bend National Park
Hiking the Bob Marshall Country
Hiking California
Hiking California's Desert Parks
Hiking Carlsbad Caverns
    and Guadalupe Mtns. National Parks
Hiking Colorado
Hiking Colorado, Vol. II
Hiking Colorado's Summits
Hiking Colorado's Weminuche Wilderness
Hiking the Columbia River Gorge
Hiking Florida
Hiking Georgia
Hiking Glacier & Waterton Lakes National Parks
Hiking Grand Canyon National Park
Hiking Grand Staircase-Escalante/Glen Canyon
Hiking Grand Teton National Park
Hiking Great Basin National Park
Hiking Hot Springs in the Pacific Northwest
Hiking Idaho
Hiking Indiana
Hiking Maine
Hiking Maryland and Delaware
Hiking Michigan
Hiking Minnesota
Hiking Montana
Hiking Mount Rainier National Park
Hiking Mount St. Helens
Hiking Nevada
Hiking New Hampshire
Hiking New Mexico
Hiking New Mexico's Gila Wilderness

Hiking New York
Hiking North Carolina
Hiking the North Cascades
Hiking Northern Arizona
Hiking Northern California
Hiking Olympic National Park
Hiking Oregon
Hiking Oregon's Eagle Cap Wilderness
Hiking Oregon's Mount Hood/Badger Creek
Hiking Oregon's Central Cascades
Hiking Pennsylvania
Hiking Ruins Seldom Seen
Hiking Shenandoah
Hiking the Sierra Nevada
Hiking South Carolina
Hiking South Dakota's Black Hills Country
Hiking Southern New England
Hiking Tennessee
Hiking Texas
Hiking Utah
Hiking Utah's Summits
Hiking Vermont
Hiking Virginia
Hiking Washington
Hiking Wisconsin
Hiking Wyoming
Hiking Wyoming's Cloud Peak Wilderness
Hiking Wyoming's Teton
    and Washakie Wilderness
Hiking Wyoming's Wind River Range
Hiking Yellowstone National Park
Hiking Yosemite National Park
Hiking Zion & Bryce Canyon National Parks
Wild Country Companion
Wild Montana
Wild Utah
Wild Virginia

■ *To order any of these books, check with your local bookseller*
*or call The Globe Pequot Press® at **1-800-243-0495**.*
Visit us on the world wide web at:
www.FalconGuide.com

FALCON®

FALCON GUIDES ®Leading the Way™

FALCON GUIDES ® are available for where-to-go hiking, mountain biking, rock climbing, walking, scenic driving, fishing, rockhounding, paddling, birding, wildlife viewing, and camping. We also have FalconGuides® on essential outdoor skills and subjects and field identification. The following titles are currently available, but this list grows every year. For a free catalog with a complete list of titles, call FALCON® toll-free at 1-800-582-2665.

SCENIC DRIVING GUIDES

Scenic Driving Alaska and the Yukon
Scenic Driving Arizona
Scenic Driving the Beartooth Highway
Scenic Driving California
Scenic Driving Colorado
Scenic Driving Florida
Scenic Driving Georgia
Scenic Driving Hawaii
Scenic Driving Idaho
Scenic Driving Indiana
Scenic Driving Kentucky
Scenic Driving Michigan
Scenic Driving Minnesota
Scenic Driving Montana
Scenic Driving New England
Scenic Driving New Mexico
Scenic Driving North Carolina
Scenic Driving Oregon
Scenic Driving the Ozarks
Scenic Driving Pennsylvania
Scenic Driving Texas
Scenic Driving Utah
Scenic Driving Virginia
Scenic Driving Washington
Scenic Driving Wisconsin
Scenic Driving Wyoming
Scenic Driving Yellowstone and
    the Grand Teton National Parks
Scenic Byways East & South
Scenic Byways Far West
Scenic Byways Rocky Mountains
Back Country Byways

HISTORIC TRAIL GUIDES

Traveling California's Gold Rush Country
Traveling the Lewis & Clark Trail
Traveling the Oregon Trail
Traveler's Guide to the Pony Express Trail

WILDLIFE VIEWING GUIDES

Alaska Wildlife Viewing Guide
Arizona Wildlife Viewing Guide
California Wildlife Viewing Guide
Colorado Wildlife Viewing Guide
Florida Wildlife Viewing Guide
Indiana Wildlife Viewing Guide
Iowa Wildlife Viewing Guide
Kentucky Wildlife Viewing Guide
Massachusetts Wildlife Viewing Guide
Montana Wildlife Viewing Guide
Nebraska Wildlife Viewing Guide
Nevada Wildlife Viewing Guide
New Hampshire Wildlife Viewing Guide
New Jersey Wildlife Viewing Guide
New Mexico Wildlife Viewing Guide
New York Wildlife Viewing Guide
North Carolina Wildlife Viewing Guide
North Dakota Wildlife Viewing Guide
Ohio Wildlife Viewing Guide
Oregon Wildlife Viewing Guide
Puerto Rico & the Virgin Islands
    Wildlife Viewing Guide
Tennessee Wildlife Viewing Guide
Texas Wildlife Viewing Guide
Utah Wildlife Viewing Guide
Vermont Wildlife Viewing Guide
Virginia Wildlife Viewing Guide
Washington Wildlife Viewing Guide
West Virginia Wildlife Viewing Guide
Wisconsin Wildlife Viewing Guide

■ *To order any of these books, check with your local bookseller
or call The Globe Pequot Press® at **1-800-243-0495**.
Visit us on the world wide web at:*
www.FalconGuide.com

FALCON®